international
review of
social history

Special Issue 30

Women's Rights and Global Socialism

Edited by Celia Donert and Christine Moll-Murata

Published by the Press Syndicate of the University of Cambridge
The Pitt Building, Trumpington Street, Cambridge, CB2 1RP
1 Liberty Plaza, Floor 20, New York, NY 10006, USA
10 Stamford Road, Oakleigh, Melbourne 3166, Australia

© Internationaal Instituut voor Sociale Geschiedenis

*A catalogue record for this book is available
from the British Library*

Library of Congress Cataloguing-in-Publication Data applied for

ISBN 9781009069960 (paperback)

Printed in the UK by Bell & Bain Ltd, Glasgow, UK.

CONTENTS

Women's Rights and Global Socialism

Edited by
Celia Donert and Christine Moll-Murata

Women's Rights and Global Socialism: Gendering Socialist Internationalism during the Cold War
Celia Donert   I

"Warphans" and "Quiet" Heroines: Depictions of Chinese Women and Children in the *Comité mondial des femmes contre la guerre et le fascisme's* Campaigns during the Second Sino-Japanese War
Jasmine Calver   23

Between National and International: Women's Transnational Activism in Twentieth-Century Chile
María Fernanda Lanfranco González   49

Radicalizing Feminism: The Mexican and Cuban Associations within the Women's International Democratic Federation in the Early Cold War
Manuel Ramírez Chicharro   75

International Solidarity as the Cornerstone of the Hungarian Post-War Socialist Women's Rights Agenda in the Magazine *Asszonyok*
Zsófia Lóránd   103

Women Labour Models and Socialist Transformation in early 1950s China
Nicola Spakowski   131

The WIDF's Work for Women's Rights in the (Post)colonial Countries and the "Soviet Agenda"
Yulia Gradskova   155

A Gendered Approach to the Yu Chi Chan Club and National Liberation Front during South Africa's Transition to Armed Struggle
Allison Drew   179

Women's Transnational Activism against Portugal's Colonial Wars
Giulia Strippoli   209

"The Call of the World": Women's Memories of Global Socialist Feminism in India
Mallarika Sinha Roy   237

IRSH 67 (2022), pp. 1–22 doi:10.1017/S0020859022000050

Women's Rights and Global Socialism: Gendering Socialist Internationalism during the Cold War

CELIA DONERT

Faculty of History, University of Cambridge
Cambridge CB2 1TN, United Kingdom

E-mail: chd31@cam.ac.uk

ABSTRACT: This Special Issue explores the complicated relationship between women's rights and global socialism during the Cold War. This Introduction describes how the articles deal with this relationship in three, partly overlapping, periods. The first set of articles looks at how the ethos of the Popular Front resonated among women's movements in Asia, Latin America, and Europe, and examines the connections between interwar anti-fascist and anti-imperialist feminisms and those that re-emerged after World War II. The second set of articles focuses on the role and development of the Women's International Democratic Federation (WIDF) and its model of internationalism in Eastern Europe, the Soviet Union, and China in the early Cold War. The final articles centre on the challenges faced by the WIDF from the 1960s, exploring issues such as the anti-apartheid struggles in South Africa, the Portuguese wars of decolonization, and the United Nations Decade for Women (1976–1985). Together with this process of decolonization, this Special Issue also examines how the consequences of postsocialism, in particular for women's rights (the loss of social rights, material security, and substantial challenges to reproductive freedoms), have triggered renewed debates about the history and legacies of communist women's liberation movements in the former socialist world.

In 1978, US feminist journal *Quest* published a forum on international feminism featuring articles by the Indian economist Devaki Jain and American writer Charlotte Bunch. It seemed a propitious moment to discuss such a topic. The United Nations had recently held an International Women's Year (1975), launched a Decade of Women (1976–1985), and was just about to adopt its historic Convention on the Elimination of All Forms of Discrimination Against Women (1979).[1] Yet, the contributors were sceptical that feminism could really become a "global ideology".[2] Women in post-colonial countries, Jain warned, viewed Western feminism as an "anti-male philosophy or a male-mimicking quest for equality which is [...] unnecessary for us and our political economies".[3] In the West, Bunch noted, women still needed to learn that a global feminism could not simply reflect a North American worldview. Postcolonial feminisms, she wrote, were shaped by a specific form of Marxism, ideas about self-determination and development, and women's status in national liberation movements or newly independent nations in the global South. At the same time, "the oppression of women in industrialized countries [has] taken a subtle and invidious turn which is some-times exported as 'women's emancipation'".[4] This was a veiled reference to the Eastern Bloc, where women's rights were often touted as proof of the success of the state socialist project. In other words, the scepticism voiced by Jain and Bunch about the possibilities of a feminist internationalism were shaped in no small part by concerns about the incompatibility of feminism and socialism. Fast forward forty years, and similar concerns are still shaping contemporary debates about global feminist solidarity.[5] These questions are also central to the articles in this Special Issue, which explores the complicated relationship between women's rights and global socialism during the Cold War.[6]

The articles in this Special Issue draw on new sources – including personal papers, private correspondence, interviews, memoirs, and institutional archives – to explore struggles over women's rights in international communist and left-revolutionary movements from the perspective of often-forgotten mid-ranking officials, functionaries, and activists. Covering the period

---

1. Jocelyn Olcott, *International Women's Year: The Greatest Consciousness-Raising Event in History* (Oxford, 2017).
2. Devaki Jain, "Can Feminism be a Global Ideology?", *Quest. A Feminist Quarterly*, 4:2 (1978), Special Issue on "International Feminism", pp. 9–15.
3. Devaki Jain would later write a canonical account of women's engagement with UN develop-ment policies. See Devaki Jain and Amartya Sen, *Women, Development and the UN: A Sixty-Year Quest for Equality and Justice* (United Nations Intellectual History Project) (Bloomington, IN, 2005).
4. Charlotte Bunch, "An Introduction…", *Quest. A Feminist Quarterly*, 4:2 (1978), Special Issue on "International Feminism", pp. 4–8.
5. Lucy Delap, *Feminisms: A Global History* (London, 2020); Dorothy Sue Cobble, *For the Many: American Feminists and the Global Fight for Democratic Equality* (Princeton, NJ, 2021); Kristen Ghodsee, *Second World, Second Sex: Socialist Women's Activism and Global Solidarity during the Cold War* (Durham, NC, 2019).
6. This Special Issue is the result of a research network hosted by the Universities of Liverpool, Cambridge, and Jawaharlal Nehru University, New Delhi, between 2018 and 2020. The work-shops were generously funded by an Arts and Humanities Research Council Leadership Fellowship ("How Women's Rights became Human Rights: Gender, Socialism and Postsocialism, 1917–2017", Grant ref. AH/P008852/2).

between the global Popular Fronts against fascism of the 1930s and the end of the Cold War, the contributors look beyond the female figureheads of international communism to illuminate the experiences of lesser-known actors, such as British journalist Charlotte Haldane, Chilean women's leader Olga Poblete, Chinese labour heroine Shen Jilan, South African socialist Elizabeth van der Heyden, Soviet functionary Zhura Rahimbabaeva, or the West Bengali writer and activist Malobika Chattopadhyay. These female activists represented a wide range of ideological positions as communists or socialists, and their views on women's rights were influenced partly by Soviet models, alongside a variety of Marxist, anti-imperialist, or nationalist approaches to women's emancipation. We thus use the term "global socialism" to refer both to the state socialist regimes of Eastern Europe, the Soviet Union, and China, and to the postcolonial socialisms that emerged in Africa, Asia, and Latin America.[7] Socialist internationalism during the Cold War enabled alternative forms of globalization in the Second and Third Worlds through transnational connections and flows of people, goods, and ideas.[8] Thus, as Paul Betts reminds us, "it is wrong to say that 1989 was the moment when globalization caught up with the Eastern Bloc. On the contrary, eastern Europe had been engaged with the Global South in countless ways since the mid-1950s, as evidenced in the spheres of trade, labour training, military assistance, education, cultural promotion and humanitarian assistance".[9] While much of the recent literature on socialist internationalism has focused on Europe and Europeans, the contributors to this Special Issue draw on archives around the world to reconstruct these alternative globalizations from the perspective of female activists from the Global South.

Women from Latin America, Asia, and Africa, as the essays in this collection demonstrate, redefined women's rights and socialist internationalism on their own terms, thus challenging the models offered by European Marxists or Soviet communism. Over the past decade, scholars such as Francisca de Haan and Kristen Ghodsee have reinserted communist women's organizations into the history of the global Cold War, arguing that the bipolar logic of that conflict, and a persistent anti-communist bias among Western feminist

---

7. James Mark, Artemy Kalinovsky, Steffi Marung (eds), *Alternative Globalizations: Eastern Europe and the Postcolonial World* (Bloomington, IN, 2020); James Mark et al., *Socialism Goes Global: The Soviet Union and Eastern Europe in the Age of Decolonisation* (Oxford, 2022).
8. Patryk Babiracki and Jersild, Austin (eds), *Socialist Internationalism in the Cold War: Exploring the Second World* (Palgrave, 2016); Łukasz Stanek, *Architecture in Global Socialism: Eastern Europe, West Africa and the Middle East in the Cold War* (Princeton, 2020); Theodora Dragostinova, *The Global Cold War from the Margins: A Small Socialist State on the Global Cultural Scene* (Ithaca, NY, 2021); Elidor Mehilli, *From Stalin to Mao: Albania and the Socialist World* (Ithaca, NY, 2017); Artemy M. Kalinovsky, *Laboratory of Socialist Development: Cold War Politics and Decolonization in Soviet Tajikistan* (Ithaca, NY, 2018).
9. Paul Betts, "1989 at Thirty: A Recast Legacy", *Past and Present*, 244:1 (2019), pp. 271–305.

activists and scholars, has erased their contribution.[10] Central to this effort has been the rehabilitation of the Women's International Democratic Federation (WIDF), an anti-fascist federation of women founded in Paris in 1945, which along with many other international non-governmental organizations (such as the World Federation of Trade Unions, the World Federation of Youth, or the World Peace Council) fell increasingly under Soviet influence after the onset of the Cold War. In an influential argument, Francisca de Haan has argued that the WIDF represented a "transnational left-feminism".[11] In parallel, there has been a much-needed re-evaluation of the history of the mass organizations for women established by national communist parties, which has resulted in a lively debate about the extent to which women in these organizations possessed "agency" vis-à-vis ruling parties or state author-ities.[12] Much of this work has drawn on the concept of "state feminism" to explain how female communist activists worked through state institutions to implement policies aimed at women's emancipation in state socialist regimes.[13]

To explore the central theme of postcolonial challenges to European or Soviet socialist models of women's emancipation, the essays in this collection pursue three lines of argument. First, we explore the limits of the category of "state feminism" as a way of demonstrating women's agency within state socialist societies and global socialist movements, in particular through a focus on mass organizations. Second, the articles presented here suggest his-tories of struggles over women's rights in the context of twentieth-century socialist internationalism in Eastern Europe and the postcolonial world need to take greater account of the hierarchies of nation, race, and ethnicity. Rather than seeing communist women as intersectional feminists *avant la lettre*, the articles in this collection seek to problematize the way in which transnational encounters within international communist movements in the age of decolonization were shaped not only by nationalism but also racial dis-courses. Third, we argue that prior scholarship has not taken sufficient

10. Francisca de Haan, "Continuing Cold War Paradigms in Western Historiography of Transnational Women's Organisations: The Case of the Women's International Democratic Federation (WIDF)", *Women's History Review*, 19:4 (2010), pp. 547–573; Kristen Ghodsee, *Second World, Second Sex.*
11. Francisca de Haan, "The Global Left-Feminist 1960s. From Copenhagen to Moscow and New York", in Chen Jian, Martin Klimke, Masha Kirasirova, Mary Nolan, Marilyn Young, Joanna Waley-Cohen (eds), *The Routledge Handbook of the Global Sixties: Between Protest and Nation-Building* (London, 2018), pp. 230–242.
12. Nanette Funk, "A Very Tangled Knot: Official State Socialist Women's Organizations, Women's Agency and Feminism in Eastern European State Socialism", *European Journal of Women's Studies*, 21:4 (2014), pp. 344–360.
13. Wang Zheng, *Finding Women in the State: A Socialist Feminist Revolution in the People's Republic of China, 1949–1964* (Berkeley, CA, 2016); Kristen Ghodsee, "Pressuring the Politburo: The Committee of the Bulgarian Women's Movement and State Socialist Feminism", *Slavic Review*, 73:3 (2014), pp. 538–562.

account of the degree to which female activists were political agents, who engaged with international women's rights from positions shaped by their political and ideological commitments rather than notions of "female solidarity" or a generalized "left-wing" orientation. From this perspective, international collaboration around women's rights was not only possible when activists chose to put to one side their political affiliations – as existing literature on women in humanitarian movements often suggests – but emerged from women negotiating their political views on both national and international levels.

GLOBAL SOCIALISM AND WOMEN'S RIGHTS: A BRIEF CHRONOLOGY

Throughout the twentieth century, communists and socialists were among the most vocal supporters of women's emancipation – and state socialist countries made significant progress in achieving legal equality and economic independence for women – yet the leadership of communist parties and mass organizations was dominated by men. This familiar paradox is reflected in the almost total absence of women from the major international histories of twentieth-century communism.[14] Women and questions of women's rights typically appear only fleetingly in scholarship exploring the transnational world of the Comintern and its associated organizations, such as Workers' International Relief or the League against Imperialism.[15] Ambivalence towards the question of women was already palpable in the early years of the Communist International. In November 1920, the Executive Committee of the Communist International (ECCI) adopted "Guidelines for the Communist Women's Movement", drafted by former social democrat and high-ranking KPD functionary Clara Zetkin. The Comintern appealed to its member parties to promote women's full participation in public and private life, and to integrate women into all levels of the "proletarian class

14. Silvio Pons, *The Global Revolution: A History of International Communism 1917–1991* (Oxford, 2014); David Priestland, *The Red Flag: Communism and the Making of the Modern World* (London, 2009). For exceptions, see Celia Donert, "Feminism, Communism and Global Socialism: Encounters and Entanglements", in Juliane Fürst, Silvio Pons, Mark Selden (eds), *The Cambridge History of Communism*, vol. 3, (Cambridge: 2017), pp. 399–421, and Donna Harsch, "Communism and Women", in Stephen A. Smith (ed.), *The Oxford Handbook of the History of Communism* (Oxford, 2014).
15. Michele L. Louro, Carolien Stolte, Heather Streets-Salter, Sana Tannoury-Karam (eds), *The League Against Imperialism: Lives and Afterlives* (Leiden, 2020); Holger Weiss, *International Communism and Transnational Solidarity: Radical Networks, Mass Movements and Global Politics, 1919–1939* (Leiden, 2017); Frederik Petersson, *Willi Münzenberg, the League Against Imperialism, and the Comintern, 1925–1933* (Lewiston, ID, 2013); Kasper Braskén, *The International Workers' Relief, Communism, and Transnational Solidarity: Willi Münzenberg in Weimar Germany* (Basingstoke, 2015).

struggle".[16] But at the same time, working-class women were viewed with suspicion. The Third Congress of the Comintern in 1921, which was largely devoted to the "woman question", concluded that "the masses of passive working women who are outside the movement – the housewives, office workers and peasant women who are still under the influence of the bourgeois world-view, the church and tradition, and have no links with the great liberation movement for communism" represented a "great danger".[17] The Comintern established a Women's International Secretariat, but it did not last long. Communist women's organizations were tied ever more tightly to party cells, and forced to compete with the unions. The international secretariat, led by Zetkin, was forced to move from Berlin to Moscow, and the Comintern monthly for women, *Die Kommunistische Woman Fraueninternationale*, was closed in 1925. The last International Congress of Communist Women took place a year later. The Women's Section of the Central Committee of the Communist Party of the Soviet (Zhenotdel) was dissolved in 1930, as the Soviet Union distanced itself from a revolutionary programme of gender and sexual emancipation, embracing a much more conservative approach to women's role as worker and mother.

This Special Issue picks up the story in the mid-1930s, when the Comintern supported the creation of a World Committee of Women against War and Fascism, presaging a broader shift towards a global Popular Front policy that allowed communists to cooperate with a wider range of non-communist, anti-colonialist, socialist, pacifist, and feminist organizations in the struggle against fascism and imperialism. The first set of articles in this collection asks how the ethos of the Popular Front resonated among women's movements in Asia, Latin America, and Europe, as well as exploring the connections between interwar anti-fascist and anti-imperialist feminisms and those that re-emerged after World War II. In this section, articles by Jasmine Calver, María Fernanda Lanfranco González, and Manuel Ramírez Chicharro explore the transnational circulation of socialist feminisms between Western Europe, East Asia, and Latin America between the 1930s and 1950s. These articles contribute to scholarship that emphasizes the role of actors from colonial and dependent territories in shaping the transnational world of the Comintern through the interwar years, despite the hierarchical system of control imposed by the Soviet Union.

The second set of articles in this Special Issue asks how the language of women's rights and socialist internationalism changed in the period of building socialism in Eastern Europe and China from the late 1940s, as well as interrogating the extent to which the WIDF's internationalism was shaped by a

16. Eriz Weitz, "The Heroic Man and the Ever-Changing Woman: Gender and Politics in European Communism, 1917–1950", in Laura L. Frader and Sonya O. Rose (eds), *Gender and Class in Modern Europe* (Ithaca, NY, 1996), pp. 311–352.
17. Brigitte Studer, *The Transnational World of the Cominternians* (Basingstoke, 2015), p. 47.

Soviet agenda during the era of decolonization. The Women's International Democratic Federation, established in Paris in November 1945, embraced anti-fascism and anti-imperialism in its early years, acting as a magnet for anti-colonial women's movements in Asia and North Africa.[18] Three years later, the Cold War was making itself felt within the Federation, as the rift between the Soviet Union and Yugoslavia resulted in the 1949 expulsion of the Antifascist Women's Front of Yugoslavia from the WIDF after the Second Cominform Resolution.[19] By 1951, along with other communist non-governmental organizations such as the World Federation of Trade Unions, the WIDF was forced to move eastwards. The Federation was stripped of its status as a non-governmental observer at the United Nations' Economic and Social Committee for its role in propaganda campaigns against UN military intervention in North Korea.[20] For the next forty years, the WIDF secretariat was located in the German Democratic Republic, coordinating peace campaigns, fact-finding missions, international congresses, and research workshops, from its offices in East Berlin.[21] The national affiliates of the WIDF tended to be mass organizations for women connected to national communist parties.

The third set of articles focuses on the challenges faced by the WIDF's model of internationalism between the 1960s and the 1980s, with a particular focus on anti-apartheid struggles in South Africa, the Portuguese wars of decolonization in Southern Africa, and the United Nations Decade for Women, which ran from 1976 to 1985. Throughout the 1960s, the WIDF was buffeted by the ideological conflicts within the Eastern Bloc, facing sharp criticism from Italian and Chinese members about its unwavering support for Soviet foreign policy. The Federation to some extent embraced development assistance as a way of supporting women's organisations in the postcolonial world, although this material assistance did not always meet

---

18. Katherine McGregor, "Opposing Colonialism: The Women's International Democratic Federation and Decolonisation Struggles in Vietnam and Algeria, 1945–1965", *Women's History Review*, 25:6 (2016), pp. 925–944; Elisabeth Armstrong, "Before Bandung: The Anti-Imperialist Women's Movement in Asia and the Women's International Democratic Federation", *Signs: Journal of Women in Culture and Society*, 41:2 (2016), pp. 305–331.

19. Chiara Bonfiglioli, "Cold War Internationalisms, Nationalisms, and the Yugoslav-Soviet Split: The Union of Italian Women and the Antifascist Women's Front of Yugoslavia", in Francisca de Haan, Margaret Allen, June Purvis, Krassimira Daskalova (eds), *Women's Activism: Global Perspectives from the 1890s to the Present* (London, 2012), pp. 59–76.

20. Celia Donert, "From Communist Internationalism to Human Rights: Gender, Violence and international Law in the Women's International Democratic Federation Mission to North Korea, 1951", *Contemporary European History*, 25:2 (2016), pp. 313–333; Michelle Chase, "'Hands Off Korea!' Women's Internationalist Solidarity and Peace Activism in Early Cold War Cuba", *Journal of Women's History*, 32:3 (2020), pp. 64–88.

21. Elizabeth Armstrong, "Before Bandung: The Anti-Imperialist Women's Movement in Asia and the Women's International Democratic Federation", *Signs: Journal of Women in Culture and Society*, 41:2 (2016), pp. 305–331.

the needs or demands of its recipients.[22] In 1975, the WIDF organized its own World Congress of Women in the German Democratic Republic, as a socialist counterpoint to the bigger UN World Conference on Women in Mexico City.[23] The WIDF provided a space for communication for left-wing women's groups that were operating illegally during the wars of decolonization. It was one of the channels enabling women from socialist countries, and from left-leaning anti-colonial movements, to participate in international discussions about women's rights during the Cold War. And, as many of the articles in this Special Issue indicate, the history of the Federation also reveals the misunderstandings, disagreements, and conflicts that were an integral part of the localized histories of "leftist" women's movements across much of the twentieth century.

WHAT IS LEFT OF LEFT FEMINISM?

The collapse of state socialism in Eastern Europe and the Soviet Union, along with China's top-down transition to state capitalism, transformed the terms of the *Quest* debate about "international feminism". Devaki Jain and Charlotte Bunch had framed their discussion of global feminism in relation to debates about Marxism, welfare, development, and self-determination, concepts that were swept away by debt crises and austerity as the Cold War stuttered to an end. Symptomatic of this shift from socialist internationalism to a new age of liberal internationalism, perhaps, was the transformation of Charlotte Bunch from a Civil Rights-era social justice feminist to the figurehead of a post-Cold War global movement to recognize "women's rights as human rights". The gendered consequences of postsocialism – including the loss of social rights and material security, and substantial challenges to reproductive freedoms – have triggered renewed debates about the history and legacies of communist women's liberation movements in the former socialist world.[24] This has diverted attention from an older narrative, in which second-wave feminism and the New Left shook up the male-dominated, hierarchical structures and theoretical orthodoxies of communist parties after 1968, above all in Western Europe.[25] Journals such as *Quest* were part of this earlier movement.

22. Elizabeth Banks, "Sewing Machines for Socialism? Gifts of Development and Disagreement between the Soviet and Mozambican Women's Committees, 1963–87", *Comparative Studies of South Asia, Africa, and the Middles East*, 41:1 (2021), pp. 27–40.

23. Celia Donert, "Whose Utopia? Gender, Ideology and Human Rights at the World Conference of Women in East Berlin, 1975", in Samuel Moyn and Jan Eckel, *The Breakthrough: Human Rights in the 1970s* (Philadelphia, PA, 2014).

24. Kristen Ghodsee, *Second World, Second Sex*.

25. See for example Maria Michetti, Margherita Repetto, Luciana Viviani, *UDI: Laboratorio di politica delle donne* (Rome, 1984); Jane Jenson, "One Robin Doesn't Make Spring: French Communist Alliance Strategies and the Women's Movement", *Radical History Review*, 23

By embracing a politics of recognition over redistribution, the philosopher Nancy Fraser has argued, women's liberation movements even helped to enable the neoliberal forms of capitalism that have flourished since the 1970s.[26] Recent scholarship has, however, sought to redefine women's political engagement in communist parties and mass organizations as a broad-based "transnational left-feminism", before the era of the New Left.[27] In this reading, the socialist past becomes a resource that could inform contemporary feminisms in an age of global capitalism.

Recent scholarship rehabilitating the role of state socialist mass organizations for women has drawn on the notion of "state feminism" to show how women worked within the structures of the socialist state to promote women's interests. Coined by students of the Scandinavian welfare state to analyse government policies aimed at removing the structural basis of gender equality by socializing reproduction and employing more women in the state sector, the concept of state feminism has also been criticized as a top-down strategy that failed to solve the problem of underrepresentation and subordination of women.[28] The term has been used to describe the policies of postcolonial welfare states in the Middle East, such as Egypt and Tunisia, which committed to public equality for women and men, and supported women's productive and reproductive roles, while leaving unchallenged women's subordinate position in the family and the political system. More recently, it has been applied to communist states, too. Wang Zheng has compellingly argued that the All-China Women's Federation operated as a socialist feminist cultural front in the People's Republic of China, and that Chinese communist party campaigns for women's emancipation should thus be seen as an example of "state feminism".[29] In the case of communist Bulgaria, Kristen Ghodsee argues that representatives of the Committee of Bulgarian Women lobbied for resources to support women's interests within the structures of the socialist state.[30] Mass

(1980), Special Issue on communist movements ("For a Social History of Politics") edited by Victoria de Grazia.

26. Nancy Fraser, "Feminism, Capitalism and the Cunning of History", *New Left Review*, 56 (2009), p. 97.

27. Francisca de Haan, "Eugénie Cotton, Pak Chong-ae, and Claudia Jones: Rethinking Transnational Feminism and International Politics", *Journal of Women's History*, 25:4 (2013), pp. 174–189; Francisca de Haan, "Continuing Cold War Paradigms; Francisca de Haan, "The Global Left-Feminist 1960s: From Copenhagen to Moscow and New York", in Shen Jilan *et al.* (eds), *The Routledge Handbook of the Global Sixties: Between Protest and Nation-Building* (London, 2018), pp. 230–242.

28. Harriet Holter, "Women's Research and Social Theory", in Harriet Holter (ed.), *Patriarchy in a Welfare Society* (London, 1984), pp. 18–24; Helga Maria Hernes, *Welfare State and Woman Power: Essays in State Feminism* (Oslo, 1987).

29. Wang Zheng, *Finding Women in the State: A Socialist Feminist Revolution in the People's Republic of China* (Berkeley, CA, 2017).

30. Kristen Ghodsee, "Pressuring the Politburo: The Committee of the Bulgarian Women's Movement and State Socialist Feminism"', *Slavic Review*, 73:3 (2014), pp. 538–562.

organisations in some cases provided sites for activism and solidarity, but also imposed hierarchies and ideological frameworks on their members, which were challenged by female activists seeking new forms of political organisation, as explored in this collection through case studies of transnational connections between Lusophone women during Portugal's wars of decolonisation, or of small socialist groups that emerged as rivals to the African National Congress (ANC) in South Africa after 1960. This also suggests that the category of "transnational left-feminism" might inadvertently obscure the political divisions and rivalries that were so crucial to the protagonists of these movements.

That the communist past of Central and Eastern Europe could be a resource used to inform future social justice feminism in the United States is an argument made strongly by Kristen Ghodsee in her recent essay, *Why Women Have Better Sex Under Socialism*.[31] The experience of Bulgarian women under state socialism is presented as a counterpoint to the lives of young American millennial women, who might have forgotten the lesson that economic independence fosters self-realization. By contrast, Miglena Todorova, who grew up in socialist Bulgaria, suggests that for post-socialist subjects, "Marx's theories of human development leading to transformed consciousness and socially useful work in the socialist public economy may not be liberation but the site of state governmentality and violence". For women who grew up in the socialist bloc, Todorova argues, the ruptures and transformations of 1989 "have produced postsocialist subjectivities, modes of consciousness, and personal and group relations marked by *doubt*", characterized by a need to "interrogate and understand how state socialism in the twentieth century enfolded race, patriarchy, heteronormativity, and violence".[32] Seen from this perspective, women might have better sex under socialism, "unless one is a poor, racialized Indigenous, Roma, or Black woman whose concern is not having satisfying sex but surviving racist patriarchal heteronormative neocolonial societies stretching from the former Soviet Union in the East to the United States and Canada in the West".[33]

Anti-fascism, anti-imperialism, and anti-racism were central to the WIDF approach to forging connections with women's movements around the world in the late 1940s, but the essays in this Special Issue remind us that socialist internationalism did not treat all women equally. The anti-racism of Soviet-supported socialist internationalism regained its appeal after the defeat of Germany and Japan, and as anti-colonial resistance gathered strength against British, French, and Dutch colonial rule in Asia during the 1940s. Across the socialist world, class was deemed to have eradicated differences based on race as well as gender,

31. Kristen Ghodsee, *Why Women Have Better Sex under Socialism and Other Arguments for Economic Independence* (London, 2019).
32. Miglena Todorova, *Unequal Under Socialism: Race, Women and Transnationalism in Bulgaria* (Toronto, 2021).
33. *Ibid.*

yet in Eastern Europe, as in the postcolonial world, race and racial difference had been central to the states that had preceded the creation of socialist regimes, whether in the Nazi New Order in Europe, or European colonial empires in Africa and Asia. As Quinn Slobodian has written, this raises the question of how "race and racialized thinking operate in a socialist society [...] that had decreed racism out of existence?"[34]

Numerous studies have shown that state socialism in Eastern Europe and the Soviet Union was anything but blind to racial or ethnic hierarchy, notwithstanding the rhetoric about working-class equality through socialist internationalism.[35] Romani, Muslim, and Jewish minorities all faced pressure to assimilate to the language and culture of the majority population across Central and Southeastern Europe.[36] Similar pressures were experienced by ethnic and national minorities in the Soviet Union. Non-European students and migrant labourers faced discrimination on the street and official restrictions on their freedom to mingle with their host societies. These racialized hierarchies were most visible in the treatment of women, and affected citizens of socialist states too, as exemplified by widespread practices of sterilization of Romani women across state socialist Europe.[37] As Miglena Todorova has argued, central and southeastern Europe were part of a "racial globality, wherein Western racial sciences, colonial technologies, Marxist-Leninist imaginations, and socialist state policies intertwined to produce socialist women belonging to privileged ethnic majorities attached to racial Whiteness and European civilization, as well as Romani and Muslim women whose Otherness marked them for state-led socialist emancipation or eradication".[38]

FROM GLOBAL POPULAR FRONTS TO THE COLD WAR

In the first article of this Special Issue, Jasmine Calver explores the *Comité Mondial des Femmes contre la Guerre et le Fascisme* (World Committee of

34. Quinn Slobodian, *Comrades of Color: East Germany in the Cold War World* (New York, 2015), "Introduction", p. 1.
35. Alena Alamgir, "Race is Elsewhere: State-Socialist Ideology and the Racialisation of Vietnamese Workers in Czechoslovakia", *Race and Class*, 54:4 (2013), pp. 67–85; Eric Weitz, "Racial Politics without the Concept of Race: Reevaluating Soviet Ethnic and National Purges", *Slavic Review*, 61:1 (2002), pp. 1–29; Francine Hirsch, "Race without the Practice of Racial Politics", *Slavic Review*, 61:1 (2002), pp. 30–43; Rossen Djagalov, "Racism, the Highest Stage of Anti-Communism", *Slavic Review*, 80:2 (2021), pp. 290–298.
36. Celia Donert, *The Rights of the Roma: The Struggle for Citizenship in Postwar Czechoslovakia* (Cambridge, 2017); Mary Neuburger, *The Orient Within: Muslim Minorities and the Negotiation of Nationhood in Modern Bulgaria* (Ithaca, NY, 2004).
37. Donert, *The Rights of the Roma*.
38. Miglena Todorova, "Race and Women of Color in Socialist / Postsocialist Transnational Feminisms in Central and Southeastern Europe", *Meridians: Feminism, Race, Transnationalism*, 16:1 (2018), pp. 114–141. See also Miglena Todorova, *Unequal Under Socialism*.

Women against War and Fascism, CMF) in relation to interwar humanitarianism as well as communist internationalism. Set up in Paris in 1934 as a sister organization of the Amsterdam-Pleyel movement, the CMF aimed to attract working-class, intellectual, socialist, and left-leaning women to the communist movement, where women were heavily underrepresented. (By the late 1920s, less than one per cent of the membership of the French Communist Party were women.) The CMF did not describe itself as a feminist organization, and its leader, Gabrielle Duchêne, did not identify explicitly as a Communist. Closely connected to the French branch of the Women's International League for Peace and Freedom (WILPF), Duchêne was a syndicalist and feminist pacifist who sympathized with the Soviet Union during the 1920s as the country of women's liberation.[39] The *Comité Mondial des Femmes* organized campaigns on behalf of women in Nazi Germany, the Spanish Civil War, in Abyssinia following the Italian invasion, and in response to the Second Sino-Japanese War. After the Japanese invasion of Nanjing in December 1937, during which tens of thousands of Chinese civilians were murdered and raped, the CMF launched a campaign to raise international awareness about the suffering of Chinese women and girls, and to support "Warphans" – children orphaned in the military conflict.

In her article, Calver draws on CMF publications and the personal papers of its members to show how both Chinese and European women drew on maternalist and humanitarian discourses alongside anti-fascist internationalism in the CMF's "Warphans" campaign. At the CMF Congress in Marseille in 1938, Loh Tsei, a Chinese sociology major and student leader also spoke in "emotive and violent language" about the rape and kidnapping of Chinese women by Japanese soldiers. Calver suggests that the CMF child sponsorship campaign for children orphaned in the Sino-Japanese War – or "Warphans" – infantilized Chinese society through its humanitarian rhetoric. Yet, her research also emphasizes that the "Warphan" was not dreamt up by the CMF, but was rather the idea of Song Meiling, wife of Nationalist leader Chiang Kai-Shek. Song Meiling had been a figurehead of the New Life movement of the 1930s, which drew inspiration from Confucianism, Christianity, and European fascism. This also involved an attempt to counter the "Modern Girl" associated with Republican China.[40] Although the CMF gave Song Meiling little credit for the Warphans campaign, Calver shows that the CMF's international socialist and anti-fascist campaigns against Japanese aggression were shaped as much by the agency of Chinese women – nationalist as well as communist – as by Europeans.

---

39. Emmanuelle Carle, "Gabrielle Duchêne et la recherche d'une autre route. Entre le pacifisme féministe et l'antifascisme", PhD dissertation (Montreal, 2005).
40. Madeleine Y. Dong, "Who is Afraid of the Chinese Modern Girl?", in Alys Eve Weinbaum *et al.* (eds), *The Modern Girl Around the World: Consumption, Modernity and Globalization*, pp. 194–219.

That the anti-fascist internationalism, maternalism, and humanitarianism of the CMF could provide a platform for cooperation between women across ideological divides was also demonstrated by a central figure in Calver's article: Charlotte Haldane, a journalist who headed the British branch for the CMF and who was sent to China by the Comintern in 1938. Haldane had been a member of the Communist Party of Britain since 1927, but maintained connections to both socialist and liberal politicians. As Calver points out, Haldane did not simply play the role of a communist delegate in China, she also delivered messages from Clement Atlee and Archibald Sinclair, leaders of the Labour and Liberal Parties. Thus, the history of the CMF bolsters Laura Beer's observation that studies of international feminism between the world wars increasingly support the revisionist view that cooperation between women across ideological divides – liberal, socialist, and communist – was possible within anti-fascist and pacifist movements to a greater extent than the narrative of socialist opposition to "bourgeois feminism" would allow.[41] Similar patterns would also emerge in the successor organization to the CMF, after the Committee dissolved at the end of 1941, its anti-fascist mission already compromised by the Nazi–Soviet pact and the outbreak of World War II. The CMF was succeeded after the defeat of Germany and Japan by the Women's International Democratic Federation, founded in Paris in late 1945.[42]

The WIDF promised to revive the anti-fascist and anti-imperialist socialist internationalism that had characterized the era of the Popular Fronts, although we still know relatively little about the personal connections that linked these two phases of anti-fascism and anti-imperialism. The article by María Fernanda Lanfranco González hints at the continuities between the two movements, drawing on a case study of the Movimiento pro-Emancipación de la Mujer Chilena (MEMCH) in Chile. Founded in 1935, the MEMCH was inspired by the 1934 World Congress of Women against War and Fascism and became the "most significant local manifestation of Popular Front feminism in Chile". A driving force behind the MEMCH was Chilean feminist Marta Vergara, who had witnessed the restrictions on women's rights by Hitler and Mussolini while serving as the Chilean delegate to the League of Nations Commission on Women's Rights and the IACW. Lanfranco González points to the many structural barriers – membership

41. Laura Beers, "Bridging the Ideological Divide: Liberal and Socialist Collaboration in the Women's International League for Peace and Freedom, 1919–1945", *Journal of Women's History*, 33:2 (2021), pp. 111–135.
42. Mercedes Yusta, "The Strained Courtship between Antifascism and Feminism: From the Women's World Committee (1934) to the Women's International Democratic Federation (1945)", in Hugo García *et al.* (eds), *Rethinking Antifascism: History, Memory and Politics, 1922 to the Present* (New York, 2016).

practices, the location of international meetings, and language differences –
that hampered Latin American women's involvement in women's international non-governmental organizations. While more than half the members
of MEMCH's local committees in the provinces had links to the Communist
Party, most of its leaders were middle-class women who were able to participate in international organizing, such as Pan-American networks protesting
against "Spanish Fascism" under Franco or the persecution of Jews in
Hitler's Germany. From 1946 to 1953, Olga Poblete (1908–1999) – a professor
of history at the University of Chile from a modest background – was
Secretary General of MEMCH and fostered links with both the WILPF and
the WIDF. While studying at Columbia University in New York in 1946,
Poblete became involved with the US branch of the WILPF and, on her return
to Chile, remained one of its few Latin American members. The onset of the
Cold War – when US foreign policy under the Truman administration made
economic aid and credits to Latin America dependent on anti-communist poli-
cies – marginalized Poblete and her fellow *memchistas* in Chile, not only com-
munist activists, but those without party affiliation in the provinces. Lanfranco
González shows through her study of Poblete's correspondence that the
WILPF leader leveraged her international networks to win protection for
MEMCH members. As Cold War tensions increased, she writes, Poblete
allied herself with the Chilean branch of the Soviet-supported World
Council of Peace even though she "did not wish for either a Soviet or
North American peace imposed by war".

As the stand-off between the United States and the Soviet Union heated up
in the late 1940s, women such as Olga Poblete faced increasingly difficult political choices when forging transnational alliances. Scholars have long recognized that Latin American feminists linked to the Inter American
Commission on Women, established in 1928 as the first intergovernmental
organization for women's rights in the world, played a crucial role in pushing
for the inclusion of women's rights in the United Nations Charter.[43] The
internationalist Pan-American feminism that emerged in Latin America during the 1930s was not simply a result of ideas being exported from the
United States and Western Europe to the "South".[44] Evolving from the
ethos of the global Popular Front against the crises of that era – the Great
Depression, the Chaco War between Bolivia and Paraguay (1932–1935), fascism's rise in Europe and Asia, right-wing authoritarianism in the Americas
and the Spanish Civil War (1936–1938) – interwar Pan-American feminism

---

43. Katherine Marino, *Feminism for the Americas: The Making of an International Human Rights
Movement* (Chapel Hill, NC, 2019; Ellen DuBois, Lauren Derby, "The Strange Case of Minerva
Bernardino: Pan American and United Nations Women's Rights Activist", *Women's Studies
International Forum*, 32 (2009), pp. 43–50.
44. Marino, ibid.

incorporated "feminist labor concerns with equal rights demands and [knitted] crucial connections between feminism, socialism, antifascism and anti-imperialism".[45] Latin American feminists, as Katherine Marino shows, dramatically expanded the contemporary focus of US feminists on legal equality to demand economic and social rights for women (including equal pay, labour rights for rural and domestic workers, rights of children born out of wedlock, paid maternity leave and childcare), as well as promoting Latin American leadership and opposition to US imperialism.

Although the WIDF offered a space for international collaboration across ideological divides in the early years of the Cold War, Manuel Ramírez Chicharro emphasizes the tensions that emerged between the European leadership of the Federation and WIDF affiliates in Latin America. In Mexico and Cuba, Ramírez Chicharro argues, tensions between the European WIDF leadership and local affiliates were compounded by the effects of US foreign policy in Latin America during the early years of the Cold War. Anti-communism in post-revolutionary, corporatist Mexico, for example, marginalized communist-affiliated women who had been active in Mexican radical feminism during the 1930s. His article examines the activities of Mexican and Cuban associations for women that were ideologically close to national communist parties, at a time when these parties had been banned. Both the Cuban and Mexican branches of the WIDF firmly opposed US imperialist intervention, and supported measures to improve the literacy and culture of female peasants. Ramírez Chicharro suggests that the Cuban Federation was more effective than the Mexican organizations, which had been excluded from government once the revolutionary period of Lazaro Cárdenas in the 1930s had ended. The corporatist Mexican state integrated left wing, reformist, and conservative women into mixed organizations, and communist women lost influence; moreover, Mexican women were not enfranchised until 1958. As a result, communist-leaning Mexican women embraced conservative gender roles, despite their radical ideological backgrounds. By contrast, he writes, the Cuban Federation "seemed to promote discourses to decolonize, or at least to radicalize, traditional conceptions of femininity linked to the nation's progress and modernization". By studying the diverse voices of Latin American affiliates of the WIDF, Ramírez Chicharro argues that Latin American women sought to expand the Federation's vision of women's rights in relation to their own priorities, for example, regarding rural women or women of colour, partly in response to perceptions of paternalism among the European leadership of the organisation.

---

45. Marino, *Feminism for the Americas*, p. 5.

"STATE FEMINISM" AND SOCIALIST INTERNATIONALISM IN THE GLOBAL COLD WAR

The second set of articles – by Zsófia Lóránd, Nicola Spakowski, and Yulia Gradskova – explore the connections between women's rights and socialist internationalism during the period of "building socialism" in Eastern Europe and China after World War II. In post-war East Central Europe, Zsófia Lóránd argues, the language of socialist internationalism meshed uneasily with older discourses of race in women's organizations that were also subject to rapid Stalinization in the late 1940s. Her article traces this argument through a detailed analysis of the women's magazine *Asszonyok*, the main publication of the Hungarian Women's Democratic Federation (MNDSz) – a Popular Front umbrella organization that swiftly became the women's section of the Hungarian Communist Party (MKP) after 1945. After the "national Christian" governments of the interwar years, German occupation and life under the fascist Arrow Cross, Hungarian feminists were seeking to redefine women's rights in the socialist state of the MKP. Lóránd argues that, in the early post-war years, the style and content of *Asszonyok* was influenced by interwar Hungarian women's movements and communist activism, especially the experience that editor-in-chief Magda Aranyossi gained while working in Paris for the magazine *Femmes* in the 1930s, where she became a founding member of the CMF and met Gabrielle Duchêne. Aranyossi was a writer and journalist from a Jewish landowning family who was forced to emigrate after the collapse of the Hungarian Soviet Republic, returning to Hungary in 1941 to join the underground communist resistance against the Axis-allied regime of Miklos Horthy. By studying the internal workings of the MNDSz and the editorial processes of *Asszonyok*, Lóránd shows how "the celebration of friendship and a broad anti-fascist alliance of women which characterised the era contrasts starkly with the series of betrayals in the Stalinisation process amongst the charismatic women of the era". Party affiliation, not class solidarity, she suggests, ultimately dictated these alliances and betrayals. At the same time, orientalism tinged the magazine's representations of anti-colonial movements, while minority women within Hungary – particularly the Roma – were absent from its pages.

While the notion of "state feminism" has been used productively to show how women worked to advance their interests within the structures of socialist states, might this concept assume too sharp a distinction between the spheres of state and society? This is the argument put forward by Nicola Spakowski in an alternative interpretation of women's agency in the early years of the People's Republic of China, suggesting that "labour" is a more appropriate lens for conceptualizing relations between women and the communist state. A Chinese labour heroine, Shen Jilan (1929–2020), emerges in Spakowski's article as a lens for understanding feminism in socialist societies through the prism of work rather than the state. Shen

Jilan was one of the most prominent Chinese woman labour models of the early 1950s, "rising to fame through her struggle for equal pay for women in Xigou village and even becoming a delegate to the Third World Congress of Women [organized by the WIDF] in Copenhagen in 1953". Spakowski argues that the "new sense of honor, dignity and acts of recognition" that Chinese women gained through their work at the local and national level were "important aspects of their 'liberation' – gains that are easily overlooked in a rights-centered discussion". Yet, this was not translated into recognition on the international level, since: "It was the educated and experienced heads of the Chinese delegation who represented New China on the congress stage and pointed to uneducated and young Shen Jilan as mere evidence of successful liberation." In contrast to the concept of a "top-down" process of state-led women's emancipation, Shen Jilan was a "central actor in the transformation of the gender order at the village level" and a "representative of the working class in China's new political order" at the national level, but on the international stage, became only a "symbol of the superiority of socialism as a society of gender equality".

The shifting scales of analysis in Spakowski's study of Shen Jilan encourage us to consider the quest for legitimacy on the international stage, as well as at home. Turning to the Soviet Union, Yulia Gradskova's article explores this issue by asking how the Soviet Women's Committee sought to influence the work of the WIDF, particularly in relation to women from newly independent countries in Africa and Asia. Drawing on the archives of the Soviet Women's Committee in Moscow, Gradskova builds on her earlier research, which used internal WIDF correspondence and reports of the Soviet Committee to reconstruct the numerous instances of women from Africa, Asia and Latin America calling on the WIDF to change its programme and structure in order better to represent the women in their countries. In many cases, it seems,

> [the] WIDF leadership, and particularly Soviet representatives, opposed their demands. This happened especially when proposed changes went against current Soviet foreign policy goals (for example, the conflict between the Soviet insistence on détente and women's participation in armed anti-colonial struggles) or when representatives of women's organizations from the Global South tried to insert their priorities on the WIDF's agenda, such as demanding women's right to be landowners.[46]

For her article in this Special Issue, Gradskova focuses particularly on the way in which the apparent success of Soviet development policies in Central Asia was used to sell the Soviet model of women's emancipation to postcolonial countries during the 1950s and 1960s, particularly in the context of growing competition between the Soviet Union and China. Importantly, however, she also argues that women

---

46. Yulia Gradskova, "Women's International Democratic Federation, the 'Third World' and the Global Cold War from the Late-1950s to the Mid-1960s", *Women's History Review*, 29:2 (2020), pp. 270–288.

from the Soviet republics in Central Asia – such as Zuhra Rahimbabaeva from Uzbekistan, who was appointed the Soviet delegate to the WIDF Secretariat in East Berlin in the late 1960s – played a significant role in reshaping and improving the Federation's relationships with women from the Global South.

THIRD WORLD SOLIDARITY, WOMEN'S RIGHTS, AND THE END OF THE COLD WAR

The final set of articles – by Allison Drew, Giulia Strippoli, and Mallarika Sinha Roy – turn their attention to southern Africa in the 1960s, and the transformation of socialist internationalism during the United Nations Decade for Women launched in 1975. Despite the crucial contributions of women to anti-colonial and nationalist movements in Africa, their role was frequently diminished after independence.[47] In South Africa, the African National Congress (ANC) refused for a long time to "acknowledge that gender discrimination needed to be addressed ahead of national liberation", believing that feminism was a bourgeois indulgence of white women in the "West" that did not apply to a radical liberation movement.[48] During the early years of the ANC's operations in exile, women activists relied on an informal "women's affairs" group led by Ruth Mompati (1925–2015) in Dar es Salaam. The 1963 WIDF conference in Moscow enabled Mompati to make contact with women from Angola's MPLA, which later resulted in further connections to women in West Africa. In 1969, an ANC conference in Morogoro created a Women's Section that would work out of ANC headquarters. The Women's Secretariat moved from Dar es Salaam to Lusaka, Zambia, in 1973. However, some ANC women were wary of getting trapped into working for the Women's Section, which they saw as focusing on welfare work shaped by conservative ideas about women's "traditional" roles rather than political issues, while the ANC leadership continued to rely on women to "fill traditional caring roles and perform the emotional labour needed to keep the movement together". Yet, South African women's opposition to long-standing racial segregation, which was institutionalized with the apartheid regime in 1948, was built on "decades of experience organising and mobilising opposition to government policies at grassroots and local levels". South African women who tried to organize both within the mixed-gender

47. Meredith Terretta, *Petitioning for our Rights, Fighting for Our Nation: The History of the Democratic Union of Cameroonian Women, 1949–1960* (Bamenda, 2013); Susan Geiger, *TANU Women: Gender and Culture in the Making of Tanganyikan Nationalism, 1955–1965* (Portsmouth, NH, 1997).
48. Emma Lundin, "'Now is the Time!' The Importance of International Spaces for Women's Activism within the ANC, 1960–1976", *Journal of Southern African Studies*, 45:2 (2019), pp. 323–340.

ANC and in women-only organizations were accused of endangering the movement's campaigns for liberation.

The ANC-aligned Federation of South African Women did not formally affiliate to the WIDF, most likely due to South Africa's 1950 Suppression of Communism Act, but it was influenced by the WIDF's "left-feminist internationalism" as well as by local concerns. At its first meeting, held in Johannesburg in April 1954, FEDSAW adopted a Women's Charter, and a year later contributed the section on women's demands to the Freedom Charter adopted by the Congress Alliance. FEDSAW's demands included rights to maternity leave, antenatal and childcare, nursery schools and access to contraception for "all mothers of all races", as well as children's rights to health and education, rights to housing, infrastructure, and food.[49] FEDSAW delegates attended the WIDF World Congress of Mothers in Lausanne in July 1955. Maternalism was the key discourse that connected "South African women and the world beyond". During the 1950s, FEDSAW organized marches and demonstrations – culminating in a 20,000-strong women's march on the Union Buildings in Pretoria in August 1956 – that delayed the implementation of pass laws for all African women, and "forced the state to see them as political agents".[50]

In South Africa, as Allison Drew points out, the experience of male political prisoners in the struggle against apartheid has been universalized, while women's experiences have been marginalized. To counteract this narrative, Drew's article focuses on two tiny socialist mixed-sex groups established on South Africa's Cape Peninsula during the first years of armed struggle against apartheid in South Africa: the little-known Yu Chi Chan Club and National Liberation Front, which split from the Non-European Unity Movement, a rival of the African National Congress. The State of Emergency imposed in March 1960 after the Sharpeville massacre marked a new phase in the anti-apartheid struggle, in which women had to find different ways to assert themselves. The ANC and PAC were banned and driven into exile. The YCCC and NLF were active on the Cape Peninsula from April 1962 until their members were arrested in mid-1963. Drawing on interviews, court records, and NLF publications, Drew argues that the group's "relatively flat organizational structure and non-gendered activities facilitated women's participation", in contrast to the hierarchical organization of the South African Communist Party. She suggests that "the NLF's focus on learning and its small horizontally-organized cells allowed women to participate", meaning that "its history has a significance beyond its tiny numbers and ephemeral existence, one that stands as a critique of the sexism that has characterized the South African left". After their arrest, eleven members of the NLF received

49. Meghan Healy-Clancy, "The Family Politics of the Federation of South African Women: A History of Public Motherhood in Women's Antiracist Activism", *Signs: Journal of Women in Culture and Society*, 42:4 (2017), pp. 843–866.
50. *Ibid.*

prison sentences of five to ten years. Four of these were women. And yet, as female political prisoners, their experiences have been erased from histories of anti-apartheid activism. Drew argues that reconstructing the history of groups such as the NLF can demonstrate the extent to which the experience of male political prisoners in the struggle against apartheid has been universalized, while women's experiences have been marginalized.

This was notably the case, Giulia Strippoli argues, for one of the last European colonial powers to relinquish its territories in Africa: Portugal. The importance of understanding transnational alliances between women as a political resource, rather than emphasizing women's dependent relations on male-dominated political parties, emerges from Strippoli's study of connections between the Portuguese Movement of Democratic Women (*Movimento Democrático de Mulheres;* MDM), and women's organizations in Cabo Verde, Guinea-Bissau, Angola, and Mozambique during the Portuguese anti-colonial wars of the 1960s and 1970s. Existing studies have either analysed these associations within a national frame, or highlighted the relations between anti-colonial movements in Portuguese territories and the Soviet Union. By contrast, Strippoli argues women associated with anti-Salazar and anti-colonial movements in Portugal and Africa were forging connections already in the 1950s. The WIDF acted as a crucial space where Lusophone women could make connections, she suggests, even before the formation of oppositional women's movements such as the MDM within Portugal itself. Strippoli resists an explanation based on party or ideological affiliation, in which women's activism is interpreted in relation to male-dominated communist or socialist parties, instead emphasizing the importance of transnational female solidarity in connecting anti-colonial movements to oppositional movements in Portugal.

Finally, Mallarika Sinha Roy's article about Malobika Chattopadhyay's experiences as Secretary of the Asian Commission in the headquarters of the Women's International Democratic Federation in East Berlin between 1984 and 1987, explores the "dreams Indian socialists held concerning European socialism" in the final years of the global Cold War. Chattopadhyay had been part of the Indian communist movement since her university studies in Calcutta in the 1950s, and remained active in Leftist women's organizations in West Bengal from the 1960s. Sinha Roy's article draws on diaries and memoirs that Chattopadhyay published during and after her journey to the GDR, situating her experiences within a longer history "of travel from colony to the metropole, and later from the postcolonial locations to European metropolitan centres", but one that also involved "making sense of the vast gap between 'real' and 'imagined' socialist Europe". The importance of travel differentiates her texts from the genre of Bengali memoirs of socialist women. Sinha Roy suggests that the memoir has not received much attention as an example of Indian women's writing due to the "delayed attention to the creative and experiential worlds of women in the Leftist political parties, literary and cultural organisations in India".

Sinha Roy's article could thus be located in a broader drive to challenge the absence of communists in studies of Indian writing and gender, "partly because of their declining political fortunes in recent years and partly because they are associated with sorry narratives of political compromise as well as an unimaginative, and at times outright hostile, approach to questions of feminist agency and sexuality".[51] Greater attention has been paid to Marxists outside the CPI. Yet, Loomba warns that we should not "oversimplify the political commitment or subjectivities of those who stayed within the Party fold. Party affiliations do not necessarily guarantee radical commitment, nor do they automatically denote radicalism compromised". "Communist self-fashioning did not take place in an ideological or social space of its own. Especially when it came to questions of gender and sexuality, communists were as deeply influenced by nationalist ideas and practices as they were by Marxist and revolutionary ones; indeed, the former provided the lens through which they viewed and appropriated the latter." Chattopadhyay's travels to East Berlin, Moscow, Athens, and the UN World Conference on Women in Nairobi in 1985, as Sinha Roy so insightfully demonstrates, show this process of socialist feminist self-fashioning also unfolding through encounters with the real and imagined worlds of European socialism.

CONCLUSION

In 2009, Malobika Chattopadhyay returned to Berlin, now the capital of unified Germany. The WIDF, which had institutionalized the camaraderie of socialist feminism that had brought her to the GDR more than twenty years earlier, had vanished from the city. Her former colleagues and friends were reluctant to discuss unification. The international world of "global socialism", of which the WIDF had been one small part, had disappeared, bringing to an end the institutions and disrupting the biographies of several generations of internationally minded communist women. Across the postsocialist world, from Eastern Europe and the former Soviet Union to China, "gender" displaced the older focus on women's emancipation as the theoretical lodestar of feminism.[52] Gender was presented as a concept enabling a clean break with the socialist past.[53] The concept of gender, as developed by Western feminists, was disseminated by transnational networks of individuals, non-governmental organizations, and Western foundations. Postsocialist

---

51. Ania Loomba, *Revolutionary Desires: Women, Communism and Feminism in India* (London, 2018).

52. Nicola Spakowski, "Socialist Feminism in Postsocialist China", *positions: asia critique* 26:4 (2018), pp. 561–592.

53. Susan Zimmermann, "The Institutionalization of Women's and Gender Studies in Higher Education in Central and Eastern Europe and the Former Soviet Union: Asymmetric Politics and the Regional-Transnational Configuration", *East Central Europe*, 34–35:1–2 (2008), pp. 131–160.

experiences of inequality, which were felt disproportionately by women as the privatization of economies was accompanied by the privatization of families, fostered a sense of nostalgia for the egalitarian structures of socialism.[54]

But, as the essays in this collection demonstrate, the socialist past is not simply a resource for contemporary feminisms. Many of the questions raised by the authors have been the subject of long-standing debates, which have re-emerged in recent scholarship about the history of "global feminisms" in the twentieth century.[55] This collaborative project has suggested that a history of struggles over women's rights in the global communist movements of the short twentieth century should look beyond the narrative of solidarity that those movements themselves constructed. Race, political affiliation, and geography were not erased by international communist movements, but constituted the relations between the women who sustained them throughout the twentieth century.

54. Enzo Traverso, *Left-Wing Melancholia: Marxism, History, and Memory* (New York, 2016); Alastair Bonnett, *Left in the Past: Radicalism and the Politics of Nostalgia* (London/New York, 2010).
55. Lucy Delap, *Global Feminisms*; Dorothy Sue Cobble, *For the Many*; Kristen Ghodsee, *Second World, Second Sex*.

IRSH 67 (2022), pp. 23–47 doi:10.1017/S0020859021000675

"Warphans" and "Quiet" Heroines: Depictions of Chinese Women and Children in the *Comité mondial des femmes contre la guerre et le fascisme's* Campaigns during the Second Sino-Japanese War*

Jasmine Calver ⓘ

Faculty of Arts and Creative Industries
University of Sunderland
St Peters Campus, St Peters Way
Sunderland SR6 0DD, United Kingdom

E-mail: jasmine.calver@sunderland.ac.uk

Abstract: The *Comité mondial des femmes contre la guerre et le fascisme* (CMF) was an international organization formed under the direction of the Communist International in 1934 in response to the threat of Nazi fascism. However, it did not restrict its activities to tackling issues in Germany; it expanded its remit to confront many of the crises that marked the mid- to late-1930s across the globe. This article analyses the CMF's work to aid civilians and refugees during the Second Sino-Japanese War. It discusses how the predominantly European committee perpetuated some essentialist and imperialist assumptions in its work and how they utilized violent and emotive language in the "Warphans" child sponsorship fundraising scheme. However, the committee also provided spaces for Chinese women to vocalize their experiences to women in the West, creating an effective humanitarian aid strategy.

INTRODUCTION

In March 1939, the British section of the *Comité mondial des femmes contre la guerre et le fascisme* (CMF) used its journal, *Woman To-day*, to appeal to members to contribute to its most recent campaign: a child sponsorship

---

* I am very grateful to Celia Donert for inviting me to participate in such an exciting Special Issue. I also thank Celia, Nicola Spakowski, and the anonymous reviewers for their feedback on this article. Thanks also go to the other contributors to this Special Issue for their suggestions. This article is the result of research done during my PhD at Northumbria University and I thank my supervisor, Charlotte Alston, and my examiners, Laura O'Brien and Laura Beers, for the suggestion that this section of my thesis be reworked into an article.

initiative for Chinese children orphaned by the Second Sino-Japanese War. To convince readers to donate, the journal stressed the increasingly globalized world in which they were living:

> China – so far away, people say – what has it to do with us? That may have been so many years ago, but to-day China is near us and so are her people. (Charlotte Haldane, Special Delegate to China from the Women's Committee for Peace and Democracy, flew from London to Hong Kong in five and a half days.)[1]

The CMF endeavoured to forge connections and collaboration between the Western European centre of operations and the rest of the world in the 1930s. A communist, anti-fascist organization targeting women, the CMF viewed the expansion of women's activism into Africa, Asia, and the Americas as integral to the success of its mission. As such, the carnage of the Second Sino-Japanese War and its impact on women and children drew the committee's attention. Estimates of Chinese casualties in the war vary from fifteen to twenty million, occurring alongside an internal refugee crisis on an unprecedented scale as tens of millions of civilians were forced from their homes.[2] In many cases, women and children were the focus of aggression from the invading Japanese troops: the most infamous example of this aggression was the massacre in Nanjing over the winter of 1937/38, in which Chinese estimates state that 300,000 civilians were murdered and as many as 80,000 women and girls were raped.[3] The overwhelmingly gendered nature of the violence and its impact on children was the main concern of the CMF.

The first section of this article will consider how imperialist rhetoric clashed with feminism in CMF work, as it invoked stereotypical depictions of Chinese women as quiet, stoic mothers, while simultaneously allowing Chinese women a platform through which to dispel these assumptions and articulate their experiences. In addition, there were frank discussions of the mass rape that they experienced, but no attempts to construct a feminist strategy to confront it. In the second part of this article, I will discuss how the CMF utilized maternalist rhetoric to forge connections between Western and Chinese women as a humanitarian strategy, which often ignored the nationalist

---

1. "Introducing the 'Warphans'", *Woman To-day* (March 1939), p. 20; The CMF became the Women's Committee for Peace and Democracy in 1939. To prevent confusion, I will use the abbreviation CMF throughout the article.
2. Lloyd E. Eastman, "Nationalist China during the Sino-Japanese War, 1937–1945", in John K. Fairbank and Albert Feuerwerker (eds), *The Cambridge History of China, Volume 13: Republican China 1912–1949, Part 2* (Cambridge, 2008), pp. 547–608, 547; and Maura Cunningham, "Shanghai's Wandering Ones: Child Welfare in a Global City, 1900–1953" (Ph.D., University of California, 2014), pp. 106 and 121 [hereafter, "Shanghai's Wandering Ones, 1900–1953"].
3. This is the highest Chinese estimate, while some Japanese sources claim that fewer than 100 were killed and "very few" were raped; Joshua A. Fogel, *The Nanjing Massacre in History and Historiography* (Berkeley, CA, 2000), p. 6.

priorities of the Chinese population. Third, I will examine how the CMF used the concept of child sponsorship to fundraise for children orphaned by the war, known colloquially as "Warphans" in the press. The "Warphans" campaign was also gendered along traditional, Western lines to encourage women as (potential) mothers to contribute, as well as employing violent language to create a short but successful humanitarian campaign.

Before the globalization of women's activism, which occurred in the post-1945 period, exemplified by organizations such as the Women's International Democratic Federation (WIDF, which Mercedes Yusta has presented as a successor to the CMF), CMF activists were actively facilitating processes of mobility and exchange across borders, in this case between Western Europe and China.[4] The CMF's China campaign bore clear similarities with the WIDF's mission to North Korea in 1951 as socialist women activists travelled to a nation that was devastated by war and experiencing a vast refugee crisis. Celia Donert has argued that WIDF used "maternalist language to legitimate women's 'independent' role as observers in conflict" and graphic descriptions of violence against women and children in its report on the Korean conflict, both of which were key tactics in the CMF's work in China.[5]

This article will be the first study on how the CMF conducted its campaigns; there has not been much examination of the CMF in the historical literature, and what has been written has tended to give a surface level overview of the committee without examining its processes or its campaigns on issues faced by women across the globe.[6] This article rectifies this gap in the literature, as it offers new opportunities through which to study the practice of women's socialist activism on a global scale in the 1930s. It will highlight processes of information exchange and the contradictions inherent in them to demonstrate that, while Chinese women gained an international voice by publicizing their struggle in CMF spaces, colonialist tropes, maternalist language, and a certain infantilization of the Chinese people were invoked to stimulate sympathy despite the committee's ideological and political positions.

---

4. Mercedes Yusta, "The Strained Courtship Between Antifascism and Feminism: From the Women's World Committee (1934) to the Women's International Democratic Federation (1945)", in Hugo Garcia *et al.* (eds), *Rethinking Antifascism: History, Memory and Politics 1922 to the Present* (Oxford, 2016), pp. 167–184, 167.

5. Celia Donert, "From Communist Internationalism to Human Rights: Gender, Violence and International Law in the Women's International Democratic Federation Mission to North Korea, 1951", *Contemporary European History*, 25:2 (2016), pp. 313–333, 323–324.

6. For further information on the CMF, see Jasmine Calver, "The Comité mondial des femmes contre la guerre et le fascisme: Anti-Fascist, Feminist, and Communist Activism in the 1930s" (Ph.D., Northumbria University, 2019) [hereafter, "The Comité mondial des femmes contre la guerre et le fascisme"].

A BRIEF HISTORY OF THE *COMITÉ MONDIAL DES FEMMES CONTRE LA GUERRE ET LE FASCISME*

Formed in 1934, in Paris, the *Comité mondial des femmes contre la guerre et le fascisme* was an international communist front organization that provided communists with new opportunities to reach working-class women who were heavily underrepresented in their parties. To take one example, the *Parti communiste français* had a female membership of just 200 in 1929, totalling 0.6 per cent of its members.[7] The CMF was created, in part, as an attempt to shift this imbalance by engaging with women deemed prime for political conversion to communism: socialists; Labour Party women; left-leaning non-party women; intellectuals; and working women in particular. However, this desire to attract non-communist women to the committee served another purpose. The CMF publicly declared itself to be above parties and was therefore used by the Comintern to test the Popular Front strategy of collaboration between parties on the left before adopting it as official policy. Like its sibling organization, the Amsterdam-Pleyel movement, the CMF was developed to discover whether left-wing activists could pool their strengths and coordinate actions against the threat of fascism effectively, despite the conflicts that had ravaged the left after 1917. This policy achieved some success in attracting socialist women to work with communist women in the CMF. Most notably, the Belgian socialist women's leader, Isabelle Blume, led the Belgian national section in tandem with the communist municipal councillor, Marcelle Leroy. However, continued concerns about communist influence on the CMF prevented it from becoming a fully effective Popular Front movement.

The CMF aimed to unite women from across the globe against fascism and imperialism and tried to reconcile the conflict between socialism and "bourgeois" feminism that had raged since the late nineteenth century. It differed from larger international women's organizations, including the Women's International League for Peace and Freedom (WILPF) and the International Council of Women, for two key reasons: first, it was deeply influenced by the politics of communist internationalism and second, it did not oppose warfare in the quest for national independence, communist revolution, or defeating fascism. It offered socialist women an avenue through which to work with feminists and utilized the "rhetoric of internationalism" (to borrow from June Hannam and Karen Hunt), specifically anti-fascist internationalism, to encourage feminist women to eschew their reservations about the influence of communism on the committee.[8] The CMF's approach to gender was complex, as the group simultaneously espoused maternalist conceptions of

---

7. Christine Bard and Jean-Louis Robert, "The French Communist Party and Women, 1920–1939", in Helmut Gruber and Pamela Graves (eds), *Women and Socialism – Socialism and Women: Europe Between the World Wars* (Oxford, 1998), pp. 321–347, 323.
8. June Hannam and Karen Hunt, *Socialist Women: Britain 1880s–1920s* (London, 2011), p. 196.

women's role in the home and championed women's right to work by necessity or choice. Further, it celebrated those women who took up arms in the fight against fascism and war and supported traditional feminist demands, including the fight for women's suffrage.

In its short lifetime (it disbanded circa 1940), the CMF had representatives and national committees on every continent, all of whom were committed to confronting the threat of the far right, to developing the socialist consciousness of working women in their own countries, and to creating an organization that united women from "all points of the earth" against a common enemy.[9] The International Executive Committee of the CMF was based in Paris and the group's largest national section was the French group; by March 1937, the French section totalled 200,000 women in 2,000 local committees and contributed to and organized events on a variety of topics, from strikes to women's enfranchisement.[10] It also had substantial support in Belgium and amongst German and Italian refugees.

The CMF was led by women who held important roles in the international communist and international feminist movements. Of particular importance here is Charlotte Haldane, the leader of the British section of the CMF, whose visit to China in 1938 made her an important witness to the suffering faced by Chinese civilians during the war. Haldane was a journalist for the *Daily Express* newspaper in the 1920s and published the dystopian science fiction novel *Man's World* in 1926. By 1927, Haldane had joined the communist party; she organized volunteers for the International Brigades in Paris for the Comintern and acted as a guide for important people who toured Spain during the Civil War, including the American entertainer Paul Robeson. She was charged with visiting China by the CMF and the Comintern, but her role extended beyond being a communist delegate; she also represented the China Campaign Committee, was a special correspondent in China for the *Daily Herald*, and relayed letters and sentiments to the Chinese leadership from Clement Attlee and Archibald Sinclair, leaders of the Labour Party and Liberal Party in Britain, respectively. She also published a report on the "situation in China and the Far East" for the House of Commons on her return to Britain.[11] Haldane's connections with major politicians and newspapers despite her communism were significant and provided a greater sense of legitimacy to her work for Chinese women and children.

9. "Manifeste vote au Congrès Mondial des Femmes contre la Guerre et le Fascisme", Portail Archives Numériques et Données de la Recherche (hereafter, PANDOR], 543_2_1, fos 120–122, p. 1.

10. "Information on the Work of the National Women's Anti-War and Anti-Fascist Commissions" (1937), PANDOR, 543_2_21, fo. 84, pp. 1, 4, and 8.

11. Charlotte Haldane, *Truth Will Out* (London, 1949), pp. 145–146; and Charlotte Haldane, "Report on the Situation in China and the Far East" (1938), Fabian Colonial Bureau Papers [hereafter, FBC], Bodleian Library, University of Oxford, Box 165, p. 1.

The CMF Executive Committee was primarily concerned with the threat that fascism and war posed to women and children. It organized aid and information campaigns based on the experiences of women in the Spanish Civil War, Nazi Germany, and during the Italian invasion of Abyssinia by employing a dichotomous discourse that positioned women as either the caring mother or the masculinized fighter, with little overlap between the two. For a committee that publicized and attempted to alleviate the impact of war and fascism-related violence on women, the Second Sino-Japanese War (1937–1945) was a source of anxiety that mobilized them to consider new strategies to ameliorate the situation of their Chinese "sisters" and their children.

THE CONTRIBUTIONS AND CONSTRUCTION(S) OF CHINESE WOMEN IN CMF DISCOURSE

The personal experiences of Chinese women during the war were integral to CMF efforts to raise consciousness about Japanese aggression in China. The committee worked with various Chinese women to stimulate strong enough bonds of "sisterhood" and sympathy across borders to pledge donations of money, food, or clothing. It gave Chinese women the opportunity to speak for themselves and to recount their experiences in graphic detail. Of particular importance, the committee provided a space for discussion of the mass rapes perpetrated by Japanese soldiers on Chinese women. Rape has been a feature of warfare for millennia, but it became more apparent in the public consciousness with the widespread sexual assault of French and Belgian women by German soldiers during World War I. However, contemporary propaganda discourses on the "Rape of Belgium", as this event has become known, tended to conflate the violated female body with the nation, minimizing the personal trauma of women who had been the target of these attacks as a result.[12] The CMF, however, blended its socialist feminism and internationalism to highlight the real impact of sexual trauma during wartime on its female victims and their children in its humanitarian propaganda.

The Nanjing Massacre in late 1937 was the subject of a speech given by a Chinese sociology student, Loh Tsei, at the CMF's Marseille Congress in 1938 (Figure 1). She had gained a reputation as "China's Joan of Arc" in the American press for her role in the Chinese student movement and was particularly well-known for her contribution to the demonstration against Japanese imperialism that took place on 16 December 1935 in Beijing, during which

---

12. Nicoletta F. Gullace, "Sexual Violence and Family Honor: British Propaganda and International Law during the First World War", *The American Historical Review*, 102:3 (1997), pp. 714–747. See also Philippa Read, "'I am expected to say something. I know not what' (Vivanti 1918, 146): Silence and Working through in Rape Narratives of the First World War", *Modern and Contemporary France*, 27:3 (2019), pp. 309–321.

Figure 1. Loh Tsei, the Chinese student activist, photographed by Carl Van Vechten in New York on 16 September 1939. Labelled as China's "Joan of Arc" by the press during her propaganda tours of America, she was a key figure in the December 9th student movement in 1935. I thank the Carl Van Vechten Trust for kindly giving me permission to use the image in this article. Carl Van Vechten / Beinecke Library, ©Van Vechten Trust.

she opened a gate to allow between 2,500 and 8,000 students to join the protest.[13] Arrested and "beaten with gun butts", she became a leader in the Chinese student movement after her release and was sent to Europe and the United States to advocate for support.[14]

Loh Tsei spoke graphically about the Nanjing massacre, in which Chinese women suffered "humiliations which exceed the imaginations of civilized peoples". In a "moving" speech, Loh Tsei told of how "Japanese soldiers [...] search from house to house for all the women and inflict a terrible fate on them: raped, tortured, sometimes almost killed", with husbands shot if they tried to help their wives.[15] She utilized emotive and violent language to expose the horrors of the massacre, citing a missionary who wrote that he had seen a woman in the hospital who "had been raped twenty times" and whose head the Japanese soldiers had attempted to remove, "resulting in a serious throat injury". Tsei stated that "100 cases of rape" at the University of Nanking were reported in just one night, including two girls of eleven and twelve years of age.[16] She utilized this language not only to report the incidents of violence towards Chinese women accurately, but also to induce a response in the women who were listening in person and who read the congress report; it was intended to create a sense of horror among the audience, which would propel them to act on behalf of the victims.

The kidnapping of Chinese women by Japanese soldiers was similarly highlighted by the CMF during its humanitarian activism. During the "Warphans" campaign (which will be explored in detail later in the article), the committee revealed that some of the children orphaned by the Second Sino-Japanese War had witnessed a particularly gendered, violent attack on their families, in that they saw their mothers kidnapped (and sometimes killed) by Japanese soldiers. Japanese soldiers kidnapped Chinese women, girls, elderly, and pregnant women frequently during the Second Sino-Japanese War to rape, use as sex slaves, or to force them to work in "comfort stations" established for institutional sexual slavery. The first official "comfort station" was established in Shanghai in 1932 shortly after the Japanese invasion of Manchuria.[17]

13. "Loh Tsei, in Spite of Her Size, is 'Joan of Arc' to Thousands", *Columbia Daily Spectator* (23 April 1937), pp. 1 and 4; and Jessie G. Lutz, "December 9, 1935: Student Nationalism and the China Christian Colleges", *The Journal of Asian Studies*, 26:4 (1967), pp. 627–648, 637.

14. Nancy Bedford-Jones, "China's Joan of Arc", *The Woman Today* (February 1937), p. 8. *The Woman Today* is a Communist Party of the US publication and not affiliated with the CMF. *Woman To-day* is the journal of the British section of the CMF.

15. "LES FEMMES DU MONDE ENTIER AU SERVICE DE LA PAIX ! Compte rendu de la Conférence internationale des femmes, Marseille 13–14–15 Mai 1938" (1938), Centre d'histoire sociale des mondes contemporains [hereafter, CHS], Archives Bernadette Cattanéo, 1-BC2-L1, p. 13.

16. Loh Tsei, "TOUT LE POUVOIR DES FEMMES AU SERVICE DE LA PAIX ET DE LA DEMOCRATIE" (1938), PANDOR, 543_2_26, fos 23–24, pp. 1–2.

17. Peipei Qiu *et al.*, *Chinese Comfort Women: Testimonies from Imperial Japan's Sex Slaves* (Vancouver, 2013), p. 22.

Chinese women were not only targeted for mass sexual violence because of the sexual deviancy of the Japanese forces, but also because they represented the "body of the nation" and rape stood as a "gesture of conquest", as Belgian women had been twenty years earlier.[18]

By March 1939, Western observers would have known, to some extent, that mass sexual violence was occurring in China. However, it is not clear how far CMF members would have understood the subtext of rape in the description of mothers being "abducted" or "taken away" by Japanese soldiers. However, the result was still horrifying, even if readers of Loh Tsei's report did not fully understand that the kidnap of Chinese women ultimately meant their sexual assault. In addition, an article in the CMF's French journal, *Femmes dans l'action mondiale*, profiled four Chinese children who had seen the kidnap and murder of their mother by Japanese soldiers, demonstrating the extreme violence that the children had witnessed. It also suggests that the children interviewed for this article had witnessed the entire attack on their mother, from kidnap to rape and murder, a fact that some of the more informed readers would have understood and that may have encouraged them to act out of horror and sympathy for the children.[19]

However, the committee's discourse on sexual violence had several limitations. Although it publicized a traumatic and often overlooked aspect of war and gave Chinese women the opportunity to discuss it on their terms, the group used these descriptions of gender-based atrocities entirely as propaganda for its humanitarian work. It did not engage with feminist politics to examine the motivations behind these atrocities or to suggest solutions, nor did it collaborate with other international groups on campaigns on civilian protection. Beyond some participation in women's delegations to the League of Nations and cooperation with organizations in a national context, the CMF tended to work unilaterally. Despite the group's resolute commitment to exposing all the horrors of the war between China and Japan, in practice its frank portrayal of sexual assault served little purpose other than consciousness-raising amongst Western women.

The involvement of several Chinese women provided a sense of legitimacy and ensured the international character of CMF work. The most renowned name attached to CMF work in China was Soong Ching-ling. As the wife of the first President of the Republic of China, Sun Yat-sen, and an important figure in Chinese politics in her own right (including being named the Honorary President of the People's Republic of China shortly before her death in 1981), Soong had broken with the nationalist Kuomintang party in 1927 after its leader, Chiang Kai-shek, expelled communists from the party and ordered the slaughter of "thousands" of communist cadres in

---

18. Timothy Brook, *Collaboration: Japanese Agents and Local Elites in Wartime China* (Cambridge, MA, 2005), p. 24.
19. "Écoutez-les ! …", *Femmes dans l'action mondiale* (March 1939), p. 15.

Shanghai.[20] In 1927, she spent a few months in Moscow and Berlin, making contact with representatives of the Comintern through whom, it is likely, she became involved with the CMF. She held a position on the *Comité d'honneur* for the group's founding congress in 1934, although neither she, nor any other Chinese delegate attended the meeting in person.[21] Her involvement lent legitimacy to the success of CMF work; for example, the Cantonese pottery that she provided for the CMF's China Bazaar in the winter of 1938 raised £400 to send to the Chinese International Hospital.[22] When Charlotte Haldane travelled to China under the auspices of the Comintern, Soong Ching-ling travelled from her home in Hong Kong to Canton (Guangzhou) to meet her, demonstrating a personal commitment to the CMF. The two had "several long and intimate talks" about the Sovietization of China and Soong's concerns about the growing "fascist" nature of the Kuomintang under Chiang's leadership.[23] These discussions were not published at the time, with the committee focusing entirely on the threat of Japanese imperialism and ignoring the internal conflicts of the Chinese nationalist movement in its publications.

Depictions of Chinese women's experiences during the war in CMF journals often reinforced the Western stereotype of Chinese women as having "little or no freedom", which had, by the interwar period, transformed into a "more complete political and social freedom than any country in the world excepting the Soviet Union". Charlotte Haldane, for example, emphasized the contribution of women to the war effort with their "unsurpassed record for physical valour and courage", evidenced by the "Chinese Florence Nightingales, Joan of Arcs, Judiths, Boadiceas, and Nurse Cavels by the dozen". However, even here Haldane described Chinese women as serene and unassuming, performing their valiant actions with a "quiet 'take it for granted, it's all in the day's work' type of heroism". She also made claims that were disputed by Chinese women themselves. Haldane asserted that the Second Sino-Japanese War had "hastened the development [of Chinese women's rights] which began in 1919", while some Chinese communist women writing for a Chinese audience claimed the opposite; for example, Pan Yihong cited Jun Hui, a member of the Chinese Communist Party, who argued that the men "responsible for defending the country" had established "tighter supervision and control over women's every move" alongside their withdrawal in the face of Japanese troops.[24]

20. Jung Chang and John Halliday, *Mme Sun Yat-sen* (New York, 1986), p. 56.
21. "Rassemblement mondial des femmes ! Contre la guerre et le fascisme : Compte rendu des travaux du congrès" (1934), CHS, Archives Bernadette Cattanéo, 1-BC2-A, p. 5.
22. "Our China Bazaar was a Success", *Woman To-day* (January 1939), p. 5.
23. Haldane, *Truth Will Out*, pp. 155–156.
24. Charlotte Haldane, "Heroines of China", *Woman To-day* (February 1939), pp. 9–10; and Pan Yihong, "Feminism and Nationalism in China's War of Resistance against Japan", *The International History Review*, 19:1 (1997), pp. 115–130, 117.

The height of women's emancipation in China had come in the mid-1920s, as some Chinese women adopted the image of the emancipated "New Woman" in terms of style and political engagement. Women from the Kuomintang and revolutionary parties alike worked to encourage peasant women to engage with politics, and some women began to crop their hair into bobs and wear masculine clothes. However, in April 1927 the Kuomintang turned against revolutionary parties, including feminists; some women with bobbed hair were persecuted or even killed as they "symbolized a liberated woman".[25] Concurrently, the dual conflicts between the nationalists and the communists, and between China and Japan, made women's emancipation less of a priority than the emancipation of the nation. It is important to note that "party-political cleavage was never a defining feature of elite women's public communication and engagement in the 1930s" in China, as women's groups formed a "united front" to fight for national salvation, regardless of party.[26]

Still, this desire for national sovereignty clashed with the main principles of international women's organizations. Many non-Western women supported military action to achieve independence, which was inherently at odds with the total pacifism of the largest women's groups. Mona Siegal has identified "feminist orientalism" on the part of Western women activists, the "recalcitrant nationalism" of Chinese women, "differing understandings of war and political violence, and the relationship of each to feminism" as barriers to collaboration between the WILPF and Chinese women in the interwar period.[27] However, these factors did not present much of an impediment to collaboration between the CMF and Chinese women; although there were orientalist and nationalist aspects to CMF work on China, it by no means negatively impacted the extent to which women from one group cooperated with women from the other. Further, Chinese women and the CMF shared a much closer understanding of the use of warfare than the WILPF did, as the CMF actively encouraged violent struggle against fascism and imperialism and for revolutionary purposes. Thus, the CMF's Chinese campaign had an integral consonance and alignment of philosophies that was lacking in previous associations between Chinese women and international women's groups.

---

25. *Ibid.*, p. 116.
26. Vivienne Xiangwei Guo, "Forging a Women's United Front: Chinese Elite Women's Networks for National Salvation and Resistance, 1932–1938", *Modern Asian Studies*, 53:2 (2019), pp. 483–511, 500 and 511.
27. Mona L. Siegal, "Feminism, Pacifism and Political Violence in Europe and China in the Era of the World Wars", *Gender and History*, 28:3 (2016), pp. 641–659, 649. See also Leila J. Rupp, "Challenging Imperialism in International Women's Organisations, 1888–1945", *NWSA Journal*, 8:1 (1996), pp. 8–27; and Marie Sandell, "Regional versus International: Women's Activism and Organisational Spaces in the Inter-War Period", *The International History Review*, 33:4 (2011), pp. 607–625.

MOTHERHOOD AS A MARKER OF SOLIDARITY

Western writers also heavily relied on essentialist tropes of motherhood to simulate bonds between women separated both by geographical space and by cultural differences. Harriet Hyman Alonso has argued that women did not have to be mothers because "just possessing the proper biology or the emotional capacity to 'mother'" was enough.[28] Moreover, contemporary feminists argued that women could understand emotions, show compassion, and "envision peace" better than their male counterparts because of their maternal instinct to nurture. It was one of the dominant discourses in twentieth-century feminism, socialist or otherwise, as the potential for motherhood represented one of the few characteristics shared by women across the globe. The CMF's appeals to women as mothers were therefore part of a longer tradition of maternalism as a feminist strategy. For example, Marie Hoheisel argued in the International Council of Women *Bulletin* that the "power to mother the world was inherent in all women, whether or not they had borne a child", and groups like the WILPF "embraced maternalist rhetoric to advance a pacifist agenda and claim a place for women on the global stage".[29] Maternal language was used to generate "a sense of global affinity among women and mothers" by international socialist women's organizations in the post-war period, too. For example, activism by the Women's International Democratic Federation (WIDF) in North Korea, Vietnam, and Chile employed maternalist rhetoric as an "important mobilising function" amongst women.[30] The CMF sat somewhere between these two strands of feminist thought, both chronologically and politically.

The CMF strategy of representing women suffering under fascism or war as either mothers or fighters aimed to create emotional solidarity and "sisterhood" across borders that were otherwise difficult to traverse. This was clear in many of the committee's international campaigns: female fighters were masculinized and an abstract figure of aspiration (seen most plainly in how *milicianas* in the Spanish Republican forces were presented), while maternity was something that connected women on the basest level, regardless of

28. Harriet Hyman Alonso, *Peace as a Women's Issue: A History of the US Movement for World Peace and Women's Rights* (Syracuse, NY, 1993), p. 11.

29. Leila J. Rupp, *Worlds of Women: The Making of an International Women's Movement* (Princeton, NJ, 1997), p. 86; and Siegal, "Feminism, Pacifism and Political Violence in Europe and China", p. 643.

30. Michelle Chase, "'Hands Off Korea!' Women's Internationalist Solidarity and Peace Activism in Early Cold War Cuba", *Journal of Women's History*, 32:3 (2020), pp. 64–88, 71; and Donert, "From Communist Internationalism to Human Rights", p. 333. See also Katharine McGregor, "Opposing Colonialism: The Women's International Democratic Federation and decolonisation struggles in Vietnam and Algeria 1945–1965", *Women's History Review*, 25:6 (2016), pp. 925–944; and Yulia Gradskova, *The Women's International Democratic Federation, the Global South and the Cold War: Defending the Rights of Women of the 'Whole World'?* (London, 2021).

whether one was a mother.[31] This reflected the idea, still propagated in many socialist and communist circles of the period, that a woman's most important job was as the bearer of and carer for the next generation of workers. CMF publications themselves emphasized the importance of mothers to socialize and educate children to become effective socialist citizens.[32]

In contrast, Chinese women were eager to dismantle the orientalist image of the Chinese woman as "ethereal and dainty creatures [...] with eyebrows as thin as that of a moth, and feet that move so light that they, under the rustling silk, would not even leave footprints on the dust". The playwright Yang Jiang condemned this image of her countrywomen to the "dead and irrevocable past", asserting that Chinese women had possessed "indomitable will and courage" during the war.[33] Similarly, Mrs Tsui-Tsing Chang refuted the "erroneous, but popular, notion among Western people that Chinese women are inferior to men, that they are helpless and always dependent", a notion solidified by early twentieth-century missionary reports that emphasized Chinese women's "victimization and weakness".[34] Instead, she argued that the rights of women had been enshrined in the laws of the Chinese Republic and that the modern Chinese woman desired higher education, a profession, and to make contributions to society.

For many Chinese correspondents, national salvation was key to their conceptions of feminism: only when the nation was emancipated could women be. The CMF also worked with other prominent female Chinese political figures who advocated for support for China in the war. In a letter to the CMF published in December 1936, nine prominent Chinese women argued that resistance was necessary to "support world peace and freedom by a brave national liberation war" and asked for support from anti-fascist women across the globe. He Xiangning, a committee member on the All-China National Salvation Association and a former minister for Women's Affairs, explained that the "only right we should strive for is the right to save the country", for without that there would be "no women's rights left to strive for".[35] This letter was also signed by Shi Liang, a lawyer who was the liaison director of the Women's Advisory Council, a "cross-party national women's organization for national resistance", and a member of the People's Political Council,

---

31. For the CMF's Spain campaign, see Calver, "The Comité mondial des femmes contre la guerre et le fascisme", pp. 149–163.

32. For the most explicit examples of this, see "Woman's Place? – Everywhere!", *Woman To-day* (December 1936), pp. 8–9; and Monica Pearson, "Launching your Daughter", *Woman To-day* (March 1937), p 4.

33. Yang Jiang, "Chinese Women and the Anti-Japanese Front", *Woman To-day* (November 1937), p. 3.

34. Tsui-Tsing Chang, "Chinese Women: Past and Present", *Woman To-day* (October 1937), p. 8; and Jinhua Emma Teng, "The Construction of the 'Traditional Chinese Woman' in the Western Academy: A Critical Review", *Signs*, 22:1 (1996), pp. 115–151, 121.

35. Pan, "Feminism and Nationalism in China's War of Resistance against Japan", p. 118.

an official "forum for public opinions".[36] Here, Japanese imperialism was presented as an extension of capitalism and the women acknowledged that only
after the expulsion of the imperialist aggressors could women work effectively
to achieve gender equality.[37]

Much of the CMF material generated from late 1938 focused on the plight of
Chinese women. Images of Chinese women and children with expressions of
sadness or pain often accompanied this material in conjunction with questions
like "Will You Let This Child Be Bombed?", which constructed a spectacle for
European readers. This exploitation of Chinese women's suffering was
designed to elicit a strength of feeling that would galvanize the audience
into action, either through protest or donation. This tactic was also utilized
by the Chinese women writing for the journal, however. Yang Jiang wrote
an article for *Woman To-Day* in late 1937 in which she deployed violent
and emotive language to obtain sympathy from readers. Labelling the
Second Sino-Japanese War "the cruellest war the world has ever seen", Yang
described the "thousands of peaceful homes [which] have been reduced to
ruins, women and children [...] murdered in cold blood, and [...] [those
who] survived have seen their dear ones tortured and killed before their
very eyes". Yang emphasized the "meaningless atrocity" of the war and argued
that this was why Chinese women participated in the conflict.[38] This allowed
European readers to confront the real suffering of women and children and to
feel sympathy based on their shared gender.

Maternalism was by no means the dominant discourse employed by
Chinese women, but they did, on occasion, utilize the commonality of
motherhood and the potential suffering associated with that experience to sur-
mount cultural differences between them and their European audience. They
linked motherhood with an inherently peaceable nature, creating a sympathetic image of Chinese women as non-violent and unwilling spectators to
the suffering of others. For example, "Madame Quo Tai Chi", the wife of
the Chinese ambassador to Britain, wrote that Chinese mothers had seen
their sons struggling "against the invader" and their daughters "meeting the
national crisis with every ounce of aid they can give". She used motherhood

---

36. Guo, "Forging a Women's United Front", p. 508; and Danke Li, "The Women's Movement in
the Chongqing Region During China's War of Resistance Against Japan, 1938–1945", *The
Chinese Historical Review*, 16:1 (2009), pp. 27–59, 29. For more on Shi Liang's life and work,
see also Stephen R. MacKinnon, *Wuhan 1938: War, Refugees, and the Making of Modern
China* (London, 2008), pp. 55–59.
37. See also Helen M. Schneider, "Mobilising Women: The Women's Advisory Council,
Resistance and Reconstruction during China's War with Japan", *European Journal of East
Asian Studies*, 11:2 (2012), pp. 213–236.
38. Yang, "Chinese Women and the Anti-Japanese Front", p. 3; Yang and her husband were living
in England and studying at Oxford University at this time: Cary Huang and Oliver Chou, "Yang
Jiang, Bestselling Author who Wrote on the Pain of Living through Persecution during Cultural
Revolution, Dies at 104", *South China Morning Post* (25 May 2016).

as a common identity by asking British women to understand that their Chinese counterparts hoped to witness the development of their children without interference from a foreign power, because "surely that is what all mothers desire for their sons and daughters". Similarly, the poet Lu Jingqing, who was living in Britain at the time, wrote of the millions of Chinese children "torn by Japanese bombs and shells", utilizing emotive, violent, and graphic language to appeal to the maternal instincts of the reader. She extended her sympathy to Japanese women as mothers, too, stating that, "millions of Japanese mothers mourn their sons, and wives grieve for their husbands who have been driven to war by the Japanese militarists and Fascists and have lost their lives in Chinese territory". In this depiction, Japanese women had little agency and argued that women were simply unwilling spectators in the conflict.[39] Leila Rupp has argued that "violence against women, like motherhood, had the potential to unite women across cultures, since all women were fair game, especially in war".[40] This maternal rhetoric, which emphasized the pain of mothers losing their children during wartime, was deployed by the CMF to create connections between women with few cultural bonds separated by great geographical distance, to generate support and material and moral contributions to the campaign.

CHILD SPONSORSHIP STRATEGIES: THE "WARPHANS" CAMPAIGN

The CMF combined these essentialist assumptions with imperialist stereotypes in its shortest, but most successful, humanitarian campaign. The "Warphans" child sponsorship campaign combined a focus on European women as potential mothers and inherent carers with the rhetoric of otherness to develop a charity strategy that presented Chinese children and, by extension, the Chinese population, as passive and in need of direction. It utilized a child sponsorship strategy that sometimes deployed rhetoric influenced by colonialist understandings of China, which occasionally infantilized China. Further, the CMF's "Warphans" campaign severely underplayed the role of Chinese women in organizing support for the at least two million orphans created by the conflict before 1945, as well as giving them little credit for the initial creation of the propagandized image of "Warphans" as a fundraising tactic.[41]

39. "Christmas Messages for Peace from a War-Threatened World", *Woman To-day* (December 1937), p. 3.
40. Leila Rupp, "The Making of International Women's Organisations", in Martin H. Geyer and Johannes Paulmann (eds), *The Mechanics of Internationalism: Culture, Society, and Politics from the 1840s to the First World War* (Oxford, 2008), pp. 205–234, 223.
41. Cunningham, "Shanghai's Wandering Ones, 1900–1953", p. 106.

However, these strategies were incredibly effective and made a substantial contribution to the humanitarian effort surrounding the crisis.

The charitable strategy of child sponsorship was still in its infancy by the late 1930s, although its exact origins have been the subject of debate. Henry Molumphy traced the origins of child sponsorship to the Foster Parents Plan for Children in Spain during the Spanish Civil War in 1937 (later Plan International), while Larry Tise asserted that the China's Children Fund was the originator of child sponsorship initiatives during the Second Sino-Japanese War (later ChildFund).[42] However, recent scholarship by Brad Watson and Emily Baughan has presented Save the Children as the true innovator of the child sponsorship model. Formed in response to the 1919 famine in Austria, Save the Children presented children as apolitical, passive actors to encourage its British patrons to donate to citizens of their recent enemy; Save the Children portrayed children as innocent and helpless, surmounting difficulties of "nationality", "ambition", and "material wealth".[43] Baughan has argued that Save the Children positioned children as "objects of innate pathos" and "extra-national figures [...] entirely removed from questions of nationality or politics", which fostered the myth that child sponsorship strategies "existed beyond self-interest, political concerns, and international diplomacy".[44]

The CMF's child sponsorship activities were heavily inspired by Save the Children. By April 1938, 37,253 children were reported as orphans by the China War Orphans Relief Commission, creating a humanitarian crisis that fit the CMF's raison d'être as an activist organization.[45] In its child sponsorship campaign, the CMF effectively utilized the sympathetic figure of the child not only to place children in an apolitical space that existed beyond national borders, but also to elicit a gendered response from its membership based on maternal feeling. For the CMF, too, these children represented "the standard-bearers of 'internationalism'", both politically and geographically. The sponsorship of children from across the globe not only reinforced CMF claims of being "international" but contributed to ideas of a socialist internationalism, which wanted to safeguard the next generation of humanity.[46]

42. Henry Molumphy, *For Common Decency: The History of Foster Parents Plan, 1937–1983* (Warwick, RI, 1984); and Larry Tise, *A Book About Children: Christian Children's Fund 1938–1991* (Falls Church, VA, 1992).
43. Brad Watson, "Origins of Child Sponsorship: Save the Children Fund in the 1920s", in Brad Watson and Matthew Clarke (eds), *Child Sponsorship: Exploring Pathways to a Brighter Future* (Basingstoke, 2014), pp. 18–40, 22.
44. Emily Baughan, "'Every Citizen of Empire Implored to Save the Children!' Empire, Internationalism, and the Save the Children Fund in Inter-War Britain", *Historical Research*, 86:231 (2013), pp. 116–137, 124.
45. Brook, *Collaboration: Japanese Agents and Local Elites in Wartime China*, p. 24.
46. Emily Baughan, "International Adoption and Ango-American Internationalism, c.1918–1925", *Past and Present*, 239 (2018), pp. 181–217, 203.

The first mention of the "Warphans" was in the January 1939 edition of *Woman To-day* in an article penned by Charlotte Haldane following her visit to China, during which she visited an orphanage in Chengdu, Sichuan province. Her account alternates between graphic, violent language, when recounting the experiences of the orphans, and sympathetic descriptions of the orphans themselves, thereby constructing the children as tragic symbols deserving of compassion. With the "Warphans", this violent language was inherently linked with the idea of children as innocent witnesses. Haldane wrote:

> Imagine the plight of one little child, which has seen its home bombed, its mother raped and then murdered by the Japanese soldiery, its father clubbed on the head, or shot in cold blood, when trying to defend her. There are millions of little Chinese children whose eyes bear the memory of such sights that no child should ever be allowed to look upon.[47]

Establishing refugee status was key to this construction of children as objects of pathos. Haldane explained how the orphans had undertaken a nearly 2,000-km journey between Anhui province (where most of the children originated from) and the orphanage in Sichuan, but qualified that it was the only option "to save their poor little lives and limbs from the pitiless massacre of Japanese bombs".[48]

Haldane's construction of these violent experiences and her construction of individual children as figures of pathos were inextricably linked. When telling CMF members about a specific child, she attempted to create a sense of familiarity for her readers, based on their personal experiences as mothers and carers. For example, Haldane described an eleven-year-old boy as a "pale-faced, keen-eyed little chap; intelligent but not in the least precocious", stating that the Chinese orphans were "not in the least different from our own children, except that they are somewhat quieter and better behaved, a concomitant, unfortunately, of all that they have been through". Here, she constructed a personal connection between her readers and the children of China; she was encouraging women to view the "Warphans" as reflections of their children and children they knew in order to foster certain maternal, and subsequently charitable, feelings. However, these descriptions of children were also infused with stereotypes about the Chinese nationality influenced by imperialist assumptions about race. Haldane demonstrated her Western prejudices by claiming that a boy who related his story to her had the "natural dignity and politeness of his race, but without a trace of conceit or self-satisfaction". Haldane then demonstrated some explicitly hierarchical attitudes towards the children. She wrote of how impressed she was that the boy chosen to talk to her had "no trace of vanity" for being chosen and that his "comrades"

---

47. Charlotte Haldane, "Rescuing China's Children", *Woman To-day* (January 1939), p. 2.
48. *Ibid.*, p. 2.

showed no "envy" that they were not, suggesting that she felt that the child was lucky to talk to her, a European woman with important international contacts.[49]

The origin of the term "Warphan" was in Chinese nationalist propaganda. The nationalist Kuomintang needed to convince the Chinese people that the welfare of children was a national responsibility, not solely the responsibility of the family as traditional discourse had asserted. Traditionally, the family system instilled appropriate behaviours in children within the home, which were then extended to interactions with society. However, during the war, orphans were "elevated to a national priority" for whom the state was responsible and around whom a concomitant debate was formed. M. Colette Plum has traced how attitudes towards orphans in China developed during the war with Japan and argues that they became a "potent cultural symbol infused with nationalist ideology" as they became threatened by Japanese influence or extermination. Before the war, orphans were often seen as problematic for the state as they represented a threat to societal harmony. They came to be viewed as especially open to manipulation by the Japanese occupiers, which would threaten the *minzu* (nation, the building of the nation) that the Kuomintang had carefully cultivated since the 1911 Revolution. Those orphaned by war were placed into children's homes and instilled with values to create an inherently nationalist society; this had long-term effects on orphans living in the state children's homes, who grew to maturity with a "strong sense of national belonging and with images of themselves as contributing members of what was described to them during their childhoods as a 'future China'".[50]

The "Warphan" was the focal point of child sponsorship initiatives by Chinese women activists before European women launched their campaigns. Key to these Chinese driven initiatives was Soong Mei-ling, who was the first woman to harness the propagandized image of the "Warphan" for foreign fundraising opportunities. The wife of Chiang Kai-shek and the sister of Soong Ching-ling, Soong Mei-ling's most important public work during the conflict was with war orphans; she set up the first orphanage for the children of soldiers in Nanjing and established the Chinese Women's National War Relief Society to care for them. It was Soong Mei-ling who coined the name "Warphan" to refer to those children who lost their parents during the war. She shaped the ideological direction of the children's homes, ensuring that the children felt a belonging to the nation through their common experiences. According to Soong Mei-ling, "Warphans" all spoke Mandarin, dressed uniformly, ate "the same food, [sang] the same songs, [and recited] the same lessons". She directed the "Warphans" campaign in China itself, imploring her

49. *Ibid.*, pp. 2 and 4.
50. M. Colette Plum, "Orphans in the Family: Family Reform and Children's Citizenship During the Anti-Japanese War, 1937–45", in James Flath and Norman Smith (eds), *Beyond Suffering: Recounting War in Modern China* (Vancouver, 2011), pp. 186–208, 188–191.

fellow Chinese to care for the "future citizens" of the nation and asking them to "Adopt a warphan for a month!" or to "Adopt as many warphans as your income will allow!"[51] She was also a frequent visitor to the number one children's home in Chongqing where she ensured "that money and food allocated to the refugee children were not embezzled by corrupt officials".[52]

The CMF gave Soong Mei-ling little credit for her activism for "Warphans". Beyond acknowledging that Soong Mei-ling had coined the term, the CMF ignored her role in campaigning and fundraising amongst the Chinese people, giving the impression that the origins of Chinese child sponsorship lay with the CMF. This perpetuated the idea, intentionally or otherwise, that the Chinese people depended on European activism and aid to protect their children, reflecting negative images of Chinese people as helpless, depoliticized, and unable to direct their aid. The criticism of the CMF's erasure of Chinese activism towards children can, and has, been levied against modern child sponsorship organizations, particularly those operating in the 1980s, which deployed "destructive stereotypes" of those in need of aid in the Global South that did not reflect the true extent of their agency.[53]

One of the key narratives in the CMF's "Warphans" campaign positioned donors as "foster parents" who had some level of parental responsibility for their "adopted" child. The "Warphans" child sponsorship scheme was inaugurated in the March 1939 editions of *Woman To-day* and *Femmes dans l'action mondiale* with a brief article couched in terms of parenthood and the discourse of adoption. Potential "foster parents" were encouraged to give three pounds a year to adopt a "Warphan", which would ensure that the parental task of making sure a child was "well-looked after" was carried out by securing "food, shelter, education and medical attention" for their chosen orphan.[54] Potential donors were approached by deploying language that positioned European "parents" as the saviours of these children; articles told readers "why you must rescue them", to convince them that they could, as white Europeans, positively alter the course of a child's life by giving only three pounds a year.[55]

The structure of these articles was simple: a short paragraph informing the reader what a "Warphan" was, several images of Chinese children accompanied by a sentence or two explaining their situation to the audience, and a final paragraph explaining how those interested could find out more information about adopting a "Warphan". These articles, like other CMF campaigning on the Second Sino-Japanese War, used language that reflected the emotional

51. Kevin Wong Scott, *Americans First: Chinese Americans and the Second World War* (Cambridge, 2005), pp. 93–94.
52. Danke Li, *Echoes of Chongqing: Women in Wartime China* (Chicago, IL, 2009), p. 71.
53. Brad Watson and Matthew Clarke, "Introduction to Key Issues in Child Sponsorship", in Watson and Clarke, *Child Sponsorship: Exploring Pathways to a Brighter Future*, pp. 1–17, 9.
54. "Introducing the 'Warphans'", *Woman To-Day* (March 1939), p. 20.
55. "Écoutez-les ! …", p. 15.

and violent experiences of the children to appeal to the common identity of motherhood that was so integral to the CMF's attempts to create connections across continents.

In this case, though, the CMF also deployed images of children to reinforce efforts to personalize its child sponsorship campaign. These images did not exploit the suffering of children in the same way that images of Chinese women did. Rather, the committee went to great lengths to depict the children as presentable and well-looked after by the orphanages. *Woman To-day* predominantly published images of girls in traditional Chinese dress with neat hair trimmed into a bob, while *Femmes dans l'action mondiale* published photographs of both male and female orphans dressed in the uniform of their orphanage, with bobbed hair for the girls and shaved heads for the boys (Figure 2). This was standard in child sponsorship initiatives in the interwar period; Save the Children provided "respectable head-shots" of children who were "properly clothed and groomed" so that potential donors could visually link the child in need with their own child. These images encouraged potential "foster parents" to select their child personally based on the idea that, provided "food, clothing, nurture, and a reason to smile", the child would be like their own children.[56] The CMF borrowed this tactic because it ensured that "foster parents" would take a greater interest in choosing a child, thereby increasing the effectiveness of the campaign in attracting sponsors.[57]

The CMF similarly found that including images of orphans for sponsorship allowed potential "foster parents" to envision the child they wanted, based on the limited photographs that they had seen. Letters received from potential sponsors, which emphasized the child's appearance as the reason for choosing them above other factors, reinforced the importance of the image of the innocent, youthful orphan for European audiences. For example, one sponsor asked for an orphaned girl but lamented that he supposed that "all the chubby boys and pretty girls have been taken", supposing that other sponsors would already have asked for children fitting this description, leaving only the "less desirable" children. In response, the committee found a girl whose "face portrayed the suffering she had gone through" for the donor.[58] That the CMF provided sponsors with photographs that amplified the pain of the child commodified them in a way that was predicated on concepts of pity and patronage, resembling the "pornography of poverty critique".[59] The sponsor responded

56. Heide Fehrenbach, "Children and Other Civilians: Photography and the Politics of Humanitarian Image Making", in Heide Fehrenbach and Davide Rodogno (eds), *Humanitarian Photography: A History* (Cambridge, 2015), pp. 165–199, 205 and 214.

57. Brad Watson, "The Origins of International Child Sponsorship", *Development in Practice*, 25:6 (2015), pp. 867–879, 876.

58. Maud Brown, "Here are the 'Warphans'...", *Woman To-day* (April 1939), p. 15.

59. Ian Smillie, *The Alms Bazaar: Altruism under Fire. Non-Profit Organizations and International Development* (Bradford, 1995), p. 136.

Figure 2. An article from the French CMF journal featuring some of the images of 'Warphans' published by the committee for fundraising purposes. "Écoutez-les ! ...", *Femmes dans l'action mondiale* (March 1939), p. 15. I thank Gallica and the Bibliothéque nationale de France for open and free usage of this image.
gallica.bnf.fr / BnF.

to the photograph of his "Warphan" by comparing her experience to that of children in the West; he wrote of the thirteen-year-old Chinese girl that he had adopted that: "In this country, a parent would be waiting until their children are 14 so that the money they earn will swell the family pool. This Chinese girl will have a better chance in life."[60] The sponsor of this child genuinely believed that his five shillings a month, or three pounds a year, would dramatically improve the child's situation and affect her life for years to come, showing a lacklustre understanding of both the war itself and the corresponding political situation.

Although it did not publish graphic images of injured children, the CMF can certainly be accused of perpetuating Chinese children as spectacle; the CMF emphasized the suffering of the "Warphans" by creating a contrast between photographs that portrayed them as innocent and "naturally dignified" and the accompanying paragraphs which often deployed graphic, emotive language. Miriam Ticktin has argued that innocence became "the necessary accompaniment to suffering, required in order to designate the sufferer as worthy", with children, as blameless figures, representing the "ideal recipients of care".[61] On the other hand, Timothy Brook has argued that many children came out of the Sino-Japanese conflict relatively unscathed, beyond having their "innocence exploited for propaganda photographs".[62]

Still, there were differences between how the British and French journals presented the children they featured. *Woman To-day* preferred to keep the "Warphan's" stories short and avoided explicit language. For example, Yu Lan Tuan, a fourteen-year-old girl from Henan province, told the publication that her "village was flooded by the Yellow River" and she had been sent to the orphanage as a result. This description neglects to explain the circumstances around the flood and drastically underplays its catastrophic nature; the Chinese military command had ordered the breaching of the southern dyke of the Yellow River in an attempt to stop the Japanese army from advancing further west, which killed somewhere in the region of 500,000 people and further exacerbated the refugee crisis.[63] The majority of the children featured became orphans because their fathers had joined the army as their mothers had died before the war; an eight-year-old boy from Sichuan province and a ten-year-old boy from Henan were both sent to government orphanages for this reason. However, some children had witnessed the violence of the conflict first-hand, like twelve-year-old Yu Fang, who had witnessed the kidnap (and presumably the murder) of her mother by Japanese soldiers. Despite her

60. Brown, "Here are the 'Warphans'...", p. 15.
61. Miriam Ticktin, "The Gendered Human of Humanitarianism: Medicalising and Politicising Sexual Violence", *Gender and History*, 23:2 (2011), pp. 250–265, 259.
62. Brook, *Collaboration: Japanese Agents and Local Elites in Wartime China*, p. 25.
63. Diana Lary, "Drowned Earth: The Strategic Breaching of the Yellow River Dyke, 1938", *War in History*, 8:2 (2001), pp. 191–207, 206.

happiness at being in the government orphanage, she wanted desperately to see her mother. The author of the article commented pityingly that Yu Fang did not understand that "she will never again see her mother", again utilizing language designed to appeal to a shared motherhood to alleviate the suffering of the Chinese "Warphan".[64] Even when the language used by *Woman To-day* to tell the individual stories of "Warphans" was not graphic or explicit, it was emotive and designed to elicit maternal sympathy from readers. In the case of Fu Mao Wei, a fourteen-year-old boy from Hubei province, this attempt to create a link based on the potential motherhood of the readers was clear. Fu Mao Wei recounted that he had been forced from his mother who, "with tears in her eyes kissed [him] goodbye because she was too ill to be evacuated from the city", a story designed to affect CMF members emotionally as mothers or potential mothers.[65]

On the other hand, the article introducing the "Warphans" in *Femmes dans l'action mondiale* was more graphic in its quest to stimulate support for the cause. Every story featured in the article described some level of violence personally witnessed by the child. Five of the twelve children featured in the March 1939 issue had survived a Japanese aerial bombing on their home in which either or both of their parents or guardians had died. Children from Anhui and Jiangxi provinces experienced their houses being "burned down in the course of a bombing by plane"; two of the children featured had seen their mother die during the attack, two had seen their entire families perish, and one witnessed his aunt die while she was acting as his guardian. Chang Hsun Lo, a thirteen-year-old boy from Jiangxi, had seen his father leave to join the army, and used his story to reflect the isolation that many "Warphans" felt: he expressed that he remained all alone following the death of his family with "nobody to take care of me".[66] A solitary child with no parental support was a particularly effective tactic for appealing to the maternal instincts of women, who, it was assumed, would want to alleviate the damaging isolation of children like Chang Hsun Lo. Lone children presented what Emily Baughan has described as a "logic of incompleteness", which generated a feeling of "parental responsibility" from the sponsor to the child.[67]

The "Warphans" campaign yielded excellent results. Within a month, women's organizations, university students, schoolteachers and pupils, and convents had already adopted more than fifty orphans out of the one hundred funded by the committee.[68] A group of women from the central branch of the

64. "Écoutez-les ! …", p. 15.
65. "Introducing the 'Warphans'", p. 20.
66. "Écoutez-les ! …", p. 15.
67. Baughan, "International Adoption and Ango-American Internationalism, c.1918–1925", p. 195.
68. "Angleterre. Rapport sur le Comité pour la Paix et la Démocratie" (1939), PANDOR, 543_2_35, fos 1–4, p. 2.

Association of Women Clerks and Secretaries adopted a "Warphan" as a collective, "several sections" of the Labour Party adopted "Warphans" through the CMF, and some students from Oxford University sponsored Chinese children. Somewhat surprisingly considering the inherently gendered nature of the CMF, several men also came forward to be "foster parents", a trend that the committee was keen to encourage. Highlighting the inequality for men when adopting domestically, the CMF wrote that the British authorities:

> did not encourage men to adopt children, but our committee does. We do not mind who adopts a "Warphan"; from the lowest to the highest-paid worker. We would not refuse the Prime Minister, nor his wife.[69]

The committee did not want to be exclusionary in whom it targeted, despite their entirely female, left-leaning membership. It was more concerned about the success of the campaign in general, including engaging traditional opponents of communism and socialism; for example, the British committee wanted to extend their "Warphans" activism to the public by targeting churches, through whom they could "obtain the aid of their congregations". The "Warphans" campaign received donations and sponsorships totalling 17,500 francs in March alone, rendering it a rousing success. For comparison, the monetary aid collected for Spain by the CMF between March 1938 and the end of March 1939 (the month that the Warphans campaign began) totalled 55,000 francs, meaning that the CMF had collected around thirty per cent of the amount collected for Spain in a year for China in a month.[70]

CONCLUSION

CMF campaigning in China in the late 1930s gives a new perspective on how socialist women engaged in international activism during the 1930s. The CMF was a transnational communist front organization that subverted communist rhetoric on gender equality by utilizing traditionally feminine symbols to yield what it expected to be the best outcomes. The processes of information exchange and mobility resulting from increasing communications between Europe and China gave Chinese women a unique opportunity to publicize the specific hardships that they faced during the war and to enhance Western understandings of the conflict. It also exposed European women to the gendered violence perpetrated against women in China, including the graphic sexual violence they endured. This, in conjunction with the involvement of prominent female Chinese political figures to legitimize the CMF's campaign, meant that the committee could raise consciousness about the

---

69. Brown, "Here are the 'Warphans'...", p. 15.
70. "Angleterre. Rapport sur le Comité pour la Paix et la Démocratie", PANDOR, 543_2_35, fos 1–4, pp. 2 and 4.

situation amongst its members and fundraise for aid for China effectively. For example, the China Bazaar that Soong Ching-ling contributed pottery to raised 50,000 francs because of her involvement.[71] The "Warphans" child sponsorship initiative also raised an incredible amount of money in a short time, meaning that the Chinese campaign was one of the CMF's most successful despite lasting eight months at most (compared with the three years of the Spanish campaign).

However, the CMF also relied on both stereotypical and essentialist tropes to achieve this success. Chinese women and children were presented as always quiet, dignified, and innocent despite their inherent emotional strength. The committee's reliance on motherhood as the commonality between its members and Chinese women dominated almost all its discourse on the conflict, which reduced women to mothers only and failed to discuss the political work of women.[72] This also presupposed that European women involved with the organization would be more likely to respond to emotional appeals based on motherhood as opposed to more rational appeals based on politics or the international situation. Criticisms can also be made of the group's decision to present the experiences and images of Chinese women and children as a spectacle for their readers, to create pathos to encourage people to commit financially. The CMF's campaign in China was an effective means of sourcing monetary aid for a population struggling with the impact of an intensely violent war. However, it also demonstrates how the activism of the CMF, which was supposedly predicated on socialist notions of equality, including amongst races and genders as well as class (if we are to be somewhat reductive about the ideology's fundamental tenets), was much more influenced by traditional gender discourses than would initially have been expected, to attract the greatest number of supporters and therefore the largest amount of money.

71. *Ibid.*, p. 2.
72. For an examination of the political work of Chinese women, see Vivienne Xiangwei Guo, *Women and Politics in Wartime China: Networking Across Geopolitical Borders* (London, 2018).

IRSH 67 (2022), pp. 49–74 doi:10.1017/S0020859021000687
© The Author(s), 2022. Published by Cambridge University Press on behalf of
Internationaal Instituut voor Sociale Geschiedenis

Between National and International: Women's Transnational Activism in Twentieth-Century Chile

MARÍA FERNANDA LANFRANCO GONZÁLEZ ⓘ

Pontificia Universidad Católica de Valparaíso
Av. Brasil 2950, Valparaíso, Chile

E-mail: fernandalanfranco@gmail.com

ABSTRACT: This article explores the transnational dimension of women's mobilization in twentieth-century Chile and the connections they established with women's international non-governmental organizations, particularly the Women's International League for Peace and Freedom (WILPF) and the Women's International Democratic Federation (WIDF). It sheds light on the political choices women made when forging transnational alliances to expand and make their activism more effective, together with the material and ideological dynamics that shaped their collaboration. The article analyses this topic by focusing on key but little-explored figures of women's activism in Chile – especially, but not solely, feminist academic Olga Poblete – and their personal communications with the leadership of women's organizations in the US and Europe. The article contends that, although both the WILPF and WIDF shared strengths and weaknesses in promoting their ideas and establishing links with activists in Chile, the alliances that Chilean women chose to pursue were mostly defined by their own political priorities and local contexts.

INTRODUCTION

This article explores the transnational dimension of women's mobilization in Chile and the connections they established with women's international non-governmental organizations (WINGOs), particularly, the Women's International League for Peace and Freedom (WILPF) and the Women's International Democratic Federation (WIDF).[1] The study sheds light on the political choices women made when forging transnational alliances to expand and make their activism more effective, together with the material and ideological dynamics that shaped their collaboration. The article analyses this

1. I am most grateful to Celia Donert and participants in the workshop "Women's Rights and Global Socialism", as well as to Lawrence Black, Henrice Altink, and Tanya Harmer, and to the reviewers for their helpful comments and suggestions. An early version of this manuscript was part of my thesis: "Women's Activism and Feminism in the Chile Solidarity Movement" (Ph.D., University of York, 2020), which was funded by CONICYT.

topic by focusing on key, but little-explored, figures of women's activism in Chile – especially, but not solely, the feminist academic Olga Poblete – and their personal communications with the leadership of WINGOs in the United States and Europe. The focus on the personal and political relations of women and local women's groups in Chile provides first-hand accounts of their choices of transnational alliances, and what impact such connections had on women's activism locally and internationally.

Although historical research in the field of women's transnational activism has expanded our knowledge about the ways in which Latin American women advanced feminist goals during the first half of the twentieth century and the early stages of the Cold War,[2] the relations between activists themselves and WINGOs remain under-researched. The most well-known WINGOs, all founded between the late nineteenth century and early twentieth century, are the International Council of Women, the International Women's Suffrage Alliance (later the International Alliance of Women), and the WILPF. More recently, the WIDF has also drawn scholarly attention, after Francisca de Haan observed how lingering Cold War narratives had prevented historians from exploring the WIDF's pivotal role in international feminism after World War II.[3]

This is not to discount the valuable insights historians have provided in the role played by WINGOs in the region and the influence of Latin American women within them, or their stress on the importance of personal connections and friendships in the development of international feminism. Such research has given due weight to local contexts in explaining the foundation of national branches, and explores the tensions and disagreements between Latin American women and their European and North American counterparts.[4]

2. Francesca Miller, "The International Relations of Women of the Americas 1890–1928", *The Americas*, 43 (1986), pp. 171–182; Katherine Marino, *Feminism for the Americas. The Making of an International Human Rights Movement* (Chapel Hill, NC, 2019); Ellen DuBois and Lauren Derby, "The Strange Case of Minerva Bernardino: Pan American and United Nations Women's Right Activist", *Women's Studies International Forum*, 32 (2009), pp. 43–50; Ann Towns, "The Inter-American Commission of Women and Women's Suffrage, 1920–1945", *Journal of Latin American Studies*, 42 (2010), pp. 779–807; Cassia Roth and Ellen DuBois, "Feminism, Frogs and Fascism: The Transnational Activism of Brazil's Bertha Lutz", *Gender & History*, 32 (2020), pp. 208–226.

3. Francisca de Haan, "Continuing Cold War Paradigms in Western Historiography of Transnational Women's Organisations: The Case of the Women's International Democratic Federation (WIDF)", *Women's History Review*, 19 (2010), pp. 547–573.

4. Christine Ehrick, "Madrinas and Missionaries: Uruguay and the Pan-American Women's Movement", *Gender & History*, 10 (1998), pp. 406–424; Jadwiga E. Pieper Mooney, "El antifascismo como fuerza movilizadora. Fanny Edelman y la Federación Democrática Internacional de Mujeres (FDIM)", *Anuario IEHS*, 28 (2013), pp. 207–226; Katherine Marino, "Transnational Pan-American Feminism: The Friendship of Bertha Lutz and Mary Wilhelmine Williams, 1926–1944", *Journal of Women's History*, 26:2 (2014), pp. 63–87; Adriana Valobra and Mercedes Yusta (eds), *Queridas camaradas. Historias iberoamericanas de mujeres comunistas* (Buenos Aires, 2017).

Indeed, these studies have brought new awareness about the effects of WINGOs' networks and politics for feminism in the region, especially in comparison to the more extensively researched historical realities of the Global North.[5] However, even with this regional research, the historiography is unbalanced: some national cases are explored more than others.[6] Beyond the passing mentions of the National Women's Council,[7] or of the role played by WINGOs in the activism against the Pinochet dictatorship in the 1970s,[8] the transnational dimension of women's activism in Chile has not received sufficient attention in the literature.

To this end, the article explores personal correspondence between Chilean women and activists abroad, the official documentation of women's organizations, and audiovisual sources to elucidate the structural, political, and ideological factors that shaped the relationship between Chilean women's activism and WINGOs in the 1940s and 1950s. It takes particular advantage of the Chilean National Archive's new collection Archivo Mujeres y Géneros, which made available the papers of feminist activists that had been kept private with limited access for researchers. From these, it examines Chilean women's shifting alliances with WINGOs after World War II, which laid the foundations for women's activism beyond the 1940s. The study contends that, although both the WILPF and WIDF shared strengths and weaknesses in promoting their ideas and establishing links with activists in Chile, the alliances that Chilean women chose to pursue were mostly defined by their own priorities and local contexts. Ultimately, the way in which Chilean women aligned themselves vis-à-vis the Cold War ideological projects and leftist women organizational forces defined the level of success WINGOs enjoyed inside the country. This focus on the transnational angle also illuminates the rich political activities of women's groups beyond the

---

5. The literature is too extensive to be cited here, but a pioneering and influential work on the topic may be found in Leila J. Rupp, *Worlds of Women: The Making of an International Women's Movement* (Princeton, NJ, 1997).
6. Mexico, for example, has received more attention. See Megan Threlkeld, *Pan American Women: US Internationalists and Revolutionary Mexico* (Philadelphia, PA, 2014); Sara Sanders, "The National Union of Mexican Women and Maternalist Alternatives in Global Women's Politics", in Sara Sanders and Yulia Gradskova (eds), *Institutionalizing Gender Equality: Historical and Global Perspective* (Lanham, MD, 2015), pp. 61–81.
7. Corinne A. Pernet, "Chilean Feminists, the International Women's Movement, and Suffrage, 1915–1950", *Pacific Historical Review*, 69 (2000), pp. 663–688, 669; Ericka Kim Verba, "The Círculo de Lectura de Señoras [Ladies' Reading Circle] and the Club de Señoras [Ladies' Club] of Santiago, Chile: Middle- and Upper-Class Feminist Conversations (1915–1920)", *Journal of Women's History*, 7:3 (1995), pp. 6–33, 10.
8. Jadwiga Pieper Mooney, "Women's Rights as Human Rights: Exile, International Feminist Encounters, and Women's Empowerment under Military Rule in Chile, 1973–1990", in Niels Bjerre-Poulsen, Helene Balslev Clausen, and Juan Gustafsson (eds), *Projection of Power in the Americas* (New York, 2012), pp. 154–179; María Fernanda Lanfranco González, "Women's Activism and Feminism in the Chile Solidarity Movement" (Ph.D., University of York, 2020).

late 1940s, challenging the common narrative that women's activism in Chile withered away in the 1950s.[9] As we will discuss later, the establishment of the Comité Nacional Femenino de Unidad (later Unión de Mujeres de Chile) – linked to the WIDF and more firmly aligned with a socialist vision – shows that the women's movement kept active in the face of political fragmentation and ideological polarization. Women remained organized as women, foregrounding gender as a political identity while intersecting it with other ideological identifications.

THE MOVIMIENTO PRO-EMANCIPACIÓN DE LA MUJER CHILENA

Chilean women were active players in pan-American feminism and international women's activism. While campaigning for women's full suffrage in Chile (only achieved in 1949), they participated in international politics, endorsed initiatives that supported international women's rights, and joined international women's conferences and organizations.[10] In the 1930s, the mobilization of women reached new levels of activity. Latin American feminists believed that American republics had a duty to stand against both fascism and the global curtailment of the advancement of women.[11] Transnational connections among women in these countries were vital to creating – and prioritizing the goals of – a Latin American feminist project both nationally and internationally. Indeed, Katherine Marino explained how *feminismo americano* peaked with the development of what she calls "Popular-Front Pan-American feminism, defined as an internationalist feminism that combined social democratic labour concerns with international 'equal rights' demands, in the context of an anti-fascist inter-American solidarity".[12] This international project would not only be significant for the Inter-American Commission of Women (IACW) during World War II, but also served to further Latin American feminist efforts in advancing the idea of women's rights as human rights at the United Nations' foundational meeting in 1945.[13]

The Movimiento pro-Emancipación de la Mujer Chilena (MEMCH) was the most significant local manifestation of Popular Front feminism in Chile. Founded in 1935, it became a multi-class nationwide organization during

---

9. This interpretation follows the idea of "feminist waves", and was initially proposed by the Chilean sociologist Julieta Kirkwood in *Ser política en Chile. Las feministas y los partidos* (Santiago, 1986).

10. Pernet, "Chilean Feminist", p. 664.

11. *Ibid.*, pp. 679–680.

12. Marino, *Feminism for the Americas*, p. 122; Katherine Marino, "Marta Vergara, Popular-Front Pan American Feminism and the Transnational Struggle for Working Women's Rights in the 1930s", *Gender & History*, 26 (2014), pp. 642–643.

13. Francesca Miller, *Latin American Women and the Search for Social Justice* (Hanover, NH [etc.], 1991), p. 116; Marino, *Feminism for the Americas*; Marino, "Marta Vergara", p. 655.

the late 1930s and early 1940s. Although it was led by an executive committee located in Santiago, MEMCH established dozens of local committees throughout the capital and provinces. At its highest point in the mid-1940s, it had around fifty local committees spread across Chile. While *memchistas* were of diverse social origin, most held progressive views involving women's political, civil, labour, and reproductive rights. Naturally, not all MEMCH members shared the same priorities or even held the same vision of feminism; yet, rather than a hindrance, this diversity fostered campaigns over a wide range of issues: full suffrage; married women's rights over their children and property; women's access to more and better-paid jobs (including equal pay and paid maternity leave); the regulation of consumer prices; sex education; contraception; and abortion rights. In the provinces, where committees were mainly composed of working-class women, campaigning also focused on improving the material, cultural, and social conditions of their families and the wider communities.[14]

Transnational ideas and connections were significant in the creation and subsequent evolutions of MEMCH. While the movement originated from Chilean domestic political developments, MEMCH took inspiration from the involvement of women in anti-fascist struggles in Europe embodied in, for example, the 1934 World Congress of Women against War and Fascism.[15] Composed of communists, socialist reformers, and women's rights activists, the World Congress was one of the earliest signs of women's international opposition to fascism, predating the official creation of the Popular Front in 1935.[16] The Chilean feminist Marta Vergara was instrumental in establishing MEMCH following inspiration from leftist ideas and women's mobilization in Europe. Having already served as the Chilean delegate to the League of Nations' Commission on Women's Rights and the IACW, Vergara witnessed the curtailment of women's rights by Hitler and Mussolini and – supported by Communist Party (CP) members – persuaded the feminist lawyer Elena Caffarena to join her in the creation of MEMCH to promote women's rights and anti-fascist and working-class activism.[17]

In Chile, the political milieu was fertile for this kind of initiative. Socialist and communist ideas had been gaining force during the challenging social and economic conditions experienced during the 1929 crash and following economic recession.[18] Progressive organizations such as MEMCH gained

14. This description of MEMCH follows Pernet's work. Corinne A. Antezana-Pernet, "Mobilizing Women in the Popular Front Era: Feminism, Class, and Politics in the Movimiento Pro-Emancipación de la Mujer Chilena (MEMCh), 1935–1950" (Ph.D., University of California, Irvine, 1996).

15. Pernet, "Mobilizing Women", p. 67.

16. Marino, "Marta Vergara", pp. 647–648.

17. Pernet, "Mobilizing Women", pp. 77–82.

18. Brian Loveman, *Chile: The Legacy of Hispanic Capitalism* (New York, [1979] 2001), pp. 197–201.

traction just as the Popular Front project was uniting centrist and leftist political forces in the late 1930s and 1940s. The Communist, Socialist, and Radical Parties established a set of political alliances of significant popular support. This resulted in control of the executive branch of the state, shaped state policies, and influenced social – and feminist – movements.[19] In this context, relationships between MEMCH and political parties were multifaceted and complex. MEMCH supported the Popular Front coalition because they believed it was their best chance of influencing politics and improving the status of women, even if this involved exerting a fair amount of pressure on politicians. A significant number of *memchistas* were also active members of the Popular Front parties, especially the CP. Women linked to the CP (although not necessarily party members) dominated local committees in the provinces, accounting for more than half of all MEMCH members by 1940.[20] Never a party member herself, the MEMCH leader, Elena Caffarena, believed that women's double militancy – struggling for both specific reforms benefiting women and general party goals – was possible, and even desirable.[21] However, this also meant that changing political alliances and inter-party conflicts were poised to negatively affect MEMCH: the parties' goals to bolster their women's sections and their desires to influence the women's movement through the participation of their female members were often at odds.[22]

Beyond local dynamics, access to overseas political organizations, transnational activism, and first-hand experiences of the achievements (and difficulties) of the women's movement in other countries gave Chilean women insight into or even inspiration to pursue political activism in their home country. International pioneers, such as Marta Vergara, were somewhat representative of MEMCH leadership. Most of its leaders were middle-class professionals who enjoyed the opportunity of participating in women's international organizing.[23] The government functionary Graciela Mandujano and teacher Aída Parada, for example, lived in the US and became involved in pan-American women's activities before becoming part of MEMCH leadership in Santiago.[24] This meant that MEMCH consistently showed an awareness of the importance of the transnational arena for women's activism, the struggle against fascism, and the protection of peace. MEMCH, for example,

---

19. Karin Alejandra Rosemblatt, *Gendered Compromises: Political Cultures and the State in Chile, 1920–1950* (Chapel Hill, NC [etc.], 2000), p. 4.
20. Pernet, "Mobilizing Women", pp. 326–327.
21. Anna M. Travis, "Consolidating Power: Chilean Women in the Political Party System, 1950–1970" (Ph.D., Ohio State University, 2007), pp. 1, 91.
22. On the relationship between political parties and the women's movements, see Travis, "Consolidating Power".
23. Pernet, "Mobilizing Women", p. 106.
24. Marino, *Feminism for the Americas*, pp. 80–87; Pernet, "Mobilizing Women", pp. 96–99.

collaborated with "the movement of Spanish Women" against "Franco's terror" and "Spanish Fascism". In 1938, MEMCH organized a public protest against the persecution of Jews outside the German Embassy in Santiago,[25] and widely and actively participated in transnational networks, sending delegates to international gatherings and maintaining contact with several women's organizations abroad.[26]

In the mid-1940s, WINGOs became part of MEMCH's transnational networks. Both WILPF and WIDF displayed global ambitions, trying to expand their activism to Latin America. Of the former, established in 1915 after 1,200 women met in The Hague to discuss putting an end to World War I, WILPF has since advocated for peace and women's rights, including goals such as women's suffrage, equal nationality rights for married women, permanent peace, the rule of international law, and humanitarian relief. In the interwar period, although WILPF had reached nearly 50,000 members in forty countries, there were almost no national sections in Latin America.[27] Of the latter, WIDF was founded in Paris at the end of World War II to promote an "alternative feminist internationalist political identity" aligned with socialist principles.[28] It became a "counter-point to the Western led" WINGOs, in which the Soviet Union wielded the most state influence on the organization. Notwithstanding, this dominant role should not be exaggerated to the point of disregarding women's own agency and diversity.[29] Indeed, WIDF women from across the world effectively organized to promote peace, anti-colonialism, and women's and children's rights.[30] As for Latin America,

25. Olga Poblete to Marie Claude Vaillant-Couturier, October 1948, Archivo Nacional de Chile, Fondo Elena Caffarena [hereafter ANCFEC], 5, 2; "Enérgica protesta de las mujeres de Chile", November 1938, ANCFEC, 5, 1. All translations are the author's.

26. Edda Gaviola Artigas et al., *"Queremos votar en las próximas elecciones"*. *Historia del movimiento femenino chileno 1913–1952* (Santiago, 1984), p. 44.

27. Sarah Hellawell, "Feminism, Pacifism and Internationalism: The Women's International League, 1915–1935" (Ph.D., Northumbria University, 2017); Rupp, *Worlds of Women*; Laura Beers, "Advocating for a Feminist Internationalism between the Wars", in Glenda Sluga and Carolyn James (eds), *Women, Diplomacy and International Politics since 1500* (New York, 2016), pp. 202–221; Threlkeld, *Pan American Women*, pp. 39–42.

28. Karen Garner, *Shaping a Global Women's Agenda: Women's NGOs and Global Governance, 1925–85* (Manchester [etc.], 2010), p. 3.

29. Quote from Garner, *Shaping a Global Women's Agenda*, p. 168. About the role of the Soviet Union and the communist world in WIDF, see Francisca de Haan, "Continuing Cold War"; "Eugénie Cotton, Pak Chong-ae, and Claudia Jones: Rethinking Transnational Feminism and International Politics", *Journal of Women's History*, 25:4 (2013), pp. 174–189.

30. Francisca de Haan, "The Women's International Democratic Federation (WIDF): History, Main Agenda, and Contributions, 1945–1991", in Thomas Dublin and Kathryn Kish Sklar (eds), *Women and Social Movements (WASI) Online Archive* (2012), pp. 1–25, 11. Available at: http://alexanderstreet.com/products/women-and-social-movements-international; last accessed 2 April 2018.

Figure 1. Olga Poblete at a ceremony of the MEMCH (front row, fifth from the left), date unknown.
Archivo Nacional de Chile, Archivo Mujeres y Género. Available at: https://www.archivonacional.gob.cl/616/articles-86872_recurso_1.jpg; *last accessed 15 September 2021.*

De Haan has described how the organization showed an interest in reaching out to the region from its inception.[31]

Both WINGOs found their key contact in Chile to be the MEMCH leader Olga Poblete (Figure 1). Especially during her period as Secretary General between 1946 and MEMCH's dissolution in 1953, Poblete was willing to foster collaboration with WILPF and WIDF to strengthen peace activism and gather support for MEMCH's campaigns in Chile. To some extent, Poblete's life story was not dissimilar from that of other MEMCH leaders. As a member of the emergent professional middle class – which benefited from the development of public institutions and the expansion of the state – and born to a modest background in Tacna in 1908 as the daughter of a single mother, Poblete took advantage of the educational opportunities that allowed her to become a history teacher in 1929.[32] In 1952, after developing a prominent career as educator in secondary education, Poblete began to work at the University of Chile, specializing in the history of "the far East and Africa".[33] In 1939, she became involved in MEMCH through a colleague, who asked her

31. Francisca de Haan, "La Federación Democrática Internacional de Mujeres (FDIM) y América Latina, de 1945 a los años sesenta", in Valobra and Yusta, *Queridas camaradas*, pp. 17–44.
32. Pernet, "Mobilizing Women", pp. 103–104.
33. María Teresa Larraín, "Olga Poblete. La mujer aún no levanta la mano". Available at: https://www.genero.patrimoniocultural.gob.cl/651/articles-28923_archivo_02.pdf; last accessed 21 April 2021.

to help with an exhibition on women's activities. This collaboration introduced Poblete to feminist politics and MEMCH circles.[34]

WILPF AND CHILE

The collaboration between MEMCH and WILPF began in 1946. While Poblete was studying new pedagogical schools of thought at Columbia University in New York, she was introduced to WILPF's work and became involved with the organization.[35] In the US, Poblete met Heloise Brainerd, who had vast experience working on the inter-American sphere and was a long-time member of WILPF. At the time she met Olga Poblete, Brainerd had been the chair of the WILPF Committee on the Americas (CA) for eleven years. Before taking the challenge of leading WILPF's inter-American project, she had worked at the Pan-American Union between 1909 and 1935, becoming Chief of the Division of Intellectual Cooperation in 1929. Her professional career and the experience of living and working in Mexico for four years meant that she had good knowledge of the Latin American region and was fluent in Spanish.[36] While there is not much information available about their encounter in the US, this initial contact between Poblete and Brainerd led to sustained communication between WILPF and MEMCH over the next few years.

Upon her return to Chile, Poblete became one of only a few associate members of WILPF in Latin America – thirteen in 1948 – and, as such, worked to disseminate "the concepts of peace, democracy, international relations, and organisation of the United Nations, in several women's groups and academic organisations".[37] Poblete considered both her work in MEMCH and her role as teacher as her "contribution to the work of the League". Through these activities, Poblete believed it achievable to "form an opinion and create favourable attitudes of peace and the strengthening of an organization of world government", showing the significance of internationalism for her. Thus, despite not organizing "a group or committee of the League as such, [she] acted in these areas as a member and pointed out that this work is part of the movement's inspiration and its purposes".[38]

Since at least the 1920s, WILPF members were actively promoting the organization's principles in hemispheric politics.[39] In the late 1930s, Brainerd

34. Pernet, "Mobilizing Women", pp. 92–104.
35. Poblete to Baer, 10 June 1950, ANCFEC, 7, 8; Pernet, "Mobilizing Women", p. 104.
36. Threlkeld, *Pan American Women*, pp. 176–177.
37. Poblete to Brainerd, 17 March 1948, ANCFEC, 5, 1; WILPF, "Interim Report to International Executive Committee of WILPF by Chairman of the Americas (Heloise Brainerd, USA)", 1948. Available at: https://archive.org/details/xcollection807b; last accessed 26 October 2020.
38. Poblete to Brainerd, 10 February 1949, ANCFEC, 7, 8.
39. Miller, *Latin American Women*, pp. 84, 260 (n. 65).

visited Chile as part of a Latin American tour where she "[established], with the help of the Círculo Pro-Paz de Valparaíso [Peace Circle of Valparaíso], other Circles in Santiago and Concepción". WILPF had worked with the peace circles in the 1930s before associating with MEMCH, yet little is known about the nature, scope, and connection of the circles to WILPF.[40] However, despite WILPF's early interest in Latin America, Megan Threlkeld has noted that the organization not only struggled to include new members from the region, but also persisted in considering it as part of the periphery of international politics.[41] Given her prior knowledge of the region, her language skills, and experience living in Latin America, Brainerd's appointment was undoubtedly beneficial in helping to overcome some of these difficulties. Nevertheless, structural barriers to incorporating Latin America women remained firmly in place. Indeed, the broader relationship between WILPF and Latin America was still troubled by persistent elements of an "orientalist ethos",[42] which permeated Poblete's relation with the WILPF.

These structural barriers – membership practices, the locations of international meetings, and language differences – hampered Latin American women's involvement in WINGOs. For instance, Poblete struggled to keep up with WILPF membership payments (set in US dollars), which may have been quite high for a female teacher in Chile. In a letter to Brainerd, she explained that:

> due to the dollar shortage and the high price on the market […], it has not been possible for me to pay the League fee. I do not know if I will be in a position to do it soon, but I wish not to be removed from the League. Believe me that I will do everything I can to continue contributing and secure all valuable information that I have been receiving so far.[43]

Similarly, while replying to an invitation extended by WILPF to the eleventh International Congress in Copenhagen, Poblete asserted that "it would certainly be impossible to attend from Chile".[44] Indeed, WINGOs' meetings were normally held in Europe and North America, and so travelling from the southern continent was fraught with difficulties. Additionally, if members wished to send written reports or statements in advance as an alternative, long-distance means of participating in international gatherings, language arose as another barrier. In considering her willingness to participate in WILPF's eleventh congress despite the myriad challenges, Poblete explained that she "would enthusiastically contribute with any report or work […] of interest

40. Brainerd to Mistral, 29 January 1939, Biblioteca Nacional Digital de Chile, Archivo del Escritor [hereafter BNDAE]. Available at: http://www.bibliotecanacionaldigital.gob.cl/bnd/623/w3-article-151184.html; last accessed 26 January 2020.
41. Threlkeld, *Pan American Women*, p. 9; for a wider explanation about the "exclusiveness" of WINGOs, see Rupp, *Worlds of Women*.
42. Threlkeld, *Pan American Women*, p. 9.
43. Poblete to Brainerd, 1950, ANCFEC, 6, 4.
44. Poblete to Brainerd, 10 February 1949.

for the Congress".[45] Brainerd helpfully explained that while she could translate the document if written in Spanish, additional time constraints would need to be put in place, and lamented that "the tongues of our League do not include Castilian, and to get the attention it needs, the report has to be in English".[46]

Although not always successful, partial solutions were put forward to advance the participation of Latin American women, most notably under the leadership of Brainerd. As previously mentioned, she was the first chair of WILPF's CA who was fluent in Spanish, meaning that newsletters and correspondence in WILPF's regionally organized body for the Americas could be composed in that language. This strongly facilitated contact, although the Committee remained small, with only nine members in 1946 (six from Latin America and three from the US).[47] Additionally, Brainerd herself translated documents to facilitate communication with other League members, as suggested by her offer to translate Poblete's report.

Another important inclusion mechanism was the organization of meetings for WILPF members and local women's groups. Indeed, regional conferences – and the personal encounters, exchanges of information, and informal socializing therein – were undoubtedly considered the most optimal means for encouraging cooperation and finding common ground.[48] In February 1946, for example, a "Meeting of Inter-American Women" was held in Washington DC to discuss the organization of the First Inter-American Congress of Women sponsored by WILPF. Representatives from several countries, including Argentina, Bolivia, Brazil, Colombia, Cuba, Venezuela, Chile, and the US, met to discuss future congress guidelines, programmes, timing, location, invitations, and funding (including participant travel expenses). Marta Vergara, at the time living in Washington, chaired one of the sessions and was elected as the organizing committee's South American delegate.[49] Brainerd also invited Gabriela Mistral, the influential Nobel Prize-winning Chilean poet (awarded in 1945), to be a congress sponsor.[50] She explained to Mistral that Vergara was part of the organizing committee so "you may take it that it deserves your trust".[51] Vergara and Mistral's support helped Brainerd to navigate the

45. *Ibid.*
46. Brainerd to Poblete, 21 February 1949, ANCFEC, 7, 9.
47. WILPF, "Interim Report".
48. Threlkeld, *Pan American Women*, pp. 35–36.
49. "Reunión de mujeres interamericanas para discutir la posibilidad de un Congreso Interamericano. Acta de las sesiones efectuadas", 1946, ANCFEC, 7, 8. According to Patricia Harms, Poblete was part of the initial steering committee established by Brainerd in the US to organize the congress. It seems that Vergara took her seat at some point. Patricia Harms, *Ladina Social Activism in Guatemala City 1871–1954* (Albuquerque, NM, 2020), p. 190.
50. On Mistral's international influence, see Nicola Miller, "Recasting the Role of the Intellectual: Chilean Poet Gabriela Mistral", *Feminist Review*, 79 (2005), pp. 134–149.
51. Brainerd to Mistral, 14 March 1946, BNDAE. Available at: http://www.bibliotecanacionaldigital.gob.cl/bnd/623/w3-article-151187.html; last accessed 26 January 2020.

lack of awareness regarding WILPF's activities in Latin America, and to advertise the importance of organizing a successful international meeting. While
Brainerd recognized that the organizing committee "is relatively unknown in
Latin America", she expected that "if your name [Mistral's] is on the letterhead,
the association will know that is a serious movement".[52]

In August 1947, the congress was finally held in Guatemala. Against
the background of the aftermath of World War II and the escalation of
Cold War tensions, the congress posed a direct challenge to US foreign
policy and rising militarization promoted by the Inter-American Treaty
of Reciprocal Assistance signed the same month in Rio de Janeiro.[53]
Organized into six committees, the delegates – representing organizations
from nineteen countries – discussed a wide range of topics: the consequences
of the atomic bomb; democratization; the struggle of human rights; the problems in inter-American politics; European immigration; refugees and victims of
war; and the civil and political rights of women.[54] The Chilean doctor María
Rivera, one of MEMCH's founders, attended the congress as a representative
of the Círculo Pro-Paz de Valparaíso and other Chilean women's organizations,
and chaired the Committee on Nuclear Weapons and Peace.[55] Poblete herself
could not travel to the meeting, but professed her staunch support of the congress resolutions, especially after living the experience of arriving in the US
while "Hiroshima and Nagasaki were still burning".[56]

WILPF's CA and the organizing committee put a considerable amount of
effort into coordinating and funding an accessible international congress. As
shown by the participation of Chilean women such as Vergara, Mistral, and
Rivera, Latin American women had an active role in both the planning and
the conference itself. Furthermore, initiatives in the same spirit followed in
the years to come. The second Inter-American Congress of Women took
place in Mexico in 1951; and, two decades later, a similar initiative in
Colombia saw the organization of the third Congress of American Women,
in 1970.[57] However, none of WILPF's sponsored congresses in Latin
America succeeded in greatly advancing the League's primary interest in the
region, namely, to create national sections. At times, they may even have
been detrimental: the organization of the 1970 congress in Colombia has
been discussed as possibly having debilitated the WILPF section in that

52. *Ibid.*
53. Harms, *Ladina Social Activism*, p. 186.
54. Miller, *Latin American Women*, p. 125.
55. Brainerd to Poblete, 22 October 1947, ANCFEC, 7, 8; Brainerd to Poblete, 17 July 1947,
ANCFEC, 7, 8.
56. Luis Alberto Mansilla, "Autorretrato de Olga Poblete", *Punto Final* (1986). Available at:
https://www.genero.patrimoniocultural.gob.cl/651/articles-28923_archivo_03.pdf; last accessed
13 May 2021.
57. *MEMCH. Antología para una historia del movimiento femenino*, 1983; Liga Internacional de
Mujeres Pro Paz y Libertad, "III Congreso de mujeres de América", n.d., ANCFEC, 7, 8.

country.[58] Ultimately, by the end of the 1940s, and despite the CA's decade-long effort to create national organizations, solely Brazilian women – and only just – had a WILPF national section in the region.[59]

Indeed, improving membership figures through the creation of national sections proved an extremely challenging task. In February 1949, when Brainerd asked Poblete her thoughts on creating a national organization in Chile, she replied: "I would not know if National Sections are convenient. I think they can be constituted upon reaching a greater stage of growth. I believe in unified movements and actions, not divided into blocks."[60] Certainly, Poblete's opinion was grounded in her local reality. By the end of the 1940s, the women's movement in Chile was riddled with political squabbles and divisions influenced by the recent realignments of the Cold War.[61] Furthermore, in January 1949, President González Videla had signed the law that granted women the vote in national elections, one of the main goals of the women's movement. However, achieving female enfranchisement also removed one of the main incentives to organize, triggering the further fragmentation of the women's movement.[62] The previous year, in 1948, Brainerd had reported that "a section is in the process of formation in Chile"; however, its official creation came twenty-four years later.[63] And Poblete herself was too overburdened to undertake more activities. While explaining the situation of the women's movement to a friend, she claimed: "I am the national leader of a women's institution of great activity, the MEMCH, and because of that I have a lot of extra work additional to, of course, my professional activities."[64] Despite this, Poblete remained enthusiastic about improving international connections despite political and personal constraints, and was open to Brainerd's suggestion "of creating a Latin American branch [...] which would have a lot to learn from the Sections in US and Canada".[65]

After this, the failed aspirations for WILPF's national sections in Latin America led to the design and implementation of alternate membership methods. Specifically, participation outside of nation-based organizing appeared to

58. Catherine Foster, *Women for All Seasons: The Story of the Women's International League for Peace and Freedom* (Athens, 1989), p. 59.
59. Heloise Brainerd, "Report to International Executive Committee by Chairman of Committee on the Americas", June 1950, ANCFEC, 7, 8.
60. Poblete to Brainerd, 10 February 1949.
61. Corinne A. Pernet, "Peace in the World and Democracy at Home. The Chilean Women's Movement in the 1940s", in David Rock (ed.), *Latin America in the 1940s: War and Postwar Transitions* (Berkeley, CA, 1994), pp. 166–183, 178–182.
62. *Ibid.*, pp. 181–182.
63. WILPF, "Interim Report".
64. Poblete to Annemarie L. Robinow, 15 February 1950, ANCFEC, 7, 8.
65. Poblete to Brainerd, 10 February 1949. Her exact words are: "una rama Latino Americana, que debe estar en formación y que tendría mucho que aprender a la de los Estados Unidos y el Canadá".

be a productive way of attracting more members and to better foster integration. Given these conditions, Brainerd suggested forming a regional WILPF branch in 1949. Women belonging to any country lacking a national section could join the League's Latin American branch by paying a reduced fee (two dollars, instead of the five usually asked of associate members). Optimistically, she stated that, "it is our idea that many Latin American women feel deep sympathy for the League's work and they will be pleased to accept the opportunity of affiliating if the dues are modest, and in due course national committees will be formed, and maybe Sections".[66] The plan began to be implemented in 1949, and Brainerd hoped that, "eventually this would lead to the formation of more National Sections of the League".[67]

In spite of such concessions, instead of creating – or transforming MEMCH into – a national section, Poblete opted for an alternative path of transnational collaboration. In her capacity as both MEMCH's secretary and member of the League, Poblete used her position to closely affiliate both organizations without sacrificing MEMCH's autonomy as an independent group. This cooperation was underpinned by Poblete's belief that WILPF's ideals coincided with MEMCH's principles of democracy, peace, and women's rights.[68] An essential part of this exchange consisted of sharing information about the organizations' experiences, goals, and, above all, common interests.[69] Materials pertaining to WILPF were sent to Poblete by the CA, the International Headquarters, and WILPF's sections. These were then studied and summarized by MEMCH's secretariat with a view to be disseminated among local committees. WILPF's international events were also publicized by the MEMCH in its own activities; for example, in International Women's Day celebrations, and through radio and printed media.[70] Thereby Poblete believed that MEMCH could effectively implement the activities carried out by WILPF's sections without actually becoming one. In her own words: "As you see, we have a lot of activities even though there is not a WILPF section constituted as such."[71]

These initiatives were positive steps in furthering collaboration between WILPF and Latin American women. In Poblete's case, she considered the connection to WILPF not only profoundly stimulating, but also valuable for MEMCH's local agenda. Especially after World War II, when political polarization and anti-communist sentiment grew, Poblete turned to her

---

66. Heloise Brainerd, "Circular al comité de las Américas", 10 October 1949, ANCFEC, 7, 8.
67. Brainerd, "Report to International Executive Committee".
68. Poblete to Baer, 10 June 1950.
69. Threlkeld makes the same point regarding contact between US and Mexican women's groups. Threlkeld, *Pan American Women*, p. 34.
70. Poblete to Robinow, 15 February 1950; Poblete to Baer, 10 June 1950; Olga Poblete to Heloise Brainerd, 25 August 1950, ANCFEC, 7, 8.
71. Poblete to Robinow, 15 February 1950.

transnational networks for support. MEMCH appealed to their contacts in WILPF to denounce political repression affecting its affiliates, members of the CP, and leftist sympathizers. The Popular Front strategy of seeking broader alliances had meant that, by the late 1930s, there were consolidated communist organizations in most Latin American countries. Growing industrialization, urbanization, and support for the allies during the war – including the prominent role gained by the Soviet Union – also helped to strengthen class mobilization and communist parties.[72] Nonetheless, the political scenario changed rapidly with the beginning of the Cold War. In 1947, President González Videla, who had been elected with support from the CP, changed his policy and began to support US foreign policy after the Truman administration made economic aid and credits dependent on anti-communist loyalty.[73] As a result, Poblete and her fellow *memchistas* were being marginalized from the political mainstream owing to their opposition to the government's restriction of civil liberties and the repression of labour, communist, and leftist leaders.[74] This affected not only the communist activists among MEMCH members, but also those *memchistas* without party affiliation, especially in the provinces.[75]

Facing this adverse political climate, this kind of international support became increasingly important for women's activism. In September 1948, Poblete wrote to Brainerd explaining that MEMCH's actions had been stifled through fear: all MEMCH activities were deemed by authorities to be "at the service of the [CP]", and so "people are terrified, and nobody wants to risk detention or exile".[76] Two months later, Poblete explicitly asked WILPF members to "intervene with their prestige and moral strength before the government of Chile [...] [so that] rational, and not brutal, means are employed against the political opposition".[77] WILPF, and Brainerd in particular, responded positively, addressing the Chilean Ministry of Labour to inquire about the internment camps. She also wrote to the chair of the United Nations Human Rights Commission, Eleanor Roosevelt, to inform her of the "cruel treatment of women communists, communist sympathizers, and even humanitarians", and requesting "that the situation be investigated and the proper steps taken to correct these abuses" and that "preferential attention" should be given "to the plight of Chile's working women".[78]

72. Victor Figueroa Clark, "Latin American Communism", in Norman Naimark, Silvio Pons, and Sophie Quinn-Judge (eds), *The Cambridge History of Communism*, 3 vols (Cambridge, 2017), II, pp. 388–413, 397–399; David Priestland, *Bandera roja. Historia política y cultural del comunismo* (Barcelona, 2017), p. 339.
73. Andrew Barnard, "Chile", in Leslie Bethell and Ian Roxborough (eds), *Latin America Between the Second World War and the Cold War, 1944–1948* (Cambridge, 1992), pp. 66–91.
74. Pernet, "Mobilizing Women", pp. 361–365.
75. *Ibid.*, p. 366.
76. Poblete to Brainerd, 18 September 1948, ANCFEC, 2, 5.
77. Poblete to Brainerd, November 1948, ANCFEC, 2, 5.
78. Brainerd to Roosevelt, 20 October 1948, ANCFEC, 8, 7.

Here, Poblete leveraged her women's international networks to advance MEMCH's goals, or at least to attempt some protection for its members. She appreciated Brainerd's support in such difficult times, explaining that, "contact with you [...] is very valuable for me as a woman, [a woman] determined to defend the same ideals that you uphold, and as the leader of [...] MEMCH, which, in these trying times for democratic convictions, is proud to stand by persecuted and abused people".[79]

SHIFTING ALLIANCES: WIDF'S INROADS IN CHILE

WILPF supported Poblete and MEMCH during a high point of women's activism in Chile and a pivotal moment of political transformation after World War II. Nonetheless, Poblete's search for international support and the expansion of her transnational network, together with her desire to preserve MEMCH's autonomy (not seeking to transform MEMCH into a WILPF branch), also set boundaries to the endorsement that WILPF was willing to give. This is clear when we highlight Poblete's connection with other international groups. Poblete established diverse contacts within international organizations, particularly among those initiatives linked to the communist movement. In contrast, during the 1940s, WILPF was extremely cautious about not being linked to international communism. The practice of associating WILPF's goals with radicalism and socialism as a way of discrediting its members began with WILPF's opposition to World War I.[80] However, this issue became more pressing after the end of World War II. As Patricia Harms notes, WILPF's advocacy of peace and Brainerd's opposition to US military policies in the Americas made the organization particularly vulnerable to allegations of being on the "wrong side" of the Cold War.[81] Brainerd, however, repeatedly denied such claims. Corresponding with Mistral in 1946, she explained that, "we [WILPF] are liberals, but not communists".[82] The next year, when a delegate to the Guatemala congress walked out on the grounds of it having been tainted by communism, she again clarified that accusations suggesting "communist influence" were "unfounded" since "the point of view [...] against any totalitarianism is precisely that which the League espouses".[83]

Such accusations were also present in Chile. The newspaper *El Mercurio* published the declarations of the Costa Rican delegate, who protested the

79. Poblete to Brainerd, 17 March 1948.
80. Threlkeld, *Pan American Women*, p. 22.
81. Harms, *Ladina Social Activism*, p. 196.
82. Brainerd to Mistral, 14 March 1946.
83. Brainerd to Mistral, 20 September 1947, BNDAE. Available at: http://www.bibliotecanacionaldigital.gob.cl/visor/BND:151238; last accessed 26 March 2020.

alleged "pro-Soviet" loyalties of the meeting.[84] The Federación Chilena de Instituciones Femeninas (Chilean Federation of Women's Institutions, FECHIF) – a national umbrella organization for more than 200 hundred different women's groups established in 1944 – also echoed such claims, and accused WILPF of being a communist group.[85] Owing to the political tensions stemming from the onset of the Cold War, FECHIF had moved to the right and expelled all the communists from its ranks. In a forceful response, MEMCH renounced the federation in 1947.[86] Thus, amid growing polarization, Brainerd tried to persuade Poblete and MEMCH to avoid Soviet-linked initiatives advocating peace. Indeed, she lamented that "the Soviet Union has sponsored so many initiatives in the name of peace that the world suspects those who use the word" and advised that, "we need to be careful not to identify with Soviet initiatives, however good they seem, because their methods do not agree with their declarations. This means, we only support *true* democracy". She concluded her message by saying: "I am sure the MEMCH is aware of this particular danger of our times."[87]

However, Poblete had her own convictions. In her years as a *memchista*, she had worked closely with communist women and, although never a party member herself, was considered an ally. In Poblete's words, "they [the CP] had a lot of trust in me, I was not an infiltrator".[88] As MEMCH entered a period of decline, Poblete threw herself into the organization of the Movimiento Chileno de Partidarios por la Paz (Chilean Movement of Partisans for Peace), a local section of the World Peace Council (WPC). The WPC was an international organization that endorsed an idea of peace linked to Soviet interests against the militarism and imperialism displayed by the West, especially the US, and had a significant presence in Latin America.[89] The Chilean section held its first national congress in 1950 and Poblete was appointed vice-president – a decision not without controversy within WILPF.[90] Her fellow League members were apprehensive about her appointment and relationships became strained. For example, replying to Poblete's calls for aid in pressuring the Chilean government after authorities had declined to issue her passport to attend the Second World Congress of Partisans of Peace in Sheffield, Brainerd warned her that, "this group falls

84. Pernet, "Peace in the World", p. 179.
85. Poblete to Brainerd, 1950. On FECHIF, see Pernet, "Peace in the World", p. 176.
86. Pernet, "Peace in the World", p. 180.
87. Brainerd to Poblete, 3 November 1950, ANCFEC, 7, 8; original emphasis.
88. Mat de Cámara. Sra. Elena. 3era Olguita (Lotty). Entrevista 7/92. [Video]. Archivo Eltit-Rosenfeld [hereafter Mat de Cámara]. Available at: https://archivospatrimoniales.uc.cl/handle/123456789/31573; last accessed 14 June 2021.
89. Patrick Iber, *Neither Peace nor Freedom: The Cultural Cold War in Latin America* (Cambridge [etc.] 2015), p. 2.
90. On the Chilean congress, see *Primer Congreso Nacional de los Partidarios de la Paz. 29 y 30 de Septiembre y 1° de Octubre de 1950* (Santiago de Chile, 1950).

under" those "dominated by the Soviet Union; not tending sincerely towards peace, but to the USSR's purposes, which sometimes are imperialistic". Thus, instead of accepting Poblete's request for help, she suggested that, "if it was not possible for you to go to the Congress, maybe it is for the better".[91] Thus, WILPF's members – along with other non-aligned pacifists – distanced themselves from the communist-led peace campaign and refused to support it. Although WILPF leaders explained that, "it was difficult, and sometimes painful, to cast doubts on expressions of solidarity in the cause of peace" through the WPC, it was "impossible not to do so when these movements were so at variance of life behind the Iron Curtain and so lacking in criticism of provocative actions by communist governments".[92]

Despite WILPF's attempts at persuasion, Poblete aligned herself with the WPC after attending the 1950 Warsaw Congress (which had moved from Sheffield because of intervention from Attlee's government) and visiting socialist Czechoslovakia. Not just asserting her own position, she further attempted to influence Brainerd to shift hers towards the inclusion of communists in the peace movement. In an emotional letter expressing her "love, respect and memories full of admiration", Poblete recognized the "true esteem" she had for Brainerd's "noble spirit" and work for the ideals of peace and freedom. However, she also believed that her "mistrust" of working with communists and her "well-intentioned and honest" compatriots were blinding her to the fact that the peace movement, with or without communists, was composed of people "holding different convictions". As one of those people with independent ideas, she claimed to "not be afraid of the company of communists". While travelling in Eastern Europe, she "clarified her position toward the problem of peace" and championed "the enormous responsibility [...] of fighting against the curtains of silence and evil misrepresentations". From her writings, it is clear that Poblete sincerely believed in the possibility of political independence and collaboration within the WPC. She urged Brainerd to question the ostensibly "objective information" given by Western magazines, such as *Time* or *Life*. Faced with Cold War polarization, Poblete "did not wish for either a Soviet or North American peace imposed by war". Nevertheless, she was completely convinced of the negative consequences of North American economic imperialism, President's Truman newly launched technical assistance programme that benefited "a handful of usufructuaries", and the shift towards a hemispheric defensive policy based on anti-communism. Poblete made clear to WILPF that her support of the WPC was honest and not politically motivated, but the vision of peace promoted by the USSR – in her eyes – was "more linked to reality" and carried

91. Brainerd to Poblete, 25 November 1950, ANCFEC, 7, 8.
92. Quoted in Lawrence Wittner, *Confronting the Bomb: A Short History of the World Nuclear Disarmament Movement* (Stanford, CA, 2009), p. 27.

"more meaning for the people than the peace put forward by US foreign policy".[93] While Brainerd and Poblete kept in touch in the years that followed, the end of MEMCH and different Cold War standpoints held by their leaders limited WILPF's influence in Chile.

While detrimental to her alliance with WILPF, Poblete's gravitation towards the communist-backed peace movement further encouraged her relationship with WIDF. As Celia Donert has remarked, the onset of the Cold War marked the association between WIDF and the Soviet-supported peace campaign. Not only did they share a common socialist definition of peace (linked to social justice and self-determination), but also many members of the WIDF held positions in the WPC.[94] Indeed, when Poblete took a leading role in the Chilean section of the WPC, she had been directly in touch with WIDF's leadership for at least two years (see below). Thus, this shift in Poblete's position shows the limits of collaboration across opposite ideological lines. As De Haan illustrated with the experiences of the feminist leaders Cécile Brunschvicg and Ceza Nabaraouy, Poblete's personal trajectory also reflects the intimately connected but increasingly antagonistic positions of WINGOs during the Cold War.[95]

The interest WIDF founders showed towards Latin America developed early, reflecting the organization's global reach. In Chile, FECHIF was the first institution officially in contact with them, while MEMCH and communist women were still part of it. In 1945, FECHIF received "repeated invitations" to the 1945 International Congress of Women in Paris.[96] The organization appointed two delegates who were in Europe at the time: Irma Salas, a prominent Chilean educator and member of the Asociación de Mujeres Universitarias (Association of University Women); and Margot Duhalde, the first Chilean female military pilot, who had served in World War II. On returning to Chile, Salas reported on WIDF's foundational congress, stressing the importance of the experience of war in developing women's consciousness and role in maintaining peace.[97] Emphatically, she explained how "women had learned to join forces […] to convert the principles of democracy into a reality for women […] and to overcome their subordinate position in society".[98] In 1946, WIDF also sponsored a visit from Marie Claude Vaillant-Couturier – a member of the French Resistance and a communist member of parliament after the end of the war – in her tour of Chile,

93. Poblete to Brainerd, 16 June 1951, ANCFEC, 7, 8.

94. Celia Donert, "From Communist Internationalism to Human Rights: Gender, Violence and International Law in the Women's International Democratic Federation Mission to North Korea, 1951", *Contemporary European History*, 25 (2016), pp. 313–333, 316.

95. De Haan, "Continuing Cold War", p. 554.

96. FECHIF, *Boletín*, 4 (September 1947), p. 10, ANCFEC, 6, 4.

97. *Ibid.*

98. Pernet, "Peace in the World and Democracy at Home", p. 176.

Argentina, Uruguay, and Brazil.[99] Vaillant-Couturier became the organization's secretary general in the same year, a fact suggestive of the attention
paid to the region. Her talks made a strong impression on the Chilean audience, who "enthusiastically paid homage" and observed her "bravery", "spirit
of sacrifice", and "elevated doctrine". Indeed, according to FECHIF's *Boletín*,
Vaillant-Couturier's words "touched the hearts of all women".[100]

It is unclear whether Poblete met Vaillant-Couturier during her visit to
Chile, but their correspondence began, at least, in 1948, and covered several
topics: the women's movement in Chile and Europe, the situation in Spain
under Franco's rule, and the international peace movement, among other
things. Communication with WIDF opened another window for
MEMCH's participation in international affairs and constituted not only
"the possibility to connect with another sector of the global women's movement", but also "a valuable source of news and suggestions".[101] MEMCH's
members were keen to know more about women's activism in other parts of
the developing world, possibly because their communication with international women's organizations had so far only focused on activities in the
Americas and Europe. Poblete, for instance, described the great interest
awakened by the WIDF-sponsored 1949 Congress of the Women of Asia
held in Beijing: "For many of our associates, the knowledge about this
Congress of Women in Asia establishes a true revelation, since it means an
extraordinary development of the women's movement in the East and a positive contribution to the world women's movement." Poblete added, "we are
highly interested in receiving all information that you could send about
such Congresses, as well as the one in Budapest, because MEMCH sustains
an active educational campaign for our women about all salient problems
both nationally and internationally".[102]

Early contacts and mutual interest in communicating were fruitful, although
collaboration remained problematic. As mentioned, for instance, FECHIF
could not send delegates to the 1945 Paris Congress directly from Chile, despite asking the government for monetary support, and instead had to rely
on women already in Europe for representation. However, geographical distance was not an insurmountable obstacle. WIDF women developed alternative methods of communication to advance connections with the region and
create bonds across the continents, similar to the strategies developed by
WILPF, such as organizing congresses in the region and exchanging materials
and letters in Spanish. Indeed, one year after WIDF's foundation, women's

99. WIDF, *Second Women's International Congress* (Paris, 1949), p. 54.
100. FECHIF, *Boletín*, 4, p. 11.
101. Poblete to Vaillant-Couturier, October 1948.
102. *Ibid.* On the 1949 Conference of the Women of Asia, see Elisabeth Armstrong, "Before
Bandung: The Anti-Imperialist Women's Movement in Asia and the Women's International
Democratic Federation", *Signs: Journal of Women in Culture and Society*, 41:2 (2016), pp. 305–331.

groups in Chile were receiving their *Boletín de Información* (Informational Bulletin) and, later, *Mujeres del Mundo Entero* (Women of the Whole World), WIDF's monthly (and from 1966, quarterly) review, in their own language. As noted by De Haan, these publications, "served to create bonds and an imagined community of progressive women worldwide, in addition to providing information about WIDF and its activities, its congresses, national affiliates, and specific events and political causes".[103]

These efforts quickly bore fruit, and the Comité Nacional Femenino de Unidad (CNFU) was established in 1947. There is little information about its initial years, but Poblete explained during an interview that the organization emerged after the "rupture of the women's movement due to repression and the Cold War". It seems that the committee, established to counteract the marginalization of leftist women, had direct support from the CP.[104] Its supporters were also probably encouraged by results of the 1947 council election in which the CP performed well, becoming the third most voted-for party (16.5 per cent of the ballots) and securing up to 11.8 per cent of the women's vote.[105] This convergence of domestic conditions likely encouraged communist support for the newly formed committee, which increased the chance of influencing women while the CP was illegal.[106] However, as shown by WIDF's global actions, women organizing CNFU were not only responding to local events but were also stimulated by communist internationalism. Mercedes Yusta highlighted this process of transnational mobilization when explaining the connection between Spanish communist women's organizing and the creation of WIDF.[107] Thus, it was a combination of both internal and external factors that galvanized Chilean communist women; those who, in turn, became instrumental to CNFU's success.

CNFU became a national organization, with local chapters in La Serena, Valparaíso, Talca, and Concepción.[108] The committee grouped "women's institutions across Chile" and strove to "improve childhood living standards, to support modest women, working women, middle-class women, in whom anguish is felt in excess, to provide them a better life, less filled with misery, with more dignity, and more humanity".[109] Over the years, the organization

---

103. De Haan, "The Women's International Democratic Federation", p. 12.

104. Mat de Cámara.

105. Erika Maza Valenzuela, "Catolicismo, anticlericalismo y la extensión del sufragio a la mujer en Chile", *Estudios Públicos*, 58 (1995), pp. 137–195, 194.

106. McGee Deutsch notes a similar dynamic regarding the Argentinian CP and the women's organization la Junta de la Victoria. Sandra McGee Deutsch, "Mujeres, antifascismo y democracia. La Junta de la Victoria, 1941–1947", *Anuario IEHS*, 28 (2013), pp. 157–175, 166.

107. Mercedes Yusta, "Las mujeres en el Partido Comunista de España (1921–1950). La estrategia internacional", in Valobra and Yusta, *Queridas camaradas*, pp. 45–69.

108. Mat de Cámara.

109. Mercedes Fuentealba and Luisa Vicentini to Gabriela Mistral, 23 May 1951, BNDAE. Available at http://www.bibliotecanacionaldigital.cl/bnd/623/w3-article-137702.html; last accessed 27 July 2018.

developed a complex structure that included an executive committee, a governing body, fee-paying provincial and local committees, and affiliated organizations.[110] They also periodically organized national, provincial, and local assemblies, together with national congresses every three or four years.[111]

Poblete collaborated with CNFU while she was leading MEMCH, bringing the two organizations together and emphasizing their "anti-war discourse".[112] In the late 1940s and early 1950s, part of this joint work consisted of supporting WIDF's petitions and campaigns, such as activism against the use of nuclear energy, international campaigns for the protection of children, and work on behalf of women's rights.[113] The prominence of WIDF was highlighted in these activities. In 1951, for example, in celebrating International Women's Day, Poblete gave a talk entitled "The Women's Movement in Europe", in which she underlined the role of WIDF's international leaders, Cotton, Vaillant-Couturier, and Maddalena Rossi (the president of the Union of Women of Italy and later WIDF's vice-president), and the "notable" role of women in Poland and Czechoslovakia.[114] Their high esteem for women's activism related to the communist movement and socialist regimes built from their past loyalties to the anti-fascist struggle (an important feature of organizations such as MEMCH), but also showed how WIDF stoked new life into leftist women's activism, even in spite (or perhaps because) of a hostile political environment. As Poblete recalled, CNFU's purpose was to "struggle for the defence of human rights [in] a time of very intense political persecution".[115]

While MEMCH entered a period of decline until its dissolution in 1953, CNFU remained active in strengthening its international ties. It is not clear when CNFU officially became affiliated with WIDF, but in 1948, it sent a report to the WIDF International Congress hoping for "its official admittance, as soon as possible".[116] At the same meeting, Fanny Edelman, the Argentine member of the WIDF executive committee, explained that Chilean women had not been able to attend owing to heavy repression in Chile.[117] A couple of months earlier, the Law of Permanent Defence of Democracy (also known as the Damned Law) had been promulgated, resulting in harsher

---

110. WIDF, *Second Women's International Congress*, p. 12.

111. *Ibid.*, p. 23.

112. Mat de Cámara.

113. Marie-Claude Vaillant-Couturier to Olga Poblete, 2 October 1948, ANCFEC, 7, 8; Olga Poblete, "Apoyo a la realización de la Jornada internacional de defensa de la infancia", 11 May 1950, ANCFEC, 6, 5; Olga Poblete, "Carta enviada por Olga Poblete de Espinosa. Presidente comando pro Jornada internacional de defensa de la infancia", n.d., ANCFEC, 6, 5; Poblete to Elisa Uriz, 26 May 1950, ANCFEC, 6, 5.

114. Poblete to Arcelina M. Goto, 12 March 1951, ANCFEC, 7, 11.

115. Mat de Cámara.

116. WIDF, *Second Women's International Congress*, p. 83.

117. *Ibid.*, p. 210.

persecution against communists. The CP was outlawed and excluded from the political system and from trade unions, which disenfranchised around 23,000 members.[118] Ultimately, however, the CNFU remained active and, following the style of other WIDF national sections, changed its name to the Unión de Mujeres de Chile (UMC) in 1956. This also coincided with the easing of the repression against communists and leftists in the early 1950s, although the "Damned Law" was not abolished until 1958.[119] Thus, in less than a decade, WIDF established a national section in Chile as it had already done in Argentina, Brazil, Mexico, Peru, and Cuba.[120]

The development of this national structure allowed for sustained involvement in WIDF's international activities. While influence from women in the Global South on the organization's leadership remained limited,[121] regional conferences were nonetheless crucial to attracting local leaders and enhancing local organization. Lia Laffaye, for instance, became president of the UMC in 1956 after being introduced to WIDF's work in a conference in Brazil. Representing the Partido Femenino (Women's Party), Laffaye had been elected to parliament in 1953, becoming the second woman to hold a congress seat in Chile's history. In 1954, she attended the first WIDF-sponsored conference of Latin American women held at Rio de Janeiro, where she developed ties to the organization.[122] The next year, she crossed the Atlantic to participate in WIDF's council meeting in Vienna. After having attended these meetings, she explained how she realized that, "the WIDF was a great force" and noted that, before participating in the Brazil Conference, she had "always worked alone and in an independent way".[123] In the Vienna council meeting, Laffaye was captivated by the international gathering, where "the problems which have been discussed [...] closely [follow] the concerns of all women. The speeches have been extremely interesting and are a revelation to me. I am particularly interested in this unity of women all across the world, and I think that is a very important step forward".[124] Inspired by these international assemblies, she not only became UMC's president, but went on to sustain

118. Barnard, "Chile", pp. 88–89.

119. Rolando Álvarez, *Forjando la vía chilena al socialismo. El Partido Comunista de Chile en la disputa por la democracia y los movimientos sociales (1931–1970)* (Valparaíso, 2020), p. 71.

120. WIDF, *Second Women's International Congress*, p. 21.

121. Yulia Gradskova, "Women's International Democratic Federation, the 'Third World' and the Global Cold War from the late-1950s to the mid-1960s", *Women's History Review*, 29:2 (2019), pp. 270–288.

122. The Women's Party was dissolved in 1953 and Laffaye became an independent member of congress. Felícitas Klimpel, *La Mujer Chilena* (Santiago de Chile, 1962), p. 109. On the Rio de Janeiro Congress, see Branca Fialho, "From the Conference of Latin American Women to the World Congress of Mothers", *Women of the Whole World* [hereafter *WWW*], 2 (February 1955), p. 7.

123. "Their Impressions of Our Council Meeting", *WWW*, 4 (April 1955), p. 9.

124. *Ibid.*

active participation in international conferences throughout the 1950s and 1960s.

Following MEMCH's tradition, the UMC advanced its programme of peace, women's emancipation, and children's rights, by establishing connections with international organizations, presenting their views about international issues to the United Nations, and maintaining an active presence at international events. In 1960, for instance, Laffaye explained that, despite facing great difficulties, the organization had been "present in almost all international meetings convened by the WIDF".[125] Indeed, the UMC was able to send delegates to the International Congress of Women in Vienna (1958), the International Assembly of Women to commemorate fifty years of International Women's Year in Copenhagen (1960), the International Congress of Women in Moscow (1963), and the World Conference for Children (1966). Its members also regularly attended council meetings (China, 1956; Helsinki, 1957; Sofia, 1965; Salzburg, 1955; Budapest, 1970) and held a seat on the WIDF's bureau.[126]

Once WIDF's national section in Chile was firmly established, and its leaders had gained a fair amount of international experience, the UMC began to sponsor regional Latin American women's conferences. Santiago was designated the host city of the First Conference of Latin American Women in November 1959.[127] This aimed to convene a wide and diverse group of participants and supporters and was organized by the UMC together with women of the CP, fellow travellers, and other public figures. According to the UMC's report, the congress was a success, with representatives from every country in the region and "all members assuming the task as their own".[128] The UMC came to the fore again during the winter of 1968, when it organized a WIDF South American Seminar and presented the report "The Growing Participation in Economic, Social, Cultural and Political Life".[129] The five-day seminar gathered more than a hundred participants from nine countries, with the aim of showcasing "the increasing activity of the women of these countries studying and solving their problems". The participants also considered the activity a contribution to the 1969 WIDF World Congress of Women in Helsinki and the International Year for Human Rights (1968).[130] These high-profile seminars sought to garner women's support for

---

125. 2° Congreso Nacional Unión de Mujeres de Chile, p. 11. ANCFEC, 6, 4.

126. *WWW*, 6 (1956); *WWW*, 8–9 (1957); *WWW*, 8 (1963); *WWW*, 1 (1966); *WWW*, 4 (1966).

127. Strictly speaking, the First Conference of Latin American Women was held in Brazil in 1954; however, it was organized under a different name (Conferência Nacional sobre o Trabalho entre as Mulheres). This conference had links with WILPF but was organized by the Communist Party of Brazil. Adriana María Valobra, "'Mujeres-sombra' y 'Barbudas'. Género y política en el Primer Congreso Latinoamericano de Mujeres, Chile-1959", *Anuario del Instituto de Historia Argentina*, 14 (2014), pp. 1–17, 2.

128. See: 2° Congreso Nacional Unión de Mujeres de Chile, p. 6. ANCFEC, 7, 11.

129. "Regional Seminars in Latin America", *WWW*, 1 (1968), p. 49.

130. Cecile Hugel, "Two Notable Events in Latin America", *WWW*, 1 (1969), pp. 3–4.

social change projects and, more specifically, WIDF. Indeed, such conferences were an effective way of connecting and involving Latin American women with communist-inspired women's transnational activism.

CONCLUSION

The personal and political relationships developed by the leaders of the Chilean women's movement and WINGOs shed light on the increasing (yet incomplete) participation of women from outside the "centres" of international politics in a particular space of women's transnational activism. Even though WILPF and WIDF shared strengths and weaknesses in promoting their ideas and establishing links with women in Latin America, they fundamentally differed in their level of success in creating national sections. Even in the fruitful collaboration developed between MEMCH and WILPF from 1946 to 1951, Poblete, as Chilean leader, articulated it from a position of autonomy. When MEMCH was dissolved in 1953 – theoretically providing a space for the establishment of a WILPF national section – Cold War realignments and impacts on the Chilean women's movement limited the organization's national influence. Conversely, WIDF's success in Chile – first, rapidly establishing a local committee in 1947, and then a national section – was due to several aspects. WIDF began as a more global organization, with one of its main aims to extend their influence worldwide. In Chile and elsewhere, WIDF's success was partly achieved by dovetailing with previous traditions in women's mobilization, particularly anti-fascism and pacifism. Those elements were vital to the initial configuration of the Chilean women's movement, and so there was a degree of continuity between MEMCH and WIDF's Chilean section. The fact that many communist women had double militancy was a tendency that also strengthened WIDF. Indeed, as Poblete explained in the 1980s, many *memchistas* became active members of the CNFU (including herself). The growing support for the CP in Chile – becoming one of the biggest political forces despite severe repression in the late 1940s and 1950s – naturally reinforced this trend.

Ultimately, the political and ideological trajectories of activists such as Poblete show that both the relationships and friendships they sought to prioritize, and their participation in women's transnational activism, were shaped by their local reality and their own political alignments and goals. Poblete appealed to her personal connections with the leadership of WINGOs to denounce the curtailment of civil and political liberties and protect leftist women affected by government repression. As political polarization grew with the onset of the Cold War, and WILPF consciously avoided associations with communism, Poblete and other activists further cultivated their relationships with communist internationalist organizations, including WIDF, to foster leftist women's activism for peace and women's rights. These relationships were not only crucial for the projection of WIDF's activities within Chile in the following decades but would also shape the fundamental role of WINGOs in the anti-dictatorial international solidarity developed in the 1970s and 1980s. In January 1974, for example, WIDF was one of the first organizations to send a fact-finding mission to Chile to investigate human rights violations, only four months after Pinochet's coup d'état. Throughout the dictatorship years, transnational connections also gave a platform to Chilean exiles to speak against the regime, including Salvador Allende's widow Hortensia Bussi, who became WIDF's honorary president.[131] Thus, such networks of women's solidarity and activism, which became prominent during the dictatorship years, had a longer history, which this article has aimed to unveil.

---

131. Lanfranco González, "Women's Activism and Feminism".

IRSH 67 (2022), pp. 75–102 doi:10.1017/S0020859022000025
© The Author(s), 2022. Published by Cambridge University Press on behalf of
Internationaal Instituut voor Sociale Geschiedenis

Radicalizing Feminism: The Mexican and Cuban Associations within the Women's International Democratic Federation in the Early Cold War*

Manuel Ramírez Chicharro ⓘ

*Comparative Studies Group of Caribbean and Atlantic World – CSIC
University Institute for Research on Latin American Studies
University of Alcala, Spain*

E-mail: manuel.ramirez.chicharro@gmail.com

ABSTRACT: This article analyses the interactions between the Women's International Democratic Federation (WIDF) and its Mexican and Cuban national chapters and affiliated organizations. Focusing on the National Bloc of Revolutionary Women, the Democratic Union of Mexican Women, and the Democratic Federation of Cuban Women, this article studies the ideological foundations these organizations defended and the action programmes they used to materialize them. One of its main contributions is to argue that Mexican and Cuban socialist and communist women contributed to the struggle for women's emancipation within the Eastern Bloc through grass-roots contributions that did not simply emulate European communist organizations, but drew on, and were informed by, national contexts, material conditions, and historical backgrounds. The increasing number of requests, demands, and proposals emerging from Latin America, and more specifically from Mexico and Cuba, ultimately fostered a steady process of decentralization that broadened visions of women's progress within the global leftist feminist movement during the early Cold War.

INTRODUCTION: THE WIDF IN LATIN AMERICA

In the late 1940s, Vaillant de Couturier – the General Secretary of the Women's International Democratic Federation (WIDF), the most important communist-oriented feminist organization of the twentieth century – expressed a paternalistic, ethnocentric, and doctrinal attitude towards her

---

* This research was supported by the National Autonomous University of Mexico's Fellowship Program in Humanities and by the research projects "El orden y sus desafíos en el Circuncaribe hispano, 1791–1960" (Ministerio de Asuntos Económicos y Transformación Digital, Spain. Ref: RTI2018-094305-B-100) and "How Women's Rights Became Human Rights: Gender, Socialism and Postsocialism in Global History, 1917-2017" (Arts and Humanities Research Fellowship, Ref: AH/P008852/1).

Latin American colleagues before the executive committee of her organization.[1] The so-called egalitarian globalism of her feminist socialism masked her historicist and teleological understanding of women's liberation. Underneath it, she seems to have believed that there was one single path to achieving liberation, which could only be headed and disseminated by European communism, pacifism, and antifascism. In this way, the French leader obscured the long history of Latin American feminists, which was constructed in dialogue with crises and revolutions in their national contexts, and which laid the foundations for their adherence to and involvement with the WIDF. By contrast, this article argues that Latin American women did not just emulate the guidelines issued by the WIDF's European leadership in their struggles for liberation but contested and enriched them with demands rooted in their specific material reality. To make this argument, this article draws on case studies from the Cuban and Mexican chapters of the WIDF, as representative of socialist feminist organizations in Latin America during the early Cold War.

The Women's International Democratic Federation (WIDF) has been studied from various points of view and with various different methodologies. Kadnikova and De Haan analyse the content and proposals made at the WIDF's international congresses from the perspective of political history, giving preference to associations and meetings in Europe.[2] McGregor and Armstrong examine the WIDF's position and actions surrounding the process of decolonization in Asia,[3] while Gradskova has an understanding of the

---

1. Madrid, Archivo Histórico del Partido Comunista de España (Historical Archive of the Communist Party of Spain; AHPCE), Women's Organizations, 116, Folder "Executive Committee", "Informe sobre el viaje a la América Latina por Maria-Claude Vaillant Couturier" (p. 273 of that file): "the results of the trip are extremely positive, as it has created a great current of sympathy around our Federation and has widely popularized our objectives and our tasks, in countries where women's organizations are still very young, but where all conditions exist for its development. Now it is necessary for us to follow them very closely to help them develop and to make an effort at the same time to create sections of our Federations where they do not yet exist". Concerning the same outcome, another document in the same file, p. 348, considers that: "We need to send authorized representatives to these meetings. But the sending of the representations of our Federation must be done, not by decision of each national section, but in agreement with the Executive Committee which, in each case, will study the manner and the convenience of assistance."
2. Francisca de Haan, "Continuing Cold War Paradigms in Western Historiography of Transnational Women's Organisations: The Case of the Women's International Democratic Federation (WIDF)", *Women's History Review*, 19 (2010), pp. 547–573; and Ana Kadnikova, "The Women's International Democratic Federation World Congress of Women, Moscow, 1963: Women's Rights and World Politics during the Cold War" (Ph.D., Central European University, 2011).
3. Katharine McGregor, "Indonesian Women: The Women's International Democratic Federation and the Struggle for 'Women's Rights', 1946–1965", *Indonesia and the Malay World*, 40:117 (2012), pp. 193–208; Elizabeth Armstrong, "Before Bandung: The Anti-imperialist Women's Movement in Asia and the Women's International Democratic

expansion of the WIDF's focus toward the so-called Third World, explaining the conflicts and clashes that arose in this process.[4] Some scholars – such as Yusta, Donert, and Goodman – examine the WIDF as a primary force in the creation of a female, antifascist, international human rights and peace movement.[5] However, despite recent research on leftist women's groups in Mexico, Chile, Brazil, and elsewhere, the exchanges between the WIDF's general secretary and the Latin American associations affiliated with it – as well as these association's participation in the international congresses organized by the WIDF during the early Cold War – have not received proper attention.[6] Studies of Latin American communist movements in the Cold War neglect Latin American women's associations and women within trade unions.[7] Some books focus on the links formed by Black international communism between the US and Latin America in the interwar period and on Black women's engagement in global freedom struggles.[8] However, the circulation and exchange of ideas between communist women in Latin American and Europe within the WIDF has not been significantly studied. Adriana Valobra and Mercedes Yusta's excellent book gives a broad understanding of the structure, militancy, and ideology of communist women linked to the WIDF throughout the continent. Departing from here, this paper seeks to shed light on the contributions made by its Mexican and Cuban chapters. It

Federation", *Signs: Journal of Women in Culture and Society*, 41 (2016), pp. 305–331; Katharine McGregor, "Opposing Colonialism: the Women's International Democratic Federation and Decolonisation Struggles in Vietnam and Algeria 1945–1965", *Women's History Review*, 25 (2016), pp. 925–944.

4. Yulia Gradskova, "Women's international Democratic Federation, the 'Third World', and the Global Cold War from the late-1950s to the mid-1960s", *Women's History Review*, 29 (2020), pp. 270–288.

5. Mercedes Yusta, "The Mobilization of Women in Exile: The Case of the *Unión de Mujeres Antifascistas Españolas* in France (1944–1950)", *Journal of Spanish Cultural Studies*, 6 (2005), pp. 43–58; Celia Donert, "From Communist Internationalism to Human Rights: Gender, Violence and International Law in the Women's International Democratic Federation Mission to North Korea, 1951", *Contemporary European History*, 25 (2016), pp. 313–333; Joyce Goodman, "International Women's Organizations, Peace and Peacebuilding", *The Palgrave Handbook of Global Approaches to Peace* (Cham, 2019), pp. 441–460.

6. Adriana Valobra and Mercedes Yusta (eds), *Queridas camaradas. Historias iberoamericanas de mujeres comunistas* (Buenos Aires, 2017).

7. Robert J. Alexander, *International Labor Organizations and Organized Labor in Latin America and the Caribbean* (Santa Bárbara, 2009); Vanni Pettinà, *Historia Mínima de América Latina en la Guerra Fría* (Mexico City, 2018); Kevin A. Young, *Making the Revolution: Histories of the Latin American Left* (Cambridge, 2019); Thomas C. Field, Stella Krepp, and Vanni Pettinà, *Latin America and the Global Cold War* (Chapel Hill, NC, 2020).

8. Margaret Stevens, *Red Internationalism and Black Caribbean: Communists in New York, Mexico and the West Indies, 1919–1939* (London, 2017); Keisha N. Blain, Tiffany Gill, and Michael West (eds), *To Turn the Whole World Over: Black Women and Internationalism* (Urbana, IL, 2019).

aims to decentralize the history of international feminist activism at the beginning of the Cold War.

At the WIDF's Foundational Congress in November 1945, General Secretary Dolores Ibárruri – who was forced to leave Spain after the Civil War – explained the need to strengthen ties with Latin America. Representatives from Argentina, Brazil, Chile, and, forming a majority, Cuba and Uruguay attended this first meeting. Ibárruri announced that there would be more representatives from the region at the next congress. In fact, there was a special interest in incorporating Mexican activists as the Communist Party of Mexico was, by that time, a forceful entity.[9] However, the Mexicans did not send a delegation to the international congresses and conferences of the WIDF until the Copenhagen Congress in 1952. Shortly after, in 1956, a CIA report noted that several organizations linked to, or supporting, the WIDF had spread throughout Latin America (Figure 1). This confidential document reveals that the most important delegations came from Brazil, Argentina, Chile, Uruguay, and Guatemala, though it notes that affiliated organizations also existed in less populated countries, such as Jamaica and British Guiana. The relevance of countries from the Global South to the WIDF rebalanced very significantly during the Cold War. Of all WIDF chapters, the percentage in Europe decreased from 47.1 in 1948 to 26.4 in 1975. In contrast, during the same period in Asia this grew from 21.6 to 23.6 per cent, in Africa from 13.7 to 23.6 per cent, in North America it fell from 3.9 to 1.9 per cent, and in Oceania it remained around two per cent. For its part, the proportion of Latin American sections skyrocketed from 11.8 to 22.6 per cent in the same historical period, it was the region with the highest growth within the WIDF.[10]

This article confirms De Haan's argument that the mutual, growing interest between the Executive Committee and Council of the WIDF and Latin American communist and socialist organizations was caused by a paradigm shift that took place between 1945 and 1948. However, clashes between the executive committee and the national chapters of countries in the Global South were especially bitter in the 1940s and 1950s, as Graskova argues.[11] The WIDF had been conceived during World War II, when defending democracy against fascism was its driving force. Once fascism was defeated, the

---

9. Francisca de Haan, "La Federación Democrática Internacional de Mujeres (FDIM) y América Latina, de 1945 a los setenta", in Yusta and Valobra, *Queridas camaradas*, pp. 17–45.

10. This information has been taken from two main sources in which the list of attendants and organizations affiliated is shown. Concerning 1948, *Second Women's International Congress: Account of the Work of the Congress which Took Place in Budapest (Hungary) from the 1st to the 6th of December, 1948* (WIDF, Paris, 1949), p. 21. Concerning 1975, see Paulina Mateus Nkonda, "Informe de la Comisión de Mandatos al 7° Congreso de la FIDM", *VII° Congreso de la F.D.I.M.* (Berlin, 1976), p. 65.

11. Yulia Gradskova, "Women's international Democratic Federation".

political paradigm of the Cold War moved from democracy to anti-communism. Additionally, the movements for independence in Asia and Africa instilled in Latin American left-wing activists a renewed anti-colonial militancy against US foreign policy in the region. Fearing a conflict in Latin America, communist and socialist women began to position themselves against military escalation and the rising price of basic foods, and to argue for women's and children's rights. These paradigms and ideological positions were not just the result of top-down programmes established by the WIDF, but of very complex interactions between women's associations affiliated with the WIDF, and between these groups and the communist forces within their countries.[12]

The Cuban and Mexican branches of the WIDF are fruitful objects of study for several reasons. Within the WIDF, they questioned, informed, and enriched global discussions about women's emancipation with disruptive ideas drawing on their specific material and political conditions. The complex and strained relationships between Latin American countries and the US concerning government institutions led Latin American leftist feminist militants to shape and share similar fundamental values and objectives. Communist Cuban and Mexican women both rooted their political discourses in similar nationalist revolutionary processes and in opposition to American imperialism and authoritarianism. Concerning women's political status – irrespective of when they gained the right to vote in national elections (respectively 1934 and 1953) – left-wing feminists from Cuba and Mexico were able to join and become militants in the WIDF in the context of a global Cold War. In addition, understanding the programmes and proposals made by Cuban and Mexican communist women at this time allows us to discover that "Latin American communist feminism" was not a consistent ontology. For instance, Cuban members of the WIDF emphasized the issues faced by Black women, while Mexican members barely mentioned the question of the diverse indigenous women in their country in publications and conferences.

This article takes as its object of study the activities of the National Bloc of Revolutionary Women (1941–1950) and its successor, the Democratic Union of Mexican Women (1950–1963) in Mexico, and the Democratic Federation of Cuban Women (1946–1956/61) in Cuba. It is commonly accepted that the WIDF displayed little interest in Latin America before the triumph of the Cuban revolution in 1959. But archival evidence suggests that a desire to strengthen political ties between leftist women from Mexico and Cuba and the Central Council and Executive Committee of the WIDF had existed since the foundation of the organization in 1945. From this date – instead of the European-based Council and Committee issuing top-down guiding principles and programmes to the Mexican and Cuban associations affiliated with

---

12. Francisca de Haan, "La Federación Democrática Internacional de Mujeres".

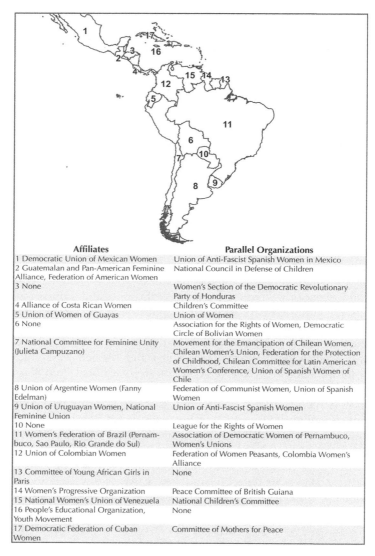

Affiliates	Parallel Organizations
1 Democratic Union of Mexican Women	Union of Anti-Fascist Spanish Women in Mexico
2 Guatemalan and Pan-American Feminine Alliance, Federation of American Women	National Council in Defense of Children
3 None	Women's Section of the Democratic Revolutionary Party of Honduras
4 Alliance of Costa Rican Women	Children's Committee
5 Union of Women of Guayas	Union of Women
6 None	Association for the Rights of Women, Democratic Circle of Bolivian Women
7 National Committee for Feminine Unity (Julieta Campuzano)	Movement for the Emancipation of Chilean Women, Chilean Women's Union, Federation for the Protection of Childhood, Chilean Committee for Latin American Women's Conference, Union of Spanish Women of Chile
8 Union of Argentine Women (Fanny Edelman)	Federation of Communist Women, Union of Spanish Women
9 Union of Uruguayan Women, National Feminine Union	Union of Anti-Fascist Spanish Women
10 None	League for the Rights of Women
11 Women's Federation of Brazil (Pernambuco, Sao Paulo, Rio Grande do Sul)	Association of Democratic Women of Pernambuco, Women's Unions
12 Union of Colombian Women	Federation of Women Peasants, Colombia Women's Alliance
13 Committee of Young African Girls in Paris	None
14 Women's Progressive Organization	Peace Committee of British Guiana
15 National Women's Union of Venezuela	National Children's Committee
16 People's Educational Organization, Youth Movement	None
17 Democratic Federation of Cuban Women	Committee of Mothers for Peace

Figure 1. According to the CIA, by 1956, the WIDF received extensive support from several communist, socialist, and left-wing women's organizations throughout Latin America. Among them there were two types of groups. The "affiliated", which had requested to join the WIDF, and the "parallel", that sympathized and helped the WIDF's national chapters. Likewise, women's groups supporting the WIDF turned up in countries such as Nicaragua or Peru in the following years.

Central Intelligence Agency, "Women's International democratic Federation (WIDF). A compilation of Available Basic Reference Data. Affiliates and Parallel Organizations, Strength, Officers, Addresses, Publicaciones", 1956. Open access, https://www.cia.gov/readingroom/docs/CIA-RDP78-00915R000600140010-9.pdf

the WIDF – fluent bottom-up proposals, initiatives, and petitions counterbalanced, enriched, and complicated the guidelines set up at the international congresses. The circulation of people, publications, and ideas between Latin America and Europe – together with those from Asian and African communist women – contributed to the creation of a truly transnational network of socialist feminism. The Eastern-bloc oriented WIDF focused on women's rights, peace, anti-colonialism, and children's rights, but its interactions with non-European activists brought decentralized, national perspectives into its discussions, which ultimately discredited allegedly universal assumptions concerning women's empowerment.

My research uses three main primary sources. First, the personal correspondence between the Executive Committee and General Secretary and the Mexican and Cuban representatives of the WIDF. Second, the minutes of the WIDF's international congresses held in 1948 (Budapest), 1953 (Copenhagen), and 1958 (Vienna), in which members of both countries delivered speeches and conferences on women's issues. And third, reports and letters published by Mexican and Cuban women in the English and Spanish version of *Women of the Whole World*, the main journal published by the WIDF. This information has been collected from the General Archive of the Nation in Mexico, the National Archive of Cuba, the Alexander Street foundation in Massachusetts (US), and the Historical Archive of the Spanish Communist Party. The theoretical frame applied to this analysis uses the postcolonial feminist perspective of Curiel (2009), Ochoa (2019), and Lugones (2020), which proposes that the study of feminist movements in Latin America for women's emancipation is a reaction against the combined sexual, racial, and religious norms and stereotypes that arise from postcolonial structures.[13]

This paper first analyses the Mexican chapters and their relations to the Mexican Communist Party as well as to the WIDF. Secondly, the Cuban chapters are studied following the same structure. Finally, the conclusion gives some insights into the similarities and disparities between both groups of women to add further complexity to the idea of "Latin American women" in the WIDF, but also to re-evaluate their contributions to the federation.

MEXICAN WOMEN'S ASSOCIATIONS AFFILIATED TO THE WIDF

The two Mexican women's organizations affiliated with the WIDF after 1946 were the National Bloc of Revolutionary Women (BNMR, 1941–1950) and

---

13. María Lugones, "Colonialidad y género", *Tabula Rasa*, 9 (2018), pp. 73–101; Ochy Curiel, "Descolonizando el feminismo. Una perspectiva desde América Latina y el Caribe", *Primer Coloquio Latinoamericano sobre Praxis y Pensamiento Feminista* (Buenos Aires, 2009); Karina Ochoa Muñoz (ed.), *Miradas en torno al problema colonial. Pensamiento anticolonial y feminismos descoloniales en los Sures globales* (Mexico City, 2019).

the Democratic Union of Mexican Women (UDMM, 1950–1963). Both were, to some extent, successors of the first nationwide women's federation in Mexican history: the United Front for Women's Rights (FUPDM). But, while the FUPDM was a broad front of left-wing, reformist, and Catholic women, the BNMR and the UDMM were organizations composed exclusively of communist women. The political plurality of the FUPDM in the 1930s was in line with the worldwide geopolitical pattern of Popular Fronts fostered by the Communist International (Comintern) during the interwar period, when progressive and nationalist forces sought alliances against the rise of fascism as a common threat. That historical moment coincided in Mexico with the presidency of socialist-sympathiser Lázaro Cárdenas Del Rio, who radicalized the revolutionary project embedded in the 1917 Constitution in 1934 (Figure 2).[14] Throughout the period studied in this article, the political influence of left-wing feminists in Mexico depended on the party discipline imposed by the presidencies of Lázaro Cárdenas Del Rio (1934–1940), Manuel Ávila Camacho (1940–1946), Miguel Alemán Valdés (1946–1952), and Adolfo Ruiz Cortines (1952–1958). The FUPDM was dissolved after the 1940 federal elections, when President Cárdenas backtracked on his promise to introduce an electoral reform allowing women to vote, even though this had already been approved by both Senate and Parliament. Mexican women did not gain the right to vote until 1953.[15] To some extent, both the BNMR and the UDMM tried to keep the radical legacy of the FUPDM alive in the early Cold War.

The BNRM joined the WIDF shortly after it was founded in Paris in 1945.[16] Established in 1941 as the women's section of the Communist Party of Mexico (PCM), shortly after the dissolution of the FUPDM, the BNMR was the most

14. There are several interpretations of the ideological nature and political aims of the Mexican revolution. A summary is available in Luis Anaya Merchant, "La construcción de la memoria y la revisión de la revolución", *Historia Mexicana*, 44 (1995), pp. 525–536.

15. Detailed information about the FUPDM is available in Esperanza Tuñón Pablos, *Mujeres que se organizan. El Frente Único Pro Derechos de la Mujer 1935–1938* (Mexico City, 1992). Concerning Refugio García, see Verónica Oikión Solano, *Cuca García (1889–1973) por las causas de la mujeres y la revolución* (Zamora, 2018). For a gender-political analysis of the debates on women's rights to vote, see Gabriela Cano, *Democracia y género. Historia del debate público en torno al sufragio femenino en México* (Mexico City, 2018), pp. 57–79. There is more about communist women in Mexico in the interwar period in Natura Olive, *Mujeres comunistas en México en los años treinta* (México D.F., 2014).

16. According to the CIA and WIDF's documents, there were other relevant left-wing women's association supporting the WIDF's activities in Mexico, such as the Union of Spanish Women at Mexico integrated by Veneranda Manzano, Regina Lago, Emilia Elias de Ballesteros, Matilde Cantos, and María Velasco among others. Further information is available in Pilar Domínguez Prats, "Mujeres españolas en México (1939–1950)" (Ph.D., Universidad Complutense, 1992); Pilar Domínguez Prats, "La actividad política de las mujeres republicanas en México", *Arbor. Ciencia, Pensamiento y cultura*, 185:735 (2009), pp. 75–85; and Enriqueta Tuñón Pablos, *Varias voces, una historia... Mujeres españolas exiliadas en México* (Mexico City, 2011).

Figure 2. A group of militants of the United Front for Women's Rights (FUPDM) marching through the Zocalo, the main square in Mexico City, while waving banners of their organization. This demonstration took place in the context of the campaigns for women's right to vote under the government of president Lázaro Cárdenas.
National General Archive (Mexico), Photographic Collection, Enrique Díaz Delgado y García, Box 59/19. From Verónica Oikión Solano, Cuca García (1889–1973). Por las causas de las mujeres y la revolución *(San Luis, 2018).*

important left-wing Mexican women's association of the 1940s.[17] At the Second International Conference of the WIDF in Budapest, Madame Vaillant-Couturier presented an affiliation request from the "National Bloc of Revolutionary Women" for ratification by the general assembly; this was approved unanimously, although records show that collaboration payments from the BNMR to the WIDF had existed since 1946.[18] Both the BNRM and UDMM tried to preserve the political and social networks created by the FUPDM, and supported women workers and peasants through their contacts with existing rural women's leagues and trade unions.[19] Women on the

17. Concerning the foundation of the BNMR, see Mexico City, General Archive of the Nation in Mexico (AGN), President's Collection-Avila Camacho (AC), box 1183, folder 707, file 3 (1183, 707/3). The "BNMR" founded in the 1940s and linked to the Communist Party of Mexico must not be confused with the "BNMR" established in 1929 under the rule of President Plutarco Elias Calles as a part of the National Revolutionary Party, the first national political party.
18. WIDF, *Second Women's International Congress: Account of the Work of the Congress*, p. 544.
19. Dionisio Encina, "Por un amplio movimiento popular en defensa de la soberanía del país y por el avance de la Revolución Mexicana", 30th document, VIIIth National Congress of the Communist Party of Mexico, in Elvira Concheiro and Carlos Payán Velver (eds), *Los congresos*

BNMR national executive committee, some of whom had been FUDPM members in the 1930s, tried to keep the feminist programme of the Federation alive. For example, BNMR General Secretary Estela Jiménez Esponda, who headed the FUPDM education secretariat in the 1930s, unsuccessfully tried to counteract the influence of the Mexican Communist Party (PCM) and conserve the feminist programme of the FUPDM by putting gender ahead of class interests.[20] Adelina Zendejas, BNMR's Secretary of Press and Propaganda, had been an active syndicalist and supported José Vasconcelos[21] in the 1920s, but joined the PCM in the 1930s. As well as managing the PCM's official magazine, *El Comunista*, she was a founding member of the FUPDM and campaigned for women's rights (Figure 2).[22] Another prominent member of the organization was Esther Chapa, the Secretary of Political Action. She spent her life balancing her political activism with her professional responsibilities as a surgeon at Juárez Hospital and a professor of microbiology at the UNAM. From the early 1930s she took part in the Sufragist Femenine Movement and the FUPDM as a strong advocate of separate jails for women in Acatitla. As a member of the PCM she defended both children's and women's rights. For twenty-two years, she asked the Congress to give women the right to vote every political term. But, in the early 1940s, Chapa moved away from the PCM to focus exclusively on women's issues. In addition, she got involved in the Mexican Committee to Aid the Children of the Spanish People.[23]

Mexican women's emancipation was inextricably connected to deeper structural reforms. It is no coincidence that the letters and reports sent to

---

comunistas. México 1919–1981, 2 vols (Mexico City, 2014), I, p. 437; and in Verónica Oikión Solano, "Las comunistas mexicanas, herederas de revoluciones", *Memoria Revista Crítica Militante*, 10 November 2019. Available at http://revistamemoria.mx/?p=2995; last accessed 5 January 2021.

20. Joel Estudillo García, Ana Lau Jaiven, and José Edgar Nieto Arizmendi (eds), *Diccionario enciclopédico del feminismo y los estudios de género en México* (Mexico City, 2019), pp. 224–225.

21. José Vasconcelos was a renowned and prominent Mexican politician and writer (1883–1959). He was Rector of the National Autonomous University, Secretary of Public Education, and director of the National Library of Mexico. He ran for presidency in 1929 but lost to Pascual Ortiz Rubio. He was the author of *The Cosmic Race*, in which he abrogated for the mixing of races as a desirable improvement of humankind, nonetheless at the expense of cultural assimilation of Mexican minor ethnic groups.

22. Gabriela Cano, "Adelina Zendejas. Arquitecta de su memoria", *Debate Feminista*, 8 (1993), pp. 387–400. In the 1960s, Adelina Zendejas, together with Clementina Batalla Bassols, was a prominent member of the Unión Nacional de Mujeres Mexicanas.

23. Ana María Portugal Speedle, "Esther Chapa Tijerina, 22 años buscando el voto", in VV.AA., *Las indispensables. Recuperando la memoria* (Mexico City, 2018), pp. 237–249. The Executive Committee of the BNMR also included María Guadalupe Arballo (Secretary of the Organization), María Concepción Aviña (Sub-Secretary of the Organization), Prof. Carmen de la Fuente (Secretary of Social Action), Prof. Consuelo Aguirre Córdova (Secretary of Cultural Action), and Gregoria Mirazo (Secretary of Popular Action).

both the federal government of Mexico and the WIDF by the BNMR were signed with the slogan, "For the liberation of women and for the progress of Mexico". BNMR petitions in 1946 called for female suffrage and equal rights for men and women, but the organization also campaigned for women's rights in employment, welfare, education, and associational life. These campaigns were influenced by the broader movements of Latin American women, within the Inter-American Commission of Women, which pushed for women's rights as human rights in the UN Universal Declaration of Human Rights in 1948. In addition, the Organization of American States, encouraged by the IACW, passed two conventions encouraging governments to ensure that civil and political rights for women were constitutionally guaranteed.[24]

Correspondence between Mexican representatives of the BNMR and the WIDF Secretariat in Berlin demonstrates how Mexican women sought to insert their specific concerns into the WIDF's political guidelines on women's rights, world peace, and child protection. The WIDF guidelines largely dictated the topics of BNMR meetings, as illustrated in a letter from Esthela Jimenez to Marie-Claude Vaillant-Couturier. Jimenez wrote that Mexican women were organizing "the National Assembly of the BNMR with representatives coming from every state of the country. The fundamental problems of Mexican women (economic, social, cultural, and judicial) will be discussed, and the problem of Spain, the one concerning Greek women, etc. [...] in accordance with the instructions you gave us in your notes and circular letters".[25] However, at the same time, the BNMR also raised their own specific concerns stemming from the Mexican and Latin American contexts. In 1946, Esponda sent a report to the WIDF defining Mexico as a "semi-feudal" and "semi-colonial" country, indicating a primary aim to fight for national liberation and economic independence. She emphasized the BNMR's opposition to the right-wing Mexican groups Synarchism, National Action, and Spanish Falange. In the same way, she pointed out that Truman's foreign policies posed a serious threat to the independence of Latin America and, more concretely, of Mexico. Moreover, Esponda let the WIDF know that the BNMR had approximately 30,000 members and that they were committed to the fight to improve

---

24. The Mexican women's rights to vote in local election was approved by the Federal Congress under the government of Miguel Alemán Valdés (the original document is on page 3 of: https://www.dof.gob.mx/index_113.php?year=1947&month=02&day=12). It was not until 6 October 1953, with President Adolfo Ruiz Cortines, that the Chamber of Representatives passed their right to vote in federal elections by modifying the 34th and 115th articles of the Mexican constitution (the amendment may be consulted here: https://www.dof.gob.mx/index_113.php?year=1953&month=10&day=17); last accessed 10 January 2021

25. Historical Archive of the Communist Party of Spain (AHPCE), 115.3, "Letter from Esthela Jiménez Esponda to Marie-Claude Vaillant-Couturier, "Lettre du 'Bloque National de Mujeres Revolucionarias'", Mexico City, 14 November 1946.

the living standards of Mexican people, with a focus on children and women.[26] The exchange of information, activities, letters, and reports shows a desire to be connected and to make the basic shared feminist agenda set out by the WIDF more complex by adding the national viewpoints of women from different parts of the world.

To translate the WIDF's international agenda into the national arena, the BNMR developed a complex propaganda apparatus of meetings, articles, brochures, and radio broadcasts.[27] For instance, in December 1946, the BNMR organized a national assembly gathering approximately 300 representatives from women's associations in several states of the nation.[28] This paved the way for a Mexican Women's Unity Committee.[29] The BNMR's political position towards the peace movement embodied the guiding principles of the Mexican Communist Party.[30] In the frame of these political connections, the BNMR's members organized several international campaigns at a national level, such as the Childcare Week and the International Day of Women, among others.[31] Notably, they established the need to consolidate democracy in order to fight fascism and stop it spreading throughout America and into Mexico. The BNMR was committed to the anti-authoritarian fight inside Spain, and supported anti-Franco guerrilla warfare.[32] The organization tried to gain sympathizers for that campaign by strengthening the coordination of its regional branches through internal circular letters. In this correspondence, the executive committee wrote that "all of us can do anything in favour of the Spanish detainees. A letter, a protest, a visit to consulates, talk about the problems in assemblies and rallies, in union and popular meetings, make our people feel this question helps save one of those lives that is in danger".[33] Likewise, the BNMR tried to support the clandestine fighters in Spain by sending products such as clothes and food to finance an international lottery promoted by the left-wing French Women's Union in 1946.[34]

26. AHPCE, 116, "Revista. Prensa de Mujeres", "Compte rendu de l'activité de la Federation Democratique Internationale des Femmes depuis son Congrès Constitutif", *Bulletin d'Information*, 14–15 (March–April 1947), p. 8.
27. Although national archives and libraries in Mexico seem not to keep any, the BNMR published regular or special volumes of a journal called *Nosotras* ("We, the women"), see AHPCE, 115.3, "Circulaire Urgente a toutes nos Organisations nationales", 14 November 1946.
28. AHPCE, 115.2, "Annexe Au Compte-Rendu d'Activité", and "Compte-Rendu d'Activité de la F.D.I.F. depuis le Conseil de la Fédération Democratique Internationale des Femmes" (approx. March/April of 1947), p. 18.
29. AHPCE, 115.3, "Report from Esthela Jiménez Esponda and Consuelo Hernández to Marie-Claude Vaillant-Couturier", 11 August 1947.
30. Horacio Crespo, "El comunismo mexicano y la lucha por la paz en los inicios de la Guerra Fría", *Historia Mexicana*, 66 (2016), p. 262.
31. AGN, AC, 266, 234.2/10, 21 December 1944.
32. Report by Nina Popova concerning the "The Progress of the Anti-Francoist Campaign" (n.d., approx. late 1946), in AHPCE, 116, "Executive Committee of the WIDF, Moscow, 1956".
33. AHPCE, 115.3, "Very Urgent Circular Letter" (n.d., approx. November 1946).
34. "El mundo femenino. Lotería", *El Nacional*, 15 August 1947, p. 9.

The BNMR also took part in the First International Congress of Women organized by the Women's International League for Peace and Freedom in Guatemala in 1947. In this meeting, the BNMR's representatives advocated for a strong position against arms race escalation and in favour of human rights, and the approval of migration laws in relation to war victims from Europe. Coupled with this, they emphasized the need to enforce equality in the civil and political rights of men and women and the right of women to hold leadership positions in their respective governments. At the end of the congress, the Mexican delegation backed the final communication in favour of building an enduring peace process in the world.[35]

The archival documentation shows that the BNMR kept the WIDF informed about their activities supporting women and reported to the WIDF general secretary on the main conclusions of their national assemblies. For example, in November 1946, representatives from all the Mexican states met in Mexico City to discuss social issues concerning women: their participation in the industrialization of the country; their fight against low standards of living and the high price of basic products; their demands for clean, affordable, and hygienic accommodation; the necessary cultural improvement and participation of Mexican women in the civic life of their country; equal rights with men, and other topics. The BNMR also reported that they were to open canteens, refectories, and small first aid centres for the unemployed and people with no financial assistance, and that they had made donations to a Rehabilitation Bank so that the BNMR's affiliates could invest substantially in low-price houses. Likewise, the association promoted a periodic craft fair selling objects made by women members from the regional branches, with the proceeds of the sales going to the craftswomen.[36]

The BNMR's position was strengthened and its activity throughout Mexico increased – alongside its capacity to follow the WIDF's guidelines – after the transition from Manuel Avila Camacho's government (1940–1946) to the presidency of Miguel Alemán Valdés (1946–1952).[37] As a result, the BNMR

35. Verónica Oikión Solano, "Mujeres comunistas en México. Desigualdad social y lucha política, 1935–1955", in Valobra and Yusta, *Queridas camaradas*, pp. 153–173. Concerning the programme of the Panamerican Congress of Women organized by the Women's International League for Peace and Freedom, see AHPCE, 115.3, "Projet de programme pour le congrès Pan American des Femmes".

36. AHPCE, 115.3, "Letter from the BNMR to all the National Organisations"; and "Letter from the BNMR to the Organizations in (México) DF", 14 November 1946. The BNMR also informed federal institutions of their demands concerning the government's responsibilities to fight speculation in the selling of basic food and to guarantee that workers and poor women had access to basic accommodation, AGN, ÁC, 513–462.1/15.

37. A conservative turn occurred under Ávila Camacho, which promoted the "Unidad Nacional" policy that reinvigorated the idealization of maternity as a destiny that would fulfil women's ambitions, Martha Santillán, "Traditionalist Discourse on Motherhood: *Excélsior* and Prolific Mothers during Ávila Camacho's Administration", *Secuencia*, 77 (2010), pp. 91–110.

were able to support other Mexican women's associations. In the Mexican Valley, they helped some members of the Liga Femenil Eufrosina Camacho Viuda de Avila, who were at risk of losing their homes, by intervening with the ruling party to secure land properties for them in Ixtacalco. Likewise, they helped the Federación de Organizaciones Femeninas in Yucatán to create protective homes for women in Merida that provided reading clubs, training centres for sewing classes, and services such as childcare and maternity centres.[38] In the north-western state of Sinaloa, almost 200 small women's organizations, which had already been created under the FUPDM in 1937, sought the support of the BNMR executive committee in Mexico Federal District. They needed to request a loan from the Federal government to set up houses for women social workers to strengthen their technical skills and for other urban improvements, such as hospitals for children, maternity centres, and mills to grind maize for "tortillas". Sinaloan women also requested some "communal sewing shops and technical schools in which peasant women learn to make their family's clothes and obtain additional income for the same family by selling cheap clothes".[39]

Women affiliated with the BNMR did not aim for political rights alone, but for technical knowledge to gain economic independence and to enforce "the revolution turned into a government".[40] Regional associations gave women the opportunity to deliver joint proposals and leapfrog state organisms by using civic platforms such as the BNMR to intercede with federal institutions. Women of the BNMR were able to exploit the language of the Mexican Revolution itself and to align with its objectives to obtain some benefits for women, and for their relatives and neighbours.

In accordance with the gendered preconceptions of both the WIDF and the PCM, the BNMR suggested ways to boost women's autonomy without completely breaking traditional gender patterns. Within the conservative paradigm of maternity promoted by Manuel Ávila Camacho, the BNMR sought to extract feminist emancipatory potential from women's traditional daily duties and expertise. During World War II, the BNMR claimed that "democracies must achieve an improvement in the life of the people, because otherwise fascism will always find a fertile ground for hatred and violence". In that context,

38. AGN, ÁC, 513-462.1/15, Letter sent on 26 August 1946, letter sent in October 1945.
39. AGN, AC, 900-562.4/24. Some of them were peasants who worked in the so-called "ejidos", which in the Mexican system of government and production were areas of "cultivated land, pastureland, other uncultivated lands, and the fundo legal (townsite). In most cases the cultivated land is divided into separate family holdings, which cannot be sold although they can be handed down to heirs" (https://www.britannica.com/topic/ejido). For an overview of "ejidos" in the twentieth century, see Eric P. Perramond, "The Rise, Fall, and Reconfiguration of the Mexican 'Ejido'", *Geographical Review*, 98 (2008), pp. 356–371; and under Lázaro Cárdenas, see Patricia Arias, "Los ejidos en 1935. Diversidad espacial, recursos naturales y organización social", *Sociedad y ambiente*, 7/10 (July–October, 2019), pp. 153–186.
40. AGN, AC, 900-562.4/24.

women had to assume two maternal roles: mother of their biological children and symbolic mother of the sons and daughters of the nation. The BNMR's General Secretary, Jiménez Esponda, stated that women disproportionately struggled with social problems because of their responsibilities for housework and childcare. As most Mexican women had to fetch water for washing and cooking, Jímenez Esponda claimed, improving water provision in towns and cities would reduce the need for them to use natural rivers or pumping wells water sources. Since women prepared and cooked tortillas, the BNMR argued that providing *nixtamal* mills would help free them from some of their gendered responsibilities, allowing them to spend more time on personal development.[41] And, finally, better medical infrastructure would reduce the amount of time women spent at their nearest health centre.

To overcome some of these constraints, the BNMR and the female section of the PRM promoted schools of Domestic Economy and Social Work for women. If the "domestic economy" reinforced links between women and duties such as managing the family's income and expenses, "social work" described the care work that women undertook because of a presumed natural impulse. However, placing due emphasis on these gender-biased but technical skills by asserting their benefits to the whole of society meant the BNMR elevated the importance of a women's professional trajectory, redirecting its place in society in line with the PRM's political philosophy concerning women.[42] The BNMR encouraged the government to create schools for domestic sciences, small-scale industries, technical training, and social assistance schools for women workers, old age and children's homes, as well as credit unions for farming chickpeas, sesame oil, tomatoes, and corn. More specifically, they requested state economic support to help them open communal factories and markets for women to sell their hand-made textile products. This initiative led them to envision and create new ways for women to achieve economic empowerment in rural and local areas.[43] To sum up, although they kept within the limits of women's normative roles in the public sphere, these initiatives met the WIDF's objectives of empowering women as well as the state's directive to further the progress of the country, a motto of both the PRM until 1946, and the Institutional Revolutionary Party (PRI) since then.

During the Ninth Congress of the PCM in 1950, the UDMM replaced the BNMR as the main affiliate of the WIDF in Mexico, taking on the responsibility of implementing the WIDF's aims: to fight for peace and against imperialism; for women's civil and salary equality; for women's labour and trade union rights; and for children's rights. The executive committee of the UDMM attempted to adopt a multi-ideological militancy – like the

---

41. *Ibid.*, 26 September 1946.
42. AGN, AC, 266–234.2/10, 21 December 1944.
43. The *nixtamal* mill was a machine used to dry and smash corn seeds to make the "tacos" tortillas, which constituted, and still do constitute, a Mexican dietary staple.

FUPDM had in the interwar years, when the Popular Fronts policy fostered by the Communist International had made that stance easier. However, the rise of the PRI at the expense of the PCM in the early Cold War affected the political capacity of the women's section of the communist party to recruit members from other political backgrounds or with no political position. The PCM's directive board seems to have been more concerned with the triumph of the proletariat and ultimately the establishment of a communist society. The Twelfth Congress of the PCM in 1954 noted that the core number of communist women in Mexico was very small and that the organic structure of the party lacked female cadres. Nonetheless, according to the CIA – which was closely tracking communist political activism in America by the early 1950s – the UDMM maintained several branches throughout most of the states of the Mexican Federation. Mexican women affiliated with the WIDF were strongly committed to the international human rights and the peace movement, and the need to improve women's living conditions and political status at the national level. Esther Chapa was very influential, nationally, but the UDMM's most prominent leaders before the WIDF were Mireya B. de Huerta, Paula Medrano, Paula Gómez Alonso, and Socorro Burciaga. Despite the PCM's lack of support, the UDMM attempted to meet the instructions of the WIDF and attracted women into its structure. To do so, the UDMM increased propaganda efforts, enhanced cooperation with trade unions, and brought the worries of common people into their regular meetings, giving priority to women's problems.

The UDMM had stronger and more extensive links with the WIDF than the BNMR. These links proved increasingly important during the 1950s as the conflict between capitalism and communism escalated, exerting influence on the Latin American region, especially after the US-supported coup d'état in Guatemala in 1954.[44] At the Third International Congress in Copenhagen in 1953, UDMM representative Paula Medrano stressed the involvement of the organization in the opposition to imperialism inside Mexico and imperialist agreements between the Mexican and the US governments. American imperialism, claimed Medrano, threatened to destroy Mexican sovereignty and independence. To face this international threat, the UDMM opposed the mobilization of Mexican soldiers in the US-led invasion of Korea. Mexican women ultimately made the government interrupt these negotiations with the US. Shortly afterwards, the UDMM created the Female Committee for Guatemala in response to a global military escalation and an increasingly aggressive US foreign policy in the region. This committee gave political asylum to people fleeing the country after the US-led military invasion. In her

---

44. Esther Chapa and María Lagunes published short letters in *Women of the Whole World*, 1 (1960), p. 4, and *Women of the Whole World*, 4 (1960), p. 4, explaining that they had received the magazine for a long time, and that it was of great utility to know and discuss, within meetings of the UDMM, women's problems in other parts of the world.

speech to the WIDF Copenhagen conference, Medrano also drew attention to the specific problems faced by Mexican peasant women. For instance, in the Lagunera region, between Coahuila and Durango, many peasant men migrated to the US due to a lack of water and the scarcity of national credits in the region to secure their jobs. She explained that the "women tried to save their land by drilling wells. They formed committees and applied to the Collective Bank for Peasant Communities, to the Department of Agriculture, and mobilized other women, with the result that the wells are drilled". She also explained that the UDMM had agreed with the Association for the Protection of Children to set up crèches and schools in working class neighbourhoods, holiday camps and open-air schools for tubercular children, and medical services for infant and children of school age. In so doing, the UDMM implicitly sought to follow the PRI's national project of modernization, as well as the WIDF's global agenda for women's and children's rights.[45]

The following year, Elvira Trueba was the Mexican representative at the Fourth Congress of the WIDF in Vienna. Although she was not a communist or a member of the UDMM, Trueba had been one of the few women representatives of the trade union of the Mexican National Railway since the 1920s and an active antifascist activist in the Union of American Women, created in Mexico in the 1930s. In Vienna, she addressed the existing differences between men and women, despite the fact that Mexican women had been enfranchised for five years, and stressed that her organization – also linked to the WIDF – was pushing for the abolition of any discrimination against women, especially salary inequality. In her speech, Trueba emphasized how the "social services developed by women's organizations, independently of the one attended by the State, aimed to solve the problems affecting women, children, and elderly people". She also affirmed that left-wing women were pushing the government for an increase in teachers' salaries, the expansion of the primary education system, and for training centres where women could improve their technical skills and become more competitive in the labour market.[46]

The UDMM broke with the Mexican Communist Party in 1964 and was re-established as the National Union of Mexican Women (UNMM), which began a new period of Mexican women's activism closer to the New Left.[47]

45. Report by Paula Medrano, General Secretary of the UDMM, in *As One! For Equality, For Happiness, For Peace: World Congress of Women, Copenhagen, June 5–10 1953* (Berlin, 1953), pp. 205–206.
46. Conference paper by Elvira Trueba, WIDF, "IV Congreso de la Federación Democrática Internacional de Mujeres", p. 108.
47. Verónica Oikión Solano, "Resistencia y luchas femeniles. La Unión Nacional de Mujeres Mexicanas en el verano del 68: una historia desconocida", *Legajos. Boletín del Archivo General de la Nación*, 17 (September–December, 2018), pp. 55–84. For the international connections between Mexican women's associations and the WIDF in the 1960s, see Verónica Oikión Solano, "Las organizaciones de mujeres de la izquierda mexicana. Su acción contestataria y sus

At the Sixth International Congress in Helsinki, 1969, the General Secretary of the WIDF, Cecile Hugel, noted that Mexican and Chilean women had led the Latin American mobilization for women's rights in the continent during the 1960s. Hugel specifically remarked on the success of the Seminar on "the defence of the rights of women and children to life, well-being and education" convened by the WIDF in Mexico (22–25 July 1968) with the financial support of UNESCO.

The report also noted that the UNMM, its president, Marta López Portillo de Tamayo, and its honorary president, Clementina de Bassols, "stimulated considerable activities throughout the country on the preparation of the meeting". Most significantly, the WIDF acknowledged that Mexican women made "an important and specialized contribution to the enrichment and approval of the studies already existing on the status of women and children; they also resulted in a deeper knowledge of the international documents of the UN and its specialized bodies". The WIDF was confident that its network of contacts and meetings "made it possible to emphasize the universal nature of the (women's) problems to be resolved", but it also indicated "the need for wide discussions of them". The WIDF's assessment implicitly recognized the need to keep working, but showed that it had listened to left-wing Latin American, African, and Asian women, whose contributions were key to challenging the assumption that women's problems around the world mirrored those in Europe.[48]

However, as we will see in the following pages, the FDMC had a greater presence, influence, and autonomy in the domestic political scene than the BNMR and the UDMM. This could be explained by three factors. Firstly, the Mexican organizations were subject to a corporative state that excluded communist forces from government once the revolutionary period led by Lázaro Cárdenas in the 1930s had ended. Secondly, given the corporative nature of the state, national women's organizations in Mexico were diverse, comprising left wing, reformist, and even conservative women. This made it very difficult for members to reach unanimous decisions. And, thirdly, after Cárdenas left office and the FUPDM was dissolved, communist women lost influence within women's state-sponsored organizations, which made it

conexiones transnacionales con la Federación Democrática Internacional de Mujeres en el contexto de la guerra fría, 1955–1968", in Santiago Aránguiz Pinto and Patricio Herrera González (eds), *Los comunismos en América Latina y el Caribe. Recepciones y militancia, 1955–1991*, vol. IV, pt. 1, Mujeres y Vanguardias (Santiago de Chile, 2022), and Ana Lau Jaiven, "La Unión Nacional de Mujeres Mexicanas entre el comunismo y el feminismo. Una difícil relación", *La ventana*, 40 (2014), pp. 165–185.
48. Bethseda, Maryland, Alexander Street Collection, Collection "Women and Social Movements, International 1840–Present", Madame Cecile Hugel, WIDF General Secretary, "Report on the Activities of the WIDF", Sixth congress of the WIDF, Helsinki, 17 June 1969, pp. 11–18.

more difficult for them to bring their ideology and objectives to the fore in international meetings.

THE DEMOCRATIC FEDERATION OF CUBAN WOMEN (FDMC)

In 1945, a Cuban delegation attended the founding meeting of the WIDF, which included Uldarica Mañas and Herminia del Portal (both from the Lyceum), Mercedes Alemán (Office for Children's Defense and Protection), Dolores Soldevilla (Female Service for Civil Defense), and Nila Ortega (Confederation of Cuban Workers). One year later, Ortega and Soldevilla wrote to the WIDF in Paris to explain that it had not yet been possible to create a national organization of progressive and leftist Cuban women, but that they were committed to doing so in the short term; they had already arranged several events to raise feminist awareness and explain the WIDF's political programme.[49]

Almost 200 women established the FDMC on 15 November 1948 in Havana. From that time, it operated as the Cuban branch of the WIDF and, to some extent, as the women's section of the PCC. Its founding document declared adherence "to the Women's International Democratic Federation established in Paris (France) in December 1945". The FDMC aimed to organize women as workers, peasants, and liberal arts and domestic workers regardless of race, religion, or political affinities and to fight for real equality between men's and women's rights in every social, economic, and legal realm. The document also embedded both the WIDF's and the PCC's programmatic objectives, such as the improvement of Cuban citizen's living conditions, state-funded social assistance services, and a labour insurance system.[50] Some of these ideological assumptions drew on the political background of its executive committee. For instance, Esperanza Sánchez Mastrapa had taken part in the Third National Congress of Women in 1939, which had been the first to organize a round table on Black women's experiences; and Clementina Serra and Nila Ortega had organized the Provincial Association for Women's Popular Education. Both García Buchaca and Mastrapa were also members of the PCC, while Ortega was an appointed representative of the Confederation of Cuban Workers. Some of the PCC and FDMC leaders were also personally connected.[51]

49. AHPCE, 115.3, "Letter from Nila Ortega and Lola Soldevilla to the WIDF", 28 October 1946, and "Letter from Nila Ortega to Marie-Claude Vaillant-Couturier", 28 October 1946.
50. Havana, National Archive of Cuba (ANC), Associations Register (AR), 215–5225.
51. Manuel Ramírez Chicharro, *Más allá del sufragismo. Las mujeres en la democratización de Cuba, 1933–1952*, (Granada, 2019), pp. 105, 106, 111, 125, and 251. García Buchaca was first the wife of Carlos Rafael Rodríguez, and then of Joaquín Ordoqui, while Maria Josefa Vidaurreta was Juan Marinello's wife.

Cuban women had been enfranchised in 1934; the law that passed their right to vote was ratified in the new democratic Constitution in 1940, much earlier than Mexico (1953). A liberal feminist movement had emerged in Cuba between 1912 and 1917. It was strengthened in the 1920s owing to the two national congresses organized in 1923 and 1925. During that decade, a progressive political shift occurred within Cuban civic society. Mass organizations such as the National Confederation of Cuban Workers, and political parties like the Cuban Communist Party (PCC) were founded. After a moderately democratic term, General Gerardo Machado established an authoritarian regime between 1928 and 1933. Under his presidency, the feminist movement split into two main factions: moderate feminists demanding the right for women to elect and be elected; and radical feminists who considered the measure "stale from the source" in a non-democratic regime, and demanded deeper changes in the political structure to grant women's full emancipation.[52] Among these women, some were socialists and communists affiliated with the now clandestine PCC, such as Ofelia Domínguez Navarro: founder of the Labour Women's Union and the Radical Women's Union. Shortly after, in 1940, a more democratic constitutional text was approved because of the work of several grass-roots assemblies – including the III National Congress of Women – and the increasing circulation of international ideas during the early Cold War, which claimed women's rights were human rights and significantly reshaped feminism in Cuba.

Once suffrage was approved, according to Michelle Chase, the feminist movement did not disappear, but moved from liberal to socialist and communist principles.[53] The PCC once regarded moderate feminists as bourgeois, as they exclusively focused on gender issues and overlooked the class constraints affecting female industrial and domestic workers. Communist women gained influence in the PCC from the 1930s onwards, when the party created female sections in their youth wing and trade unions and selected women as Parliamentary candidates.[54] In the 1940s, female candidates for the Autentico and Republican parties obtained, on average, five per cent of the votes, while women of the PCC received up to twenty per cent in 1944.[55]

---

52. Julio César González Pagés, *En busca de un espacio. Historia de mujeres en Cuba* (Havana, 2003), and Kathryn Lynn Stoner, *De la casa a la calle. El movimiento cubano de la mujer en favor de la reforma legal (1898–1940)* (Madrid, 2003).
53. Michelle Chase, "La Federación Democrática de Mujeres Cubanas: de la República a la Revolución", in Valobra and Yusta, *Queridas camaradas*, p. 205.
54. Manuel Ramírez Chicharro, "De la participación a la acción política. Las secciones femeninas de los partidos políticos en Cuba, 1925–1959", accepted for publication in *Historia Caribe*.
55. Manuel Ramírez Chicharro, "Beyond Suffrage: The Role of Cuban women in the State-Building Years of a Failed Democracy (1940–1952)", *Women's History Review*, 27 (2018), pp. 754–777. It is noteworthy that, between 1942 and 1944, two communist representatives were appointed Ministers without portfolio within the democratically elected government led by colonel Fulgencio Batista.

Women lacked influence in mid-century Cuban state institutions, but wielded power in civic society as feminist activists. While long-lasting and well-known women's cultural associations – such as the Lyceum and Lawn Tennis Club – still existed in the early Cold War, the most important Cuban women's feminist organization in the 1940s and 1950s was the Democratic Federation of Cuban Women (FDMC).[56]

The FDMC achieved influence among Cuban women because of its extensive structure. It existed on national, provincial, and local levels, and was made up of different social classes, faiths, and "races", unlike other female white-collar associations. Within the lowest ranks of the organization, management committees integrated by women workers represented several industries, such as tobacco, sugar, telephone, laundry, and ironing. Domestic workers, who did not have the right to unionize – in contrast with industrial and commercial women workers – were also represented. Like the BNMR, the FDMC had its own journal, *Mujeres Cubanas*, but the Cuban group also regularly published a column in the national newspaper, *Noticias de hoy*, as well as broadcasting regularly on the radio, which increased its ability to reach a broader audience in the countryside.

FDMC members' commitment to the fight against racism in Cuba was unique among Cuban women's organizations, and very innovative even within the WIDF. For instance, one of the leaders of the organization until 1951, Sánchez Mastrapa, highlighted the failure of the new Cuban Constitution to erase the enduring racial boundaries that excluded most women of African descent from better living and labour conditions. At the Second International Congress of the WIDF in Budapest, Mastrapa emphasized the tripartite oppression of Black Cuban women "500,000 coloured women in our country hope that this great Congress pass resolutions tending to fight against discrimination wherever it exists as a part of the struggle to establish true democracy".[57] Statements like this were repeated at the FDMC's national congresses and local assemblies. In this way, the organization raised awareness, both inside and outside the island, of the problems that Black and mulatto Cuban women faced in their daily lives.

However, according to scholars such as Mackinnon and Chase, the FDMC did not meaningfully challenge the gender gap in labour markets or succeed in depicting the family as the basic mechanism blocking women's emancipation. Their demands were focused – in order of importance – first on class, then on

56. Rosario Rexach, "El Lyceum de La Habana como institución cultural", in Sebastian Neumeister (ed.), *Actas del IX Congreso de la Asociación Internacional de Hispanistas*, 12–23 August (Berlin, 1989).

57. *Second Women's International Congress WIDF 1948*, pp. 356–362. For further information on Mastrapa, see Manuel Ramírez Chicharro and Michelle Chase, "Black Left Feminism in Pre-Revolutionary Cuba: The Life and Work of Esperanza Sánchez Mastrapa (1901–1958)", *Women's History Review* (2021), https://doi.org/10.1080/09612025.2021.1996555.

women, and then on race. In other words, this organization asked for better labour conditions for working families, addressed the position and rights of women workers, and, occasionally, demanded that men and women workers' opportunities were placed on the same level regardless of race or perceived phenotype. However, the FDMC demanded, with little success, that the international agreement on "equal salary for equal work" be enforced at a national level. This was eventually signed into law by the Cuban government once the International Labor Organization passed it in 1951.

Not surprisingly, the demands formulated by the FDMC in relation to women's emancipation and international peace were portrayed as a necessary precondition for children's rights. Alongside groups in the so-called first wave of feminism – and in line with the WIDF's political programme – the FDMC proposed several measures to ensure good living conditions for Cuban children once World War II had ended. The threat of nuclear war strengthened their commitment to peace, and to women and children's safety. The FDMC arranged a national conference on this issue and some of its members, such as Esther Noriega, took part in the Childhood World Congress in 1952. Prior to this international meeting, attendees discussed issues such as the main causes of infant mortality, childhood diseases, solutions to rates of childhood illiteracy, and regulations for existing child reformatories.[58]

The political and gender discourse of the FDMC helped to redefine the image of women as "new women", in fact, as "super-women" *avant la lettre*: able to juggle jobs and "their" housework. As opposed to the "female literature" focused on women's beauty and entertainment that was represented by journals such as *Vanidades*, the FDMC-funded *Mujeres Cubanas* defended the emancipation of women by increasing their literacy rates. In the late 1940s, the organization helped set up a night school, so that women workers could study after their working day. According to Chase, the FDMC revolutionized the gender/class divide in Cuban society by suggesting that women workers and peasants should be incorporated into political networks of solidarity and activism outside the fight for women's rights. For the FDMC, women's emancipation was mainly subject to the power relations structuring and sustaining class relations.[59]

As for its international militancy, the WIDF appreciated the FDMC's actions concerning the civil defense of Cuba in the face of the expected war between the USSR and the US, and its support of the clandestine groups

58. "Conferencia Nacional por la Defensa de la Infancia", *Mujeres Cubanas*, 2–10/12 (1951); "Comité Gestor de la Conferencia Nacional de la Infancia", *Mujeres Cubanas*, 1–11 (July-August, 1951); "Esther Noriega marcha a la Conferencia Internacional de Defensa de la Infancia", *Mujeres Cubanas*, 2–15 (May, 1952).
59. Michelle Chase, *Revolution within the Revolution: Women and Gender Politics in Cuba, 1952–1962* (Chapel Hill, NC, 2015), pp. 77–105.

opposing the Franco dictatorship in Spain.[60] At the Second International Congress of the WIDF in Budapest, García Buchaca, a Cuban representative, emphasized that "submission to the interests of imperialism is the way to war. [...] And each step towards war will bring, as an inevitable consequence, less democracy".[61] In that sense, the onset of the Korean War made all women more aware of the need to demand rights and provide protection for children affected by military conflicts. Following WIDF and PCC guidelines on the international context, the FDMC's leaders launched a high-profile campaign for nuclear disarmament and against President Prío Socarrás's decision to support the US by sending Cuban soldiers to the Korean War. According to the FDMC's official magazine, the organization managed to collect up to 700,000 signatures against the president's project, which was finally discarded. Likewise, the Cuban Mothers' Commission for Peace, encouraged and supported by the FDMC, wrote to Socarrás seeking this annulment. In this letter, they wrote "Mr. President, it is our children who are going to die if you send them to Korea".[62] The reaction of Cuban communist women and mothers to the Korean War and the potential involvement of their colleagues and children in it enacted a maternal feminism that regarded global peace, anti-authoritarianism, and anti-imperialism as unavoidable structural preconditions for women's empowerment, children's rights, and social justice (Figure 3).

In 1952, the military uprising led by Fulgencio Batista against Socarrás's democratic government moved the horizon of war and authoritarianism into Cuba. Several nationalists, reformists, democratists, and left-wing activists spoke up, marched, and fought against the military dictatorship until 1959. The FDMC was one of the few opposition groups exclusively made up of women, together with the radical nationalist Pro Martí Women's Civic Front (Frente Cívico de Mujeres Martianas, FCMM) and the leftist United Oppositionist Women (Mujeres Oposicionistas Unidas, MOU). The FDMC was in the opposition movement, but, as well as the PCC, it is thought that it was not as active as these other women's groups – due to its lack of participation in violent actions and attacks on state institutions. However, as a left-wing group like the PCC, it was monitored by the Political Bureau for the Repression of Communist Activities that was created in 1955. Although the FDMC did not disappear during the insurrection against Batista, its

---

60. AHPCE, 115/2, "Annexe Au Compte-Rendu D'Activite", and "Compte-Rendu D'Activite de la F.D.I.F. depuis le Conseil de la Fédération Democratique Internationale des Femmes" (approx. March/April 1947), p. 8.

61. *Second Women's International Congress WIDF 1948*. Buchaca, pp. 233–240. Concerning the speech by Mastrapa, see pp. 356–363. To read the conference by María Argüelles, see pp. 438–442.

62. ANC, Secretary of Presidency, 50/6, "Comité de Madres habaneras partidarias de la Paz, Comunicado del 26 de febrero de 1951", and "Carta de un grupo de mujeres al Presidente de la República, 20 marzo de 1951".

Figure 3. This cartoon was published almost a year after the end of the Korean War (1950-1953). It shows a group of Cuban women marching and carrying banners and flags (some on the left even carry a child in their arms) calling for an international peace agreement and protesting the bacteriological war. In the background we see a typical Cuban countryside with log cabins and palm trees. *FDMC, "Programa de la FDMC", Mujeres Cubanas, April 1954, pp. 14–17.*

capacity to operate was severely limited, exemplified by the fact that it had to stop publishing its magazine in 1956. It is important to note, however, that FDMC was not demanding the establishment of a communist system once Batista was defeated, but rather the restoration of democracy; in their view, the 1940 Constitution provided a radical enough framework for reforming Cuban society and improving women's political status and living conditions.[63]

Despite the atmosphere on the island, a Cuban representative with no official affiliation, María Antonia González, managed to attend the Fourth International Congress of the WIDF in Vienna.[64] María González declared that she was speaking on behalf of the clandestine United Oppositionist Women (MOU) group rather than the FDMC. Her speech to the WIDF Congress focused on the repression exercised by the authoritarian regime since 1952. She described how women were used to trap opposition leaders,

63. Manuel Ramírez Chicharro, *Llamada a las armas. Las mujeres en la revolución cubana, 1952–1959* (Madrid, 2019), pp. 134–141.
64. Although there is no conclusive proof, she might have been the same Cuban activist, María Antonia González, who hosted both Fidel and Raúl Castro after they fled to Mexico City from Cuba once freed by Colonel Batista and before they invaded and initiated the guerrilla warfare of December 1956, Manuel Ramírez Chicharro, *Llamada a las armas*, pp. 202–203.

while others were assaulted, tortured, and raped when suspected of helping the guerrillas and clandestine groups. González also reported that women's organizations such as the MOU – although unable to fight for women's rights due to the extreme political climate – were assisting the imprisoned activists, sometimes with the support of their wives, mothers, sisters, and female relatives. MOU also supported prisoners on hunger strike and lobbied the Cuban High Court to liberate those illegally sent to prison. The conclusions she offered to the WIDF highlighted the significant role women played in every part of the world in the fight for democratic liberties and against the terror.[65]

In summary, the FDMC was more important to the WIDF than traditional historiography has commonly recognized. As Chase discovered, the foundation of the still-extant Federation of Cuban Women (FMC) in August 1960 probably owes more to "old leftist/radical" women (of the FDMC) than to the "new leftist/radical" women (of the "26th of July Revolutionary Movement", founded by Castro and his colleagues to fight the dictatorship of Fulgencio Batista). However, Vilma Espín, a secret participant in the "26th of July Revolutionary Movement" and Raúl Castro's wife, did later become a noteworthy member of the WIDF. Chase argues that the FDMC's ideological foundations – alongside the participation of its members in the First Congress of Latin American Women through the Revolutionary Female Union – marked a turning point in radical women's activism in Cuba a long time before the foundation of the FMC under the revolutionary government.[66]

CONCLUSIONS: SIMILARITIES AND DISPARITIES BETWEEN THE CUBAN AND MEXICAN BRANCHES OF THE WIDF

This article has argued that Latin American women did not just emulate, but also contested and enriched the guidelines issued by the WIDF with demands rooted in their specific material reality. However, several differences between the Cuban and Mexican chapters of the WIDF are worth comparison and further explanations. Both countries are close to the US, and US foreign policy exerted a strong influence on their domestic agendas during the early years of the Cold War. Indeed, both the Cuban and Mexican Communist Party

65. WIDF, "IV Congreso de la Federación Democrática Internacional de Mujeres, 1–5 de junio de 1958 Viena" (Berlin, 1959), pp. 49–51.
66. The grass-roots initiative to create the FMC that was fostered by revolutionary women and took part in the insurrectional movement against the dictator Fulgencio Batista, and the relationship between the birth of the FMC and the spread of the WIDF in Latin America have been studied by Michelle Chase, *Revolution within the Revolution*, pp. 115–134. The strong feminist precedent set by the members of the FDMC during the Constitutional period and the historical background of feminist militancy in Cuba after the approval of women's suffrage have been researched by Manuel Ramírez Chicharro, *Llamada a las armas*, 2019.

were persecuted and banned. This was due to the influence of the
"McCarthyist" victimization of (real and supposed) Marxists in America during the 1950s. The BNMR–UDMM, and the FDMC were, respectively,
formed by members of, or ideologically close to, the Cuban Communist
Party and the Mexican Communist Party. Likewise, both the Cuban and
Mexican WIDF branches were firmly against US imperial policy and its interference in other countries' national agendas. Both of them had a strong commitment to the development of rural areas and, more specifically, to improving
the literacy and access to culture of women peasants.

   Neither the BNMR nor the UDMM sought to seriously disrupt gender
roles and archetypes, despite their radical ideological backgrounds. Most of
their requests concerned women's rights to join representative institutions;
they saw maternity and traditional femininity as core ideas. They did not
seek to dissolve or challenge the family as the foundational structure of social
organization, nor did they seek to overcome the traditional paradigm of
women as reproductive beings whose main duty and purpose was to take
care of their biological children as a way of looking after the children of the
nation. They were less radical feminists than their Cuban colleagues. The
Cuban feminists followed traditional female archetypes, and, like the
Mexican women, proposed modest new ways to understand femininity and
suggested that a woman could have a role within society as an educated worker
or peasant, but also as a technician or a liberal arts professional. Nevertheless,
the Cuban branch seemed to promote discourses that decolonized, or at least
radicalized, traditional concepts of femininity linked to the nation's progress
and modernization. In fact, while the FDMC demanded further improvements for Black women, the Mexican groups had made no noticeable mention
of Indigenous or Afro-Mexican women by that time. This was linked to the
widespread idea, defended by Vasconcelos, that "the mestizo" was the universal race of Mexico. This famous concept attempted to intentionally erase the
existence of indigenous people in Mexico. By arguing that all Mexicans were
a product of miscegenation between indigenous people and Spaniards, it inti-
mated that there was no need to recognize the existence of a stratified social
system that marginalized and excluded people on the basis of race in post-
revolutionary Mexico.

   Additionally – in line with the communist parties that they were attached to
or had close relations with – both women's organizations defended complex
discourses about agrarian reform and the need to fight against material depri-
vation, the lack of vital products, and enable access to vital sources of welfare
and happiness such as food, water, health, and education. In this regard,
Cuban and Mexican communist women used traditional concepts of maternity as a strategy to mobilize and bring more women into activism. In fact,
these organizations developed associations for the Protection of Children as
a way of ensuring the safety of all citizens and the future of the nation.
Because of this and their shared Marxist ideology, they proposed to build

new crèches and day care centres in working class districts. With respect to peasants, they demanded equality between men and women, as well as their rights to be landowners and to have access to water, and they requested the extension of medical services for school-age children.

It would be wrong to depict Latin American feminists as a consistent onto-logical mirror-image of European socialist feminists. Within the framework of the WIDF, there was no political bloc of socialist or communist feminists unit-ed by a Latin American identity or with a common programme for Latin America as a differentiated entity. Nor could it be argued that Latin American communist women worked without hierarchies, free from cultural prejudices. In fact, in a travel story published by FDMC member, Justina Álvarez, after a trip to America, Cuban feminists show a sense of superiority over colleagues from other Latin American countries such as Guatemala, Colombia, Ecuador, or Mexico.[67] In the same way, another FDMC member, Sarah Pascual, portrays Mexican women as illiterate, powerless, unprotected, and poorer than Cuban ones.[68]

This image contrasts with how Cuban reformist feminists estimated left-wing Mexican women in the 1930s. Prominent Mexican feminist leaders of the FUPDM, such as Refugio García and Adelina Zendejas, were honoured guests at the Third National Congress of Women in Cuba (1939). They spoke about Cárdenas' revolutionary policies and how Mexican feminists had con-tributed to enhancing women's living standards and political status.[69] During the interwar period, Mexico had become the paradigm of revolution in America, while, in contrast, Cuba was embroiled in a period of transition into a constitutional convention in which military warlords, such as Fulgencio Batista, still controlled short-lived civil presidents. However, in the late 1940s, Cuban communist women might well have regarded Mexico as a much less revolutionary country because of the corporative turn of the PRM under Manuel Ávila Camacho, who abolished some of the most radical measures approved by Cárdenas and tried to gain greater control over mass organizations like trade unions, youth associations, and feminist groups.

In spite of these disparities, it is worth noting that the convergence between European and Latin American socialist and communist women within the WIDF strengthened the internationalization of feminism in the twentieth century. This analysis has used personal letters, journals, and the records of international meetings in the early Cold War to show the changing, but increasing, alignment of Mexican and Cuban women to the top-down princi-ples of the WIDF on antimilitarism and women's and children's rights.

---

67. Justina Álvarez, "Relato de un viaje a centro y sur América", *Mujeres Cubanas* (April 1954), pp. 12–13.
68. Sarah Pascual, "Así trabajan, sufren y luchan en el corazón de México miles de mujeres", *Mujeres Cubanas* (June 1951), p. 6.
69. Manuel Ramírez Chicharro, *Más allá del sufragismo*, p. 93.

However, the convergence also sped up the decentralization of that era's feminist paradigm. These meetings and dialogues resulted in a rich exchange of ideas and discussions that also opened the door to grass-roots proposals and demands. Transnational interaction in para-diplomatic circles within the socialist bloc expanded and made more complex the WIDF's political agenda defined in Europe by bringing alternative ideological understandings of women's emancipation together.

To sum up, this article seeks to encourage a reassessment of the role of Latin American left-wing women within the WIDF during the Early Cold War. Although the WIDF created the institutional possibility of an international socialist network of feminist associations in 1945, the success of its development relied not just on the initiatives of its executive committee, council, and secretariat, but even more on the existing logistical structure and disposition of its affiliated national sections. Both Cuban and Mexican communist and socialist women's groups were willing to openly inform the WIDF about their particular problems and challenges, as well as to collaborate in the finance and organization of campaigns launched by other groups associated with the WIDF, such as petitions against military action, authoritarian regimes, or colonial policies in Africa and Asia. As has been argued, the guiding principles of their European colleagues were implemented by Mexican and Cuban socialist and communist women, who always remembered their own national contexts, material conditions, and the historical background of feminist activism. The main programme for women's emancipation within the WIDF could have first been overwhelmingly outlined by European leaders in the mid-1940s. However, this article shows that the increased number of exchanges and contributions made by Latin American left-wing women affiliated with the WIDF during the late 1940s and 1950s paved the way for a true decentralized globalization of women's fights and rights within the Eastern bloc.

IRSH 67 (2022), pp. 103–129 doi:10.1017/S0020859022000049

International Solidarity as the Cornerstone of the Hungarian Post-War Socialist Women's Rights Agenda in the Magazine *Asszonyok**

ZSÓFIA LÓRÁND ⓘ

Faculty of History, Cambridge University
Cambridge CB2 1TN, United Kingdom

E-mail: zsofia.lorand@gmail.com

ABSTRACT: This article analyses five years of the magazine *Asszonyok* (Women) the main forum for discussing women's rights between 1945 and 1949 in Hungary. The magazine was published by the Magyar Nők Demokratikus Szövetsége (the Hungarian Women's Democratic Federation), an umbrella organization created mostly by women from the communist movement. This analysis is centred around the idea of internationalism and how it became a means for socialist women's emancipation, proof of the political power of the new women's organization, and a platform of political education. It also symbolized the new era of peace after the war, peace becoming one of the slogans of the socialist women's movement globally. The broadening international platform of transfers became a terrain where political languages about race, class, and gender were slowly but steadily taking shape. Solidarity with women across the globe became one of the main tenets of communist women in Hungary. However, solidarity had its limits. As is shown here, identification with the right political agenda was even more important than aspects of race and class. This was one of the most important ways in which socialist women's rights and feminism were diverging from each other, despite the broad spectrum of shared elements on their agenda.

* This project has received funding from the European Union's Horizon 2020 research and innovation programme under the Marie Skłodowska-Curie grant agreement MSCA-IF-EF-ST 841489 hosted by the University of Cambridge. I would like to warmly thank Celia Donert and Michael Kozakowski for their unrelenting support and always wise input, and the generous and most ingenious community of scholars brought together by Dr Donert around the AHRC project "How Women's Rights became Human Rights: Gender, Socialism, and Postsocialism in Global History, 1917–2017", as well as the two anonymous reviewers for the time and effort they took to improve this paper. I have also received invaluable help from the archivists at the Institute of Political History and Hungarian National Archives, for which I am immensely grateful. All translations from the Hungarian sources are mine, if not indicated otherwise (ZsL).

"From this point on, we were members of the family of hundreds of millions of democratic women of the world", concludes Boris Fái, one of the leaders of the communist Hungarian women's movement, her account about the first Women's International Democratic Federation (WIDF) congress of socialist women from all over the world, which took place in Paris in 1945.[1] The time between the immediate aftermath of World War II and the establishment of a single-party communist regime in 1949 was a phase full of hope, fascination, transformation, solidarity, and betrayal for the Hungarian women's movement. The freshly founded women's organization, the Magyar Nők Demokratikus Szövetsége (the Hungarian Women's Democratic Federation, MNDSz), which joined the WIDF, played a crucial role in channelling the Hungarian women's movement into one strand of international women's rights. This article analyses the role internationalism and women's solidarity played in *Asszonyok* (Women),[2] the main public forum of the politics of the MNDSz, which also served as a platform of women's political education and of public representation of a new form of female internationalism. Despite the almost complete lack of other published sources on women's rights from this time, the magazine has not been researched in detail until now.[3] Between 1945 and 1949, Hungary experienced a transition to democracy and then to Stalinism, while the MNDSz, first a popular front umbrella organization, became by 1949 the women's section of the Magyar Kommunista Párt (Hungarian Communist Party, MKP). I explore this process through five years of *Asszonyok*, focusing on reports about big international meetings on the one hand, and reports and correspondences about bilateral relations with women and their organizations from other countries on the other hand. In particular, with a combined approach of social and intellectual history, the article analyses the sidelining of pre-war feminism by the communist Hungarian women's movement after World War II, as well as tensions between the emerging discourse of socialist internationalism and notions of race and racism.

Despite initially serving as the voice of the popular front women's movement, *Asszonyok* was predominantly edited and written by communist women. It documented the political and social processes of the time, but its role went way beyond creating a communist women's sensibility. While it served as a propaganda tool, it was also a platform of debates about women's

---

1. Memoirs of Boris Fái, Politikatörténeti Intézet Levéltára [Archives of the Institute of Political History, hereafter PIL], 906, f. 29, p. 70.

2. IPA transcript: [ɒsːoɲok]. I have translated the titles of the articles from the magazine, as these are often highly relevant for their interpretation. Not all issues have page numbers. Where page numbers could not be given accurately, I indicate "n.p.".

3. A recent publication about gender, media, and communication made an important contribution to Hungarian historiography, but ignores the immediate post-war period: Balázs Sipos and Lilla Krász (eds), *A női kommunikáció kultúrtörténete* (Budapest, 2019).

rights, where arguments about the desired form of women's emancipation took shape. Women's rights were scarcely discussed elsewhere in the main intellectual forums of the time. For example, the most important social science journal of the time, *Társadalmi Szemle* (Social Science Review) did not have a single article about women between 1946 and 1949, and only a handful were written by women. This makes *Asszonyok* an indispensable source that should be researched systematically in order to understand the processes by which the discourse on women's rights changed in the immediate post-war era.

The five years when *Asszonyok* was published were formative for the socialist women's emancipation discourse, and this is well documented in the magazine. The editors of the magazine, as well as the women in the MNDSz, debated fiercely with the anti-fascist, yet in several aspects conservative, Christian Women's League on issues such as divorce, the rights of children born out of wedlock, women's role in society, and the conflict between women's employment and women's traditional role within the family. The relationship with the feminists of the pre-war Feministák Egyesülete (Association of Feminists; FE), who were fighting not only for women's suffrage, but also for labour and education rights, and were taking a stance on issues such as prostitution, trafficking, and illegitimacy, was more ambivalent owing to the similarities in the political demands between socialist women and the feminists. These shared interests did not prevent them from having severe clashes over the years, however.[4] In 1912, the FE accepted new legislation that expanded suffrage to women with limitations according to educational and property criteria; this created an irreversible abyss between feminists and social democrats.[5]

First marginalized and then forced into illegality during the Horthy regime (1920–1944), the FE was re-established in 1945, but dissolved in 1949. Attempts by the FE to find a place in relevant and visible public forums such as *Asszonyok* were largely ignored by the MNDSz,[6] and their ideas of solidarity among women were quickly marginalized by the communist women's agenda of women's class- and work-based emancipation. In light of the complicated history of socialist and feminist women, a story that started in the early twentieth century and continued in the aftermath of World War II, I will rely here on a clear distinction between feminism and socialist women's emancipation politics as two separate strands of political thought. Although the communist women's

4. About the history of FE, see Judit Szapor, "Sisters or Foes: The Shifting Front Lines of the Hungarian Women's Movements, 1896–1918", in Sylvia Paletschek and Bianka Pietrow-Ennker (eds), *Women's Emancipation Movements in the 19th Century: A European Perspective* (Stanford, CA, 2004), pp. 189–205; and Dóra Czeferner, "Túlélési stratégiák, alkalmazkodás, nemzetközi beágyazottság. A Feministák Egyesülete két világháború közötti történetének kutatási lehetőségei", *Per Aspera ad Astra*, 2 (2020), pp. 107–122.
5. Szapor, "Sisters or Foes", p. 199.
6. See letter of Margit Izsáky to the FE, 28 August 1947, Magyar Nemzeti Levéltár [Hungarian National Archives, hereafter MNL], P 999, t. 5, no. 29.

goal was to address all women, they prioritized class and loyalty to Marxism-Leninism over gender alliances, and clearly distanced themselves from feminism. They either treated the history of the FE as the past, acknowledging some of its merits,[7] or were opposed to feminism as the ideology responsible for creating a gender cleavage that carried the danger of breaking up the class struggle.[8] Socialist women's emancipation politics introduced substantial changes in women's lives, and the history of the women and women's organizations working for these changes deserves to be thoroughly researched and discussed. However, I suggest using the term "feminism" for individuals and groups who embraced this label and will refer to the women in the MNDSz as communist and socialist women, and their politics as socialist women's emancipation politics. I therefore diverge from the term "left feminism" recently suggested by Francisca de Haan and others for the activities of communist women in Eastern and East Central Europe, while acknowledging the merits of their research in re-evaluating the complexities of women's lives in this part of the world during state socialism.[9] By this move, I am also hoping to divert discussions from the directions set by recent debates and the struggle over heavily contested concepts such as agency.[10]

THE MNDSz AND *ASSZONYOK*

After the years of illegality, the immediate post-war period carried the promise of democratization and thus was a fascinatingly ambiguous time for the women's movement.[11] The MNDSz was founded in 1945 and by 1949 became

---

7. Letter of Boris Fái to Mrs Oszkár Szirmai in the FE, MNL, P 999, t. 5, no. 561.

8. For an early statement about this, see Magda Jóború, quoted in Mária Palasik, *A jogállamiság megteremtésének kísérlete és kudarca Magyarországon 1944–1949* (Budapest, 2000), p. 131.

9. See Francisca de Haan, "Continuing Cold War Paradigms in Western Historiography of Transnational Women's Organizations: The Case of the Women's International Democratic Federation (WIDF)", *Women's History Review*, 19:4 (2010), pp. 547–573.

10. W.B. Gallie, "Essentially Contested Concepts", *Proceedings of the Aristotelian Society*, 56 (1955–1956), pp. 167–198. For the debate: Nanette Funk, "A Very Tangled Knot: Official State Socialist Women's Organizations, Women's Agency and Feminism in Eastern European State Socialism", *European Journal of Women's Studies*, 21:4 (2014), pp. 344–360; *idem*, "(K)not So: A Response to Kristen Ghodsee", *European Journal of Women's Studies*, 22:3 (2015), pp. 350–355; Kristen Ghodsee, "Untangling the Knot: A Response to Nanette Funk", *European Journal of Women's Studies*, 22:2 (2015), pp. 248–252; Francisca de Haan, "Ten Years After: Communism and Feminism Revisited", *Aspasia: The International Yearbook of Central, Eastern, and Southeastern European Women's and Gender History*, 10 (2016), pp. 102–168.

11. About the complexity of this period, see Péter Kenéz, *Hungary from the Nazis to the Soviets: The Establishment of the Communist Regime in Hungary, 1944–1948* (Cambridge, 2006); Éva Standeisky, *Demokrácia negyvenötben* (Budapest, 2015); and Palasik, *A jogállamiság megteremtésének kísérlete és kudarca*.

the only women's organization in the country.[12] Its founders were women from the illegal communist movement, but their aim was to recruit as many women as possible, in the spirit of the "coalition era".[13] As the leadership of the organization described their objectives to the MKP leadership in April 1945, the goal was "to gather all women into one organization, no matter what social status, party affiliation, profession, religion, all the women and girls who love their country and want to work". It is important to note here that women's "willingness to work" already carried a heavy political weight. It meant much more than simply taking up employment, it meant the willingness to embrace the values of socialism, as debates about "bourgeois women", prostituted women, or the Roma show. At the same time, as the letter to the party leadership continues, "in order to be able to fulfil the programme of our Association, we need to implement a comprehensive programme of women's education, and for that, we indispensably need a *centrally controlled* magazine that covers the entire country to present our work for society and women's (political) education".[14] A letter from a year later is more explicit about the kind of political education that is to be expected from the MNDSz: one "in the spirit of the party, but without its terminology", wrote Magda Aranyossi, the editor in chief of *Asszonyok*.[15]

The activities of the MNDSz were becoming more systemic over time. In Boris Fái's retrospective account (probably from the 1960s), the work of the MNDSz had three directions, focusing on healthcare and social issues, cultural activities, and politically enlightening educative work.[16] The communist women in the MNDSz were aligned with the MKP agenda, but had their own ideas and preferences driven by their personal knowledge "from the field". They were the ones working with women from all walks of life and were aware of their needs as well as the possibilities to recruit them to the communist cause. One article about the organization locates the 1946 congress of the MNDSz as the moment when the organization became more "politicized", in

---

12. For the story of the MNDSz, see Andrea Pető, *Nőhistóriák. A politizáló magyar nők történetéből* (Budapest, 1998), pp. 88–121; and Andrea Pető, *Women in Hungarian Politics, 1945–1951* (Boulder, CO, 2003), pp. 29–60.

13. Kenéz, *Hungary from the Nazis to the Soviets*; and Ignác Romsics, *Magyarország története a XX. században* (Budapest, 2005), pp. 271–333. English translation: Ignác Romsics, *Hungary in the Twentieth Century*, transl. Tim Wilkinson (Budapest, 1999).

14. MNDSz to the MKP, MNL, f. 274, cs. 19, őe. 15, p. 3 (emphasis mine). Andrea Pető quotes different sources with similar ideas in Pető, *Women in Hungarian Politics*, pp. 29–60.

15. Letter of Magda Aranyossi to the MKP's Department of Mass Organisation, MNL, f. 274, cs. 19, őe. 15, pp. 5–6.

16. Boris Fái, "A magyar nőmozgalomért 1945-ben", PIL, 906, f. 29, p. 62. Also in Eta Nagy and Katalin Petrák (eds), *Tanúságtevők 5* (Budapest, 1975), pp. 180–193.

other words more explicitly performing MKP ideology.[17] There were several rounds of power transfer within the organization, though. As a result of these, the intellectual women who founded both the MNDSz and *Asszonyok* disappeared from the leadership, and by 1952, all MNDSz activities were subordinated to the trade unions.[18] In 1948, all other women's organizations were abolished or merged into the MNDSz. Moreover, progress on the organizational level necessarily affected the ideological level as well, as the women's rights discourse and politics was dominated by the communist women. These changes were directly reflected in *Asszonyok*, the editorial team and the content of the magazine following the changes within the MNDSz.

ASSZONYOK AND THE WOMEN BEHIND IT

Asszonyok, published first in the summer of 1945, was created by a couple of fascinating women, and was heavily shaped by a range of inter- and transnational transfers. A few years later, in 1949, when the MKP solidified its power, it was transformed into *Nők Lapja* (Women's List), a magazine still published today. The first issue of *Asszonyok* was printed in June 1945 on paper given to the women's movement by Marshall Klementin Voroshilov, the president of the Allied Control Commission in Hungary at the time (Figure 1).[19] From the outset, *Asszonyok* took on the highly ambitious task of politically educating women, without creating the impression that they were being targeted by propaganda. In common with many women's magazines, *Asszonyok* taught women about hygiene, efficient household practices, and new principles of childrearing (the latter from a rather progressive viewpoint, for the time). These themes were accompanied by articles focusing on political and social education, and these included stories about women all over the world.

Among the MNDSz women most involved in creating the magazine were Magda Aranyossi and Boris Fái. While Fái was one of the main organizers of the MNDSz and the magazine, she and her fellow activists heavily relied on the intellectual input from Aranyossi (who soon became the editor-in-chief of the magazine), as well as the protection and influence of the wives of

17. Kornélia Burucs, "MNDSZ. Magyar Nők Demokratikus Szövetsége", *História*, 4 (1991). Available at: https://regi.tankonyvtar.hu/hu/tartalom/historia/91-04/ch09.html; last accessed 19 August 2021.

18. See Pető, *Women in Hungarian Politics*, pp. 58–60; and Júlia Orosz, "A Magyar Nők Demokratikus Szövetségének szerepe Magyarország újjáépítésében a második világháború után (1945–1946)", *Debreceni Szemle*, 22:4 (2014), pp. 302–310. About the restricted possibilities of the new leadership, see Anna S. Kosztricz, "A nők mobilitásának vizsgálata a part- és az állami vezetésben a Magyar Dolgozók Pártja káderanyagai alapján (1948–1956)", in Mária Palasik (ed.), *A nő és a politikum* (Budapest, 2007), pp. 145–165; and Mária Schadt, "Struktúra és funkcióváltozások az MNDSZ-ben 1950 és 1953 között", in Palasik, *A nő és a politikum*, pp. 167–189.

19. Fái's memoirs, PIL, 906, f. 29, p. 67.

Figure 1. The cover of the first issue of *Asszonyok*, published in June 1945.

prominent communists, such as Júlia Rajk, the wife of the future minister of interior and creator of the state secret police, László Rajk,[20] and Lili Révai,

20. Júlia Rajk's biography: Andrea Pető, "De-Stalinisation in Hungary from a Gendered Perspective: The Case of Júlia Rajk", in Kevin McDermott and Matthew Stibbe (eds),

the wife of the cultural and intellectual ideologue of the MKP, József Révai. Fái and Aranyossi took different paths to the Communist Party. Fái was born into a middle-class family in Budapest. She was engaged in women's mobilization from an early age, having participated in the work of the FE with her mother. While, over time, she embraced communism and a class-based emancipation politics over the rights focus of the FE, organizing women for the MKP evoked memories of working with her mother in the FE.[21] Fái never disavowed her mother's feminist past, but treated it as the politics of the past, whereas communism was the future, the movement that had the potential to mobilize and emancipate masses of women – workers, peasants, bourgeois alike. As she wrote in her memoir: "Already during the time in France, in emigration, and then right before the liberation and during the siege, I was preparing to work for the women's movement."[22] On both occasions when Fái publicly talked about her ideas of women's politics, in the 1945–1949 period, and in her published recollections of the time in the 1960s, her ideas of women's emancipation always embraced all women and emphasized the importance of inter-class reconciliation.[23]

Magda Aranyossi, a writer and journalist, like many Hungarian communists spent most of the interwar period in emigration in Germany and France. In Paris, she ended up working for the magazine *Femmes*. Having come from a Jewish landowning family, Aranyossi had a solid bourgeois education and familiarized herself with Marxism after having met her husband, Pál Aranyossi. In France, she first worked as a typesetter for the newspaper of the Hungarian workers in Paris, *Párisi Munkás* (Parisian Worker). As she noted later: "This work turned out to be unexpectedly useful for me [...] this was when traits of my old, bourgeois mindset were shattered by the simple wisdom of the workers' letters."[24] Before her time at *Femmes*, she had been the editor of the newspaper for the women in the Hungarian workers' emigration with the title *Március 8* (8 March). Her husband already worked for the prestigious *Regards* (the editorial board of which included Romain Rolland, Maxim Gorky, André Gide, and Isaak Babel, among others).[25] The illustrated weekly clearly influenced Magda Aranyossi's conception of a politically educational women's magazine, and thus her work with *Femmes* and later with *Asszonyok*.

De-Stalinising Eastern Europe: The Rehabilitation of Stalin's Victims after 1953 (Basingstoke, 2015), pp. 46–66. Andrea Pető, *Árnyékban. Rajk Júlia élete* (Budapest, 2020).

21. Fái's memoirs, PIL, 906, f. 29, p. 55.
22. *Ibid.*, p. 23.
23. *Ibid.*
24. Magda Aranyossi, *Én régi, elsüllyedt világom. Rendszertelen önéletrajz.* Annotations by Boglárka Nagy and Péter Nádas (Budapest, 2018), p. 151.
25. Péter Nádas, *Világló részletek. Emléklapok egy elbeszélő életéből* (Budapest, 2017). E-book edition, without page numbers.

During her time at the Confédération générale du travail unitaire and in the French communist women's movement, Aranyossi became acquainted with Bernadette Cattanéo and Gabrielle Duchêne, and closely followed the creation of the fellow organization of the Women's International League for Peace and Freedom, the Comité mondial des femmes contre la guerre et la fascism (World Committee of Women Against War and Fascism; CMF) in 1934. This is when she got to meet, for the first time, Dolores Ibárruri (Pasionaria), who became a major supporter of the MNDSz in the WIDF. Aranyossi was a hands-on editor and organizer, with stylistic skills and vision, so she was quickly recruited to work for the new magazine *Femmes* (original title: *Femmes dans l'action mondiale*, published between 1934 and 1939, twenty-five issues in total).[26] *Femmes* was the journal of the CMF and generally envisioned the women's movement as international. The other source of inspiration for the profile of *Femmes*, besides *Regards*, was the Soviet magazine *Rabotnitsa* (The Woman Worker, first published in 1914).[27] The result was a combination of political education (and propaganda) with a large amount of visual material, and articles about traditional themes of women's magazines.

Aranyossi remembered her debates with Cattanéo and the French leadership over more representation of women from the colonies, as well as more controversial issues concerning women's rights, such as abortion. The French women considered the former less relevant, whilst the latter was much too risky in France in the mid-1930s. Aranyossi was willing to risk public outrage and felt that the women from the colonies deserved more attention, whereas the French socialist women had other priorities: "Only later did I realize that Cattanéo's resignation from not only the colonial, but also some other questions, was more than simple naïveté. They did not know history well, had childish illusions of the future, but were all the better in navigating the daily issues."[28] She was impressed by how quickly they reacted to domestic politics, with their ability to organize mass protests within hours. The knowledge Aranyossi acquired clearly shaped her view on the creation of *Asszonyok*.

During the five years of its short existence, *Asszonyok* went through several transformations, most of which followed the power dynamics and political programme within the MNDSz. The profile of *Asszonyok* was new to Hungarian readers: the earlier illustrated women's magazines targeted middle-class and wealthier women, while the political ones, such as the FE's *A Nő és a Társadalom* (Woman and Society – later simply *A Nő*) and the journal of the social democratic women, *Nőmunkás* (Woman Worker), were without

26. Aranyossi, *Én régi, elsüllyedt világom*, p. 194, fn. 193.
27. Lynne Atwood, *Creating the New Soviet Woman: Women's Magazines as Engineers of Female Identity, 1922–53* (New York, 1999), p. 25.
28. Aranyossi, *Én régi, elsüllyedt világom*, p. 196.

attractive illustrations. The innovative and experimental concept of *Asszonyok* was also far from set in stone. After an ambitious start in 1945, the concept of the magazine became subject to debates within the MNDSz. These debates led to its refashioning in 1946, and while Aranyossi remained in charge, those in the MNDSz leadership with close ties to the MKP wanted more political and professional control, including every issue to be approved by two women from the MNDSz leadership.

Lili Révai, who was in the MNDSz leadership at the time, complained to the MKP Central Secretariat that "[u]ntil this time, the paper was full of rather uninteresting content, it was insignificant, not even adequately reporting about the work of the MNDSz". She did not blame Aranyossi directly, admitting that the editor-in-chief was doing the work of an entire editorial board by herself. However, relieving Aranyossi's workload was a way to intervene in the internal affairs in the magazine. Révai was against "the original picture magazine format, which we find incompatible with the changes of the inside content".[29] Révai wanted more political propaganda, while Aranyossi believed in a more cautious and indirect approach. When the publication ceased for a few months owing to the economic difficulties created by massive inflation, Révai took her chance to implement changes. Nevertheless, the magazine eventually retained its picture magazine format, and by the autumn of 1946, a new editorial board was established on which all women were MKP members, Aranyossi remaining editor-in-chief. In her letter to the MKP, Aranyossi presented the ambitious plan to reach the print run of 50.000 copies per issue and her strategy to edit *Asszonyok* "in the spirit of the party, but without its terminology".[30]

Part of Aranyossi's plan was an entire section with focus on the "whole wide world", where also the "Soviet section" would find its place. Apart from this section, several types of articles reported on international affairs: original texts written by an editor, journalist, or activist working for the magazine, and materials received from the Soviet Union. While it is clearly noted in *Nők Lapja* (the successor of *Asszonyok*) that it reprinted materials from the Soviet magazine founded in 1945, *Soviet Woman*, this was often the uncredited source in *Asszonyok* too. On other occasions, materials sent directly by the Antifashistskii Komitet Sovetskikh Zhenshchin (Soviet Women's Anti-Fascist Committee, AKSZh) were used.[31] *Soviet Woman* was edited by the AKSZh, led by Nina Popova.[32] The magazine "was an artifact of both wartime internationalism and Cold War competition", and over time, it was widely distributed in multiple languages (Russian, English, French, and

29. All references to Lili Révai's letter, see MNL, f. 274, cs. 19, őe. 2, pp. 8–9.
30. Aranyossi's letter, MNL, f. 274, cs. 19, őe. 15, pp. 5–6.
31. Special thanks to Alexandra Talaver for this information.
32. Alexis Peri, "New *Soviet Woman*. The Post-World War II Feminine Ideal at Home and Abroad", *The Russian Review*, 77 (October 2018): pp. 621–644, 621.

German, as well as in Hindi, Japanese, and Spanish).[33] Its Hungarian edition first appeared in 1960 with the title *Lányok, Asszonyok* (Girls, Women) and between 1960 and 1972 again as *Asszonyok*. This magazine was the translation of the Soviet edition, and it never reached the popularity of its contemporary local counterpart, *Nők Lapja*.

It needs to be emphasized that as a journalistic and political endeavour *Asszonyok* was more deeply rooted in the context of Hungarian women's movements and women's interwar communist activism, especially Aranyossi's work at *Femmes*. In this sense, it is very much a product of the 1945–1949 era, documenting the influence of interwar intellectual traditions as well as the transition to the Sovietized one-party state. Its title itself tells this story. The words *femmes* and *women* (as well as женщины/*zhenshchiny*) can be translated both as "asszonyok" and as "nők". The more inclusive one, *nő* (plural: *nők*), was used as the title of the journal of the FE. It was all the more fitting, since the word *nő* highlights women's individuality, while the word *asszony* (plural: *asszonyok*) refers to married women (and to some extent more widely to mature women). At this point, the focus on the individual woman that characterized feminism in the first half of the twentieth century belonged to the past, and even though the MNDSz activists were divided in their relationship to the FE, many acknowledging its merits,[34] an impression of being the carriers of the feminist heritage had to be avoided. The reference to marriage in the term *asszony*, while it excludes young women, suggests respectability. This was in line with *Asszonyok* targeting the broad population, with its primary mission to win masses of rural working women and women workers, first, for the cause of post-war reconstruction, and secondly and less openly, for the communist cause.

INTERNATIONALISM, RACE, THE MNDSz, AND *ASSZONYOK*

For the women in the MNDSz, one of the clearest symbols of internationalism was the newly founded WIDF.[35] It was this level of international politics and

33. Christine Varga-Harris, "Between National Tradition and Western Modernization: Soviet Woman and Representations of Socialist Gender Equality as a 'Third Way' for Developing Countries, 1956–1964", *Slavic Review*, 78:3 (2019), pp. 758–781, 763.

34. Fái was not the only one, as the FE–MNDSz correspondence shows. MNL, P999, t. 5, no. 561–565; Ilona Kasitzky from *Szabad Nép* to the FE, MNL, P999, t. 5, no. 852–853. The MNDSz-FE relations from a different angle: Pető, *Women in Hungarian Politics*, pp. 79–91.

35. A selection from the growing and fascinating literature on the WIDF: De Haan, "Continuing Cold War Paradigms"; Celia Donert, "From Communist Internationalism to Human Rights: Gender, Violence and International Law in the WIDF Mission to North Korea, 1951", *Contemporary European History*, 25:2 (2016), pp. 313–333; *Idem*, "Whose Utopia? Gender, Ideology and Human Rights at the 1975 World Congress of Women in East Berlin", in Jan Eckel and Samuel Moyn (eds), *The Breakthrough: Human Rights in the 1970s* (Philadelphia,

diplomacy on the one hand, and bilateral connections (which often grew out of the involvement with the WIDF) on the other hand that most influenced the meanings of internationalism of the MNDSz and *Asszonyok*. In her memoirs written in 1970, Boris Fái remembers receiving the invitation to the 1945 congress of the WIDF in Paris. The document reveals several aspects of how internationalism mattered to the local women's movement:

> I felt this enormous excitement. Not only because apart from our contact with the Yugoslav and Romanian women, this was our first contact with *abroad* [a külfölddel]. We didn't know much about the women's movements elsewhere, since there was no train or mail connection yet. We realized it now, from the brochure sent with the invitation, that there are women from America, China, Vietnam, Italy, [...] who fight for the same goals, and with similar means as we do. That women of the whole world fight for democracy, peace, the protection and happiness of children. *Then we saw that we were on the right path.* [...] It was a delegation of ten women. All four parties had representation. [...] From this point on, we were members of the family of hundreds of millions of democratic women of the world.[36]

Joining the WIDF and having access to the most memorable figures of the socialist women's movement worldwide was a huge step not only because of Hungary's role in World War II. Fái, Rajk, and Aranyossi all knew about life during decades of illegality, and, Fái especially, imprisonment and torture too. Being part of the WIDF congress meant an acknowledgement of their views and work in front of what seemed to them like the entire world.

The third aspect of internationalism, beyond symbolizing a clean slate after the war as well as the realization of the principles of socialism, was that of worldwide solidarity among women. *Asszonyok*'s task was to ensure that all these aspects were duly explained to Hungarian women. Articles on the subject varied between reports about the WIDF; reportage on women's lives in other, mainly socialist countries; women in socialist parties and workers' movements elsewhere; and portraits of women activists from all over the world. Anti-imperialism and anti-colonialism were already an integral part of women's socialist internationalism at this early stage. Central European women, who had previously had very little contact with the developing world/Third World, were fascinated but also generally uninformed.[37] Fái's first impression from the WIDF meeting in 1945 summarizes the good intentions as well as the lack of knowledge that was hard to overcome and often stood in the way of anti-racism and transnational solidarity:

PA, 2014), pp. 68–87; Jadwiga Pieper Mooney, "Fighting Fascism and Forging New Political Activism: The Women's International Democratic Federation in the Cold War", in Jadwiga E. Pieper Mooney and Fabio Lanza (eds), *De-Centering Cold War History: Local and Global Change* (London, 2013), pp. 52–73.
36. PIL, 906, f. 29, pp. 69–70 (emphasis mine).
37. I will use the contemporaneous terms for what we today refer to as the Global South.

Thousands of women from forty countries gathered there, and many of them came from much further away and often on much more arduous journeys than us. We found here the crème-de-la-crème of the women of the world. We did not even understand the language of most of them, still, there was a strong tie between all of us from the first moment. We were very, very different [from each other]. Not only our language, our skin colour, our clothes, our customs. There were rich and poor, highly educated and very simple women. But most of us had lived through the war, many of us the hell of prisons and concentration camps, we all hated fascism and were ready to fight for peace, independence, democracy.[38]

This sense of solidarity was the basis of their internationalism, stemming from the shared struggle against fascism and for a socialist future. Political alliances overrode other factors, such as class and race, even though class was recurringly evoked as a reason for exclusion. When talking about women in general, the MNDSz and *Asszonyok* claimed that all women would be liberated by the movement. Still, it becomes apparent from articles about women in particular life situations or as members of ethnic, national, socio-economic groups that the women who deserved sympathy and rights were those with the correct political views.

Encountering women of colour in the WIDF reveals several aspects of the complicated treatment of race in socialist theory, including the still defining work of Marx and Engels. Anti-imperialism and anti-colonialism were integral elements of the Marxism-Leninism that guided the new communist leaders in East Central Europe after World War II, and this greatly influenced their anti-racist agenda. For the USSR, differentiating its policies in Soviet Asia from the colonialism of the Russian Empire was essential for its self-identity and legitimacy; racial, ethnic, and cultural differences were a key terrain for this.[39] This approach extended to the developing world/Third World and the national struggles for independence and socialism. In 1945–1949 we cannot talk about "global communism", but alliances such as the WIDF were important first steps towards what soon became global communism.[40] The politics of anti-imperialism in this Cold War global setting was struggling with its language of anti-racism. This was before the "linguistic turn" of the language of anti-racism, and since the language of anti-racism we use today was born to the west of the Iron Curtain with the 1960s civil rights

---

38. PIL, 906, f. 29, p. 12.
39. See Yuri Slezkine, *Arctic Mirrors: Russia and the Small Peoples of the North* (Ithaca, NY, 1994); Douglas Northrop, *Veiled Empire: Gender and Power in Soviet Central Asia* (Ithaca, NY, 2004); Artemy M. Kalinovsky, *Laboratory of Socialist Development: Cold War Politics and Decolonization in Soviet Tajikistan* (Ithaca, NY, 2018); and Tobias Rupprecht, *Soviet Internationalism after Stalin: Interaction and Exchange between the USSR and Latin America during the Cold War* (Cambridge, 2015).
40. See the argument about socialist globalization in James Mark, Artemy Kalinovsky, and Steffi Marung (eds), *Alternative Globalizations: Eastern Europe and the Postcolonial World* (Bloomington, IN, 2020).

movements, it remained foreign in the "Second World" for quite some time. The language of Marxism-Leninism, starting with Marx and Engels, was influenced by nineteenth-century theories of race too. This, as Erik van Ree argues in his analysis, deserves a nuanced evaluation in its contemporary context. He concludes that though Marx and Engels can be read as racist today, they also relied on "the Lamarckian proposition of circumstance remoulding heredity",[41] and thus did not treat racial traits as unchangeable. This ambiguity nevertheless accompanies the concept of race in the period of state socialism.

While scholarship about socialist East and East Central Europe has avoided taking race as a focus of analysis in the region seriously for a long time, as Catherine Baker in her book about race and Yugoslavia emphasized, it is an unsustainable notion that "eastern Europe could have entered the twenty-first century without exposure to the global dynamics of race".[42] This becomes apparent when we read how contributors to *Asszonyok* struggled to talk about race in the immediate aftermath of the war, and the political agenda and political uses of anti-fascism of the time. In fact, internationalism in *Asszonyok* was closely tied with presenting and talking about women from the Global South, and the visible difference of these women had to be tackled in the texts. Lacking a reflective discourse about race, many of the articles, to quote Baker again, "contained a hierarchy of biological and cultural essentialism that did resemble race".[43] These hierarchies appear in the discourse about the local Roma population, even when on paper the situation of the Roma in the early period of state socialism was framed as a problem of work and class.[44]

SOCIALIST FRIENDSHIPS AND BETRAYALS

The very first issue of *Asszonyok* opened with the news that the MNDSz had been invited by Yugoslav women to the first post-World War II meeting of

41. Erik van Ree, "Marx and Engels's Theory of History: Making Sense of the Race Factor", *Journal of Political Ideologies*, 24:1 (2019), pp. 54–73, 67.
42. Catherine Baker, *Race and the Yugoslav Region: Postsocialist, Post-Conflict, Postcolonial?* (Manchester, 2018), p. 7.
43. *Ibid.*, p. 12, quoting Kesha Fikes and Alaina Lemon, "African Presence in the Former Soviet Spaces", *Annual Review of Anthropology*, 31 (1999), pp. 497–524. A paradigmatic example that I will not be able to analyse here in detail: I. M., "Ceyloni mozaik" [Ceylon Mosaic], *Asszonyok*, 3: 10 (May 1947), n.p. About communist criticism of the racial hierarchies in the US and post-imperial Western Europe, see Yulia Gradskova, "Women's International Democratic Federation, the 'Third World' and the Global Cold War from the late-1950s to the mid-1960s", *Women's History Review*, 29:2 (2020), pp. 270–288.
44. See Celia Donert, *The Rights of the Roma: The Struggle for Citizenship in Postwar Czechoslovakia* (Cambridge, 2017); and Péter Apor, "Cigányok tere. Kísérlet a kommunista romapolitika közép-kelet-európai összehasonlító értelmezésére, 1945–1961", *Aetas*, 24:2 (2009), pp. 69–86.

anti-fascist women (Figure 2).[45] This was followed by reports on the WIDF meetings, including those introducing the most charismatic women in the organization, as well as reports and portraits of women from neighbouring countries. Other reports about the international belonging of the Hungarian women's movement were written by activists and journalists visiting the countries in the region. The tone in these articles is much more personal and subjective, and the metaphor of friendship ties them all together. A new, political concept of female friendship is emerging at the time, also shaped by the Soviet "friendship of the peoples" campaign, which began in the USSR in the 1930s and was gradually entering East Central Europe in the aftermath of World War II.[46] The friendship rhetoric was crucial in distancing the USSR's international politics (and its treatment of Soviet Central Asia) from earlier imperial practices.

The letter from Dolores Ibárruri, in which she addresses Anna Kara and Boris Fái as her "dear [female] friends" was published in large script and placed prominently in the magazine, despite its otherwise uninteresting content. What mattered was the declaration of friendship.[47] The intimacy associated with friendship, and especially female friendship, was meant to bring the movement and women from all over the world closer to the readers.[48] When it came to the most famous women from the international socialist movement, *Asszonyok* approached Ibárruri, Nadezhda Popova, Eugenie Cotton, and Anna Pauker with admiration and a sense of inferiority: in contrast to them, Hungarian women "had nothing to say about the fight against fascism".[49] The support of these iconic women was a form of rehabilitation of the country itself. Ibárruri argued for inviting Hungarian women to the Executive Committee of the WIDF: "Because the Hungarian people are not identical with the Horthy and Szálasi fascists, because the real Hungarian people is the one whose heroic sons were fighting in Spain, many of them sacrificing their lives for the Spanish freedom."[50] These are Fái's words, narrating Ibárruri's statement, reflecting again on the sensitive matter of "the last satellite" status of the country. As a result of this admiration, Ibárruri and other women from the WIDF were presented similarly to film and theatre

45. "Nőkongresszus Belgrádban" [Women's Congress in Belgrade], *Asszonyok*, 1: 1 (June 1945), n.p.
46. Rachel Applebaum, *Empire of Friends: Soviet Power and Socialist Internationalism in Cold War Czechoslovakia* (Ithaca, NY, 2019); and Terry Martin, *Affirmative Action Empire: Nations and Nationalities in the Soviet Union, 1923–1939* (Ithaca, NY, 2001).
47. Dolores Ibárruri, "Kedves barátnőim!" [My Dear Friends], *Asszonyok*, 4:2 (15 January 1948), n.p.
48. For how the concept of friendship is heavily gendered *and* political, see Marilyn Yalom with Theresa Donovan Brown, *The Social Sex: A History of Female Friendship* (New York, 2015).
49. Anonymous, "A világ asszonyai Magyarországot a demokratikus országok közé sorolták" [The Women of the World Declared Hungary One of the Democratic Countries], *Asszonyok*, 3: 20 (15 October 1947), n.p.
50. Fái's memoir, PIL, 906, f. 29, p. 70.

Nőkongresszus Belgrádban

A jugoszláv nők antifasiszta szövetsége közös találkozóra hívta meg, Belgrádba, június 16–18-ra az Egyesült Államok, Anglia, a Szovjetunió, Belgium, Franciaország, Bulgária, Románia, Albánia, Lengyelország, Csehszlovákia, Ausztria és Magyarország demokratikus nőszervezeteit.

A háború kitörése óta a világ demokratikusan gondolkozó asszonyainak ez lesz az első találkozása. Büszkék és boldogok vagyunk, hogy a Magyar Nők Demokratikus Szövetségét is meghívták erre. Tudjuk, milyen fontos feladat vár ránk Belgrádban. Meg kell értetni azokkal az asszonyokkal, akik férjeik, fiaik oldalán annyi éven át harcoltak a fasizmus ellen, szóval és tettel, a szabotázs fegyverével és puskával kezükben, mint partizánok, hogy mi, magyar asszonyok szintén résztveszünk a nagy építésben. Meg kell értetnünk a világ asszonyaival, hogy milyen nehéz volt a magyar nő helyzete a reakció és fasiszta elnyomás esztendeiben. Meg fogjuk velük ismertetni munkánkat és terveinket, mi is meg akarjuk ismerni az övéiket és így közösen dolgozni az egész világ asszonyainak javán.

„ITT IS, OTT IS ASSZONYCSAPAT KAPÁL
HOL MAJD ÉLET TEREM,
MÉGIS, MÉGIS ÉLNI JÓ"
                                        Ady

Figure 2. The article about the first visit to the partisan women in Belgrade in 1945, "Nőkongresszus Belgrádban" [Women's Congress in Belgrade], *Asszonyok*, 1:1 (June 1945), n.p.

stars. *Asszonyok* proudly announced that women in the MNDSz had earned the respect of their comrades in WIDF for contributing to the maintenance of peace and democracy in Hungary.[51] The next year, in 1948, the country even hosted the next WIDF congress.[52]

The celebration of friendship and a broad anti-fascist alliance of women is in strong contrast with the series of betrayals in the Stalinization process among the charismatic women of the era. Andrea Pető writes about the role of Boris Fái in attesting against Júlia and László Rajk, family friends of Fái and her husband, during the Stalinist show trial against László Rajk.[53] In line with the verdict of the trial, Rajk was executed on 15 October 1949. *Asszonyok*'s international reporting accidentally published an image that can be read as a symbol of these betrayals, portraying three women, among them the Czech feminist lawyer Miládá Horáková (1901–1950). Horáková was one of the most important feminist thinkers of the interwar period not only in Czechoslovakia but in East Central Europe, who over the course of a couple

51. Anonymous, "A világ asszonyai…", n.p.
52. About the 1948 Budapest congress, see Éva Cserháti, "Report on the International Women's Congress, 17 December 1948", *Aspasia*, 9 (2015), pp. 126–146.
53. Pető, *Árnyékban*, pp. 92–94.

of years changed from an anti-fascist hero into an enemy of the state.[54] In the issue of *Asszonyok* from 1947, Horáková was presented as a member of the Czechoslovak delegation of the WIDF leadership.[55] The picture of the women from Czechoslovakia is included in photo reportage about "women of the wide world", republishing pictures from the 1945 WIDF meeting. Miládá Horáková is in the company of Marie Trojanová and Anežka Hodinová-Spurná. The accompanying script has several inaccuracies: the names of all three women are misspelled and their party affiliations are mixed up. Ironically, Horáková was presented as the communist representative and Hodniková as the one from the Czech National Social Party, Horáková's moderate social democratic party. There was indeed cooperation between the different women's organizations at the time, but while Horáková was executed in the first show trial in 1950, Hodinová had a steady career in the party, including leadership of the Committee of Czechoslovak Women.[56]

The most likely reason for the inaccuracies in this article is errors in the transliteration of Cyrillic script that appeared in the Russian materials that were reprinted. These inaccuracies document the scarcity of information and resources of the almost naively enthusiastic MNDSz women. The picture was important for the mission of the MNDSz as it embodied two of the most politically important messages of the time: broad party coalition (popular front-like) politics and female friendship, symbolizing women's solidarity and implying a higher level of intimacy. The case of the picture of the three Czechoslovak women allows us a glimpse into the chaotic ways in which Hungarian women were immersed in international politics on a scale not seen before. With multiple political agendas in the background, similar processes were taking place everywhere in East Central Europe: popular front women's organizations joined the WIDF, including women who would later disappear (emigrate, get imprisoned, or simply be sidelined). However, at this point, the stories about women "from all over the world" sent a political message to working-class and peasant women all over the country.

BILATERAL RELATIONS: REGIONAL FRIENDSHIPS, RACE, AND RELIGION FROM A DISTANCE

In 1947, Júlia Rajk, first secretary of the MNDSz, wrote upon meeting Josip Broz Tito: "we will prove it through our work that we are worthy of this

54. Melissa Feinberg, *Elusive Equality: Gender, Citizenship, and the Limits of Democracy in Czechoslovakia, 1918–1950* (Pittsburgh, PA, 2006), pp. 190–222.
55. Anonymous, "A nagyvilág asszonyai" [Women of the Wide World], *Asszonyok*, 3:1 (1 January 1947), n.p.
56. "Anežka Hodinová-Spurná", Wikipedia. Available at: https://cs.wikipedia.org/wiki/Ane%C5%BEka_Hodinov%C3%A1-Spurn%C3%A1; last accessed 4 February 2021.

friendship".[57] Yugoslavia, a country proud of its partisan resistance to fascism, was, along with the Soviet Union, admired by the MNDSz women. Articles in *Asszonyok* celebrated the partisan movement, speaking highly of the achievements of the (Antifašistička fronta žena (Women's Anti-Fascist Front, AFŽ) and the social transformation taking place as the result of their work. The short articles discussed a broad scale of social issues, with an undercurrent of a domestic political programme that targeted Hungarian women.

Presenting women in the Yugoslav partisan movement to a broad, still rather traditionally minded audience about women's roles required a balance.[58] It was to be shown that even amid fighting *and winning* a war, these celebrated women did not abandon their traditional gender roles. Beyond the broader readership of *Asszonyok*, the MKP was also not willing to drastically subvert the existing patriarchal relations. Thus, instead of emancipation from traditional gender roles, partisan experience was presented as a means to eliminate women's socio-economic inferiority, while they could retain their traditional feminine roles as mothers and wives. In the spirit of recruiting women across classes, there were reports about bourgeois women who joined the partisans and, through the experience of camaraderie, became supporters of the Tito regime.[59] The sense of camaraderie was even more deeply rooted in the experience of all women being mothers, daughters, and sisters of men who sacrificed their lives in the war: "And we saw the real mothers in them, the ones who worry about their children smartly and who know how to act. The congress of the anti-fascist women of Yugoslavia was nothing but the congregation of smart mothers."[60]

The idea of peace itself was closely entangled with the possibility of women returning to their traditional roles. The article about a Hungarian woman joining the Yugoslav and Polish partisans emphasized: "As good a soldier she was, she is a good mother now."[61] At the same time, the MNDSz women appreciated that in Poland and Yugoslavia, where a large number of women were active in the war, women had higher positions in politics; they even held ministerial seats.[62] These international comparisons were made rarely, but allow for criticism of the current domestic situation, such as in a report on Poland: "Here [in Hungary] they don't allow women into such high positions,

57. Anonymous, "Tito", *Asszonyok*, 3:24 (15 December 1947), n.p.
58. On Yugoslav partisan women, see Barbara Jancar-Webster, *Women & Revolution in Yugoslavia 1941–45* (Denver, CO, 1990); Ivana Pantelić, *Partizanke kao građanke. Društvena emancipacija partizanki u Srbiji, 1945–1953* (Belgrade, 2011); and Jelena Batinić, *Women and Yugoslav Partisans: A History of World War II Resistance* (Cambridge, 2015).
59. Anonymous, "Jugoszlávia asszonyai", *Asszonyok*, 3:24 (15 December 1947), n.p.
60. *Ibid.*
61. Károlyné Sásdi, "Akikre büszkék vagyunk. Magyar partizán nők" [Whom We are Proud Of: Hungarian Partisan Women], *Asszonyok*, 3:1 (1947), p. 23.
62. Dinnyés Lajosné, "Mit láttam Jugoszláviában?" [What Did I See in Yugoslavia?], *Asszonyok*, 3:21 (1947), n.p.

and I'm not saying it's because of male jealousy, but not all women get into the positions they deserve."[63] Connecting women's political advancement to prior achievements enabled talk about the lack of women in powerful political positions in Hungary. The article about Poland suggests that the lack of a significant partisan movement in Hungary should not be a reason to exclude women from political leadership.

Beyond the broad subjects of female participation in partisan struggles and its gendered consequences, the reports portraying bits and pieces of the lives of women and children involved a combination of the themes of friendship and race, women's rights, and prostitution. Work, as the most important concept for communist politics after 1945, tied women's rights, prostitution, and poverty together. The magazine reports presented Yugoslavia as a country where even the problem of beggars and prostitution had been solved by the high demand for labour.[64] In an article by Nóra Aradi (later an art historian), prostitution is not seen a matter of sexual morale, but much rather as a result of poverty (symbolized by "begging"). At the same time, the idealization of retraining prostituted women into a "useful labour force" already carried the danger of restigmatizing prostitution by placing it into a moralistic framework from the socio-economic one. In later years of state socialism, women in prostitution were again labelled asocial and amoral, as according to the official stance, the "forgivable" reason of poverty had already been eliminated.[65]

Children's well-being was a crucial barometer of the success of post-war reconstruction, and a new approach to pedagogy as well as attempts for socialized childcare accompanied the care for orphaned and sick children.[66] The newly built, modern pioneer city in Belgrade evoked admiration in the *Asszonyok* reports. However, the highlight of Yugoslav child protection policies was their approach to Roma children: "In Yugoslavia, There is No Child Beating, There are a Lot of Female Locomotive Drivers and the Gipsy Pre-Schoolers [sic] Want to Build Hungarian Train Tracks," says one lengthy title.[67] Roma children signal the progress in Yugoslavia next to the image of women in traditionally male jobs of physical labour (the unfortunate yet widespread metaphor of socialist women's emancipation). Bidding

---

63. Anonymous, "A lengyel nő mind harcolt" [All Polish Women were Fighting], *Asszonyok*, 4:3 (1948), n.p.

64. Nóra Aradi, "Jugoszláviában nem verik a gyerekeket, sok a női mozdonyvezető és a cigányóvodások magyar vasutat akarnak építeni" [In Yugoslavia, There is No Child Beating, There are a Lot of Female Locomotive Drivers and the Gipsy Pre-Schoolers [sic] Want to Build Hungarian Train Tracks], *Asszonyok* 3:20 (20 October 1947), n.p.

65. See Barbara Havelková, "Blaming All Women: On Regulation of Prostitution in State Socialist Czechoslovakia", *Oxford Journal of Legal Studies*, 36:1 (2016), pp. 165–191.

66. See Eszter Varsa, "Protected Children, Regulated Mothers: Gender and the 'Gypsy Question'", in *State Care in Postwar Hungary, 1949–1956* (Budapest and New York, 2021).

67. Aradi, "Jugoszláviában nem verik a gyerekeket", n.p.

farewell to the MNDSz delegation, "the black-eyed little ones, the children of 'Tito's country'", offer to build a railway for the Hungarian children.

In these first years of post-World-War-II socialist women's activism and *Asszonyok*, this was the first of the very few occasions when the Roma were mentioned. As Celia Donert shows us, the communist agenda for the Roma population in the immediate post-war phase was very much in the making.[68] However, already then, the acknowledgement of the Roma as fully fledged members of socialist society was tied to their participation in the labour force,[69] and the top-down emancipatory sentiments were accompanied with a discourse in which the Roma were depicted as innocent because they never supported fascism.[70] The innocence discourse, which was always tied to a romanticized ethnicization and infantilization, is what we find in this article too. While almost every issue of *Asszonyok* featured women of colour and their relationship to socialism, Romani women were missing. It seems that children (in another country) were innocent and exotic to allow for their mention, especially in light of the endearing story about the dialogue.

While Yugoslavia's ethnic, religious, and cultural diversity was celebrated as part of the new internationalism, the discussion of particular groups who stand out of the white, Christian/secular paradigm posed a challenge about the right kind of language in which they could be presented. Muslim women in Bosnia and Herzegovina were shown as the symbol of backwardness and target of top-down emancipation.[71] Their hijab was treated as the ultimate proof of this, especially in contrast to "the women of the AFŽ [who] instead of the veil, wear the 1941 star of the partisans. But the more progressed women do not look down on the retarded ones [another potential meaning: 'on those who are left behind' [*visszamaradottak*]".[72]

This kind of power hierarchy between emancipated, progressive women (women who were either educated owing to their background or received their education in the partisan movement) and "backward" women has a growing literature.[73] The appearance of Muslim women in the Hungarian context adds an extra layer, given the agenda of the *Asszonyok* editorial board of "lifting up" the backward women at home. Introducing the story of Muslim women in Yugoslavia to the Hungarian readers offered two life models: the "advanced" women of the AFŽ and those "left behind", but being "helped"

68. Donert, *The Rights of the Roma*, p. 38. Péter Apor confirms this: Apor, "Cigányok tere".
69. Donert, *The Rights of the Roma*; also Varsa, *Protected Children, Regulated Mothers*.
70. Donert, *The Rights of the Roma*, p. 50.
71. About "civilizing" and "liberating" Muslim women in Bosnia, see Ivan Simić, *Soviet Influences in Postwar Yugoslav Gender Policies* (Basingstoke, 2018), pp. 155–182.
72. Anonymous, "Nagyvilág. Belgrád" [Big Wild World: Belgrade], *Asszonyok*, 3:10 (15 May 1947), n.p.
73. See Chiara Bonfiglioli, *Women and Industry in the Balkans: The Rise and Fall of the Yugoslav Textile Sector* (London, 2019).

in their development. The readers could thus choose with whom to identify, and both choices would eventually feed into the emancipation process.

RACE AND RACISM

The bilateral encounters with Yugoslav and Polish women offer glimpses into the language of race and religious difference. The reports on the WIDF meetings are a rich source of language about race at the dawn of the era of global communism with its anti-racist agenda, a milestone in the complex and often troubled history of the concept of race in the history of socialist ideas. There is a difference in language and approach alike between the reports on individual countries and on the WIDF. In the latter, white women in leadership positions overshadow the women of colour around them, despite the wide presence of women from Africa, Asia, and the United States in group photos of the assemblies.[74] These photos are often accompanied by texts such as "colourful women",[75] and "colourful company [...] negro [*sic*], Hindu, Korean women delegates" (Figure 3).[76] The reader learns significantly less about the achievements of these women compared with the (mostly white) WIDF leadership and the women from various European partisan movements, and exceptionally, women from Central Asia representing the Soviet Union. The imbalance in the visual portrayal correlates with the language: women of colour, whether from the West or the Third World, are mostly not even mentioned by name, let alone by their position. The responsibility for this is not solely on the women in the editorial board of *Asszonyok*; even the reports from the Soviet materials perpetuated the inherent injustice.

Reporting on individual countries offers more nuance and represents a clear difference in power and hierarchies. These were mostly written by the *Asszonyok* authors, and were not translations from elsewhere. The communist women in the MNDSz were still on a quest for forgiveness after World War II. This, together with their admiration for and the expectation of guidance from the USSR, put them in an in-between position vis-à-vis the USSR and the Third World/developing world. Informing the readers of *Asszonyok* about the lives of women in far-away countries served the goal of socializing the readers into politics both by broadening their geographical horizons and by showcasing the positive change socialism and the Soviet Union carried for women's lives.

One of the most interesting pieces of writing from this period was a report by Zsuzsa Osvát about women in (North) Korea before and after socialism. A writer and journalist in the interwar period, Osvát survived the

---

74. Yulia Gradskova finds this tendency in the later phase of the history of WIDF too. Gradskova, "Women's International Democratic Federation".
75. "Nagyvilág asszonyai", n.p.
76. Anonymous, "Két esztendeje" [Two Years Ago], *Asszonyok*, 3:23 (1 December 1947), n.p.

Figure 3. "A nagyvilág asszonyai" [Women of the Wide World], *Asszonyok*, 3:1 (1 January 1947), n.p. Upper-left corner picture has the subtitle "1. Three colourful women: Mrs Mason, the American negro [sic], Mrs Handoo, the Indian lady, and Hŏ Chŏng-suk, the Korean lady cooperate to solve problems they have in common with their fellow Yugoslav and Czechoslovak women.' Part of this photo was republished in 1947 ("Két esztendeje" [Two Years Ago], Asszonyok, 3:23 (1 December 1947)). Bottom-left corner: "4. The Czechoslovak women represent the perfectly functional coalition. [...] They work together and they are best friends."

Holocaust in a "safe house"; that is, in one of the buildings in Budapest under the diplomatic protection of the neutral states. After the war, she started working for *Asszonyok*, and over time became the editor of the magazine. Her text about Korean women starts with a highly accurate and self-reflective summary of the widespread stereotypes and orientalizing language that characterized the discourse about Korean women earlier. Korean women, in the popular imagery, were frail and subservient, and either mothers of many children or worked "as draft animals on the farmlands". Moreover, they were illiterate and often used as prostitutes.[77] Osvát's exaggerated language is a critique of both the Hungarian imaginary of Korean women and Korean society before socialism. Osvát emphasizes the interconnectedness of colonial oppression (Japanese colonial rule) and gender-based oppression, resulting in women's dual subordination in colonized Korea. Moreover, she uses a sympathetic tone when talking about prostituted women, who become "geishas" or "girls of pleasure" as a result of oppression and poverty, a line of argument that characterizes almost all articles in *Asszonyok* on the subject.

The story about Korean women fits into the interpretation that communism liberates nations (from imperial and colonial rule): these women were aware of their oppression, and realized that "it is only national independence that can bring freedom to the people and only a free people can give human rights to women too". With the help of the USSR, women in socialist North Korea gained complete equality, illiteracy was eliminated, and thousands of them joined the Korean sister organization of the MNDSz. Osvát argues for the interconnectedness of gender inequality, racism and colonial oppression: "[W]omen's inferiority is just as much a fairy tale told by those in power as is the fairy tale told by the conquerors about the superiority of certain races or peoples." This is one of the most spelled-out self-critiques of orientalizing language combined with a critique of colonialism; anti-colonialism as anti-racism on the pages of *Asszonyok*.

The case of Germany was even more perplexing for the socialist women than the much less known world of the Global South. In the aftermath of World War II, solidarity with German women proved to be impossible. Some of the articles voiced the difficulty of recreating bonds with the country, an example being the emotional strength one needed to visit Berlin, the capital of the former enemy (written by Júlia Török, from the left wing of the social democratic party).[78] There is a strong contrast between treating the WIDF and communist women in general with care, enthusiasm, and intimacy (through the topic of friendship and discussion of private matters), and the way in which any woman suspected of fascist collaboration, and especially German

---

77. Osvát Zsuzsa, "Távol-Kelet asszonyai" [Women of the Far East], *Asszonyok*, 2:17 (11 December 1946), n.p.
78. Júlia Török, "Mit láttam Németországban?" [What Did I See in Germany?], *Asszonyok*, 4:13 (1 July 1948), n.p.

women, were portrayed. Women with a fascist past and upper-class women who refused to give up their class privileges were treated with animosity and were portrayed as selfish, hysterical, and often purely evil.[79]

The generic German woman was embodied by the character of "Grätchen" in an article revealing several important moments of a gendered post-war history of war brides and rape. It was written by Klára Feleki Kovács, a former actress who also wrote trivial romance novels in the interwar period. Some of the language of these returns in her reflective piece on the news that "Six thousand German girls arrived with their fiancés in England".[80] As the ban on British soldiers marrying "ex-enemy aliens" relaxed in 1946, fiancées and wives from Germany could emigrate to the UK to reunite with their partners.[81] Feleki Kovács takes on the role of an omniscient narrator and presents a story told to her by someone "who knows Grätchen and the other Grätchens very well". However, the emphasis on the plural suggests that the sensational story is more fiction than fact.[82] Grätchen's character embodies a figure of an inherently evil woman, who uses her femininity and sexuality only to destroy. She even gives away her new-born child for the Nazi cause.[83] The article emphasizes that it was black US troops with whom she traded sex for chocolate and cigarettes before escaping to the British Occupation Zone. This detail serves to prove Grätchen's hypocrisy, as she had earlier been a devoted believer in racial supremacy, but the text also addresses the existing stereotypes surrounding African-Americans and people of colour. The loose morals of "Grätchen" are in contrast to prostitution seen as necessitated by poverty and lack of proper employment.

79. The section "Vádlott" [The Accused] in *Asszonyok* focused on stories about the evil bourgeois woman.
80. Feleki Kovács Klára, "Nyugaton a helyzet megváltozott" [Not So Quiet on the Western Front], *Asszonyok*, 4:2 (15 January 1948), n.p.
81. See Christopher Knowles, "Marriage with 'Ex-Enemy Aliens': Marriages between British Servicemen and German Women After the End of the Second World War", in Peter E. Fäßler, Andreas Neuwöhner, and Florian Staffel (eds), *Briten in Westfalen 1945–2017. Besatzer, Verbündete, Freunde?* (Paderborn, 2019), pp. 217–237. About the US military in Germany and the story of war brides, see Petra Goedde, *GIs and Germans: Culture, Gender, and Foreign Relations, 1945–1949* (New Haven, CT, 2003). The relations between military personnel and women in the Western occupation zones was, however, more often violent than romantic. See Atina Grossman, *Jews, Germans, and Allies: Close Encounters in Occupied Germany* (Princeton, NJ, 2009); and Mary Louise Roberts, *What Soldiers Do: Sex and American GIs in World War II France* (Chicago, IL, 2014).
82. The name "Grätchen" is more frequently spelled as Gretchen, a colloquial diminutive for Grete, Margarete. The name "Jimmy" sounds more American than British, and the name of the British fiancée, "Mary", is misspelled as "Märy".
83. This is a probable allusion to the Lebensborn programme of Nazi Germany. See Joshi Vandana, "Maternalism, Race, Class and Citizenship: Aspects of Illegitimate Motherhood in Nazi Germany", *Journal of Contemporary History*, 46:4 (2011), pp. 832–853.

In the immediate post-war era, when Hungarian women struggled to bring home their family members held as prisoners of war, the news about happy brides from Germany travelling to the former Allied countries must have raised difficult emotions. Nevertheless, the tone of this article stands out in its misogyny and the blatant hatefulness vis-à-vis the imaginary "Grätchen", especially in this women's magazine that heralded international solidarity among women. The way the story is told, however, directs contemporary readers' attention to the silences of trauma and violence. The idea that German women in the Allied zones of occupation were happily fraternizing with military personnel stands in stark contrast to the silence around the mass rapes by the "liberating" armies.[84] In Hungary alone, tens of thousands of women were raped by members of the Soviet army. The numbers themselves suggest that it was widely known that women were victims of mass rape, even though it was an experience surrounded by silence until the 1990s.[85]

This approach stands in strong contrast to the portrayal of Yugoslav women after the Tito–Stalin split in 1948. Following this split, women's organizations in the Soviet bloc had to break ties with the until then much-admired forerunners of anti-fascist resistance and of women's emancipation.[86] After months of silence, the MNDSz sent their declaration to the WIDF, in which they pledged not to work with the AFŽ anymore. However, they expressed solidarity with the Yugoslav people and Yugoslav women, who were presented as those misled by Tito and the AFŽ. The letter was published in the news section of *Nők Lapja*, three months after it replaced *Asszonyok*:

> We know that most Yugoslav women see the true colours of Tito, and they will stand by those who fight for the free and peaceful life of the heroic Yugoslav people against the nefarious clique of Tito and his followers. We believe that we are helping the victory of the true Yugoslav patriots by debunking the current leaders of the Anti-Fascist Front of Women, who are loyal to Tito and his clique, and who spread anti-Soviet propaganda among the Yugoslav women and pursue anti-peace activities.[87]

---

84. For Germany, see Helke Sander and Barbara Johr, *BeFreier und Befreite. Krieg, Vergewaltigungen, Kinder* (Frankfurt am Main, 2005).

85. The exact numbers are still unknown, despite decades of research of the subject. Andrea Pető, *Elmondani az elmondhatatlant. A nemi erőszak Magyarországon a II. világháború alatt* (Budapest, 2018). In English: "Memory and the Narrative of Rape in Budapest and Vienna in 1945", in Richard Bessel and Dirk Schumann (eds), *Life After Death: Approaches to a Cultural and Social History during the 1940s and 1950s* (Cambridge, 2003), pp. 129–148.

86. On the break of the WIDF with the AFŽ, see Chiara Bonfiglioli, "Cold War Internationalisms, Nationalisms and the Yugoslav-Soviet Split: The Union of Italian Women and the Antifascist Women's Front of Yugoslavia", in Francisca de Haan, June Purvis, Margaret Allen, and Krassimira Daskalova (eds), *Women's Activism: Global Perspectives from the 1890s to the Present* (London, 2013), pp. 59–73.

87. Anonymous, "A Nemzetközi Nőszövetséghez" [To the International Federation of Women], *Nők Lapja*, 1:3 (5 November 1949), n.p.

Disavowing the AFŽ women, many of whom the women from the MNDSz had known personally, allowed the MNDSz and the magazine to stand by their previous writings about the greatness of Yugoslav women in general. However, women who became targets of Stalinist show trials, for example Júlia Rajk in Hungary and Milada Horáková in Czechoslovakia, were accused of Yugoslav links and of spying for Tito's regime.

CONCLUSION

During these formative years of the Cold War world order and of global communism, transfers of ideas and concepts were just as important for the solidification of the MNDSz as for the creation of its journal, *Asszonyok*. The pre-World War II debates and competition for recognition between the two progressive streams of women's rights movements, feminists and socialists, were decided during this time, feminism (together with social democracy) being pushed to the brinks of forgetting and replaced by socialist women's emancipation politics. For the MNDSz and *Asszonyok*, internationalism meant solidarity with other women; but the same way as their internationalism was defined by socialism and communism, their solidarity was not unconditional either. Even more importantly than class, political affiliation was decisive. Solidarity with women was reserved for "democratic women", as socialist women were often described. This early phase of women's internationalism made it unavoidable to think about the relations to women not only with skin colour other than white, but also from countries with a wide range of political past (including the Nazi past of Germany) and present (such as Yugoslavia after the Tito–Stalin split). As Celia Donert emphasized, between the late 1940s and 1960s the idea of "solidarity between women as women across geographical and geopolitical divides" was "more often hemmed around by national loyalties, ideological cleavages, and painful personal decisions".[88]

Even in this early phase of women's socialist internationalism, allegiances were expected to be first and foremost with the party. These expectations not only led to the disavowal of the formerly admired women in the Yugoslav AFŽ, and hostile language about German women, but also a series of betrayals among the women in the MNDSz and in the *Asszonyok* magazine's editorial board. Most women participating in founding the MNDSz and the magazine had disappeared from the women's movement by 1949. With the dismissal of all intellectual women from the movement,[89] the interwar activist memories, knowledge, and experience were also erased, and not only in cases such as Júlia Rajk's. Even Boris Fái and Magda Aranyossi,

---

88. Donert, "Women's Rights in Cold War Europe: Disentangling Feminist Histories", *Past & Present*, 218: suppl. 8 (2013), pp. 180–202, 181–182.
89. Pető, *Women in Hungarian Politics*, pp. 58–60.

who never disavowed or openly confronted the communist regime, were side-lined from women's politics and women's rights issues.

Nevertheless, this was a period in which the foundations of the new language of women's emancipation were created. As we have seen, *Asszonyok* is a valuable source for the ideas and politics of the early MNDSz, a space where ideas were created and discussed. It served as the main forum to communicate and develop ideas about women's socialist internationalism and, through these, also shape the domestic women's rights agenda. *Asszonyok's* international sections are one of the earliest places where race, gender, class, and ethnicity could be discussed and connected with. Encounters with women and children of different skin colour, religion, and culture enabled the discussion of matters of race and ethnicity when crucial issues such as the situation of Hungary's Roma population were off the official political agenda. Writing about women from all over the world, the state socialist women's rights agenda that was simultaneously emancipatory (with its access to work and education) and traditionalist (with its focus on family and motherhood) was taking shape. The period between 1945 and 1949 shaped the language of women's rights and the discourse on race and ethnicity for the coming decades, even if the women shaping the discourse would not be the same.

IRSH 67 (2022), pp. 131–154 doi:10.1017/S0020859021000705

Women Labour Models and Socialist Transformation in early 1950s China*

NICOLA SPAKOWSKI 🆔

*Institut für Sinologie, Albert-Ludwigs-Universität Freiburg
Werthmannstraße 12, 79098 Freiburg im Breisgau, Germany*

E-mail: nicola.spakowski@sinologie.uni-freiburg.de

ABSTRACT: This article investigates Chinese women labour models (or labour heroines) of the early 1950s as actors and symbols of socialist transformation. It centres on the example of Shen Jilan (1929–2020), who was one of the most prominent women labour models of the time. Shen rose to fame through her struggle for equal pay for equal work in her native village, became a delegate to China's National People's Congress, and even participated in the Third World Congress of Women in Copenhagen in 1953. The article critically engages with the concept of "state feminism" and proposes a shift in focus from state–society relations to work as a means to understanding the transformation of women's lives under socialism. Socialist society was a society of producers and work shaped people's daily lives; it was central to identity formation and constituted the regulating mechanism of social relations. Indeed, women labour models, together with related categories of working women, came to typify the new Chinese woman, who was integral to and symbolic of socialist modernity. They epitomized communist theory about women's participation in production being the mechanism of their liberation. The article has three main parts, each of which addresses a different level (local, national, international), different constellations of actors and agency, and different aspects of the relationship between working women and socialist transformation. By tracing Shen Jilan's activities in various contexts, the article reveals the complexity, contradictions, multilayered nature, and also incompleteness of socialist transformation.

* The author would like to thank Tani Barlow and Dong Limin for helpful discussions and comments on an earlier draft. Thanks also to an anonymous reviewer for suggestions and to Joleen Meiners for help with editing the footnotes. Research for this article was supported by the German Science Foundation.

On 22 March 1953, *Shanxi ribao* (Shanxi Daily), the newspaper of China's northern Shanxi province, published a one-page article titled "Zai zuguo gege zhanxian shang de funümen" (The women at the various fronts of the motherland). Fourteen photos featured women in different settings and occupations: the military front of the Korean War; fields and factories (including heavy industry); the construction site of a retaining dam; wasteland surveyed by female personnel; a maternity ward; and a kindergarten. The "theoretical front" was represented by Kang Keqing and Cao Mengjun, two prominent women's leaders, studying Stalin's "Economic Problems of Socialism in the USSR" and a document issued by the Nineteenth Congress of the Communist Party of the Soviet Union. Their equivalents at grassroots level appeared in two photos: vice cooperative leader and labour model Shen Jilan instructing her co-villagers on the upcoming autumn harvest; and vice-cooperative leader and labour model Guo Donglian discussing the production plan for 1953 with co-cadres of her cooperative.[1] Similar reportage articles centred entirely on work, making women the "new force in the cause of the construction of the country".[2]

The photo reportage and the details of its composition are of interest for two reasons. First, they indicate the central place New China envisaged for women. Second, they present concrete configurations of women's new role in society, as *working* women, instructed by the theories of communism (emanating from the Soviet Union) and guided by labour models and cadres who provided planning and organizing at village level. Indeed, women labour models, together with related categories of working women,[3] came to typify the new Chinese woman, who was integral to and symbolic of socialist modernity,[4] and who epitomized communist theory about women's participation in production being the mechanism of their liberation.

---

1. "Zai zuguo gege zhanxian shang de funümen" (The women at the various fronts of the motherland), *Shanxi ribao* (22 March 1953).
2. "Funü shi guojia jianshe shiye zhong de xin shengli jun" (Women are the new force in the cause of the construction of the state), *Xin Zhongguo funü*, 5 (1953), pp. 17–18.
3. These are the so-called firsts among women (*nüjie diyi*) in typical men's jobs and the "iron maidens" (*tie guniang*) of the 1960s. See Tina Mai Chen, "Female Icons, Feminist Iconography? Socialist Rhetoric and Women's Agency in 1950s China", *Gender & History*, 15:2 (2003), pp. 268–295; Yihong Jin, "Rethinking the 'Iron Girls': Gender and Labour during the Chinese Cultural Revolution", *Gender & History*, 18:3 (2006), pp. 613–634; Kimberley Ens Manning, "Embodied Activisms: The Case of the Mu Guiying Brigade", *China Quarterly*, 204 (2010), pp. 850–869.
4. This is also reflected in the front covers of *Xin Zhongguo funü* (Women of New China) and its successor, *Zhongguo funü* (Women of China), the organ of the All-China (Democratic) Women's Federation, in the years 1949 to 1966, forty-eight per cent of which featured working women; see Huang Jigang, "Cong 'xin nüxing' dao 'fengmian nülang'. You nüxing qikan fengmian kan xiandaixing huayu zhi shan bian" (From "new woman" to "cover girl": Front covers of women's magazines as evidence for the evolution of the discourse of modernity), *Xiangtan daxue xuebao*, 37:4 (2013), p. 133. See also Chen, "Female Icons", pp. 268–295; Ma Chunhua, "'Nüren kai

This article presents China's women labour models, or labour heroines,[5] as important actors and symbols in the construction and transformation of China in the early 1950s and work as the perspective that is best suited to understanding these processes. It is true that women's mobilization for work is at the heart of scholarship on Chinese feminism in the socialist period, but scholars are divided over their assessment of this period, both within and outside China.[6] Whereas feminists in the West initially praised Mao Zedong's China for its progressive women's policy ("women hold up half the sky"), negative voices prevailed from the 1980s. Western scholars spoke of "patriarchal socialism", and saw Chinese women as instruments and victims of the socialist state. In their eyes, the Chinese Communist Party (CCP) was not genuinely interested in the liberation of women but mobilized them for production for purely economic purposes.[7] In a similar vein, China's "new women's movement", which began to form in the second half of the 1980s, criticized the Maoist pattern of women's liberation as top-down and over-politicized, forcing women into masculinized gender roles and imposing on them the double burden of productive and reproductive work. Chinese women, these critics claimed, should develop a subjective and collective consciousness and strengthen themselves for the labour market instead of relying on the state.[8] While these

huoche'. 'Shiqi nian' wenyi zhong de funü, jiqi yu xiandaixing" ("Women drive trains": Women, machines and modernity in arts and literature of the "seventeen years"), *Wenyi zhengming*, 6 (2014), pp. 17–23; Song Shaopeng, "Jiazhi, zhidu, shijian. 'Nan nü tong gong tong chou' yu laodong funü zhuti de shengcheng" (Value, institution, event: "Equal pay for equal work between men and women" and the production of a subjectivity for working women), *Funü yanjiu luncong*, 7 (2020), pp. 108–128.

5. The two terms were used interchangeably. *Laodong yingxiong* ("labour hero") was the early expression and an import from the Soviet Union. It was soon joined by the term *laodong mofan* ("labour model"), which I prefer here because it signals what is specific about labour models' function in Chinese society, namely, to demonstrate exemplary rather than exceptional actions and attitudes.

6. See also the critical reviews of existing scholarship by Zhong Xueping, "Women Can Hold Up Half the Sky", in Ban Wang (ed.), *Words and Their Stories: Essays on the Language of the Chinese Revolution* (Leiden [etc.], 2011), pp. 227–247; Wang Lingzhen, "Wang Ping and Women's Cinema in Socialist China: Institutional Practice, Feminist Cultures, and Embedded Authorship", *Signs: Journal of Women in Culture & Society*, 40:3 (2015), pp. 589–622.

7. See, for instance, Judith Stacey, *Patriarchy and Socialist Revolution in China* (Berkeley, CA, 1983); Harriet Evans, "The Language of Liberation. Gender and *Jiefang* in early Chinese Communist Party Discourse", *Intersections: Gender, History and Culture in the Asian Context*, 1 (1998). Available at: http://intersections.anu.edu.au/issue1/harriet.html; last accessed 23 November 2013.

8. Nicola Spakowski, "Women Studies with Chinese Characteristics? On the Origins, Issues, and Theories of Contemporary Feminist Research in China", *Jindai Zhongguo funüshi yanjiu* (Research on women in modern Chinese history), 2 (1994), pp. 297–322; Nicola Spakowski, "'Gender' Trouble. Feminism in China under the Impact of Western Theory and the Spatialization of Identity", *positions: east asia cultures critique*, 19:1 (2011), pp. 31–54; Tani E. Barlow, *The Question of Women in Chinese Feminism* (Durham, NC [etc.], 2004), pp. 253–301; Liu Jie, "'Nan nü pingdeng' de yihua yu wudu. Yi jitihua shiqi Taihang shanqu funü canjia

negative voices mirrored a desire for self-determination after years of political campaigning, they also suited the needs of a market economy free of state intervention and cashing in on the consumption of autonomous subjects.[9] No wonder that, since around 2010, a new group of feminists formed that attributed women's discrimination in Reform China to neoliberalist structures and called for intervention at the level of political economy.[10] As for working women under Mao, these new socialist feminists point to the voices of women who have experienced socialism and claim to have profited from socialist gender policies, were proud of their work, and were positively affected by the propaganda of labour heroines and other progressive female role models.[11] These Chinese debates are not unique, but echo the discussions on "state feminism" in the former socialist countries of Eastern Europe.[12] Indeed, state feminism has become a concept in China Studies as well,[13] and scholars outside China Studies use the Chinese state feminists described in Wang Zheng's book *Finding Women in the State* as evidence of women's agency under the constraints of socialist states.[14]

While scholarship under the rubric of "state feminism" is able to defend state intervention on behalf of women as a plausible strategy, and while recent research has highlighted moments of women's agency even in the context of strong socialist states,[15] I do not adopt the term because I find it misleading

---

shehui shengchan wei li" (Alienation and misunderstanding of "equality between men and women": A case study of women's participation in social production in the mountain areas of Taihang during the period of collectivization), *Dang shi yanjiu yu jiaoxue*, 1 (2014), pp. 17–27.

9. See Barlow, *The Question of Women*, pp. 253–301.

10. Nicola Spakowski, "Socialist Feminism in Post-Socialist China", *positions: asia critique*, 26:4 (2018), pp. 561–592.

11. Zhong, "Women Can Hold Up Half the Sky", pp. 244–245. Not all authors respect subjective voices, though. Huang Xin, "In the Shadow of Suku (Speaking Bitterness): Master Scripts and Women's Life Stories", *Frontiers of History in China*, 9:4 (2014), pp. 584–610, for instance, tries to explain away subjective assessments of interviewees and "re-educate" them to assume a more "feminist" viewpoint.

12. Francisca de Haan (ed.), "Ten Years After. Communism and Feminism Revisited", *Aspasia*, 10 (2016), pp. 102–168.

13. For an early use of the term, see Mayfair Mei-Hui Yang, "From Gender Erasure to Gender Difference: State Feminism, Consumer Sexuality, and Women's Public Sphere in China", in Mayfair Mei-Hui Yang (ed.), *Spaces of Their Own: Women's Public Sphere in Transnational China* (Minneapolis, MN, 1999), pp. 35–67.

14. Wang Zheng, *Finding Women in the State: A Socialist Feminist Revolution in the People's Republic of China, 1949–1964* (Oakland, CA, 2017), Kristen Ghodsee, *Second World, Second Sex: Socialist Women's Activism and Global Solidarity during the Cold War* (Durham, NC, 2018), pp. 51–52.

15. For China, see Wang, *Finding Women in the State*. The difference between my own and Wang Zheng's perspective lies in the role and conceptualization of the state. While Wang rightly corrects "the conventional image of a monolithic party-state" by highlighting the "subversive women" within the state apparatus (pp. 7–8), I suggest abandoning fixation on the state as an isolated entity (and thus also the term "state feminism") in the first place. See also Wang, "Wang Ping and

in two respects. First, the term "state feminism" implies a generic feminism that is non-statist. The qualification of socialist feminism as statist not only entails a hierarchy between the two forms of feminism – feminism as the norm, state feminism as deviation from this norm – but it also excludes the possibility of a continuum between purely liberal and purely statist feminist formations. In addition, the "state" in state feminism explicitly or implicitly tends to follow a conceptualization of state and society as autonomous spheres. The state, in this view, is marked by "coherence, integrity, and autonomy".[16] Societies, on the other hand, are conceived as self-regulating entities, composed of individuals who are protected by law, have "authentic" selves, make rational choices, are autonomous in their decisions, and act accordingly ("rights, choice, agency").[17] These concepts have been contested from various angles,[18] but they still leave their traces in literature on women and the state. They force us to make either/or choices in the allocation of actors to one of the two spheres and to produce clear-cut assessments of gains and losses along notions of autonomy or repression.

The second reason for my reservations about state feminism as a focus of investigation is that privileging the state hides aspects that might be equally or even more important for understanding feminism in socialist societies. In my view, work, the very material and social basis of socialist societies, is such an alternative. Socialist society was a society of producers, and "socialist

---

Women's Cinema"; Chen, "Female Icons"; Zuo Jiping, "20 shiji 50 niandai de funü jiefang he nannü yiwu pingdeng: zhongguo chengshi fuqi de jingli yu ganshou" (Women's liberation in the 1950s and equality of duties between men and women: Experiences and feelings of Chinese urban couples), *Shehui*, 1:239 (2005), pp. 182–209. For Central and Eastern Europe, see Shana Penn *et al.*, *Gender Politics and Everyday Life in State Socialist Eastern and Central Europe* (New York, 2009).

16. Joel S. Migdal *et al.*, "Rethinking the State", in Klaus Schlichte (ed.), *The Dynamics of States: The Formation and Crises of State Domination* (Aldershot, 2005), pp. 1–40.

17. Amy Borovoy *et al.*, "Decentering Agency in Feminist Theory: Recuperating the Family as a Social Project", *Women's Studies International Forum*, 35:3 (2012), pp. 153–165, 153.

18. In China Studies, Jake Werner, "Global Fordism in 1950s Urban China", *Frontiers of History in China*, 7:3 (2012), pp. 415–441, 438, speaks of a "social totality" that comprises both state and society. In political science, scholars have proposed to see the state as a process; see Joel S. Migdal *et al.*, "Rethinking the State", in Schlichte, *The Dynamics of States*, pp. 19–20. Bob Jessop, *State Power: A Strategic-Relational Approach* (Cambridge [etc.], 2008) proposes a "strategic-relational approach" to the state, which he sees as a social relation. Olle J. Fröde, "Dissecting the State: Towards a Relational Conceptualization of States and State Failure", *Journal of International Development*, 24 (2012), pp. 271–286, 272, speaks of the state as "structures of interaction". In sociology, scholars have stressed relationality in the formation of subjectivity; see, for instance, Norbert Ricken, "Anerkennung als Adressierung. Über die Bedeutung von Anerkennung für Subjektivationsprozesse", in Thomas Alkemeyer, Gunilla Budde, and Dagmar Freist (eds), *Selbst-Bildungen. Soziale und kulturelle Praktiken der Subjektivierung* (Bielefeld, 2013), pp. 69–99; Norbert Ricken, "Zur Logik der Subjektivierung. Überlegungen an den Rändern eines Konzepts", in Andreas Gelhard, Thomas Alkemeyer, and Norbert Ricken (eds), *Techniken der Subjektivierung* (München, 2013), pp. 29–47.

man" was conceived of as a working man or woman. Work shaped people's daily lives and was central to identity formation. It constituted the regulating mechanism of social relations and, as such, was also the point of departure for the liberation of women.[19] One does not have to be an advocate of the communist theory of women's liberation through work in order to acknowledge that "the work-originated changes in women's lives and belief system fundamentally changed women's social position and traditional views about them".[20] The concept of work as social basis emanated from state ideology, of course, and the state was a strong actor in the field of work. But women's lives were shaped by socialism in various ways, not only in terms of the (beneficial or negative) effects of an intervening state.[21]

In this article, I continue earlier research on women and feminism in the process of China's "socialist transformation",[22] with transformation defined as the "deliberate and intended attempt of a radical and systemically steered social change".[23] By using the term "socialist transformation", I place Chinese feminism in a broad and multidimensional process that affected women in a multitude of ways, not just as subjects and objects of feminism. In addition, socialist transformation included actors at all levels of society. These actors, in most cases, cannot be neatly assigned to either the state or society, or separated into winners and losers of the new conditions, nor can their individual experience be easily divided into gains and losses. Rather, relations between actors and the effects of socialism upon actors should be conceived of as complex and even contradictory. Finally, transformation as an intended process includes the possibility of unintended outcomes or incomplete change. Shen Jilan, the labour model featured in the photo reportage on "Women at the Various Fronts of the Motherland", is an excellent example of the complexity, contradictions, multilayered nature, and incompleteness of socialist transformation.

---

19. For a more extensive discussion of the significance of work, see Nicola Spakowski, "Moving Labor Heroes Center Stage: (Labor) Heroism and the Reconfiguration of Social Relations in the Yan'an Period", *Journal of Chinese History*, 5:1 (2020), pp. 1–24; Nicola Spakowski, "Yan'an's Labor Heroines and the Birth of the Women of New China", *Nan Nü: Men, Women and Gender in China*, 22:1 (2020), pp. 116–149.

20. Zhong, "Women Can Hold Up Half the Sky", p. 239.

21. See Dong Limin, "'Lishihua' xingbie. 'Guanlian' ruhe keneng ("Historicizing" gender: How can a connection become possible), *Wenyi zhengming*, 4 (2012), pp. 31–35, 34, on the many factors and dimensions that shaped the phenomenon of women's participation in production.

22. Nicola Spakowski, *"Mit Mut an die Front". Die militärische Beteiligung von Frauen in der kommunistischen Revolution Chinas (1925–1949)* (Cologne: 2009); Nicola Spakowski, "Die Frauenpolitik der Kommunistischen Partei Chinas und das Problem der 'Frauenbefreiung' (1920er bis 1940er Jahre)", *Jahrbuch für historische Kommunismusforschung* (Berlin, 2015), pp. 1–16.

23. Raj Kollmorgen, "Gesellschaftstransformation als sozialer Wandlungstyp. Eine komparative Analyse", Sozialwissenschaftlicher Fachinformationsdienst, *Politische Soziologie*, 1 (2006), pp. 1–30, 19.

This article investigates Chinese women labour models of the early 1950s as actors and symbols of socialist transformation, centring on the example of Shen Jilan (1929–2020). Shen Jilan was one of the most prominent women labour models at the time, rising to fame through her struggle for equal pay for women in Xigou village and even becoming a delegate to the Third World Congress of Women in Copenhagen in 1953. Her case is well documented and allows us to address all levels and contexts where labour models mattered: the local, the national, and the international. My main sources are texts on Shen published in the state media in the early 1950s, such as newspaper reports and interviews.[24] Even though these texts presented an image of women labour models shaped by the preferences of the state, we should not dismiss them as mere propaganda, unrelated to women's experience. Rather, as Tina Mai Chen has pointed out in her work on women in typically male fields of occupation, the representation and experience of these women were inseparable, based on "a tripartite process linking representation of model women in CCP propaganda, language of experience employed by and for these women, and actions undertaken by women in response to such representation".[25]

The article has three main parts, each of which addresses a different level, different constellations of actors and agency, different aspects of the relation between working women and socialist transformation, and particular evidence of the incompleteness of the process. The first part introduces the system of labour models and provides biographical information on Shen Jilan. It focuses on Xigou village and work as Shen Jilan's true spaces of activity and identification, and on her fight for equal pay for equal work, the episode that brought her fame. It reveals the upsetting effect of women's participation in production on the traditional gender order, and shows how the particular ideals and interests of various actors – state, local cadres, village women – converged in the demand for equal pay. The second part moves to the national level and the political order, where male and female labour models were appointed delegates to the National People's Congress (NPC; China's "parliament") and figured in the CCP's efforts to legitimize communist rule. It highlights women's new sense of honour, dignity, and acts of recognition as important aspects of their "liberation" – gains that are easily overlooked in a rights-centred discussion. The third section is dedicated to Shen Jilan's participation in the Third

24. Interviews, oral history, and autobiographical texts are valuable sources for social history. However, in a Chinese context, authors and interviewers be careful not to touch upon issues that are outside the politically acceptable. What constitutes a sensitive issue depends on the subject and varies over time, though. See also my discussion of the use of memoirs for social history in Spakowski, *"Mit Mut an die Front"*, pp. 25–30, and on subjectivity in memoirs in Nicola Spakowski, "Destabilizing the Truths of Revolution: Strategies of Subversion in the Autobiographical Writing of Political Women in China", in Marjorie Dryburgh and Sarah Dauncey (eds), *Writing Lives in China, 1600–2000: Histories of the Elusive Self* (Basingstoke, 2013), pp. 133–158.
25. Chen, "Female Icons", p. 271.

World Congress of Women in Copenhagen in 1953, a stage shaped by Cold War constellations and a discourse of socialism's superiority over capitalism. China posed – and was praised – as a forerunner of women's liberation, with women's right to work and equal pay as ultimate yardsticks of equality. One would have expected a central role for Shen Jilan in this display of socialist progressiveness but this was not the case. It was the educated and experienced heads of the Chinese delegation who represented New China on the congress stage, and they pointed to the young and uneducated Shen Jilan as mere evidence of successful liberation.

FEMINISM AT THE GRASSROOTS

The system of labour models was established in the communist border regions in 1942 and was extended to the entire country in 1949, when the CCP came to power.[26] Labour models were not important in their individual contribution to economic output, but rather as models for everybody to learn from. They were models of concrete practices of work in the fields and factories, and they exemplified the attitudes and behaviour expected of socialist citizens. As intermediaries between the Party and the people, they functioned as quasi-cadres and were responsible for organizing work. Women labour models, in addition, were examples of women's liberation through production, based on the logic that their contribution to family income earned them the respect of their husbands and mothers-in-law.[27] Many of these women, however, also assumed responsibility for mobilizing their female co-villagers and acquired formal positions in the local organizations of Party and government.[28] And a few

26. For the formation of the system in the 1940s, see Patricia Stranahan, "Labor Heroines of Yan'an", *Modern China*, 9:2 (1983), pp. 228–252; Spakowski, "Moving Labor Heroes Center Stage", and Spakowski, "Yan'an's Labor Heroines". For labour models after the founding of the PRC, see Gao Xiaoxian, "'The Silver Flower Contest': Rural Women in 1950s China and the Gendered Division of Labour", *Gender and History*, 18:3 (2006), pp. 594–612; Gail Hershatter, *The Gender of Memory: Rural Women and China's Collective Past* (Berkeley, CA, 2011), pp. 210–235; Gail Hershatter, *Women and China's Revolutions* (Lanham, MD, 2019), pp. 197–199, 234–235; Guang Meihong *et al.*, "1950 nian quango funü laomo xingxiang zai tantao" (A re-exploration of the images of woman labour models in the 1950s), *Shanxi shida xuebao*, 43:5 (2016), pp. 27–31.
27. Spakowski, "Yan'an's Labor Heroines". For the early 1950s, see, for instance, Lan Cun, "'Laodong jiu shi jiefang, douzheng cai you diwei'. Li Shunda nong lin chu mu shengchan hezuoshe funü zhengqu tong gong tong chou de jingguo" ("Work means liberation, but only through struggle one can gain status": The course of the fight for equal pay for equal work by the women of Li Shunda's production cooperative of farming, forestry, animal husbandry and pastoral economy), *Renmin Ribao* (People's Daily), 25 January 1953, hereafter *RMRB*.
28. For female labour models in political functions, see Liu Weifang, "Quanmian jianshe shehuizhuyi shiqi funü canzheng yizheng chutan" (Women's political participation in the period of all-round socialist construction), *Zhonghua nüzi xueyuan xuebao*, 1 (2010), pp. 98–103.

labour models even rose to national fame, owing to the breakthroughs they achieved in their respective field of work. One example from the early 1950s is textile worker Hao Jianxiu, who invented a new method to prevent thread breaking, a serious problem in textile production.[29] In agriculture, Shen Jilan is among the most prominent women labour models, owing to her fight for "equal pay for equal work" (*tong gong tong chou*) in Xigou village.

Shen Jilan was typical in her origins as a poor peasant woman but untypical in her exceptional political career. Born in 1929 into a poor family in Shanxi Province,[30] marriage in 1947 brought her to Xigou, a hotspot for introducing new cooperative forms under the guidance of Li Shunda. Li was the founder and head of the renowned "Production cooperative of farming, forestry, animal husbandry and pastoral economy of Li Shunda" and also among the most prominent male labour models of the time. In 1952, Li appointed Shen Jilan to the post of co-leader of the cooperative, probably for two reasons. First, Shen could work – she had unbound feet that allowed her to move easily, and she was used to working outside the home from the age of fourteen. Second, she was active in the local women's association, which was headed by Li Shunda's mother.[31] Besides, appointing women as co-leaders of cooperatives was a policy supported by regional authorities.[32] As co-leader, Shen was responsible for mobilizing Xigou's women for work in the fields. She succeeded, but it was only the principle of equal pay that convinced the village's women that work outside the home was worthwhile. Shen Jilan's unrelenting fight for equal pay for equal work soon gained her national fame.[33] Owing to her role and achievements in Xigou and the publicity she received, she was

---

29. Thousands of articles featured the "Hao Jianxiu method". Hao was even mentioned by Zhang Yun in her speech to the Third World Congress of Women; see "Wo daibiaotuan futuanzhang Zhang Yun zai shijie funü dahui yanshuo. Zhongguo funü yonghu heping jiejue guoji wenti" (Speech to the World Congress of Women by Zhang Yun, the vice head of China's delegation: The women of China support the peaceful solution of international problems), *RMRB*, 12 June 1953.

30. For monographic biographies of Shen Jilan, see Mai Tianhe, *Bense rensheng. Shen Jilan* (A life with a distinctive character: Shen Jilan) (Taiyuan, 2007); Zhong gong Shanxi sheng weiyuan xuanchuanbu (Propaganda department of the party committee of Shanxi province) (ed.), "Shiji renmin daibiao. Shen Jilan" (The delegate of a century: Shen Jilan) (Beijing, 2014). For interviews with Shen Jilan and oral history protocols, see Ma Shexiang, "Fu jin yi wang 60 nian. Danren li jie quanguo renda daibiao jingli he ganshou – Shen Jilan fangwenlu" (Reflecting on the past 60 years in the light of the present: The experience and feelings of a NPC delegate of several legislative periods – an interview with Shen Jilan), *Dang de wenxian*, 6 (2009), pp. 106–109; "Duihua Shen Jilan" (A dialogue with Shen Jilan), *Nan feng chuang*, 3 (2006), p. 21; Liu Chan, "Liang hui 'huohua shi' Shen Jilan. Wo de jibie shi nongmin" (Shen Jilan, "living fossil" of the two conferences: My rank is that of a peasant), *Funü shenghuo*, 3 (2016), pp. 7–9; Li Zhongyuan, Liu Xiaoli (eds), *Koushu Shen Jilan* (An oral history of Shen Jilan) (Beijing, 2017).

31. Song, "Jiazhi, zhidu, shijian", pp. 121–122.

32. *Ibid.*, p. 118.

33. For rural women's mobilization for production and the general notion of "labour is glorious", see Guang Meihong, "Guannian, jingsai, zhidu. 20 shiji 50 niandai Zhongguo nongcun funü canjia

Figure 1. Exhibit in the Shen Jilan exhibition hall in Xigou, Shanxi Province: "The path of Shen Jilan, delegate to the First to Thirteenth National People's Congress". Photograph by the author.

nominated as a labour model and appointed to a number of functions in the Women's Federation and related bodies and activities at the regional and national level.[34] In 1953, she became a delegate to the Second National Conference of Women in Beijing, and she was even appointed delegate to the first NPC in 1954. She held this position until the end of her life, and is actually the only person in China who was a delegate to the NPC for thirteen successive legislative periods (see Figure 1). After Li Shunda's death in 1983, Shen became head of Xigou and started to develop new economic opportunities for the village. When I visited Xigou in October 2019, she was still involved in village affairs. She passed away in June 2020 at the age of ninety.

Shen Jilan was a prominent person in public discourse. In the reform period, she became the object of a number of films and plays.[35] Her career was

laodong dongyin zai tantao" (Concepts, competition, system: Re-discussing the motives for rural women to participate in work in the 1950s), *Gu jin nongye*, 3 (2013), pp. 90–96.

34. For the long list of positions and distinctions Shen received, see Chang Yinting, "Gongheguo jianzhengzhe de shengming zuyi. Yi quanguo laomo Shen Jilan wei zhongxin" (The footprints of the life of a witness of the republic: A case study of national labour model Shen Jilan), *Shanxi nongye daxue xuebao*, 10 (2018), pp. 30–37, 31–32.

35. For examples, see Feng Xiang, "Jiang zhengzhi he jiaoxuefei. 'Shen Jilan' de ganga" (Talking about politics and paying tuition: The dilemma of [the movie] "Shen Jilan"), *Nanfang zhoumo*, 3 April 2014.

Figure 2. Statue of Shen Jilan in the Labour Hero Park in Changzhi, Shanxi Province. Photograph by the author.

crowned in 2019 with the Medal of the Republic, China's highest order of honour, and the local government of Pingshun County continues to honour her and other labour models of the region with a labour model park in Changzhi (see Figure 2). A museum in Xigou is exclusively dedicated to Shen Jilan's life. Critics, on the other hand, point to her peasant background and lack of education, which, they claim, made Shen a "living fossil" in the NPC.[36] Furthermore, her statement that, as an NPC deputy, she never voted against the Party, made her the object of public debate.[37] Democracy activists call her a "voting machine", and particularly excoriate her for voting

36. Liu, "Liang hui 'huohua shi' Shen Jilan".
37. Xu Zhongqiang, "Shen Jilan gai bu gai dang renda daibiao" (Should Shen Jilan be a delegate to the NPC), *Shidai renwu*, 4 (2013), p. 76.

in favour of the infamous Hong Kong security law on 28 May 2020, her last act of voting.[38]

The battle for equal pay took place in spring 1952 while Li Shunda was away for several months on an inspection tour of the Soviet Union. Only a few women were willing to join agricultural activities because they could not see how they would benefit from work outside the household – which they were expected to do on top of domestic work. Those who participated in work realized that they did not receive the same number of work points as male team members.[39] The battle for equal pay was fought in several rounds. First, Shen Jilan convinced the women of her village that working outside their homes would enhance their status in the family. She then convinced her male co-villagers that women deserved the same number of work points as men, thus giving women an incentive not to return to their homes. The resistance of male villagers was based on the claim that women worked less, performed worse, or took on less-demanding tasks. Step by step, the women of the village proved that they were able to perform as well as male team members in the same physically demanding tasks, and step by step the male villagers had to acknowledge that women could work as hard as them. Some peasants revealed a malicious streak, arbitrarily assigning tasks to women. Eventually, Xigou's women got the same pay, and upon Li Shunda's return, the arrangement was changed so that women received equal pay but were released from those jobs that were physically too demanding. In addition, the village introduced several rules and services to protect and support women. Consequently, relations between men and women improved, and "beautiful and happy families" were the result in Xigou, Shen Jilan's in-laws among them.[40]

This local event became public through a long report in *Renmin Ribao* (*RMRB*; People's Daily), a national paper and the CCP's mouthpiece, on 25 January 1953.[41] This was because Lan Cun, the author of the report, had

---

38. Shen Hua, "Zhongguo Renda 'jushou jiqi' Shen Jilan shen hou de huati (The deceased Shen Jilan, "voting machine" of China's NPC, as a topic of conversation), Voice of America, 6 July 2020. Available at: https://www.voachinese.com/a/shenjilan-npc-reform-07062020/5491539.html; last accessed 25 September 2020; and "China Detains Activists Over Criticism of the Ruling Communist Party", Radio Free Asia, 3 October 2019. Available at: https://www.rfa.org/english/news/china/criticism-10032019140459.html; last accessed 25 September 2020.

39. The introduction of the work point system was an important element in the collectivization of agriculture. Women benefited from the system because their work became countable and visible and was no longer hidden in the family economy. Countable work raised their status in the family and was the condition for exposing unequal remuneration at village level. See also Spakowski, "Yan'an's Labor Heroines".

40. Lan, "'Laodong jiu shi jiefang'".

41. *Ibid*. It was also published in "Women of New China" (Ma Ming, "Nongye shengchan zhanxian shang de nü mofan Shen Jilan" (Shen Jilan, female model at the front of agricultural production), *Xin Zhongguo funü*, 5 (1953), pp. 17–18.

been present at a local meeting where Shen had related her experience of mobilizing women for work. More importantly, the national government obviously *wanted* these events to become public. Indeed, events in Xigou mirrored a conflict that existed in other pioneer villages, where the work point system had been introduced and women were mobilized for production but earned only half the points of men. At the time when the work point system was to become national policy, the government obviously used events in Xigou to promote gender equality as a core feature of socialist society and as an incentive for women to work outside their homes. It was only in 1978, though, that the principle of equal pay for equal work was introduced into China's constitution.[42]

What was at stake when Shen Jilan demanded equal pay for women? Reports on the events in Xigou, a village famous for its pioneer role in China's transition to socialism,[43] and similar events in other places, demonstrate how grave the problem was and that it was actually work, together with marriage,[44] that decided on privileges and power in the family.[45] To mobilize women for production was a break with tradition, and had been put into effect in communist base areas in 1943.[46] Unlike the 1940s, however, when the family was still the basic unit of production, the cooperatives of the 1950s came with a system of remuneration through work points that made women's work countable. Women's contribution to the family income could no longer be hidden in a family's budget, and each family member's share in the household income affected her or his status within the family. Men's fierce resistance against women's entrance into the workforce and against the principle of equal pay reflects their fear of losing their status as household heads and sole decision-makers in family matters. Even if individual political leaders used women's mobilization for work as a mere tool for purposes other than their liberation, it was a policy that radically affected the traditional gender order. This traditional order was not easily transformed,

42. Song, "Jiazhi, zhidu, shijian"; the author debunks a number of myths related to Shen Jilan and her fight for equal pay, in particular Shen's supposed pioneering role and the claim that equal pay became a constitutional principle in 1954.

43. Chang, "Gongheguo jianzhengzhe de shengming zuyi"; "Xiang Shen Jilan xuexi" (Learning from Shen Jilan), *Shanxi nongmin*, 27 December 1952, and Lan, "'Laodong jiu shi jiefang'" emphasize this fact as proof of how grave the problem of women's discrimination was.

44. Neil Diamant, *Revolutionizing the Family: Politics, Love, and Divorce in Urban and Rural China, 1949–1968* (Berkeley, CA, 2000).

45. See the report on Wuxiang County in Shanxi Province, where the fight for equal pay was "a process of bitter struggle". Men are reported to have behaved in a particularly obstinate way and women seem to have developed a group consciousness. When the men demanded ever-increasing proof of women's capacities, women asked in return whether men could bear children; see "Nan nü tong gong tong chou fahui le funü qianli" (Men and women's equal pay for equal work brings women's potential into play), *Shanxi ribao*, 16 January 1953.

46. Spakowski, "Yan'an's Labor Heroines". For women and work before that time, see Guang, "Guannian, jingsai, zhidu".

though; indeed, it required "bitter struggle".[47] Newspaper articles reporting women's fight for equal pay noted success in some places but failure in others. Women succeeded usually as a consequence of struggles similar to those in Xigou.[48] Besides equal pay, women's increasing share in production (in Xigou, their work amounted to thirty-five per cent of the total sum of work days),[49] the high percentage of locally appointed women labour models, women's appointment to the post of co-leader of cooperatives, and more "harmonious" relations between husbands and wives and daughters- and mothers-in-law were presented as indicators of success.[50] In other places, the problem persisted, even though the Party pushed hard for the principle of equal pay.[51]

The basic lesson to be drawn from the story of Xigou's women was that true realization of women's rights depended on their own struggle. Indeed, the title of the *RMRB* article "Work Means Liberation, but Only through Struggle Can One Gain Status", a quote from Shen Jilan repeated in other papers,[52] indicated that the promise of liberation in state ideology was the socialist framework for a feminist struggle for rights. The concrete (and measurable) goal for women was status, but gaining status required them to directly confront their husbands and male co-villagers. The struggle for status, then, was called a matter of "self-liberation".[53] Women had to free themselves

---

47. "Xiang Shen Jilan xuexi"; "Nan nü tong gong tong chou". For a similar struggle for equal pay in the production of cotton, see Gao, "The Silver Flower Contest", pp. 602–603.

48. He *et al.*, "'Tong gong tong chou' yu funü jiefang. Yi nongye hezuohua shiqi de Heshun xian wei li" ("Equal pay for equal work" and the liberation of women: A case study of Heshun County during the period of organizing agricultural cooperatives), *Shandong nüzi xueyuan xuebao*, 4:140 (2018), pp. 50–56; Li Jinzheng and Liu Jie, "Laodong, pingdeng, xingbie. Jitihua shiqi Taihang shanqu nan nü 'tong gong tong chou'" (Work, equality, gender: Men's and women's "equal pay for equal work" in the mountain areas of Taihang during the period of collectivization), *Zhonggong dangshi yanjiu*, 7 (2012), pp. 53–61.

49. Lan, "'Laodong jiu shi jiefang'".

50. *Ibid.*; Peng Fei, "Nongcun funü canjia shengchan de yi mian qi" (A flag in peasant women's participation in production), *Shanxi ribao*, 26 December 1952. See also He *et al.*, "'Tong gong tong chou' yu funü jiefang" on the positive effect of the policy on women's access to positions in government and the Party. For the combination of mobilizing women for work and establishing democratic and "harmonious" family structures, see Spakowski, "Yan'an's Labor Heroines". The necessary link between both strategies is also emphasized in "Huzhu shengchan zhong nan nü bixue tong gong tong chou" (In production through mutual aid men and women have to receive equal pay for equal work), *Shanxi ribao*, 26 December 1952. See also Shen Jilan, "Gei renmin dang hao daibiao" (Being a good representative of the people), *Shanxi nongmin*, 21 August 1954. She speaks of her "harmonious family" where everything is negotiated between family members and her parents-in-law treat her with an attitude of respect.

51. In Wuxiang County, only a minority of cooperatives gave women equal pay ("Nan nü tong gong tong chou"). According to He *et al.*, "'Tong gong tong chou' yu funü jiefang", p. 55, the principle was realized only in model cooperatives.

52. Peng, "Nongcun funü canjia shengchan"; "Xiang Shen Jilan xuexi".

53. See, for instance, Peng, "Nongcun funü canjia shengchan"; "Xiang Shen Jilan xuexi". "Huzhu shengchan zhong" speaks of women's "mentality of considering themselves as weak" (*zi ruo sixiang*).

from a traditional understanding of their role and, step by step, prove their abilities vis-à-vis men. The particular sequence of events – with women meeting ever increasing challenges from male peasants – makes the story of Shen Jilan's fight for equal pay a manual of how to approach gender conflict at the local level.[54] In a nutshell, newspapers made women's status a matter of performance. The burden of proof lay with the women,[55] and the standard was men's.[56] This strategy of education fitted the Party's identification of the causes of the practice of unequal pay, namely the "feudal" mindset still effective in agrarian China.[57] One article classified the conflict as a "struggle within the working population" ("laodong renmin neibu de douzheng"),[58] an equivalent to "side contradictions" in Marxism. Defining the problem as a mere side contradiction and relegating its solution to women's own struggle certainly left the transformation of the gender order incomplete.

Even though the central state intervened only half-heartedly at the village level, it set up a legal framework that truly enhanced the status of women.[59] Indeed, among the first laws promulgated by the newly founded state were those that were intended to enhance the status of women: the Marriage Law of 1950, which gave women the right to divorce and prohibited marriage practices that violated women's freedom of marriage, and the Land Reform Law of the same year, which stipulated that each individual, irrespective of gender, was entitled to the same acreage of land. Many additional stipulations and services improved women's lives, in particular health and education. Finally, state propaganda advocated equality and new roles for women in public life.

For Shen Jilan, the events in Xigou were the starting point for her career in the Women's Federation, which forced her to leave Xigou. This is also why Shen, an icon of women's fight for equality, did not really identify with this

---

54. This is also true for a picture story published in the daily newspaper *Shanxi nongmin* (Peasants of Shanxi) in October 1953: Zhang *et al.*, "Shen Jilan", *Shanxi nongmin*, 17, 21, and 24 October 1953. The paper obviously wanted to reach illiterates among the population. In "Nü gongchandang yuan Jia Guoyong tongzhi lingdao funü zhengqi tong lao tong chou" (Female Party member Jia Guoyong leads women in their struggle for equal pay for equal work), *Shanxi ribao*, 11 November 1953, a woman is portrayed who took Shen Jilan as a model to fight for equal pay also in her village. This fight very much resembles the one in Xigou.

55. This is particularly evident in the editorial of *Shanxi nongmin*, which calls for learning from Shen Jilan ("Xiang Shen Jilan xuexi").

56. Some Chinese scholars are particularly critical of women's adaptation to men's standards; see, for instance, Liu, "'Nan nü pingdeng' de yihua yu wudu".

57. Ma, "Nongye shengchan zhanxian shang de Shen Jilan"; "Huzhu shengchan zhong"; "Xiang Shen Jilan xuexi" compares this feudal mindset with a "wandering ghost" that lives on in people's "backward brains".

58. "Huzhu shengchan zhong". See also "Xiang Shen Jilan xuexi", an editorial that speaks of "social reform" (*shehui gaige*).

59. For state policy on women after 1949, see Hershatter, *Women and China's Revolutions*.

career. From interviews, we know that her genuine space of interaction was Xigou and her primary field of identification was "work" (*laodong*), manifest in her role as a labour model. She respected Li Shunda and "the Party" and appreciated her in-law family as her major network of support.[60] Asked about her appointment to the position of provincial head of the Women's Federation in 1973, she said:

> I didn't feel I could do that. I have no education; it was the Party which fostered me to be a labour model. Labour model, labour model – only if you take the lead in work you are called labour model. How could I be called labour model if I was sitting in an office and not working?[61]

In another interview, she said: "As a labour model, I do have to work. And as an NPC delegate for Xigou, I cannot leave Xigou."[62] Shen Jilan's stance confirms the fact that feminism cannot be easily isolated from socialist transformation.

(WOMEN) LABOUR MODELS AND THE PARTY

While Shen Jilan's fight for equal pay was a village affair that was limited to local Party members, her career as a labour model and representative of women's issues brought her onto the national stage and into direct contact with the Party leadership. From interviews, we know that assuming roles on the national stage lay beyond the horizon of labour models, and meeting Mao Zedong in person was an absolute highlight in their lives. These events are all the more important because they explain labour models' loyalty to the Party as well as their symbolic function in the Party's efforts to legitimize communist rule.

Labour models had good reason to be loyal to the Party. In interviews, Shen Jilan and her labour model sisters express deep gratitude for the tremendous improvement that revolution effected in their individual lives and the Party's care for their concerns as people with particularly poor origins.[63] At a fundamental level, liberation to them meant being able to earn a living. In addition, it brought release from repressive family structures and humiliating practices in

60. See, for instance, Ma, "Fu jin yi wang 60 nian"; Xia Lina, "Shen Jilan. Renmin daibiao dahui de 'huohuashi'" (Shen Jilan: The "living fossil" of the National People's Congress), *Zhongguo Renda*, 25 May 2009, pp. 50–51; Chang, "Gongheguo jianzhengzhe de shengming zuyi".
61. "Duihua Shen Jilan".
62. Ma, "Fu jin yi wang 60 nian", p. 108.
63. See, for instance, the interviews with Shen Jilan in Zhu Xianli *et al.*, "Ganxiang yu yuanwang" (Reflections and aspirations), *Nongye kexue tongxun*, 30 March 1954, pp. 509–511; Tian Liu, "Lai zi renmin, weile renmin" (From the people, for the people), *RMRB*, 18 September 1954; Ma, "Fu jin yi wang 60 nian", and one with Shanghai textile labour model Yi Shijuan (Xia Lina, "Zhenzang ban ge duo shiji de minzhu jiyi" (Democratic memories that were collected for more than half a century), *Zhongguo Renda*, 16 November 2014, pp. 53–55).

the workplace.[64] Representatives of the state and the Party even instilled them with a sense of self-esteem. Women labour models spoke (and still speak) of the dignity installed in them and the honour they received. Shen Jilan stated: "The Party and Chairman Mao gave us so much attention and care, what reason did we have not to work hard for this heroic country and this mighty Party?"[65] These women's commitment to their tasks can probably best be explained with a mix of benefits (material, symbolic, legal). The symbolic gains and the "dignity" that women from the lower strata of society felt seem to have played a prominent role in this mix.[66]

Interaction with Mao Zedong was marked by mutual recognition and was reported in newspapers as evidence for the particularly close relationship between Mao and the people. This charismatic bond was a matter of careful orchestration by the Party and practised from the beginning of the labour hero movement in the 1940s. Indeed, labour heroes' glorification of Mao was an important element in the establishment of a Mao cult.[67] Shen Jilan is a case in point, and her reverence for Mao is most evident in a report where she mentions her direct meeting with Mao in 1953. Mao appeared to her "as if a fresh red flower was blossoming out".[68] He told her "Work hard!" – words, she said, she would never forget.[69]

Charisma was a pillar of political legitimization that was meant to justify the exceptional status of Mao Zedong. It was closely intertwined with two more pillars of legitimacy, namely ideology – in particular the claim to have "liberated" the Chinese people and to have made the working class the "master" (*zhurenweng*) of the state[70] – and formal representation through the National People's Congress. For all three pillars, labour models figured as representatives of the working class.

Indeed, the sudden prominence of labour models, who typically originated from exceptionally poor conditions and lacked an education,[71] constituted a radical reversal of traditional social hierarchies. Biographies of labour models such as Shen

---

64. Women labour models in industry usually mention the humiliation of body searches and the foreman system. In the countryside, women were humiliated by husbands and mothers-in-law (see, for instance, Lan, "'Laodong jiu shi jiefang'").
65. Ma, "Fu jin yi wang 60 nian", p. 108.
66. See also the notion of the "decent society" in Avishai Margalit's *The Decent Society* (Cambridge, MA, 1996).
67. Spakowski, "Moving Labor Heroes Center Stage".
68. The red flower is a typical metaphor in the Mao cult. It was also employed in a letter titled "A red flower is blossoming in our heart" (Women xinli kaile yi duo hong hua) sent to Mao Zedong by the women of Li Shunda's cooperative; see "Women xinli kaile yi duo hong hua" (A red flower is blossoming in our heart), *Xin Zhongguo funü*, 7 (1953), pp. 12–13.
69. Shen, "Gei renmin dang hao daibiao".
70. Zhu *et al.*, "Ganxiang yu yuanwang", p. 509. For the discourse of "masters of the country", see Zhang Jishun, "Creating 'Masters of the Country' in Shanghai and Beijing: Discourse and the 1953–54 Local People's Congress Elections", *China Quarterly*, 220 (2014), pp. 1071–1091.
71. Guang *et al.*, "1950 nian quango funü".

Jilan provided examples of *fanshen* (literally, to turn the body), or liberation at an individual level, which testified to the successes of revolution as a collective event led by the Party. These biographies were marked by a strong contrast between people's miserable lives in the old society and their happiness in the new.[72]

Shen Jilan and other labour models also mattered in the process of establishing "representative" political forms. The NPC is China's parliament and nominally the highest organ of state power. True power lies with the Party, of course, which, in the early 1950s, sought to establish an image of the NPC as a true parliament and an image of NPC delegates as true representatives of the people. In the first NPC, which convened from 15 to 28 September 1954 and was of particular importance because it passed the first constitution of the PRC, a considerable number of delegates were labour models, three of them coming from Pingshun County: Xigou's Li Shunda and Shen Jilan and Guo Yu'en from Chuandi.[73] Nominating labour models for the NPC constituted the ultimate act of recognition, considering that they had only recently been relieved from extreme poverty and powerlessness.

Labour models were preferred subjects for interviews and features in news coverage of the first NPC.[74] Articles highlighted the sense of "honour" (*guangrong*) – a key term in these texts – and responsibility these labour models felt.[75] One such text, "Being a Good Representative of the People" (*Gei renmin dang hao daibiao*),[76] appeared under the name of Shen Jilan.[77] Shen reports how she received the news about her appointment and immediately rushed to Taiyuan, the capital of Shanxi, where delegates of the provincial People's Congress wanted to meet her. A long section is dedicated to the departure scene in Xigou, where villagers support her, help her collect her luggage, and accompany her. Shen appears as a person who is part of a community that she can rely on and that also understands the importance of representative politics. She is a deputy who really comes from the people. On her journey, she reflects on the past, listing the steps in her career from

72. Zhu *et al.*, "Ganxiang yu yuanwang"; Tian, "Lai zi renmin, weile renmin"; Shen, "Gei renmin dang hao daibiao".

73. Ma, "Fu jin yi wang 60 nian", p. 107. This shows the exceptional status of Pingshun and Xigou for agricultural policies at the national level. Among the twenty-four delegates to the NPC from Shanxi, eleven seem to have been labour models in 1954 or later.

74. In Tian, "Lai zi renmin, weile renmin", five out of six delegates mentioned by their names were labour models, Li Shunda and Shen Jilan among them. Zhu *et al.*, "Ganxiang yu yuanwang" is a collective interview with four labour models, again including Li Shunda and Shen Jilan.

75. Zhu *et al.*, "Ganxiang yu yuanwang"; Tian, "Lai zi renmin, weile renmin". An *RMRB* article pointed out that the draft of the constitution had been under discussion for three months already and that "(l)abor model delegates from the fields of industry and agriculture discussed it particularly conscientiously" (Tian, "Lai zi renmin, weile renmin").

76. Shen, "Gei renmin dang hao daibiao".

77. Since it was only later in her life that Shen learned to read and write, she must at least have been "helped" with writing the text.

joining the Party to her participation in the Second National Assembly of Women – which was also the occasion when she met Mao Zedong – to her participation in the World Conference of Women in Copenhagen in 1953. Besides the list of remarkable events in her life, she also provides a typical story of *fanshen* and women's liberation.[78] The fight for equal pay is not mentioned in this and other texts featuring her as an NPC deputy.

Texts such as this one try to portray the NPC as a true body of representation and its delegates true representatives of the common people. They also emphasize its revolutionary nature by highlighting the humble origins of its members and in particular their illiteracy (but not their gender).[79] However, readers are left in doubt about whether labour model delegates can really meet the high demands of parliamentary work. This is a sign of the incompleteness of socialist transformation.

In 2006, Shen Jilan gave an interview that focused on her role as NPC delegate, and she admitted her political naivety at the time of the First NPC. Asked how she intended to participate in the deliberation and administration of state affairs, she responded:

> I am a village woman. At that time, I couldn't even read and write, I just wanted to see Chairman Mao. When I eventually met with him, I was so excited that I couldn't say a single word. Tears were running from my eyes. Giving my vote to Chairman Mao meant that my mission was accomplished. How could I make any suggestions?[80]

It was her role as NPC delegate that provoked critical questions in Reform China and immediately after her death.[81]

WORKING WOMEN AND THE SUPERIORITY OF SOCIALISM

The most extraordinary event in Shen Jilan's life was probably her participation in the Third World Congress of Women,[82] organized by the Women's International Democratic Federation (WIDF),[83] and hosted in Copenhagen

78. For Shen Jilan as an example of women's liberation, see also Zhu *et al.*, "Ganxiang yu yuanwang", and Tian, "Lai zi renmin, weile renmin".

79. See, for instance, Tian, "Lai zi renmin, weile renmin".

80. "Duihua Shen Jilan".

81. See above.

82. For a full account of her trip to Copenhagen, see Mai, *Bense rensheng. Shen Jilan*, pp. 68–74.

83. For the history of the WIDF, see Francisca de Haan, "Continuing Cold War Paradigms in Western Historiography of Transnational Women's Organisations: The Case of the Women's International Democratic Federation (WIDF)", *Women's History Review*, 19:4 (2010), pp. 547–573; Francisca de Haan, "The Women's International Democratic Federation (WIDF): History, Main Agenda and Contributions (1945–1991)", *Women and Social Movements International, 1840 to the Present*. Available at: https://alexanderstreet.com/products/women-and-social-movements-international-1840-present; last accessed 15 June 2016; and Elisabeth Armstrong, "Before

from 5 to 10 June 1953.[84] The Chinese delegation went to Copenhagen by train, with a stop-over in Moscow, where the group was shown the sights of the achievements of socialism.[85] In the historical context of celebrating the friendship between China and the Soviet Union, propagating the Soviet Union as a model for China and emphasizing the differences between the two camps in the Cold War, Shen Jilan, a simple peasant woman of Xigou village in northern China, became a messenger for socialism and socialist feminism. Reports on the event further demonstrate that work, women's right to work, and the principle of equal pay were the core elements in the strategy of socialist feminism and its competition with the capitalist world.

WIDF was founded in Paris in 1945 as "a progressive, 'left-feminist' international umbrella organization, with an emphasis on peace, women's rights, anti-colonialism and anti-racism" and a "strong association with the communist world".[86] Francisca de Haan identifies it as "the largest and probably most influential international women's organization of the post-1945 era".[87] The All-China Democratic Women's Federation (ACDWF), later renamed the All-China Women's Federation, was among the particularly large member organizations.[88] The meeting in 1953 was the third of its kind and assembled 1,900 women from sixty-seven countries.[89] The Chinese delegation of thirty members was selected by the Second National Conference of Women and led by Cai Chang, Li Dequan, and Zhang Yun, who all held leading positions in both ACDWF and WIDF. In the list of participants published in *RMRB*, Shen Jilan appears as "agricultural labour model, vice-head of Shanxi Province Li Shunda's production cooperative of farming, forestry, animal husbandry and pastoral economy". Her equivalent in industry was Sun Xiaoju, a railway labour model.[90]

Bandung: The Anti-Imperialist Women's Movement in Asia and the Women's International Democratic Federation, *Signs*, 41:2 (2016), pp. 305–331.

84. Basic information on the conference (dates, number of participants) is taken from de Haan, "The Women's International Democratic Federation". Information in Chinese texts slightly deviate. A better understanding of China's role in the WIDF and the Copenhagen conference would have to be based on archive material, which, unfortunately, is not accessible.

85. For the trip to Copenhagen, see Mai, *Bense rensheng. Shen Jilan*, pp. 68–74; Zhong gong, "Shiji renmin daibiao", pp. 31–34.

86. De Haan, "The Women's International Democratic Federation", p. 1.

87. *Ibid.*, p. 1.

88. *Ibid.*

89. *Ibid.*, Table 2.

90. For the list of participants, see "Zhongguo di er ci quanguo funü daibiao dahui xuanchu wo guo chuxi shijie funü dahui de daibiaotuan" (China's Second National Congress of Women elects the Chinese delegation to the World Congress of Women), *RMRB*, 27 April 1953. A report on the departure of the delegation from Beijing speaks of twenty-four members and eighteen service staff; see "Chuxi shijie funü dahui Zhongguo funü daibiaotuan qicheng" (Departure of the delegation of Chinese women who participate in the World Congress of Women), *RMRB*, 20 May 1953.

Chinese coverage of the event was extensive and included translated *Pravda* articles and the speeches of delegates from countries other than China. Readers of *RMRB* and *Xin Zhongguo funü* (Women of New China) learned that the assembly was an international and thus diverse and colourful event, but that the world and women's lives therein were divided into two: "one world, two ways of life".[91] In countries of the capitalist world, colonies, or dependent countries, women were in a "miserable situation" (*beican chujing*), whereas in "the Soviet Union, China, and other countries of people's democracy", they were leading a "happy life" (*xingfu shenghuo*).[92] Articles with an international focus gave the "big picture" of this divided world. They focused on work and made women's right to work and the principle of equal pay a yardstick for assessing their situation. This is also true for the final resolution, which put provisions related to work at the top of a long list of rights.[93] The ideal of these and similar texts was a working woman who fully participated in the economic and political life of her country.

A second type were articles on the situation of women in China that substantiated the superiority of socialism with facts. This is the case with speeches by leaders of the Chinese delegation, Li Dequan and Zhang Yun, which, the papers claimed, were enthusiastically received by the audience of the congress.[94] While Li Dequan outlined the situation of women in China, Zhang Yun focused on matters of war and peace, with only brief sections on China's economic recovery after the war and women's contribution to economic progress. But even Zhang mentioned two labour models by name.[95] My emphasis here is on Li Dequan's speech because it is a good example of

---

91. Shen Zijiu, "Shijie funü dahui buji" (Notes on the World Congress of Women), *Xin Zhongguo funü*, 8 (1953), pp. 18–22, 20.

92. Lu Cui, "Yonghu shijie funü dahui de zhaokai. Zai Zhongguo di er ci quanguo funü daibiao dahui shang de fayan zhaiyao" (Embrace the convocation of the World Congress of Women: Excerpts of the speech at China's Second National Congress of Women), *RMRB*, 26 April 1953; Shen, "Shijie funü dahui buji", "Shijie funü dahui (jieshao)" (The World Congress of Women (introduction)), *Xin Zhongguo funü*, 7 (1953), pp. 6–7; "Ba shijie funü dahui de jingshen daihuiqi" (Bringing back the spirit of the World Congress of Women), *Xin Zhongguo funü*, 8 (1953), pp. 23f. For the quotes, see "Shijie funü dahui (jieshao)", p. 7. For more articles and speeches in *RMRB*, see the issues of 5, 7, 8, 10, 11, 13, and 15 May.

93. "Shijie funü dahui tongguo de xuanyan ji jueyi" (Resolution and decisions adopted by the World Congress of Women), *Xin Zhongguo funü*, 7 (1953), pp. 5–6.

94. For the enthusiasm of the audience, including standing ovations for Li Dequan, see Shen, "Shijie funü dahui buji", p. 21.

95. "Wo daibiaotuan". Zhang Yun gives the example of Hao Jianxiu, the most prominent labour model in the textile industry of the early 1950s, and Gong Zhaozhi, a technical worker in the famous Anyang Steel Company. The latter is introduced as an example of all those women who work in fields conventionally regarded as men's work. For both examples, Zhang highlights the inventiveness of women in production and their important contribution to a rise in quality and quantity in the production of the respective field.

official Chinese rhetoric on women under socialism and because she mentioned Shen Jilan by name.[96]

Li, the first Minister of Health in the PRC and a woman with roots in a pre-1949 social and cultural elite,[97] spoke to the delegates as a representative of "the women of New China", and the contrast between "new" and "old" constituted the framework of her speech:

> As is well known, in semicolonial-semifeudal Old China, women didn't have any political or economic rights or the right to education; they didn't even enjoy rudimentary human rights. They had the double status of being oppressed and being enslaved [...] Today, China's women are the master of New China who enjoy the same rights as men, they are active builders of free and happy New China.[98]

Li's long report included sections on the equality of women and men as a constitutional right; women in leadership positions at all political levels; women's right to vote; women's economic participation and the rights and welfare provisions pertaining to their status in the world of production; education; the marriage law; and, finally, the improved situation of children. Summing up, Li could claim spectacular progress for China's women: "In only three years our country and the women of our country forged ahead not for a few years or decades, but for an entire era!"[99]

Shen Jilan and her equivalent in industry, Sun Xiaoju, figured as examples of the advancement of women under socialism. In the brief paragraph on women in rural China, Li Dequan mentioned women's right to land, their equality in agricultural production, equal pay for equal work, and women's enthusiasm for learning agricultural and administrative skills, resulting in responsible positions and government awards.[100] To Shen Jilan, she devoted only one short sentence: "Shen Jilan, a delegate to this congress, is a woman who in the old society was oppressed and looked down upon, but now she is the vice head of the famous production cooperative of farming, forestry, animal husbandry and pastoral economy of Li Shunda."[101] Speaking on behalf of Shen Jilan, Li Dequan rendered her a symbol of socialist China's progressiveness. She mentioned her as co-head of a cooperative named after its male leader, Li Shunda, and omitted her fight for equal pay altogether. Obviously, Shen

---

96. "Wo guo chuxi shijie funü dahui daibiaotuan tuanzhang Li Dequan zai shijie funü dahui shang de yanshuo" (Speech to the World Congress of Women by Li Dequan, head of the Chinese delegation to the World Congress of Women), *RMRB*, 10 June 1953.
97. Kate Merkel-Hess, "A New Woman and Her Warlord: Li Dequan, Feng Yuxiang, and the Politics of Intimacy in Twentieth-Century China", *Frontiers of History in China*, 11:3 (2016), pp. 431–457.
98. "Wo guo chuxi".
99. *Ibid.*
100. For the under-representation of peasant women's interests in the WIDF and the efforts of Asian women to get them on its agenda, see Armstrong, "Before Bandung".
101. "Wo guo chuxi".

Jilan was not allowed a voice on the international stage and certainly did not claim one. In interviews during her later years, she admitted: "Back then, I followed the others, I didn't dare to speak much."[102] Furthermore, she described herself as a misfit in the delegation, lacking knowledge of diplomatic decorum, for the first time in her life wearing a *qipao*,[103] not knowing how to paint her face, and not managing to walk in high-heeled shoes.[104] Biographers also highlight the gap between Shen Jilan's rural origin and the modern urban environment she found herself in,[105] and they mention the gifts Shen bought with the pocket money she received at the stopovers on the trip: in Berlin, a doll that could blink its eyes, and a couple of toy cars and rubber balls in Moscow.[106] Shen Jilan might have symbolized the liberation of women in China, but China's representation on the international stage was left to an educated and sophisticated elite – yet another element of incomplete socialist transformation.

In the travel report published under her name in the national magazine *Xin Zhongguo funü*,[107] Shen Jilan posed as an advocate of the superiority of socialism, based on her tour through Moscow and the insights she gained at the congress. Among the railway workers she spotted from the window of the train to Moscow, a majority were women. She stated: "Indeed, in the Soviet Union women do the same work as men; their life is very happy." Moscow educated her on the boons of progress; and the congress provided her with insights into the lives of women outside China, those from the capitalist, colonial, and semi-colonial world, who "are oppressed like we were before liberation", and those from socialist and "new-democratic" countries, "which are totally different". The principle of equal pay is also an important yardstick in her report, in which the United States appears as a backward country, with women receiving only sixty to seventy per cent of men's wages for the same work.[108] This article and others made women's liberation a matter of social progress, with national models showing others the way towards the future. While the Soviet Union constituted the ultimate model of equality between men and women, China could claim status as a model (*bangyang*) as well.[109] International delegates' enthusiastic reactions to Li Dequan's speech, according to one article,

---

102. Li Zhongyuan, Liu Xiaoli, *Koushu Shen Jilan*, p. 101.
103. A close-fitting dress with high neck and slit skirt. The entire delegation had been equipped with *qipaos*, skirts and high-heeled shoes by the Women's Federation, see Xia, "Shen Jilan", p. 51.
104. Xia, "Shen Jilan", p. 51.
105. Mai, *Bense rensheng. Shen Jilan*, pp. 68–74; Zhong gong, "Shiji renmin daibiao", pp. 31–34.
106. Mai, *Bense rensheng. Shen Jilan*, pp. 73–74.
107. Shen was practically illiterate and not in a position to write these kinds of texts.
108. Shen Jilan (recorded by Yang Yi), "Cong shijie funü dahui guilai" (Back from the world conference of women), *Xin Zhongguo funü*, 8 (1953), p. 18.
109. Shen, "Shijie funü dahui buji", p. 21. See also "Shijie funü dahui (jieshao)", p. 7.

reflected that the situation described by Li "showed them their own future".[110]

CONCLUSION

This article has presented women labour model Shen Jilan in the context of China's socialist transformation. Work was the core field in this process, as the basis of socialist "construction" and the point of departure for creating new social relations. Labour models mattered not so much for their concrete contribution to production but as actors and symbols of change. Women labour models, in particular, represented the new logic of women's liberation through participation in production. They mobilized women for work and figured as examples of successful liberation. Indeed, work, women's obligation or right to work, and gender equality in the workplace were core concerns in feminist discussions at the time, both within and outside China, and they still are.

The example of Shen Jilan also helped to illustrate core features of socialist transformation: its multilayered nature, complexities, contradictions, and incompleteness. Shen Jilan assumed different roles at different levels of interaction, from central actor in the transformation of the gender order at the village level, through representative of the working class in China's new political order, to symbol of the superiority of socialism as a society of gender equality at the international level. To her and to her labour model sisters, women's rights mattered – but so did recognition, honour, and dignity. Women labour models cannot be attributed to clear-cut spheres of either state or society, nor are they clear-cut cases of either instrumentalization or liberation. Shen Jilan was and remains a controversial figure to this day.

---

110. Shen, "Shijie funü dahui buji", p. 21. See also the report on non-Chinese participants who had arrived in China together with the Chinese delegation; a participant from Ecuador is quoted who saw "the Soviet Union and China as examples to learn from" ("Ba shijie funü dahui de jing-shen", p. 23).

IRSH 67 (2022), pp. 155–178 doi:10.1017/S0020859022000062

The WIDF's Work for Women's Rights in the (Post)colonial Countries and the "Soviet Agenda"*

Y U L I A   G R A D S K O V A ⓘ

Department of History, Stockholm University
SE-106 91 Stockholm, Sweden

E-mail: yulia.gradskova@sh.se

ABSTRACT: The primary aim of this article is to problematize the WIDF's interpretations of the rights of women from (post)colonial countries and its tactics in working for and together with these women. It shows that, in the context of rapid geopolitical changes – the growing anti-colonial struggle and Cold War competition – the WIDF had to change its ideology, ways of working, and communication strategies in order to keep its leading position in transnational work for women's rights and to maintain the sympathies of women from countries outside Europe. The main focus is on the contradictions, negotiations, and adjustments inside the WIDF with respect to the new political situation and the demands of women from Africa and Asia, in particular, during the highest period of anticolonial transformation (1950s to early 1970s). This article also pays attention to Soviet ideas on the emancipation of women and, in particular, to the influence of Soviet experiences of emancipating women from non-Slavic (Eastern and Southern) parts of the USSR on the WIDF's perception of and policies for the improvement of the situation of women in Asia and Africa. This article is based primarily on analysis of the WIDF's archival documents preserved in the State Archive of the Russian Federation (GARF) in Moscow, along with the WIDF's official publications.

This article deals with the history of the Women's International Democratic Federation's (WIDF) promotion of women's rights in the countries of Asia and Africa during the period of decolonization; it pays special attention to the Soviet role in this endeavour. The WIDF was created in Paris in 1945, and, as previous research has shown, was an important actor in the anti-

---

* The research that this article is based on was supported by the Swedish Research Council (Vetenskapsrådet, pr. 2017-00947).

imperialist struggle.[1] For example, Elisabeth Armstrong comes to the conclusion that, thanks to the WIDF's activities, "the older playbook of the Western enlightened charity model of feminist internationalism was turned upside down".[2] Katherine McGregor demonstrates that the WIDF facilitated contacts between women's organizations in Algeria and Vietnam during the period of their struggle for independence and that it contributed to global solidarity with these countries.[3] However, neither author pays much attention to the internal process of WIDF decision-making or to the Soviet role in the organization. Yet, both authors carefully state that historical sources on the WIDF's activities are incomplete and invite further discussion of the WIDF's work advancing women's rights and opposing colonialism.

Research on the WIDF (including in connection to women's rights in the "Third World") could not, historically, avoid the question of how much the Soviet Union and countries under state socialism influenced the Federation.[4] Indeed, Francisca de Haan, the first academic to write about this organization, argues that researchers often view it as one of the pro-Soviet organizations without evaluating the WIDF's role more seriously.[5] According to her, this was a continuation of the Cold War in women's history.

However, during recent years, the Cold War itself has started to be explored differently. New approaches to the history of the Cold War stress its global character,[6] while some common developments and even exchanges between the main adversarial actors have been explored.[7] These approaches have

1. See Francisca de Haan, "The Women's International Democratic Federation (WIDF): History, Main Agenda and Contributions (1945–1991)", in *Women and Social Movements (WASI) Online Archive*, edited by Thomas Dublin and Kathryn Kish Sklar, 2012. Available at: http://alexanderstreet.com/products/women-and-social-movements-international; last accessed 19 May 2021; Elisabeth Armstrong, "Before Bandung: The Anti-imperialist Women's Movement in Asia and the Women's International Democratic Federation", *Signs*, 41 (2016), pp. 305–331; Katherine McGregor, "Opposing Colonialism: The Women's International Democratic Federation and Decolonisation struggles in Vietnam and Algeria 1945–1965", *Women's History Review*, 25 (2016), pp. 925–944; Adriana Valobra and Mercedes Yusta (eds), *Queridas Camaradas. Historias iberoamericanas de mujeres comunistas* (Buenos Aires, 2017).
2. Armstrong, "Before Bandung", p. 328.
3. McGregor, "Opposing Colonialism", pp. 931–932.
4. See Francisca de Haan, "Continuing Cold War Paradigms in Western Historiography of Transnational Women's Organizations: The Case of the Women's International Democratic Federation (WIDF)", *Women's History Review*, 19:4 (2010), pp. 547–573; Valobra and Yusta, *Queridas Camaradas*; Celia Donert, "From Communist Internationalism to Human Rights: Gender, Violence and International Law in the Women's International Democratic Federation Mission to North Korea, 1951", *Contemporary European History*, 25 (2016), pp. 313–333.
5. See De Haan, "Continuing Cold War Paradigms".
6. Odd Arne Westad, *The Global Cold War: Third World Interventions and the Making of Our Time* (Cambridge, 2005); Mark Mazower, *No Enchanted Palace: The End of Empire and the Ideological Origins of the United Nations* (Princeton, NJ [etc.], 2008).
7. Giles Scott-Smith & Hans Krabbendam (eds), *The Cultural Cold War in Western Europe, 1945–1960* (London, 2003).

opened the possibility of questioning the WIDF's full dependence on Moscow. Nevertheless, the question of Soviet and "Eastern bloc" political interests in the Federation continues to be important, several researchers have recently indicated that countries under state socialism had a special place in the Federation.[8] My own research also suggests that the Soviet Union attempted to control the WIDF's work.[9] However, I show that these attempts had different modalities and degrees of success in different periods of the WIDF's history. In particular, I demonstrate that Soviet representatives in the WIDF's governing bodies had to use alliances and negotiations to realize their politics. These negotiations were important, not least in relationships with female communists from other countries, including countries of the "Eastern bloc". In this article, I return to the theme of the "Soviet agenda" in the WIDF's promotion of women's rights, with a special focus on a particular period and geographical region: the anti-colonial struggle and early postcolonial transformation of Asia and Africa (late 1940s–early 1970s).

Researchers studying the Soviet Union's relationships with newly independent countries in the postcolonial era and its developmental aid to the countries of Asia and Africa show that Soviet encounters with the postcolonial world, and with women from Asia and Africa, were full of contradictions and misunderstandings.[10] On the one hand, the Soviet achievement of fast industrialization, in particular in Central Asia, as Artemy Kalinovsky shows, was an attractive example for the elites of the newly independent countries of Asia and Africa: many saw industrialization as a path towards the broader transformation of their societies.[11] Changes in women's roles in society were an important component of this transformation.

---

8. See Donert, "From Communist Internationalism to Human Rights", pp. 313–333; Celia Donert, "Whose Utopia? Gender, Ideology and Human Rights at the 1975 World Congress in East Berlin", in Jan Eckel and Samuel Moyn (eds), *The Breakthrough: Human Rights in the 1970s* (Philadelphia, PA, 2014), pp. 68–87; Mercedes Yusta, "The Strained Courtship Between Antifascism and Feminism: from the Women's World Committee (1934) to the Women's International Democratic Federation (1945)", in Hugo Garcia *et al.* (eds), *Rethinking Antifascism* (New York, 2016), pp. 167–186.
9. Yulia Gradskova, *The Women's International Democratic Federation, the Global South and the Cold War: Defending the Rights of Women of the "Whole World"?* (London, 2021), pp. 23–62.
10. In particular, the capacity of the Soviet economy to provide assistance to postcolonial countries is questioned by Oscar Sanchez-Siboney, while James Mark, Artemy Kalinovsky, and Steffi Marung's book shows the complex political and economic reasons for the involvement of East European countries in developmental programmes in the "Third World". See Oscar Sanchez-Siboney, *Red Globalizations* (Cambridge, 2014); James Mark, Artemy Kalinovsky, and Steffi Marung, *Alternative Globalizations: Eastern Europe and the Postcolonial World* (Bloomington, IN, 2020). On women, see Elisabeth Banks, "Sewing Machines for Socialism? Gifts of Development and Disagreement between the Soviet and Mozambican Women's Committees, 1963–87", *Comparative Studies of South Asia, Africa and the Middle East*, 41 (2021), pp. 27–40.
11. Artemy Kalinovsky *Laboratory of Socialist Development: Cold War Politics and Decolonization in Soviet Tajikistan* (Ithaca, NY, 2018), p. 74.

However, whether the Soviets and "Eastern bloc" successfully cooperated with postcolonial countries (including women) remains an open question. Some researchers show that the Soviets and "Eastern bloc" raised expectations of assistance in postcolonial countries that they did not entirely fulfil. For example, students from these countries who came to study in the USSR learned about the successes of the state socialist system, but also about its problems, including issues in the education system and racism.[12] On the other hand, Kristen Ghodsee, who analyses the cooperation between the Bulgarian women's organization and women from Zambia in the 1980s, has a positive evaluation of mutual understanding.[13] However, her study also shows tensions and hesitations from both parties (including in the use of finances and working habits), as well as a devaluation of and failure to remember the work of women involved in the cooperation surrounding the post-Cold War transition. However, Ghodsee avoids a specific discussion of the role of the Soviet Union in the Federation's work with women from (post)colonial countries. Unlike Ghodsee, a recent article by Elizabeth Banks explores the cooperation between the Committee of Soviet Women and the Organization of Mozambican Woman (OMM) and insightfully shows that large-scale Soviet thinking in combination with narrow provisions did not correspond to the expectations of African women. Indeed, the results of this cooperation demonstrate different values, rather than mutual understanding.[14] This scholarship makes further exploration of the WIDF's work for women's rights in (post)colonial countries, and the Soviet's role in this work, particularly pertinent.

The main aim of this article is to explore how the WIDF worked to further women's rights in (post)colonial countries with a focus on the contradictions, negotiations, and adjustments inside the WIDF at this time. This article pays special attention to Soviet attempts to influence the federation and Soviet ideas concerning the emancipation of women and, in particular, Soviet experiences of emancipating women from the non-Slavic (Eastern and Southern) parts of the USSR.

This article is based primarily on an analysis of the archival documents preserved in the State Archive of the Russian Federation (GARF) in Moscow, unlike many previous publications on the WIDF, which focused mainly on its official activities.[15] However, I also use the WIDF's official publications, including its journal, published from 1951 in several languages.

---

12. Constantin Katsakioris, "The Lumumba University in Moscow: Higher Education for a Soviet-Third World Alliance, 1960–91", *Journal of Global History*, 14 (2019), pp. 288–289.
13. Kristen Ghodsee, *Second World, Second Sex: Socialist Women's Activism and Global Solidarity during the Cold War* (Durham, NC, 2018).
14. Banks, "Sewing Machines for Socialism?", p. 37.
15. The fond 7928 only partly consists of the documents of the CSW, many documents in this fond constitute the original documents (and/or their Russian translations) sent from WIDF

The archival materials of the WIDF preserved in Moscow – in the collection of the Soviet member organization of the WIDF, the Committee of Soviet Women (CSW; before 1956 the organization was called the Antifascist Committee of the Soviet Women, ACSW) – can play an important role in further research on the WIDF.[16] The collection has several thousand folders containing the WIDF's documents as well as the correspondence of the CSW with other organizations that were members of the Federation. The WIDF materials in this archive include not only Russian language translations of the protocols of the Federation's meetings and congresses, but also the original letters, notes, and drafts of these documents in different languages. These less-official materials have a lot of information, not only on the Soviet role in the Federation, but also on some member organizations from other countries aimed for internal use in the Federation. Finally, the archive also includes internal Russian-language correspondence between Soviet representatives in Moscow and the WIDF's headquarters. These documents have not been analysed before and are often classified. They allow us to discover some of the internal conflicts and problems in the organization that are not visible in official WIDF publications or draft documents and notes. Using these different types of documents, it is possible to reconstruct the ways in which the Soviet Union attempted to influence the Federation.

The WIDF's periodical publication, *Women of the Whole World*, was another source in this study of the WIDF's history.[17] However, while this journal and some of the WIDF's other official publications can be unproblematically used to reconstruct the WIDF and CSW's activities, their use for an evaluation of the WIDF requires knowledge of state socialist propaganda technologies as well as special tools for investigation.[18] While some archival documents can be interpreted as the "historical truth" per se, the documents in the Soviet archives and the publications of the official journals produced inside or

---

headquarters. Before, the materials of this GARF archival fond were used mainly for research on the CSW and its international cooperation with countries in the Global South. See Christine Varga-Harris, "Between National Tradition and Western Modernization: Soviet Woman and Representations of Socialist Gender Equality as a 'Third Way' for Developing Countries, 1956–1964", *Slavic Review*, 78 (2019), pp. 758–781; Galina Galkina, *Komitet sovetskiskh zhenshchin* (Moscow, 2013); Timothy Nunan, *Humanitarian Invasion: Global Development in Cold War Afghanistan* (Cambridge, 2016).

16. See Melanie Ilic, "Soviet Women, Cultural Exchange and the Women's International Democratic Federation", in S. Autio-Sarasmo and K. Miklóssy (eds), *Reassessing Cold War Europe* (London, 2011), pp. 157–174.

17. *Women of the Whole World* (hereafter *WWW*) was published in several languages with almost identical content. The Russian version was called *Zhenshchiny mira* (hereafter *ZM*).

18. On the Soviet ideological language, see Natalia Kozlova and Irina Sandomirskaja, "*Ya tak khochu nazvat kino*". *'Naivnoe pismo': Opyt sotsio-lingvisticheskogo chteniia* (Moscow, 1996). On researching Soviet official publications and their dominant codes, see Catriona Kelly, "A Laboratory for the Manufacture of Proletarian Writers", *Europe-Asia Studies*, 54 (2002), pp. 573–574.

in cooperation with the "Eastern bloc" usually suffer from distortions, censorship, and silences.[19] Soviet publications for women can seem quite convincing. For example, Christine Varga-Harris states in her study of the journal *Soviet Woman*, published by the CSW, that it is easy to believe in the truthfulness of the information it provides.[20] However, I think this apparent "truthfulness" needs to be thoroughly investigated. It has been established that, during its history, the WIDF and its Soviet member organization were very careful with their international image and regularly published self-written accounts of their own history in their journal and as separate publications.[21] These were produced with the aim of celebrating the achievements of both organizations and some of their prominent leaders. One of the veteran members of the CSW, professional historian Galina Galkina, published the last of these accounts recently.[22] Like those in the WIDF's official periodicals, these accounts suffer from limitations because they present a selective and manipulated version of reality, while also containing a lot of important factual information. I suggest that official accounts of the WIDF's history should be used in combination with the classified and non-classified "internal use" archival documents. I advocate a more critical perspective on both WIDF and official Soviet publications and I try to use this below.

This article falls into three parts. The first explores the WIDF's views on the rights of women in colonial and dependent territories at the beginning of its work and Soviet attempts to guide and police the Federation's collaborations with women from (post)colonial countries. Here, I analyse the promotion of the story of the Soviet emancipation of women: the narrative that the lives of women from non-Russian parts of the Soviet Union (colonial borderlands, according to Madina Tlostanova) had been transformed. I examine the ways

19. See Sheila Fitzpatrick, "Impact of the Opening of Soviet Archives on Western Scholarship on Soviet Social History", *The Russian Review*, 3 (2015), pp. 377–400; Alexei Livshin, Oleg Khlevnyuk and Igor Orlov, *Pisma vo vlast* (Moscow, 2002); Natalia Kozlova, *Sovetskie liudi. Stseny iz istorii* (Moscow, 2005).

20. According to Christine Varga-Harris, reading the journal *Soviet Woman* and some letters from its foreign readers, it is easy to come to the conclusion that Soviet women were "agents of their own fate". Varga-Harris, "Between National Tradition", p. 780. However, as we know from several publications based on memories and oral history accounts, many Soviet women often felt a lack of agency and the possibility of gaining influence. See Melanie Ilic, *Soviet Women: Everyday Lives* (London, 2020); Marfua Tokhtakhodzhaeva, Dono Abdurazakova, and Almaz Kadyrova, *Sudby I vremia. Proshloe Uzbekistana v ustnykh rasskazakh zhenshhin-svidetelnits sovremennits sobytii* (Tashkent, 2002); Zamira Yusufjonova-Abman, "State Feminism in Soviet Central Asia: Anti-Religious Campaigns and Muslim Women in Tajikistan, 1953–1982", in Melanie Ilic (ed.), *The Palgrave Handbook of Women and Gender in Twentieth Century Russia and the Soviet Union* (London, 2018), pp. 299–314.

21. For example, "Mezhdunarodnoi Demokraticheskoi Federatsii Zhenschin 20 let", *ZM*, 9 (1965), pp. 4–7; *WIDF 40 Years* (Berlin, 1985); M.G. Gryzunova, *MDFZh 1945–1975* (Moscow, 1975). On the CSW, see Galkina, *Komitet*.

22. Galkina, *Komitet*.

this story was used in the WIDF's work on the rights of women in countries fighting against colonialism.[23] The second part explores the impact of the increasing pro-independence activism of women in Asia and Africa on the WIDF's understanding of women's rights and activism. I look closely at criticisms of the WIDF's work and the conflicts and contradictions in it that became visible. The third part analyses further transformations of the WIDF's politics with respect to women's rights in (post)colonial countries in the late 1960s and early 1970s. Here, I return to the theme of Soviet women from former colonial borderlands, but my focus is on the active involvement of these women in the work of the WIDF in a later period.

THE WIDF's KNOWLEDGE OF WOMEN'S PROBLEMS UNDER COLONIALISM

I start my analysis with the Soviet report from the meeting of the WIDF Executive Committee in Prague, February 1947. The documents from the archives in Moscow suggest that the activities of the WIDF in this period (at least up to the death of Stalin) were closely monitored, not only by representatives of the Soviet women's organization, but also by the Communist Party of the Soviet Union (CPSU). The report on the meeting of the WIDF Executive Committee in Prague is among several other documents that are preserved in the file aimed for the Central Committee (CC) of the CPSU.[24] It is accompanied by Russian translations of some of the documents produced by the Federation. The primary aim of these documents seems to be to give information to the leaders of the CPSU about the meeting, namely its decisions, problems, and conflicts. For example, a document signed by Nina Popova, the head of the ACSW, gives an evaluation of a speech by the WIDF president Eugenie Cotton.[25] Popova states that Cotton gave "a correct analysis of the international situation and of the women's movement".[26] The word "correct" indicates that the vision of the situation presented by Cotton corresponded to the views of the CPSU and ACSW's leaders. Further on, the report on the meeting assures the CPSU's CC that "the decisions unanimously taken (by the meeting of the Executive Committee) generally corresponded to the guidelines that were received by the Soviet delegation".[27] This form of reporting to the CPSU indicates that the ACSW,

---

23. See Madina Tlostanova, *Gender Epistemologies and Eurasian Borderlands* (Basingstoke, 2010).
24. GARF, f. 7928, op. 4 d. 7 (in Russian, my translation).
25. Popova was the head of the organization from 1941, when it was founded; she worked as a secretary of the Communist Party district committee in Moscow at the beginning of the war. In the 1950s, Popova would become a candidate to the CC of the CPSU, see Ilic, "Soviet Women", p. 159.
26. GARF, f. 7928, op. 4 d. 7, p. 59.
27. *Ibid.*, p. 72.

the Soviet member of the WIDF, did not have independent status and was expected by the leaders of the Soviet state and the Communist party to fulfil the important task of defending Soviet interests in this transnational organization.

However, while the documents from the file – addressed to the CC of the CPSU – show the Soviet intention to control the WIDF through its representative, they also suggest that these intentions were quite far from reality, even during this period of "high Stalinism". Contrary to the theory that the WIDF was no more than an instrument of Soviet foreign policy (the "Soviet front"), the same report shows that Soviet representatives to the WIDF had limited control and could not guarantee that female WIDF leaders from different countries would behave according to Soviet expectations. The authors of the report notice several "problems", indicating that national women's organizations and individual women – including those from the nascent "Eastern bloc" – could not be controlled. For example, Hungarian participants at the Prague meeting insisted on the need to discuss the difficult situation facing the Hungarian minority in Czechoslovakia, while delegations from Italy and Bulgaria expected to draw attention to the injustices the peace agreement contained for their countries. In her letter to the participants of the meeting, written in the name of Bulgarian women, Tsola Dragoycheva – a well-known Bulgarian women's activist and member of the CC of the Bulgarian Communist Party[28] – demanded that those parts of the peace agreement that, according to her, did not bring justice to the Bulgarian people and Bulgarian women, be changed.[29]

A glance at the Soviet report from the WIDF meeting in Prague shows that, from the beginning, the WIDF was a place for women who, though members of the Communist Party, understood women's problems in their own countries and the world in different ways to Moscow. As a result, discussions about the format and priorities of the WIDF's work often led to conflicts.

The WIDF's work promoting women's rights in colonial and dependent countries was subject to different interpretations and conflicts. While representatives from several countries in the Global South (India, Algeria, Argentina, Uruguay, and others) took part in the WIDF's founding conference in Paris in 1945, from the beginning the WIDF seemed to lack information about women's experiences in some parts of the world and contact with women's organizations in many countries in Asia, Africa, and Latin America. A special WIDF Commission visited the countries of Asia to evaluate women's experiences there and establish contacts; the results of the Commission's work were presented in 1948 and reflected in the official

28. Dragoycheva could not participate at the meeting due to her illness.
29. GARF, f. 7928, op. 4 d. 7, pp. 84–85.

report.[30] The meeting in Prague also discussed more general plans for organizing work in the Global South.

This meeting discussed the circumstances of women in colonial countries and racial minorities in the US. A presentation on the first issue was made by Alice Sportisse, an Algerian communist of European descent and member of the French Parliament.[31] According to the Soviet report sent to the CC CPSU, Sportisse "totally correctly" (as in the case of Eugenie Cotton) connected the solution to the problems of women in colonies to the solution of the colonial question.[32] The WIDF's Executive Commission's meeting also discussed the statute of the Secretariat Commission dedicated to working with women in colonial countries (one of three commissions established by the Prague meeting). According to this statute, the Commission considers women in colonial countries to have full citizenship rights, political rights, and labour rights. For example, the section on economic rights discusses the prevention of discrimination against women on the basis of their social and economic status, their right to work and for equal pay, and the introduction of at least two weeks of yearly leave and six weeks of leave for working women before and after giving birth.[33] These demands were highly progressive at the time they were voiced.

At the same time, the text of the document indicates that it was not written by women experiencing colonial domination themselves, but instead expresses the commitments of women outside the system. Indeed, the statute of the Commission argues that the WIDF should lead and supervise the activities of women in Africa and Asia; in other words, the Commission should help women in colonial countries to gain their political and citizenship rights.[34] The Commission collected material on the experiences of women in colonial countries through contacts with women's organizations and visits to those countries. Using these materials, the Commission had to prepare reports for the WIDF and, later, to present information about the problems facing women in the Global South to bodies of global governance, first of all the UN:

> When the material is collected and summarized, the Commission is making reports for the WIDF's Secretariat and proposes recommendations concerning the situation of women in colonial countries and the situation of racial minorities. It will send these recommendations to the UN and to the governments of different countries, as well as to trade unions and other organizations.[35]

---

30. For an analysis of this report, see Armstrong, "Before Bandung" and McGregor, "Opposing Colonialism".

31. See Allison Drew, *We Are no Longer in France: Communists in Colonial Algeria* (Manchester, 2014).

32. GARF, f. 7928, op. 4 d. 7, p. 65.

33. *Ibid.*, p. 44.

34. *Ibid.*, p. 42.

35. *Ibid.*, pp. 42–43, article 4, originally in Russian.

Although they firmly state that women in colonies should have citizens' rights and economic rights, some of the articles defining the work of the Commission sound quite patronizing:

> The Commission helps the federation to take up the issues on the need of educational work with the women of colonial countries in discussions with progressive and democratic women, trade unions, cultural and social organizations and media. It is very important to wake up the consciousness of women [in the colonial countries] and to contribute to the elimination of their general and political illiteracy.[36]

This combination of radical demands for the rights of women in colonial and dependent territories and the assumption that they needed the WIDF's advice and assistance to acquire them characterized the WIDF's activities during its earlier years.

The achievements of countries under state socialism were an important way of showing the possibilities of a fast and successful modernization that could bring both economic development and increased women's rights. As early as the 1950s, delegations from different countries at WIDF meetings were invited to visit the Soviet Union (officially these were visits to the ACSW, but in reality the Soviet state was responsible for financing them).[37] The WIDF's official publication periodically reported with pride on Soviet women's achievements in political and working life, as well as the care of the Soviet state for mothers and children. For example, an article from 1953 reports that, together with all Soviet people, women are working to fulfil the new five-year plan and are proud of their ability to work for their motherland.[38] Issue two from the same year published a picture by Zinaida Gagarina, a member of the ACSW who held a doctorate in economic sciences and was elected to the Moscow city council.[39] However, the WIDF journal never published an article that explored the hard working conditions of Soviet women or their lack of political influence while working in elected bodies.

In the late 1950s to early 1960s, the Soviet Union and other countries under state socialism were presented by the WIDF journal as models that could be used by developing countries.[40] In particular, women from the non-Russian republics of the Soviet Union, mostly those of Central Asia, started to play an important role in the WIDF's publications and in WIDF work with the growing anti-colonial movements in Asia and Africa. Previous scholarly work has shown that Central Asia played a special role in showcasing the achievements of state socialism and in maintaining good relationships with

36. *Ibid.*, p. 45, article 6, originally in Russian.
37. Russian State Archive of Socio-Political History (RGASPI), f. 17, op. 137 d. 818, pp. 56, 65.
38. M. Ovsianikova, "The Soviet Women and a Five-Years Plan", *ZM*, 1 (1953), p. 22.
39. *ZM*, 2 (1953), p. 11.
40. See, for example, the article on maternity care in Romania: *ZM*, 2 (1961), pp. 5–6; on female students from non-European countries in Czechoslovakia, see *ZM*, 7 (1959), pp. 23–26.

the intellectual elite and some leaders from the Global South.[41] The colonial past of the Soviet republics of Central Asia, and the predominance of Islam as the traditional religion of the majority of its population, played an important role in this process. The WIDF's official publications and archive material suggest that these facts also aided the WIDF's work with women from Africa and Asia.

For example, an issue from 1958 published an article on a conference of writers from Asia and Africa taking place in Tashkent and showed on its cover three women participants in that conference from Japan, Ghana and Uzbekistan (the last presented as a poet: Zulfiia).[42] The article about the conference notes that it was attended by several famous personalities, including Professor Dubois and his spouse Shirley Graham Dubois, but that only a few women writers were present.[43] Zulfiia is described as taking part in the organization of the conference and participating in it.[44] The same issue published a poem by Zulfiia dedicated to Egypt and mentions her attending a conference of Asian-African solidarity in Cairo.[45] As in the publications on Soviet women I have discussed, Zulfiia seems to have been chosen to illustrate the achievements of the Soviet system in furthering women's emancipation. Neither her poem nor any other information about her contain any criticisms of the situation facing women in Uzbekistan. In 1959, the WIDF journalist Maria Theresa Gallo published an article under the remarkable title: "Some Time Ago Uzbekistan was the Most Backward Colony of the Russian Empire, Now a Woman is the President of Uzbekistan".[46] The article starts by recounting the hard life endured by women in Uzbekistan under the Russian colonial ("tsarist") regime. It describes women fully covering their bodies, getting no education, enclosed in their homes amid economic backwardness; it continues with textual and visual representations of female students in Soviet Uzbekistan.[47] The main

---

41. See Rosen Djagalov and Masha Salazkina, "Tashkent '68: A Cinematic Contact Zone", *Russian Review*, 2 (2016), pp. 279–298; Masha Kirasirova, "Building Anti-Colonial Utopia: The Politics of Space in Soviet Tashkent in the Long 1960s", in Chen Jian, Martin Klimke, and Masha Kirasirova *et al.* (eds), *The Routledge Handbook of the Global Sixties: Between Protest and Nation-Building* (Abingdon, 2018), pp. 53–66; Akbar Rasulov, "Central Asia as an Object of Orientalist Narratives in the Age of Bandung", in Luis Eslava, Michael Fakhri, and Vasuki Nesiah (eds), *Bandung, Global History and International Law: Critical Pasts and Pending Futures* (Cambridge, 2017), pp. 215–231; Nunan, *Humanitarian Invasion*, p. 182.
42. *ZM*, 11 (1958), cover page.
43. William Edward Burghardt Dubois is known as one of the early critics of racism and a defender of the rights of African Americans.
44. "Tashkentskaia konferentsiia pisatelei stran Asii I Afriki", *ZM*, 11 (1958), pp. 15–16.
45. Zulfiia, "Tebe Egipet", *ZM*, 11 (1958), p. 19.
46. Maria Theresa Gallo, "Neskolko let nazad Uzbekistan byl samoi otstaloi koloniei Rossiiskoi Imperii. Seichas president Uzbekistana. Zhenshchina", *ZM*, 12 (1959), pp. 19–21. The translation of the title from Russian is mine.
47. As I showed in my earlier work, this was the typical construction of texts on non-Russian Soviet women. See Yulia Gradskova, *Soviet Politics of Emancipation of Ethnic Minority Women: Natsionalka* (Cham, 2018).

protagonist of the article is the head of the Supreme Soviet of Uzbekistan (named the President in article's title): Ms. Nasriddinova. Her life is described as typical of female political leaders of her generation – she was one of the first women in the republic to attend higher education, worked as an engineer, and, finally, was elected to her current political position. The article suggests that old customs and religious fanaticism were the main barriers to the advancement of women before the Soviet state created the favourable conditions now enjoyed by women of the former colonies. Indeed, the article implies that other postcolonial countries should learn from the Soviet experience. Another article, published in issue 2 from 1963, is dedicated to Hamroh Tahirova, a construction engineer from Tajikistan. Her life story is presented as "typical" for women of the region – thanks to the Soviets, she took off her veil and got an education, first in a special school for workers (*rabfak*) and then in a university. According to this article, these successes in professional life contributed to her political career and led her to become minister of construction as well as a member of the government of Tajikistan.[48] These articles were meant to convince the reader that the Soviet Union created new opportunities for women's careers and political and cultural participation in its territories while disregarding race, ethnicity, or the former colonial or imperial status of the territory.

Representations of women from the countries under state socialism in general and of women from the Soviet borderlands in particular had a very uncritical tone and never mentioned any problems, conflicts, or contradictions in Soviet "emancipation".[49] The problems of the double burden, patriarchal family life, restrictions to religious freedoms, and Russification were hidden from readers of the journal, including those in (post)colonial countries.[50] Positive images of emancipated Soviet women from former colonies were intended to strengthen the WIDF's influence on women in (post)colonial countries, a tactic I will return to in the last part of this article.

CHANGES IN THE WIDF's STRATEGIES FOR WOMEN's (POST)COLONIAL RIGHTS

This section explores more closely the ideas surrounding the needs of women in (post)colonial countries voiced by the new organizations participating in the WIDF during the late 1950s to the early 1960s. During this period,

48. A. Chekhovskaia, "Hamroh Tahirova. Stroitel iz solnechnogo kraia", *ZM*, 2 (1963), pp. 19–20. Ivonne Quiles's article dedicated to the first Afro-Asian Women's Conference in Cairo briefly mentions that Tahirova was the head of the Soviet delegation at the conference, see *ZM*, 4 (1961), p. 8.
49. See, for example, the evaluation of the contradictory results of the Sovietization of Central Asian and other minority women in Marianne Kamp, *The New Woman in Uzbekistan: Islam, Modernity and Unveiling under Communism* (Seattle, WA, 2006), and Gradskova, *Soviet Politics*.
50. Tokhtakhodzhaeva *et al.*, *Sudby I vremia*.

decolonization rapidly gathered pace in Asia and Africa. Here, I explore some changes that took place in the Federation's everyday work as a response to the mass anticolonial movement and to the growing participation of women outside Europe in its structure. As early as 1955, the Bandung Conference of representatives from Asian and African countries showed not only the growing importance of the newly independent nations in global politics, but also their aspirations to modernize their societies and transform the world's legal and economic order.[51] While these aspirations were not free from contradictions and had different versions, a change in the status of women constituted an important part of most of them. Furthermore, women were not only active global participants in the anti-colonial struggle and postcolonial social movements, but also organizers and ideologists in campaigns for the rights for women.[52]

In the late 1950s, the WIDF's leaders found themselves in a new situation that required them to expand their programmes amid the changing political visions of women from the Global South and, as I wrote elsewhere, incorporate female leaders from Africa and Asia into the WIDF's leadership.[53]

In some cases, as the documents from the Moscow archives suggest, female activists from Africa and Asia actively looked for the WIDF's support. For example, Fatima Ahmed Ibrahim – a young representative of the Sudanese women's organization created in 1953 – visited the WIDF headquarters in Berlin in 1954. According to the brief report sent to Moscow by the Soviet representative at the WIDF's Secretariat in Berlin, in her talk with members of the Secretariat, Ahmed Ibrahim described the activities and problems that the Sudanese Women's Union faced and reacted enthusiastically to the WIDF's proposal to visit the Sudan and her organization. The Soviet representative also stressed that this conversation showed that the Sudanese organization expected different types of help from the WIDF, including help financing travel to WIDF congresses and other international meetings and advice that shared its expertise on the work of women's organizations in different countries. The Sudanese women also expected that the WIDF would support some campaigns they were organizing in the Sudan, and also establish contacts with women's organizations in countries like India as well as in the Middle East and the UK.[54]

51. Eslava *et al.* (eds), *Bandung, Global History, and International Law*; Christopher Lee, *Making a World After Empire: The Bandung Moment and Its Political Afterlives* (Athens, OH, 2010).
52. See, for example, Margot Badran, *Feminists, Islam, and Nation: Gender and the Making of Modern Egypt* (Princeton, NJ, 1995); Laura Bier, *Revolutionary Womanhood: Feminisms, Modernity and the State in Nasser's Egypt* (Berkeley, CA, 2011); Meredith Terretta, *Petitioning for our Rights, Fighting for our Nation: The History of the Democratic Union of Cameroonian Women, 1949–1960* (Bamenda, 2013).
53. Gradskova, *The Women's International*.
54. GARF, f. 7928, op. 2 d. 1482, pp. 1–2, 1954, in Russian.

In addition to fostering contact between the WIDF and women from different countries and regions, WIDF congresses played an important role in making the struggle for women's rights in (post)colonial countries in Asia and Africa visible. However, even in the late 1950s, women from Asian and African countries faced many difficulties when taking part in these international congresses. This led to a disconnect between the WIDF's self-presentation and its real presence and influence among women from (post) colonial countries at the congresses. For example, the 1958 WIDF Congress in Vienna made anti-colonialism one of its central topics and spoke in the name of women from countries fighting for and gaining independence. However, it only hosted fifteen representatives from seven African countries, including Algeria, French Sudan (Mali), Senegal, Cameroon, and Madagascar.[55] Meanwhile, the Soviet delegation alone consisted of sixteen women. Furthermore, the archival documents show that the preparation for the Congress was guided by its European leaders, while the Congress's opening speeches concerned familiar issues from the WIDF agenda, like the protection of peace.[56] The anti-colonial theme was present, however, in an opening speech by Anna Hornik – a representative of Austria's women's organization – who demanded freedom for the "Algerian heroine Djamila Bouhired", who was in prison facing the death penalty.[57] The heroism of Algerian women fighting against colonialism was praised by Mamia Chentouf, participant in the Algerian Independence Movement.[58] But the war in Algeria was also discussed in the WIDF's familiar language of fascism and anti-fascism.[59] Finally, the thematic workshops organized as the part of the Congress did not center the issue of independence, but were dedicated to the defence of life, the possibility for woman to combine work with motherhood, and the rights of children and young people to an education.[60]

The WIDF leadership used different strategies in the following years to bring powerful women from the Global South under its influence. These included participating in conferences and other events in the region, covering the travel costs and accommodation of the region's delegates at WIDF events, expanding the Federation's solidarity work, and partially changing its leadership structures. In addition, the leadership made attempts to bring the WIDF's governing bodies geographically closer to the Global South, for example,

55. GARF, f. 7928, op. 3 d. 14, pp. 58–84.
56. "A message for the International Women's Day, 8 of March 1958", GARF, f. 7928, op. 3 d. 8, pp. 6–7.
57. *Ibid.*, p. 7.
58. GARF, f. 7928, op. 3 d. 11, pp. 32–37.
59. Speech by Anna Hornik, head of the Vienna organization of the Union of Democratic Women of Austria, GARF, f. 7928, op. 3 d. 11, pp. 6–7.
60. GARF, f. 7928, op. 3 d. 9, p. 2.

through holding some bureau meetings outside Europe – in Jakarta (Indonesia) in 1960 and Bamako (Mali) in 1962.

The archive documents show that, in the early 1960s, demand for public declarations of solidarity and support for women's struggles grew so great that the WIDF systematized and mechanized their delivery. A classified letter the Soviet representative in the Secretariat, Zinaida Lebedeva, sent to Moscow in February 1961 stated:

> Due to the need to show solidarity with one or another group fighting for its freedom and national independence, apart from the bulletin we decided to elaborate a special template that could be used every time it would be necessary. […] In every case [when the WIDF would show solidarity], such a letter should be sent to corresponding addresses and to the national committees.[61]

Lebedeva's letter suggests that solidarity was only shown to those who corresponded to the ideological definition of "friends" used by the WIDF. This definition usually excluded so-called bourgeois women's organizations and those representatives of the left (such as Trotskyists) whose interpretations of socialism were considered wrong. Nonetheless, the rapid pace of decolonization in the 1960s meant that members of the Secretariat often had no information about the women's groups or situations in the regions gaining independence. This hindered the WIDF's promotion of solidarity. According to a letter from the Soviet representative in the Secretariat, when they received a request for solidarity, the WIDF Secretariat often made no decision: "We do not know what is going on there […] we have to wait".[62]

In 1960, the WIDF organized its first bureau meeting outside Europe, in Jakarta, Indonesia. A classified report by the Soviet representative, Maria Skotnikova, from the WIDF's Secretariat in Berlin, dated 23 March 1960, informed the CSW in Moscow that the WIDF general secretary, Carmen Zanti, felt the meeting would mean "the members of the Bureau could understand better the problems that women in Asia and Africa have".[63] It seems that meeting in the physical environment of the Global South made Zanti – and other participants in the WIDF – think about the differences in working conditions between women's organizations from (Western and Eastern) Europe and the Global South. Several prominent participants in the meeting expressed critical views of the WIDF's work in Asia. In a talk delivered in Jakarta, Anasuya Gyanchand – the representative of the National Federation of Indian Women (NFIW) – concisely outlined the problems women from newly independent countries encountered while attempting to cooperate with the WIDF. The Executive Committee of the NFIW's report, presented by Gyanchand, included many negative comments on the WIDF's activities

---

61. GARF, f. 7928, op. 4 d. 149, p. 15.
62. *Ibid.*, pp. 15–16, in Russian.
63. GARF, f. 7928, op. 4 d. 142, pp. 52–54.

in the Global South. Indeed, it started by stating that the WIDF had to make more of an effort if it was interested in attracting women from Asia and Africa:

> In our opinion the WIDF, [...] still was not able to find out the key slogans which would appeal to the vast masses of women of the East and was not able to work out organizations forms that would correspond to the conditions of these countries.

> It was a fact that the women of Asia and Africa did not play a leading part in the WIDF, and that, with the exception of the Chinese and some other countries, either whole countries remained outside the sphere of our organization, or the women who were elected to the leading bodies of the WIDF did not represent the leadership of the broad masses of women in our countries [...].[64]

The Indian women's organization saw a direct connection between the lack of representation of Asian (and other non-European) women in the WIDF's leadership and its difficulties formulating a programme that would attract women from the "Third World". However, their criticism was not limited to issues of representation; they emphasized important differences between the living conditions and political situations of women in Africa and Asia, of which the WIDF's leadership was not sufficiently aware. One such problem was the different attitudes among women in former colonial countries towards men. According to the report: "In our countries, men have themselves advocated reforms and encouraged women to break their shackles."[65]

The report also indicates that class structures in countries in the Global South were more complex than the (Eastern and Western) European leaders of the WIDF were used to considering.

> We feel that our friends in Europe and America are too used to looking at the different social strata of people as "industrial workers, capitalists, farmers or agriculturalists". They find it difficult to understand that different levels of social emancipation exist both in the town and country-side [...].[66]

The five pages of critical remarks on the WIDF's work written by the NFIW has a friendly tone and was intended to increase the WIDF leadership's awareness of existing problems. However, the WIDF's attempts to cooperate with women's organizations from the Global South were often met with more openly negative reactions and resistance.[67] The archival materials demonstrate that, during the 1960s, the WIDF carefully followed developments in the women's movement in Africa and tried to attract women's organizations from Africa to its side. For example, the 1963 report titled "The WIDF's Connections with the Women's Organizations in Africa" shows that it was easier to maintain contacts with some organizations than with others. The

---

64. GARF, f. 7928, op. 3 d. 410, p. 66, in English.
65. *Ibid.*, p. 67; for more on this report, see Gradskova, *The Women's International*, pp. 122–126.
66. GARF, f. 7928, op. 3 d. 410, p. 69.
67. See Gradskova, *The Women's International*, pp. 119–120.

report notes that the state-supported Tunisian women's organization – the National Union of Tunisian Women – was not interested in cooperation with the WIDF, while the WIDF did have contacts with a small clandestine organization, the Union of Tunisian Women.[68] The report demonstrates that women's organizations from the Sudan, South Africa, and Morocco participated in the WIDF; however, the Federation did not manage to preserve contacts that were established with other countries, such as the Côte d'Ivoire.[69] The document notes that, even though a delegation from this country took part in the WIDF's external bureau meeting in Bamako in 1962, the WIDF had lost contact with its members by the time the report was written.

Maintaining contacts, forming allegiances, and attracting members from among Africa's women's organizations was increasingly important for the WIDF. This was not only due to the Federation's interests in women's rights, but also Cold War competition. This is evident in the words of the WIDF's vice-president Funmilayo Ransome Kuti, a representative from Nigeria, at the WIDF's 1962 bureau meeting. This meeting was dedicated to preparations for the 1963 WIDF Congress in Moscow, an occasion that, according to Ransome Kuti, would "be an important event". She explained that "many international and other organizations want to get African women under their influence […] Thus, the WIDF should deal with the problems concerning the women of Africa and actively work with these problems".[70]

According to the same report, in the period leading up to the meeting many "bourgeois women's organizations [were] trying to establish contacts with the African countries". The document names the International Council of Social-Democratic Women, the International Women's Alliance, and the International Council of Women.[71] This confirms Ransome Kuti's comments about competition for alliances with African women and suggests that the WIDF took this competition very seriously. The same file contains another document with a short description of the activities that other transnational bodies – political, cooperative, religious, and agrarian – were organizing for women and girls in Africa. These included offering fellowships, organizing housekeeping courses, and giving healthcare lectures[72]. Among other things, this review pays attention to the activities of the UK and Israeli governments, private foundations like the Rockefeller Foundation, and the Swedish social democrats.[73]

---

68. GARF, f. 7928, op. 3 d. 799, p. 7, document in Russian.
69. *Ibid.*, p. 3.
70. GARF, f. 7928, op. 3 d. 790, p. 29, in Russian.
71. GARF, f. 7928, op. 3 d. 799, p. 10.
72. Recent research on Israel's work with women in Africa suggests that the WIDF was right to be afraid of the competition. See Daniel Kupfert Heller, "Gender, Development and the Arab-Israeli Conflict: The Politics of Study Tours for Women from the Global South in the State of Israel, 1958–1973", *History Australia*, 17 (2020), pp. 678–694.
73. GARF, f. 7928, op. 3 d. 799, pp. 13–17.

The document also indicates some discrepancies between the position of the Federation and the position of some African female activists. These African women stressed that "the solution to the problems of women and children [...] depends on the solution to the problem of national independence", and they considered that the question of détente defended by the Soviet Union occupied a "secondary place compared to independence".[74] According to the report, African women often supported the "neutralist" position of their governments. The Soviet report therefore suggests that African female activists considered both the USSR and the US responsible for the continuing arms race. Thus, in some cases, women from the Global South doubted that the WIDF could fully understand and represent their interests on the transnational stage.

The need to keep women from (post)colonial countries interested in the WIDF together with a fear of losing the Cold War competition with the "West" led the WIDF to broaden its repertoire of activities, including organizing research trips and seminars and offering fellowships for women to study in the Eastern bloc.[75] This contributed to a further strategic development in the examples of success the WIDF presented to the women of "Soviet Asia", that I discuss in the next section.

THE WIDF IN THE 1960S AND THE ROLE OF SOVIET "WOMEN OF COLOUR"

While most newly independent countries saw economic development and overcoming the legacy of colonialism as their most important tasks, the WIDF aimed to provide advice on how women's legal status and practical well-being could be improved. It is likely that the readmission of the Federation as an NGO at the Economic and Social Council of the UN (ECOSOC) in 1967 contributed to its efforts to present itself as an organization concerned with scientific expertise on women's rights rather than politics. This image of international expertise in women's rights was meant to help wash away the Federation's associations with the "Eastern bloc" and Moscow, making it more attractive for governments and women in (post)colonial countries. The WIDF's journal played a leading role in this transformation. As I have written elsewhere, from 1966 onwards the federation reviewed the concepts published in its main periodical, aiming to make it more scientific by offering increased space to contributors with doctoral degrees and university positions.[76]

---

74. *Ibid.*, p. 12.
75. See Gradskova, *The Women's International*, p. 175.
76. *Ibid.*, pp. 171–172.

For example, an article by Dr. Marguerite Thibert (France), published in 1967, is dedicated to women's influence on political decision-making; it was related to an International Seminar in Rome co-organized by the WIDF.[77] Referring to international law, Thibert states that the Declaration of Human Rights and Convention on the Political Rights of Women adopted by the UN in 1952 were important steps on the way to women's rights. At the same time, she implies that assumptions about the advancement of women's political participation cannot be fully justified on the basis of legal information alone. According to Thibert, in some cases women could be misused. Their political participation could be used to satisfy the needs of another political party or group and women taking part in elections might lack a full understanding of their responsibility and the empowering nature of this act.[78] Another article published by the WIDF journal in 1967, authored by Prof. Anita Grandke – described as a representative of the Academy of Sciences of the GDR – is titled "Women's Equal Rights and Social Progress". Grandke argues that women's rights and the development of society are interrelated; that more rights for women correspond to a more developed society.[79] However, similarly to Thibert, Grandke's conclusion implies that any change in the political conditions of women does not automatically lead to their increased influence in society and advocates for more serious reforms.

Reading the WIDF's journal it is possible to assume that education and family law were particularly important areas in the WIDF's work for women's rights in Asia and Africa. For example, the first issue from 1968 makes a comparative assessment of levels of literacy among women in different countries and contains an article by Lie Oumou, an activist from Mali, who claims that the development of the economy would be impossible without investment in "human capital". According to Oumou, illiteracy makes women in many postcolonial countries an unused reserve of workers and hinders them from contributing politically to society.[80] The second issue from the same year, with a subtitle "Women and Family", contains several articles authored by representatives of different geopolitical regions and organizations who defend the importance of equality between men and women in the family. In particular, property rights and rights preserving children's custody after divorce are advocated with references to the conventions adopted by the UN General Assembly in 1966 (The Convention on Civil and Political Rights and the Convention on Economic, Social and Cultural Rights) and the Declaration on the Elimination of Discrimination against women adopted

77. Marguarete Thibert, "Imeyut li zhenshchiny golos pri priniatii reshenii?", *ZM*, 1 (1967), pp. 18–19.
78. *Ibid.*, pp. 18–19.
79. Anita Grandke, "Ravnopravie zhenshchin i ssotsialnyi progress", *ZM*, 3 (1967), pp. 14–15.
80. Lie Oumou, "Obrazovanie zhenshchin i ego sviaz s trudom", *ZM*, 1 (1968), pp. 19–20.

by the UN in 1967.[81] The authors of these articles show that in some cases family laws even in "developed" countries did not give equal rights to women (for example, in Austria).[82] An article by Dr. Shahnaz Alami stresses that feudal-patriarchal customs and Muslim laws can hinder equality in the family.[83] Alami particularly criticizes the laws enabling polygamy and discriminating against women gaining custody of their children that were enshrined in new Family Legislation in Iran. And, finally, an article by Cristina Vrono in the same issue reports that the first Congress of Women in Guinea banned polygamy and made the elimination of female illiteracy among its most important goals.[84]

It can be assumed that, by the late 1960s, the WIDF paid attention to some of the problems voiced in the NFIW's 1960 report from Jakarta, not least through diversifying its policy. Indeed, the WIDF's defence of women as mothers and workers focused increasingly on the importance of literacy, primary education, and the professional education of women in newly independent countries. Meanwhile, its defence of family rights started to focus on the issues of property rights and the custody of children.

However, as I have already mentioned, the WIDF's publications continued to report on the Soviet advancement of women's rights, particularly in non-Russian republics, as an example for women in African and Asian countries. The struggle for independence and its new connections with women's organizations in Asia and Africa, increased the importance of non-Russian regions and women for the WIDF's work. Gradually, Central Asian women – usually high-level Soviet party and state officials – became more responsible for greeting women from Asia and Africa, including WIDF delegations, and exhibiting to them Soviet advancements in the rights and opportunities of women from "former colonies".

One example of this is connected to a seminar, supported by the WIDF, on education for women from Asia and Africa that took place in Tashkent on the 13–15 September 1962.[85] The seminar included lectures and discussions in Tashkent as well as study trips to other Central Asian Soviet republics. According to the archival reports, the guests were impressed by the educational facilities and number of female students they saw.[86] Hujuma Shukurova – the head of the Uzbekistan Society of Friendship with People of Africa and Asia and a member of the CSW – played an important role in

81. Edith Geumery, "International Documents for Protection of Family", *ZM*, 2 (1968), pp. 16–17.
82. Margarete Reinelt, "Vo imia samoi elementarnoi spravedlivosti", *ZM*, 2 (1968), p. 23.
83. Shahnaz Alami, "Iran. Chto prines zhenshchine novyi zakon o semie", *ZM*, 2 (1968), pp. 20–22.
84. Cristina Vrono, "Guinea. Vazhnoe reshenie", *ZM*, 2 (1968), p. 28.
85. GARF, f. 7928, op. 3 d. 776.
86. See more in Gradskova, *The Women's International*, pp. 102–103.

organizing the seminar.[87] While official information on the seminar does not contain many details about Shukurova's place in the Soviet hierarchy, some information about this can be found in an "In memoriam" publication from 1980.[88] According to this publication, Shukurova, born in 1927, was a member of the CPSU from 1950 and held different offices in the Soviet and Communist Party apparatus; she also wrote a dissertation on the Soviet emancipation of women in Uzbekistan. Shukurova's appointment as head of the Uzbek Friendship Society in 1962 seems to have been strategically important: the Soviet leadership considered her a loyal member of the Soviet system, while guests from non-European countries could find in her an emancipated woman from a former colony, embodying the achievements of Soviet equality.

However, the most remarkable use of the image of the "emancipated woman" of Central Asia in the work of the WIDF is probably the (unique, according to my knowledge) case of the Central Asian woman sent to represent the Soviet Union at the WIDF Secretariat in Berlin in the second half of the 1960s. This was Zuhra Rahimbabaeva from Uzbekistan, a member of the Communist Party who – like Shukurova – had a doctoral degree in history and specialized in Soviet emancipation. Her appointment in Berlin was most likely made in the hope of improving communication with women from the formerly colonized countries of Africa and Asia and improving the Soviet's position in the growing competition between the Soviet Union and China in the Global South. Indeed, as Rahimbabaeva's speeches and publications show she could speak the "Soviet language",[89] in her work, Rahimbabaeva stresses the importance of the Soviet politics of emancipation in the 1920s and 1930s.[90] In her book published in 1949 – *Women of Uzbekistan on the Way to Communism* – she stated that the "happiness of the Uzbek woman is unlimited":

> [...] the Great October has given her equal rights with men in all the spheres of economic, state and cultural life, it woke up her talents and her creativity that had been sleeping for centuries before that.[91]

87. GARF, f. 7928, op. 3 d. 776, p. 26.
88. "In Memoriam. Hujuma Samatovna Shukurova 1927–1980", *Obshchestvennye nauki v Uzbekistane*, 7 (1980), p. 56.
89. Ali Igmen, *Speaking Soviet with an Accent: Culture and Power in Kyrgyzstan* (Pittsburg, PA, 2012).
90. The story presented by Rakhimbabaeva was aimed for glorifying the Soviet politics. It did not include any critical perspective on these politics, nor did it specifically address the thousands of women who lost their lives as a result of *hujum*. On the last issue, see e.g. Kamp, *The New Woman in Uzbekistan*.
91. Zuhra Rahimbabaeva, *Zhenshchiny Uzbekistana na puti k kommunizmu* (Tashkent, 1949), p. 3.

During the approximately four years during which Rahimbabaeva worked as a Soviet representative at the Secretariat in Berlin, she participated in multiple conferences and seminars with women from Asian and African countries and visited Asian countries as an official representative of the WIDF Secretariat.[92] The interview with her and Dina Levin – a representative of the WIDF Secretariat from a "Western" country – published in the WIDF journal in 1972, suggests that Rahimbabaeva was elected for this mission not least because of an expectation that she would bring authority to sensitive discussions with Asian women concerning women's rights, religion, and anti-colonialism. Like the images of Central Asian women from the official WIDF publication I described at the beginning of this article, Rahimbabaeva could connect her status as a "former colonial subject" with her current position as a Soviet woman enjoying a prestigious place in the Soviet (multinational) state. This could contribute to the possibility of her forming connections with her interlocutors – women from Asia, Africa, and Latin America – in a different way to her colleagues from Moscow, East Berlin, or the "West". This different way of creating relationships with women from former colonies was possibly furthered by Rahimbabaeva's non-whiteness. Unlike the Russian/Slavic women who used to represent the USSR in the WIDF, Rahimbabaeva could be read as a Soviet "woman of colour" and the leadership of the CSW expected her to be particularly important in building alliances with women from Asia and Africa.

In the 1960s, the number of women from outside Europe grew both in the WIDF as a whole and in its leadership.[93] In 1975, the permanent members of the bureau included: one vice-president from Africa, Funmilayo Ransome Kuti (Nigeria); two from Latin America, Julia Arevalo (Uruguay) and Vilma Espín de Castro (Cuba); and two from Asia, Aruna Asaf Ali (India) and Fuki Kushida (Japan). The bureau included only three women from countries under state socialism, namely, Valentina Tereshkova (USSR), Ilse Thile (GDR), and Gusta Fučikova (Czechoslovakia), as well as one from Australia, Frida Brown, and one from Western Europe, Marie-Claude Vaillant-Couturier (France).[94] Although about half the leaders belonged to communist parties in their respective countries, the composition of the WIDF leadership had changed, and representatives of European countries now constituted a minority. In 1975, the Federation represented 117 women's organizations from 101 countries; representation of women's organizations from the Global South was high.[95]

92. Interview with Dina Levin and Zuhra Rahimbabaeva on their visit of women's organizations of India, Nepal, Ceylon, Pakistan, and Afghanistan, *ZM*, 4 (1968), pp. 32–38.
93. Gradskova, *The Women's International*.
94. *WWW*, 1(1975), p. 3.
95. *WWW*, 2 (1975), p. 1.

In practice, the relationships inside the organization continued to be more complex than a numerical account of its leadership and members implies. The classified correspondence between the CSW in Moscow and its representative in Berlin shows this. Rahimbabaeva, who continued working in Berlin as a Soviet representative to the WIDF Secretariat, in 1972 was tasked with lobbying for a leading role for the WIDF in the upcoming conference of the Afro-Asian People's Solidarity Organization (AAPSO). Mentioning other Soviet representatives' unsuccessful attempts to gain leading roles in the preparation of previous conference (which was attributed to China – "due to separatist activities of the Maoists"), the CSW representative, Xenia Proskurnikova, suggested that Rahimbabaeva should work with the WIDF to become "one of the organizers of this conference".[96] While the archive documents do not show how successful Rahimbabaeva was in this regard, they suggest the complex role given to Soviet women of colour in the WIDF's work with (post)colonial countries. They had to represent emancipated women from former colonies, while contributing to the realization of the "Eastern bloc's" geopolitical aspirations in the Global South.

CONCLUSION

The materials connected to the WIDF in the archive of the CSW show that we cannot ignore Soviet attempts to influence the Federation and gain support from women in (post)colonial countries. These were particularly visible in the use of the Federation's official publications to advertise Soviet achievements in emancipation. Soviet representatives in the Federation also had to make their aspirations match those of women from newly independent countries. While the Federation's official publications often make its internal conflicts and tensions invisible, the archival materials partly reconstruct them.

This study shows that the WIDF's leaders (including its Soviet representatives) significantly improved their understanding of the needs and problems of women from the Global South over the history of this transnational organization. In the beginning, women from countries outside Europe were considered to have similar problems to European women, with the addition of colonial exploitation. The incorporation of significant numbers of women's organizations from newly independent countries into the WIDF contributed to an understanding that their concerns were more specific. Unlike existing scholarship focused on the WIDF's engagement with the Bandung spirit prior to 1955, I pay attention to the composition of the WIDF's leadership in that time period and its knowledge of the problems facing women in colonial and dependent countries.

---

96. GARF, f. 7928, op. 3 d. 2941, p. 2, 15 February 1972, document in Russian.

The materials I have explored show that acknowledging the importance of national liberation for women in Asia and Africa influenced the Federation's views on alliances between women from (Western and Eastern) Europe and the Global South. If in the late 1940s the relationships between the two was seen as a form of "assistance", from the late 1950s onwards, women of the Global South were recognized as having their own agency. In the context of the Cold War, their participation in the WIDF – an organization geopolitically linked to the Soviet Union – became a particularly important resource for cultural influence. The competition between each "side" of the Cold War adversaries to attract women from Africa and Asia led to internal conflicts in the WIDF, but it also strengthened the Federation's focus on rights, including its criticism of racism and colonialism.

Finally, the new composition of the Federation and new geopolitical demands led the WIDF and its Soviet member organization (which always held an important role) to adopt new strategies for representing women from countries under state socialism. In the late 1960s, the Soviet Union was represented in the WIDF's Secretariat – and at several international events outside Europe – by a non-Russian and non-Slavic woman from the Soviet borderlands. This "woman of colour" became an important mediator between the WIDF's ideological programme and potential participants from the Global South at a time when the world order was drastically changing.

IRSH 67 (2022), pp. 179–207 doi:10.1017/S002085902100047X

A Gendered Approach to the Yu Chi Chan Club and National Liberation Front during South Africa's Transition to Armed Struggle*

ALLISON DREW ⓘ

University of Cape Town, Centre for African Studies
Upper Campus, Rondebosch 7701, South Africa

E-mail: allisonvictoriadrew@gmail.com

ABSTRACT: South Africa's anti-apartheid struggle reflected an ideal of heroic masculinity that ignored and depreciated women as active political agents. This has contributed to a post-apartheid social order that accepts formal gender equality but that perpetuates gender inequality by discounting women's experiences. This article examines the little-known and short-lived Yu Chi Chan Club (YCCC) and National Liberation Front (NLF). Tiny Cape Peninsula-based breakaways from the Non-European Unity Movement – an African National Congress rival – the YCCC and NLF were exceptional amongst early 1960s underground groups in their systematic attempts to theorize guerrilla struggle and assess its applicability to South African conditions and, in the NLF's case, to build a cell structure through political education. Although the NLF's idealized notion of revolutionary life was premised on an abstract individual with traits then associated with public and vocal male activists, nonetheless women participated as equal abstract individuals. The NLF's relatively horizontal cell structure, small cell size, and lack of hierarchy made participation easier for both women and men, allowing women to operate equally within the political space. From their gendered upbringing and early experiences in hierarchical organizations to their brief experience of equality within the YCCC and NLF, the women were then forced into a prison system with an extremely rigid and unequal gender divide. Subjected to the state's regendering project, the political space available to the NLF's women prisoners shrank far more than it did for their male comrades, whose prison experiences became the measure of anti-apartheid politics.

* Research for this article was made possible by a British Academy grant. The author is very grateful to the Academy for its support. Thanks to Celia Donert, David Howell, David Johnson, Christine Moll-Murata, and two anonymous readers for comments.

Following Elizabeth van der Heyden's release from a South African prison in 1973, after ten years for conspiracy to overthrow the state, veteran anti-apartheid campaigner Helen Suzman asked her what Robben Island prison had been like. There were no women prisoners on Robben Island, she replied.[1]

The exchange reflects a common misconception about anti-apartheid politics. Male experiences have been universalized, with those of Robben Island's black political prisoners overshadowing all others.[2] The anti-apartheid struggle was based on an ideal of heroic masculinity that depreciated women as active political agents. This has contributed to a post-apartheid social order that accepts formal gender equality but that perpetuates gender inequality by discounting women's experiences. Not surprisingly, most studies of the South African left during the early armed struggle years, focused on the African National Congress (ANC) and its allies, have neglected gender.[3]

This article examines the little-known Yu Chi Chan Club (guerrilla warfare, YCCC) and National Liberation Front (NLF), tiny socialist groups of which Van der Heyden was a member. Cape Peninsula breakaways from the Non-European Unity Movement (NEUM) – an ANC rival – the YCCC and NLF were exceptional amongst early 1960s underground groups in their systematic attempts to theorize guerrilla struggle and assess its applicability to South Africa and, in the NLF's case, to build a cell structure through political education. Despite splintering from the NEUM, the YCCC and NLF nonetheless used its educational techniques to study guerrilla struggle. The YCCC, formed around April 1962, disbanded in December to organize the NLF. But six months after the NLF's January 1963 launch, its founding members were arrested. While its members had produced theoretical analyses and begun setting up cells, they had neither developed a national network, nor taken steps towards armed activities. Eleven of its members received prison sentences ranging from five to ten years. Yet, the scholarly literature has

---

1. Helen Scanlon, *Representation & Reality: Portraits of Women's Lives in the Western Cape, 1948–1976* (Pretoria, 2007), p. 210; University of Cape Town Manuscripts & Archives [hereafter UCTMA], Neville Alexander Papers [hereafter BC1538], State versus Neville Alexander and ten others [hereafter D.5.1.1].17, Verdict, p. 1966.

2. Black male political prisoners were incarcerated in various locations, Robben Island being the best known. Black refers to all people of colour victimized by the white supremacist apartheid regime. Where relevant, I use the official categories of African, Coloured, and Indian.

3. Some exceptions using life story approaches are Scanlon, *Representation*, see esp. pp. 12–14; Arianna Lissoni and Maria Suriano, "Married to the ANC: Tanzanian Women's Entanglement in South Africa's Liberation Struggle", *Journal of Southern African Studies*, 40:1 (2014), pp. 129–50; N.P.Z. Mbatha, "Narratives of Women Detained in the Kroonstad Prison during the Apartheid Era: A Socio-Political Exploration, 1960–1990", *Journal for Contemporary History*, 43:1 (2018), pp. 91–110; Emma Elinor Lundin, "'Now is the Time!' The Importance of International Spaces for Women's Activism within the ANC, 1960–1976", *Journal of Southern African Studies*, 45:2 (2019), pp. 323–340; Shanthini Naidoo, *Women Surviving Apartheid's Prisons* (Washington, DC, 2021).

neglected – indeed, excluded – these groups. They have literally been erased from history.[4]

Despite its minute numbers, the NLF had a large proportion of women compared to other groups planning armed struggle. Four of the eleven NLF members imprisoned for conspiracy were women – Elizabeth van der Heyden, Doris van der Heyden, Dorothy Alexander, and Dulcie September. Dorothy Adams, who led an NLF cell in Wellington, was detained, released, and banned. The Namibian activist Ottilie Abrahams (née Schimming) chaired local and regional NLF meetings and edited its organ *Liberation* but returned to South West Africa [now Namibia] before the arrests. These women were intellectuals motivated by a desire to learn, yet the NLF has been overshadowed by the trial's accused number one, Neville Alexander.[5] Using interviews, political documents, and trial transcripts, this article decentres the understanding of this group by exploring how gender shaped these women's political involvement.[6] It argues that the group's relatively flat organizational structure and non-gendered activities facilitated women's participation.[7]

By contrast, the underground South African Communist Party (SACP), formed in 1953, was arranged hierarchically into area, district, and central committees. When ANC leader Nelson Mandela launched the military organization *Umkhonto we Sizwe* (Spear of the Nation, MK) in December 1961, he recruited SACP and ANC men, although ANC women's leader Dorothy Nyembe states that she was recruited that year, and communist journalist Ruth First was involved in MK discussions.[8] "You can count your lucky

4. Madeleine Fullard, "State Repression in the 1960s", in South African Democracy Education Trust (SADET), *The Road to Democracy in South Africa, Volume 1 (1960–1970)* (Cape Town, 2004), pp. 341–90, refers in passing to "Neville Alexander and 10 others", p. 367; the volume does not mention the NLF. *South African History Online*, https://www.sahistory.org.za/, is rectifying this historical omission.

5. Na-iem Dollie, "Dialogical Narratives: Reading Neville Alexander's Writings" (DLitt et Phil, History, University of South Africa, 2015), p. 90.

6. During the trial, the defence maintained that Kenneth Abrahams, then in South West Africa, pushed armed struggle against the views of other members. The defendants held in solitary made statements that were not free or voluntary and elected to make unsworn statements rather than be examined.

7. Joan Acker, "Hierarchies, Jobs, Bodies: A Theory of Gendered Organizations", *Gender and Society*, 4:2 (June 1990), pp. 139–158; Rosabeth Moss Kanter, "The Impact of Hierarchical Structures on the Work Behavior of Women and Men", *Social Problems*, 23:4 (April 1976), pp. 415–430.

8. Nelson Mandela, *Long Walk to Freedom: The Autobiography of Nelson Mandela* (London [etc.], 1994), pp. 259–262; "Dorothy Nomzansi Nyembe", *South African History Online*. Available at: https://www.sahistory.org.za/people/dorothy-nomzansi-nyembe; last accessed 3 February 2021; Ruth First, *117 Days: An Account of Confinement and Interrogation under the South African 90-Day Detention Law* (London, [1965] 2010), pp. 7, 53–57, 138–139; Paul S. Landau, "Gendered Silences in Nelson Mandela's and Ruth First's Struggle Auto/biographies", *African Studies*, 78:2 (2019), pp. 290–306.

stars that we still have respect for women in our country", First's interrogator told her when she was detained in August 1963 – referring obviously to white women. "You could have been charged in the Rivonia case. But we didn't want a woman in that case."[9] However, the state's attitude to incarcerating women activists, especially black women, was hardening. While First spent 117 days in prison, Nyembe, arrested the same year, was sentenced to three years. When communist lawyer Bram Fischer was arrested in September 1964, six of the twelve white detainees charged with him were women.[10]

The Cold War provided a convenient rationale for the 1948 launch of apartheid and the 1950 Suppression of Communism Act, which was cast so broadly that any government critic could be arrested. Political space – the environment available to individuals and groups for political activity – expanded during the early 1950s as masses of people openly protested apartheid's imposition.[11] But as state repression increased, political space contracted and moved underground. The shift from public to underground politics has generally facilitated the dominance of military factions, skewing "the gendered participation in the movement toward men".[12] However, the NLF's focus on learning and its small horizontally organized cells allowed women space to participate, although their brief experience of gender equality in these groups was cut off with their imprisonment. Thus, its history has a significance beyond its tiny numbers and ephemeral existence, one that stands as a critique of the sexism that has characterized the South African left.

THE YCCC AND NLF'S GENDERED ANTECEDENTS

YCCC and NLF members, mostly in their twenties, came from NEUM affiliates, especially the Cape Peninsula Students' Union (CPSU) and African People's Democratic Union of Southern Africa (APDUSA), and from the South West African People's Organization (SWAPO).[13] Founded in 1943 as a federal organization, the NEUM sought to attract African, Coloured, and Indian organizations around a common democratic platform in the hope of undermining the state-imposed sectional divisions. Its two main affiliates were the All-African Convention (AAC) and the Anti-CAD movement

9. First, *117 Days*, p. 139.

10. Mbatha, "Narratives", p. 105; Stephen Clingman, *Bram Fischer: Afrikaner Revolutionary* (Cape Town. [etc.], 1998), p. 337.

11. Distinguished from public space, political space exists within and across organizations and expands or shrinks horizontally and vertically, above and underground. David Howell, *British Workers and the Independent Labour Party, 1886–1906* (Manchester, 1983), pp. 129–132, 277–282, discusses expanding political space in a democratizing society.

12. M. Bahati Kuumba, *Gender and Social Movements* (Walnut Creek, CA [etc.], 2001), pp. 83–84.

13. Author interview, Kenneth Abrahams, Windhoek, February 1988.

against the Coloured Affairs Department (CAD), but factionalism culminated in a split in December 1958.[14]

The NEUM accepted the idea of gender equality, but its conception of political activism assumed an abstract individual with traits then associated mainly with men – active, public, political, and vocal – in contrast to the traits then linked to women – passive, private, domestic, and silent.[15] Point one of the NEUM's 1943 Ten Point Programme of minimum democratic demands declared: "the right of every man and woman over the age of twenty one to elect, and be elected to Parliament, Provincial Councils and all other Divisional and Municipal Councils". Point one's explanatory remarks called for "the end of all political tutelage, of all communal or indirect representation, and the granting to all Non Europeans of the same [...] ballot as at present enjoyed by Europeans". But those demands would not be sufficient to end gender inequality, as white women were also subjected to sexism. Point six called for: "Full equality of rights for all citizens without distinction of race, colour and sex". Yet, its explanatory remarks stated only: "this means the abolition of all discriminatory Colour Bar Laws".[16]

The NEUM's ambiguity towards gender was hardly unique. Unlike the NEUM, the ANC had a Women's League, but only in 1943 did the ANC accept women as full rather than auxiliary members. Its June 1955 Freedom Charter called for gender equality, albeit confusedly. Describing South Africans as a "brotherhood" and as "countrymen and brothers", it nonetheless added that "only a democratic state [...] can secure to all their birthright without distinction of colour, race, sex or belief [...] The rights of the people shall be the same, regardless of race, colour or sex". However, it concluded, "All laws which discriminate on grounds of race, colour or belief shall be repealed".[17]

The liberation movement was aware of gender inequality. The 1950s opened with mass demonstrations by African women protesting the state's efforts to impose passes on them. The Congress-aligned Federation of South African Women (FEDSAW) adopted a detailed Women's Charter at its April 1954 inaugural conference. The charter called for social provision for mothers and children and "the removal of all laws, regulations, conventions and

14. David Johnson, *Dreaming of Freedom in South Africa: Literature between Critique and Utopia* (Edinburgh, 2020), pp. 104–132; Corinne Sandwith, *World of Letters: Reading Communities and Cultural Debates in Early Apartheid South Africa* (Pietermaritzburg, 2014), pp. 86–172; Allison Drew, "Social Mobilization and Racial Capitalism in South Africa, 1928–1960" (Ph.D., University of California, Los Angeles, 1991), pp. 423–517.

15. Joan Wallach Scott, "French Feminists and the Rights of 'Man': Olympe de Gouges's Declarations", *History Workshop*, 28 (Autumn, 1989), pp. 1–21, 4.

16. *The Ten-Point Programme* [1943], in Allison Drew, ed., *South Africa's Radical Tradition: A Documentary History*, vol. II (Cape Town [etc.], 1997), pp. 62–63.

17. "The Freedom Charter adopted at the Congress of the People at Kliptown, Johannesburg on 25 and 26 June 1955", in Drew, *Radical Tradition*, vol. II, pp. 121–124, 121–122.

customs that discriminate against us as women, and that deprive us in any way of our inherent right to the advantages, responsibilities and opportunities that society offers to any one section of the population".[18]

FEDSAW's communist members facilitated its membership in the Soviet-aligned Women's International Democratic Federation (WIDF), whose overseas conferences offered FEDSAW access to international political space. FEDSAW's Helen Joseph, Lillian Ngoyi, and Dora Tamana attended the WIDF's July 1955 World Congress of Mothers in Lausanne, Switzerland. On their return, FEDSAW convened its own Congress of Mothers in August 1955.[19] But FEDSAW was denied formal membership in the ANC-led Congress Alliance, thus limiting its national political space. Nonetheless, the Women's Charter and the earlier Ten Point Programme were pressures for the Freedom Charter's adoption. The rigid sectarianism dividing the NEUM and the Congress movement made it unlikely that the FEDSAW influenced NEUM women, although they could not have missed the massive women's march on Pretoria's Union Buildings on 9 August 1956.[20]

The NEUM's anti-Stalinist leaders had no comparable international links, although they had contacts with the small, fragmented Fourth International aligned with exiled Soviet dissident Leon Trotsky. But they encouraged radical education through lectures and discussions outside formal teaching institutions and, in 1937, launched the New Era Fellowship (NEF) to provide an intellectual space for black University of Cape Town (UCT) students excluded from the university's non-academic spaces.[21] White supremacy permeated UCT's atmosphere, penetrating the psyches of its tiny numbers of black students, who, with rare exceptions, sat together at the back of lecture theatres and congregated outside at a campus spot cynically called Blackies' Corner or, optimistically, Freedom Square.[22]

NEUM-affiliated educational fellowships mushroomed around the Cape Peninsula in the 1940s and 1950s. Cape Town's laws impeded the influx of Africans, and fellowship audiences were generally people classified as Coloured with some higher education – most were teachers. In 1951, the

---

18. "Report of the first National Conference of Women held in the Trades Hall, Johannesburg, South Africa, 17 April 1954", in Drew, *Radical Tradition*, vol. II, pp. 115–121, 118; Bahati Kuumba, *Gender*, pp. 40, 81; Cherryl Walker, *Women and Resistance in South Africa* (Cape Town [etc.], [1982] 1991), part three.
19. Meghan Healy-Clancy, "The Family Politics of the Federation of South African Women: A History of Public Motherhood in Women's Antiracist Activism", *Signs* (2017), 42, 4, 843–866, 857–859.
20. Healy-Clancy, "Family", 861–862; Lundin, "'Now'", pp. 327–328. The Congress Alliance included the ANC, South African Indian Congress, Coloured People's Congress, Congress of Democrats, and Congress of Trade Unions.
21. Sandwith, *World*, pp. 157–158.
22. Deirdre Levinson, *Five Years: An Experience of South Africa* (London, 1966), p. 68.

NEUM's founding father, master orator, and thinker, Isaac Tabata, launched the Society of Young Africa as an AAC affiliate to promote political education of African township youth. Benita Parry attended NEF lectures and estimated that women constituted some thirty-five to fifty-five per cent of its audiences. Nonetheless, men dominated the discussions as they often had higher educational qualifications than women, making participation in such discussions less intimidating. The "woman question" was rarely if ever discussed – an interesting silence given that the Russian Marxists from whom NEUM leaders drew their inspiration had often discussed and written about the topic.[23]

Jane Gool was a significant exception to the male-dominated leadership. Born in 1902, as a young woman she joined the Lenin Club, and helped launch the Spartacist Club, Workers Party of South Africa, Anti-CAD, and NEUM. An organizer, newspaper contributor, pamphleteer, and public speaker, she nonetheless "had no time for other women", thought Ursula Fataar (née Wolhuter). "They saw her as strange and quirky. She would speak at their [NEUM] conferences and was part of the inner group that organized the NEUM".[24]

More generously, Benita Parry notes Gool's courage as the daughter of an elite conservative Muslim family who broke racial and religious barriers by attending the South African Native College (later University of Fort Hare) and marrying an African – Isaac Tabata. But Gool never promoted herself as a spokesperson for women or pushed the woman question. "It seems to me that she was positioned as a figure-head which confirmed the movement's commitment to a gender equality that never was", Parry recalled. She was "on all the important committees", Parry explained, and "well-versed in Marxist literature and in Trotskyites [sic] debates both national and international. She invariably contributed to internal theoretical discussion, and was also a practiced and effective public speaker".[25]

Yet, an experienced public speaker well-versed in Marxist theory was certainly not a figurehead. Neville Alexander described her as "almost my political mother [...] who, behind the scenes, played a very, very important role". Her niece, Nina Hassim, who once caught her reading a book as she cooked, saw her as an aunt, mentor, and comrade who encouraged her to read whatever she liked. She "could speak well and had a good presence [...] and saw herself as a revolutionary, devoted to politics".[26]

23. Benita Parry to author, 26 July 1996; cf. Sandwith, *World*, p. 167; Crain Soudien, *The Cape Radicals: Intellectual and Political Thought of the New Era Fellowship, 1930s–1960s* (Johannesburg, 2019), pp. 8, 128; Richard Stites, *The Women's Liberation Movement in Russia: Feminism, Nihilism, and Bolshevism, 1860–1930* (Princeton, NJ, 1978), pp. 233–277, 317–422.

24. Author interview, Ursula Fataar, 24 June 2018, Wynberg, Cape Town; J. Gool–Tabata [obituary], *APDUSA*. Available at: http://www.apdusa.org.za/book-authors/gool-tabata-j/ [n.d.]; last accessed 15 July 2020.

25. Parry to author.

26. UCTMA BC1538 A2.2–2.4, Augie Matsemela, interview, Neville Alexander, September 1988, pp. 39, 41; Author interview, Nina Hassim, Cape Town, 10 May 2019.

In contrast to Jane Gool's influential public role and behind-the-scenes power, the Scottish immigrant, author, and Marxist literary critic Dora Taylor played an extremely important intellectual role in the background – refraining, as a white person, from overshadowing the NEUM's public proceedings. She worked closely with Tabata, and her breadth of intellect profoundly influenced Neville Alexander.[27]

Tabata, indeed, encouraged women. When the NEUM organized a boycott of the April 1952 Jan van Riebeeck Tercentenary Festival commemorating the arrival of Dutch colonizers, he insisted that Phyllis Ntantala Jordan speak on a public podium. She was reticent. "But when I took up the theme of 'We have Nothing to Celebrate' and related it to the position of African women, the exploited workers in the cities and the widows of the reserves", she realized, "I was not at a loss of what to say".[28] However few in numbers, the NEUM had important women intellectuals.

STUDENT POLITICS AND POLITICAL FAMILIES

With NEUM organizations largely silent on gender, it is hardly surprising that young socialist women of those years did not directly challenge the gender hierarchy in which they had been socialized and politicized. Instead, they became activists in issue-oriented student movement politics, feeling more comfortable speaking in the small study circles popping up across the western Cape, rather than in the earlier large, hierarchically organized meetings.

Cape Town political circles were small, and politics was very much a "family business", according to activist James Marsh. One knew who the active families were, the Van der Heydens being a case in point.[29] Elizabeth van der Heyden credits growing up in a "free-thinking family [...] a big rowdy family" as crucial to her intellectual and political development. Born in December 1935, her father was a carpenter, and her mother a housewife who cleaned for a white family. They lived in Gleemoor, a working-class area of Athlone, a Coloured township. Their council house carried a stigma, but the children were fortunate in being allowed to talk and ask questions, and in this way she learned to speak in small groups. They spoke English at home and listened to BBC radio.[30]

27. Matsemela, interview, Alexander, pp. 52–53; Sandwith, *World*, pp. 66–128; Johnson, *Dreaming*, pp. 107, 119–130; Ciraj Shahid Rassool, "The Individual, Auto/biography and History in South Africa" (Ph.D., University of the Western Cape, 2004).
28. Phyllis Jordan, *A Life's Mosaic: The Autobiography of Phyllis Ntantala* (Bellville, [etc.], 1992), pp. 151–152.
29. Author interview, James Marsh, Kenwyn, Cape Town, 30 June 2018.
30. Author interview, Elizabeth van der Heyden, Elfindale, Cape Town, 8 June 2018; Scanlon, *Representation*, p. 202.

Despite her mother's warnings that men did not like smart women, Van der Heyden was a good student and voracious reader, and with her father's support she got to standard 10 – the end of high school. She attended Wynberg and Athlone High, and at both schools was strongly influenced by her NEUM teachers. Thus politicized, she began attending the Cape Flats Educational Fellowship.

Nursing and teaching were the only professions open to women classified as Coloured. Van der Heyden's younger brother, Leslie, was groomed for university, but she was expected to go to teacher training college, although later their younger sister, Doris, attended university. Elizabeth took a two-year teacher training course at Hewat Training College, where the NEF held joint meetings with the college debating society. In 1956, she began teaching at Grassy Park High, where Ursula Wolhuter taught. Wolhuter, politicized through her Livingstone High teachers, had also attended Hewat, and found Van der Heyden "very revolutionary".[31] The next year, Van der Heyden joined the NEUM-affiliated Teachers' League of South Africa (TLSA), but it was consumed by the NEUM's factionalism and scarcely did any organizational work. It was also male dominated. Although many teachers were women, most TLSA leaders were men with the higher educational qualifications prized for the top positions.[32]

The government hammered black education, introducing the Extension of University Education – University Apartheid – Bill in 1956. The NEUM had campaigned against the 1953 Bantu Education Act, but this new bill hit its Cape Town leadership particularly hard, Alexander suggested, because of the NEUM's stress on higher education and the mystique that UCT had for the western Cape's Coloured intelligentsia.[33] Heretofore, tiny numbers of black students had enrolled at UCT and University of the Witwatersrand, which together had less than 100 African students in the late 1940s. By 1958, out of 12,019 students at all English-speaking universities, 269 were African, 350 were Coloured, and 606 Indian. In 1959, University Apartheid became law, prohibiting black students from registering at formerly open universities without written permission from the Minister of Internal Affairs – an attempt to stifle the development of black intellectuals and professionals.[34]

The University Apartheid Bill had catalysed the CPSU's launch in March 1957 – despite opposition from the Anti-CAD, which was responsible for

---

31. Author interview, Van der Heyden; Author interview, Fataar.
32. Author interview, Van der Heyden; BC1538 D5.1.1. 13, Elizabeth van der Heyden, pp. 1517–1518; Scanlon, *Representation*, pp. 204–205.
33. Matsemela, interview, Alexander, pp. 57–58.
34. M.A. Beale, "The Evolution of the Policy of University Apartheid", n.d. p. 82. Available at: https://sas-space.sas.ac.uk/4228/1/M A Beale - The evolution of the policy of university apartheid.pdf; last accessed 27 May 2020; John A. Marcum, *Education, Race, and Social Change in South Africa* (Berkeley, CA [etc.], 1982), pp. 3–5.

the educational fellowships and saw the CPSU as a threat. While the National Union of South African Students (NUSAS) campaigned for academic non-segregation, the CPSU countered that academic non-segregation meant non-academic segregation or social apartheid rather than full democracy.[35]

Already teaching, Van der Heyden became an associate CPSU member. Previously, in her words, an "observer rather than participant", in the CPSU she became an activist.[36] Virtually all of the office-bearers were men. UCT medical student Kenneth Abrahams was president, and Alexander editor of its organ *The Student*; in Van der Heyden's recollection, they were the main speakers and movers. She met Ottilie Schimming, Hewat student Marcus Solomon, who had attended Trafalgar High, and UCT law student Fikile Bam, who, as a student at St Peter's in Johannesburg, had been particularly influenced by his teacher Oliver Tambo. Entering UCT in 1958, he recalled, there were "six black African students and no more than about 26 coloureds and Indians".[37]

Van der Heyden launched the CPSU's South Peninsula Branch in Grassy Park and urged her good friend Dulcie September to join. Born in August 1935, September's parents were apolitical, her father a primary school principal, and her mother a housewife. The Septembers and Van der Heydens lived around the corner from each other in Athlone, although the Septembers had a higher social standing.[38]

Dulcie's father was brutal. To avoid his beatings, she frequented the Van der Heyden home; she and Elizabeth became good friends. Not academically inclined as a child – perhaps because of the beatings – September was twice held back, so that she was in the same class as her younger sister. Like Van der Heyden, she attended Athlone High, where she was similarly politicized by her NEUM teachers. But in standard 8, her father removed her from school. He threw her out of the house, so she slept on the front stoep until she found new accommodation – learning early the price of speaking back to power.[39]

Nonetheless, she persevered, attending evening classes while working days, and passing standard 8. She began but did not finish a teacher training course at Wesley Training College, Salt River. However, her mother appealed to Dr Richard van der Ross, principal of Battswood Teacher Training College in

35. BC1538 D5.1.1.14, Neville Alexander, p. 1657; BC1538 D3.5, *The Student*, n.d. [1957].
36. Elizabeth van der Heyden, pp. 1517–1518; Author interview, Van der Heyden; Scanlon, *Representation*, pp. 204–205.
37. UCT Legal Resource Centre Oral History Project, interview, Fikile Bam, 29 November 2007, p. 3; Allison Drew, "Marcus Solomon", 13 May 2019, *South African History Online*. Available at: https://www.sahistory.org.za/people/marcus-solomon; last accessed 30 January 2021.
38. Dulcie September Biography, n.d., courtesy Michael Arendse; BC1538 D5.1.1.13, Dulcie September, p. 1583.
39. Author interview, Van der Heyden.

Figure 1. A young Dulcie September, no date.
Source: Unknown.

Wynberg. Determined, September enrolled and completed the course. In July 1956, she began teaching at Bridgetown Primary, Athlone's first primary school, where the entering students were already nine or ten years old (Figure 1). Struck by the local poverty and the overcrowded classes, she "became aware of the struggle people were facing". She joined the TLSA and attended CPSU meetings but never joined, despite Van der Heyden's urgings.[40]

40. September Biography; September, pp. 1560–1561, 1588.

In December 1960, Tabata, Jane Gool, and Alie Fataar launched the African People's Democratic Union – APDUSA from January 1961. A unitary organization allowing people to join directly, APDUSA prioritized the demands of black workers and peasants.[41] It therefore attracted a younger and more militant membership not occupationally restricted to teaching. Van der Heyden and September resigned from the TLSA because of its endless squabbles and joined APDUSA.[42]

In the meantime, Alexander had left South Africa in September 1958 to pursue doctoral studies at the University of Tübingen. In Germany, he joined the Sozialistische Deutsche Studentenbund (Socialist German Student Union, SDS), organized migrant workers for the metalworkers union, and, with the Algerian anti-colonial war in full swing, engaged in solidarity work for the Front de Libération Nationale (FLN). He fell in love with Tübingen student and SDS comrade Irmgard Bolle. But the Sharpeville-Langa massacres of 21 March 1960 confirmed his need to liberate his country. He obtained a DPhil *magna cum laude* in February 1961 and, on his way home, visited Trotsky's widow Natalia Sedova in Paris and met with Fourth International representatives. They advised him that if the NEUM sent two representatives to Paris, the Fourth International would assist with preparations for armed struggle. Alexander reached Cape Town in July 1961, convinced of the need to build international solidarity networks to help black South Africans travel overseas.[43] He had received several teaching offers in Europe, but could not obtain a post at UCT – although very few white academics then had a doctorate. So, in September 1961 he began teaching at Livingstone High.[44]

THE MOVE TO UNDERGROUND POLITICS

Spurred by the early 1950s expansion of political space, the 1956 Riotous Assemblies Act prohibited open-air public gatherings that the government deemed a danger to public peace. Shortly after the Sharpeville-Langa massacres, the 1960 Unlawful Organizations Act No. 34 outlawed organizations seen as threatening public order. Certain political leaders had already been banned – Tabata in 1956, for his oratory successes, for instance. Now, the ANC and Pan Africanist Congress (PAC) were banned.

41. Robin Kayser and Mohamed Adhikari, "Land and Liberty! The African People's Democratic Union of Southern Africa during the 1960s", in SADET, *Road*, pp. 319–339, 322–324.
42. Elizabeth van der Heyden, p. 1518; Scanlon, *Representation*, pp. 206–207.
43. Neville Alexander, p. 1651; Matsemela, interview, Alexander, pp. 35–36; Quinn Slobodian, *Foreign Front: Third World Politics in Sixties West Germany* (Durham, NC, 2012), pp. 22–24; Brigitta Busch, Lucijan Busch, and Karen Press, eds, *Interviews with Neville Alexander: The Power of languages against the language of Power* (Scottsville, Pietermaritzburg, 2014), pp. 59–66.
44. Levinson, *Five Years*, pp. 139–140; Matsemela, interview, Alexander, pp. 33–34.

Political space receded underground. Activists met secretly in individual homes. Using a methodology of reading and discussion, study groups sprang up to assess the rapidly evolving conditions. So did sabotage groups. In late May 1961, a PAC faction launched the underground *Poqo* (meaning alone, pure), its cells drawing on home-boy networks linking migrant workers in towns with their communities of origin, often one rural village. In September and October, the SACP and recently formed National Committee of Liberation (NCL) each engaged in sabotage. In December, *Poqo* distributed incendiary leaflets in African townships around Cape Town. MK incorporated the SACP military units and on 16 December 1961 launched a rolling sabotage campaign.[45]

The NEUM was already squeezed by the Congress movement's expansion and marginalized by its own reticence to engage in mass protests. Concerned that it would be further diminished if it did not plan for armed struggle, Alexander conveyed the Fourth International message to the leadership. Fearing the NEUM would be banned if it came out for armed struggle, they forbid him to speak about it. However, he was invited to a secret leadership caucus, where he "crossed swords with Jane [Gool]" and decided not to attend any further leadership caucus meetings. Kenneth and Ottilie Abrahams were SWAPO members. SWAPO came out for armed struggle, Kenneth Abrahams – by then a medical doctor – pushed the SWAPO line, and Alexander defended him. In January 1962, Abrahams and Alexander were suspended from SOYA and, as a result, from other NEUM affiliates.[46]

However, the two men had APDUSA supporters. Like the Van der Heydens, the Alexanders were a political family. Neville and his younger sister Dorothy were "live-wires".[47] Born in August 1938, Dorothy attended Holy Rosary Convent in Cradock and obtained her teaching certificate from Dower Memorial College in Uitenhage, joining the TLSA in 1956. In January 1960, she started teaching at Garden Village Methodist School in Maitland. After her brother's return, she accompanied him to lectures on international affairs, joining APDUSA around August–September. She joined an unofficial Lansdowne APDUSA group, which had several teachers and two students. Brian Landers attended the University College of the Western Cape (UCWC), a Coloured institution established under University Apartheid.

45. Monica Wilson and Archie Mafeje, *Langa: A Study of Social Groups in an African Township* (Oxford, 1963), pp. 14, 47; Bernard Magubane *et al.*, "The Turn to Armed Struggle", in SADET, *Road*, pp. 53–145, 79–90; Tom Lodge, *Sharpeville: An Apartheid Massacre and Its Consequences* (Oxford, 2011), pp. 194–195; Eddie Daniels, *There & Back: Robben Island, 1964–1979* (Cape Town, 1998), p. 105.
46. Matsemela, interview, Alexander, pp. 38, 42; Author interview, Kenneth Abrahams; Neville Alexander, pp. 1661–1662; Rassool, "Individual", pp. 465–468; Levinson, *Five Years*, pp. 149–153.
47. Author interview, Marsh; Neville Alexander, p. 1661.

Franz Lee, from an impoverished northeast Cape family, became a clerk in Cape Town. Fired and blacklisted, he enrolled at the distance-education University of South Africa (UNISA). The Lansdowne group invited Neville Alexander and Kenneth Abrahams to lecture on Algeria, Cuba and South West Africa.[48]

Neville Alexander had already joined Wolhuter's study group.[49] In March 1962, Dorothy Alexander joined an Athlone caucus of discontented Apdusans, which included Elizabeth van der Heyden, September, and Solomon. They invited Abrahams and Alexander to speak. As September put it, "the [APDUSA] leadership […] had a bureaucratic hold over the organisation […] no progressive work could be done and the suspension of Drs. Alexander and Abrahams caused a rift in the organization […] many of the members were contemplating leaving". The caucus met fortnightly to discuss revamping APDUSA.[50]

Around April, a new circle began meeting fortnightly at the Abrahamses's home. Like the Van der Heydens and Alexanders, Ottilie Schimming came from a political family. Born in September 1937, in Old Location Township near Windhoek, her father was South West Africa's first black teacher, and her mother an ardent proponent of national liberation. Multilingual, in 1952, she helped found the South West Africa Student Body – later the South West Africa Progressive Association (SWAPA) (Figure 2). She and her activist sisters Norah, Charlotte, and Isabella were sent to school in Cape Town. Exceptionally determined, in Cape Town Ottilie "made sure [she] met the right kind of people".[51] She attended Trafalgar High, also influenced by her NEUM teachers.

She began meeting with fellow Namibians at Timothy's Barber Shop in Cape Town's Sea Point suburb and, in 1957, became a founding member of the Ovambo and People's Congress [later, Ovamboland People's Organization, then SWAPO] led by Andimba Toivo ya Toivo. The NEUM and CPSU included many Namibian students, and Ottilie joined, attracted by their "atmosphere of lively debate".[52]

Graduating from UCT in 1960, she began teaching, "already clear that the man [she] was going to marry […] would have to come to Namibia". She had valued the NEUM's "constructive criticism", but when it suspended Alexander and her husband, "they came to a parting of the ways". In her words, "we were not going to get our freedom without some sort of armed

48. BC1538 D5.1.1.13, Dorothy Alexander, pp. 1548–1550; BC1538 D6, *Franz J. T. Lee*, New York: Alexander Defense Committee, n.d.
49. Allison Drew and Lungisile Ntsebeza, interview, Marcus Solomon, Rylands, Cape Town, 15 June 2018; Author interview, Fataar.
50. September, p. 1562, Elizabeth van der Heyden, pp. 1519–1520; Neville Alexander, p. 1663.
51. UCT Centre for Popular Memory [hereafter UCTCPM] BC1223, Augie Matsemela, interviews, Ottilie Abrahams, Windhoek, 31 October, 3 November 1988.
52. Matsemela, interviews, Ottilie Abrahams.

Figure 2. Ottilie Schimming, SWAPA Reception, International Hall, Windhoek, 3 July 1960. *Source: South West News*, 9 July 1960.

struggle […] we felt that this was the only way out […] it was something we grew into". Her sister Charlotte was going out with Solomon and convinced him to join SWAPO.[53]

53. *Ibid.*; Author interview, Ottilie Abrahams, Windhoek, February 1988; Author interview, Kenneth Abrahams; Yvette Abrahams, "Tribute to 'Mother of Education'", *Namibian*, 4 July 2018. Available at: https://www.namibian.com.na/179164/archive-read/Tribute-to-Mother-of-Education; last accessed 3 August 2020; BC1538 D5.1.1.16, Marcus Solomon, pp. 1930–1954.

Initially, the Abrahamses's group included Neville Alexander, Xenophon Pitt, a UCWC student and CPSU member from Queenstown, and Andreas Shipanga of SWAPO. A teacher, Shipanga had left South West Africa for further education. When ya Toivo was banished to Ovamboland, Shipanga took over his organization's Cape Town branch. He recalled that the YCCC included "South Africans and Namibians, including myself and some other current members of SWAPO. We studied Marxism-Leninism and the writings of Mao Tse-tung and 'Che' Guevara. This was only a study circle, but all the same it was forming cadre who were to become the instructors and leaders of our guerrillas".[54]

In May, Kenneth Abrahams invited Solomon to join.[55] Bam, who boarded with the Abrahamses, began attending in June, along with two other SWAPO members, migrant worker David Haufiku, and, briefly, Peter Kaluma; the three Swapos were also Liberal Party members. In mid-July, Kenneth Abrahams invited Van der Heyden after learning she had been reading independently about guerrilla struggles. The second woman in the group, she was "eager for new ideas". Bam suggested the group be called *Ingqungquthela yesizwe* [a coming together of the nation]. But they decided on YCCC, after Mao Tse Tung's book *Yu Chi Chan* [*On Guerrilla Warfare*]. According to Van der Heyden: "We felt armed struggle was inevitable and that we needed to be a part of it".[56]

They discussed building a united front and armed struggle strategies, an ongoing topic in political circles since the 1961 sabotage attacks. In addition to Mao, they read Che Guevara's *Guerrilla Warfare*, Joan Gillespie's *Algeria: Rebellion and Revolution*, and Deneys Reitz's *Commando*, about the 1899–1902 Afrikaner guerrilla war against the British. The point was not to mechanically apply these cases to South Africa, Dorothy Alexander explained, but to assess in what ways they might be applicable.[57]

They photostatted texts and published their own pamphlets, stimulating lively discussions with frequent disagreements. Neville Alexander wrote *The Conquest of Power in South Africa*; Kenneth Abrahams, *Technical and Organisational Aspects of the Yu Chi Chan Club*, and Van der Heyden, *Secret Communications*, based on the 1962 *Encyclopedia Britannica* section

54. Neville Alexander, p. 1663; Dennis Mercer, *Interviews in Depth – Namibia (SWAPO): Andreas Shipanga* (Richmond, BC, 1973), pp. 4, 6; *Namibian*, 21 February 2013. Available at: https://archive.is/20130221040735/http://www.namibian.com.na/news-articles/national/full-story/archive/2012/may/article/liberation-pioneer-dies/; last accessed 23 June 2020.
55. Drew and Ntsebeza, interview, Solomon, 15 June 2018.
56. Neville Alexander, p. 1663; BC1538 D5.1.1.11, Fikile Bam, p. 1352, has *Indqindqthela yesizwe*; Elizabeth van der Heyden, p. 1520; Ronald Dreyer, *Namibia & Southern Africa: Regional Dynamics of Decolonization, 1945–1990* (Abingdon, [1994] 2016), p. 204, n. 26; Randolph Vigne, *Liberals against Apartheid: A History of the Liberal Party of South Africa, 1953–1968* (Macmillan, 1997), p. 185.
57. Dorothy Alexander, p. 1553, Elizabeth van der Heyden, pp. 1520–1522; Neville Alexander, pp. 1667, 1700.

on "codes and ciphers".[58] The pamphlets' authorship reflected, not gender, but that some members had the scholarly training to write long complex pieces and some did not. Nor was production gendered: Neville Alexander and Landers typed; Giose stencilled; Ottilie Abrahams cyclostyled; Solomon and Bam stapled.[59]

Work in APDUSA continued: Neville Alexander and Solomon ran under-the-radar study groups; Elizabeth van der Heyden, Dorothy Alexander, and September served on its finance committee; Van der Heyden and Pitt organized; September and Wolhuter convened meetings. Similarly, the Abrahamses and Shipanga organized SWAPO study groups and published *South-West Commentator* and *SWAPO (Cape Town Branch)*. They roneoed documents at the Van der Heyden home and in the Abrahamses's garage, where production of the YCCC/NLF documents became centralized.[60]

In November–December, Haufiku left for South West Africa, Bam, to prepare for exams, and Pitt, to teach in Queenstown. Those remaining disbanded the YCCC and decided to organize a network of cells called the National Liberation Front, after the Algerian FLN. These cells would study the YCCC publications and comparative works on guerrilla warfare. This decision was confirmed at an executive committee meeting on 16–18 January 1963. But setting off on their own had consequences, Alexander conceded: "We didn't have the maturity. We didn't have the resources. We didn't have the network". MK, by contrast, had the ANC and SACP.[61]

THE NLF: STRUCTURE AND RECRUITMENT

The anonymous typescript *When, Where, Why was the N.L.F. Formed?* describes the NLF's structure and aims. The NLF aspired to link other groups into a united front, "organize in breadth not depth" and create a network of cells with ten regions, five zones, five areas, and one cell per area, i.e. *dorp*, location, or part of a town. Possibly influenced by the FLN model, cells were to have a maximum of ten members – most were smaller – and regional committees with two members from each cell would coordinate work by passing information to and from the cells.[62]

---

58. Author interview, Van der Heyden; Elizabeth van der Heyden, p. 1522; Matsemela, interview, Alexander, pp. 67–68; UCTMA, A.H. Murray Papers [hereafter BC1253], A.1.1; During the trial two pamphlets were attributed to Kenneth Abrahams.

59. Bam, pp. 1411–1412; Neville Alexander, pp. 1744, 1755.

60. Elizabeth van der Heyden, pp. 1519–1520; Neville Alexander, p. 1701.

61. Matsemela, interview, Alexander, pp. 45, 81; Neville Alexander, pp. 1701–1703, denied the NLF was named after the FLN; September, p. 1611.

62. BC1253, *When, Where, Why was the N.L.F. Formed?* (April 1962 [sic]), p. 2; Marcus Solomon to author, 3 June 2020, thought that the document was collectively discussed; Scanlon, *Representation*, pp. 208–209.

The NLF sought people with political and organizational experience keen to study guerrilla struggle and form cells. New recruits were to be vetted by two individuals, but this was not always practiced. The desired attributes were revolutionary ardour, honesty, integrity, intelligence, initiative, and fearlessness; idealistically, each member was "to devote 24 hours per day for revolution" and "to work and play only when very necessary".[63] They debated whether revolutionaries should have children; some already did.[64]

Significantly, the document stipulated: "No sex discrimination [...] No age discrimination. No discrimination on grounds of political history". Despite the stricture on age discrimination, the document stated a preference for people between the ages of 20 and 35 as students were seen as "usually too immature", and older people, "too fixed in way of thinking".[65]

Recruitment developed through personal networks, broadly following gender lines, with some exceptions. In Van der Heyden's recollection they looked at CPSU and APDUSA members who would fit into the sort of organization they were envisioning. She recruited September, whom she thought was an adept organizer and administrator; September recalled learning that the NLF was a study group in January–February 1963 and joining in March because she "was interested in learning". Van der Heyden also recruited Dorothy Alexander and Doris van der Heyden, her younger sister. A CPSU member, Doris attended Athlone High and studied librarianship at UCT. In 1961, she became a library assistant at the Cape Provincial Library Services. She joined APDUSA, but tired of its "continual bickering", she joined the new group.[66]

Elizabeth van der Heyden met Dorothy Adams at an APDUSA meeting. Born in 1928 and raised in the country town of Wellington, Adams's great-grandfather, the West Indian photographer Francis McDonald Gow, had introduced the African-American-founded African Methodist Episcopal Church (AMEC) to South Africa. Her maternal grandfather was an AMEC minister, and her mother, active in the church. The women in Dorothy's immediate family attended the AMEC, and the men, the Dutch Reformed Church, but Dorothy was not a regular churchgoer; her family saw her as opinionated and outspoken. She studied at Athlone Teacher Training College in Paarl, later returning to Wellington to teach at Pauw Gedenk Primary School.

Sorely disappointed by the failure of churches to challenge the Group Areas Act, Adams became active in the TLSA and APDUSA. In March 1963, the Wellington Apdusans invited Neville Alexander to lecture on Algeria.

63. *When, Where*, pp. 2–3, 9.
64. BC1538 D5.1.1.4, Reginald Francke, p. 380; Author interview, Van der Heyden; Lissoni and Suriano, "Married", p. 138, for a similar view of revolutionary lives.
65. *When, Where*, pp. 2–3, 9; Author interview, Van der Heyden.
66. Author interview, Van der Heyden; September, pp. 1563–1564, 1588; BC1538 D5.1.1.15, Doris van der Heyden, pp. 1880–1883.

Adams set up an NLF cell with three stable and various floating members, and Alexander and Solomon visited occasionally to drop off literature.[67] Since anyone who spoke out could be banned, Adams explained,

> we decided on this organization that could look at [...] the successful revolutions: Cuba, Algeria, China. But also there would be no public meetings, it would have to be cells, and the cells would operate in their area and [...] have a representative in that area who will meet with other representatives.[68]

Neville Alexander recruited his Livingstone colleagues Reginald Francke and Leslie van der Heyden, who knew of the group from his sister Elizabeth. Leslie attended Athlone High, graduated from UCT with a BA in Native Law and Administration, and Constitutional History and Law, and obtained a teaching certificate. He married Ursula February, whose activist brother Basil, a member of the ANC-aligned Coloured People's Congress, was planning to join MK. Basil February was well-acquainted with the NLF members: he had boarded with the Van der Heydens, was friends with Solomon, and argued fiercely about politics with Neville Alexander, some of the discussions filtering into *Liberation* (Figure 3).[69]

Alexander discussed armed struggle with lawyer and Apdusan Kader Hassim in Durban, but his overtures were rejected. He recruited Anti-CAD activist Gerald Giose, who taught with his mother Dimbiti Bisho Alexander at a Mowbray primary school; Giose's father, an AMEC minister and a communist, had ensured his children learn the Lord's Prayer and the Communist Manifesto.[70] Alexander approached Wolhuter, who was tired of endless conferences and meetings and thought guerrilla struggle was the only way forward. She was on the point of joining just before his arrest.[71]

Underground recruitment varied across the liberation movement but generally showed gendered patterns. For MK, Mandela prioritized male World War II veterans who knew sabotage techniques, while the SACP prioritized ideological commitment, with veteran communists evaluating prospective recruits.[72]

67. Scanlon, *Representation*, p. 208; Kayser and Adhikari, "Land", pp. 324–325; Neville Alexander, p. 1714; Author interview, Fataar; "Dorothy Adams", *South African History Online*. Available at: https://www.sahistory.org.za/people/dorothy-adams; last accessed 15 July 2020.

68. Quoted in Scanlon, *Representation*, p. 209.

69. BC1538 D5.1.1.10, Leslie van der Heyden, p. 1020; Author interview, Van der Heyden; Drew and Ntsebeza, interview, Solomon.

70. "Gerald Giose, National Liberation Front/Yu Chi Chan Club: ANC/Umkhonto we Sizwe (Cape Town, 6 December 1995)", in Tor Sellström, ed., *Liberation in Southern Africa: Regional and Swedish Voices. Interviews from Angola, Mozambique, Namibia, South Africa, Zimbabwe, the Frontline and Sweden* (Uppsala, 1999), pp. 122–127.

71. Nina Hassim to author, 27 July 2020; Author interview, Fataar.

72. Mandela, *Long Walk*, pp. 261–263; Joe Slovo, *Slovo: The Unfinished Autobiography* (Randburg [etc.], 1995–1996), p. 153.

Figure 3. *Liberation*, the NLF organ, appeared in 1963.
Source: Neville Alexander.

Jean Middleton and Sylvia Neame were recruited into the SACP. A young
teacher and socialist, Middleton was in the ANC-aligned South African

Congress of Democrats (COD) when Hilda Bernstein recruited her into a four-woman SACP cell. After training, including discussion of communist literature, Middleton moved to a mixed-sex cell. The cells were divided by tasks, ranging from slogan painting to distribution of flyers, to highly secretive document production. At the bottom of the SACP hierarchy were racially segregated area units and committees, reflecting residential apartheid. At the top were "mixed race" district and central committees. Women were in the lower, racially based groups, excluded from the top tiers on the preposterous grounds that their presence would enable the police to charge people under the Immorality Act, which forbade sex between people of different racial groups. "It's undeniable that the organization was dominated by men", Middleton concluded.[73]

As a Rhodes University student, Neame joined the Liberal Party, but switched to the COD when she moved to Cape Town. In August 1961, communist and trade unionist Reginald September invited her to join the SACP. She agreed, "thrilled to bits and very proud to have been asked". In January 1963, she moved to Johannesburg and joined a cell of young people in Hillbrow, before being drawn into the Rivonia network.[74]

By contrast, newly politicized UCT student Stephanie Kemp volunteered at the Defence & Aid Fund and was befriended by several older communist women – Ray Edwards, Dora Alexander, and Sarah Carneson. They lent her Eddie Roux's *Time Longer than Rope*, and she began eating supper with the Carnesons. In 1962, Fred Carneson invited her to join the SACP. "Becoming a Communist was easy [...] Marxism-Leninism provided guidelines". She joined a Party cell and read the few Marxist books she could find – many were censored. But there is no sense that the complexities of Marxism or of guerrilla struggle were discussed.[75]

That same year, Kemp joined the NCL – without telling her SACP comrades. NUSAS leader and Liberal Party member Adrian Leftwich invited her for coffee and asked if she would consider engaging in sabotage. Leftwich was "a senior and I was some small fry student, so I was highly flattered", she recalled. He insisted that she think about it, and she decided against it. But three weeks later Leftwich asked again. "I just never could bring myself to say no", she acknowledged. "I wasn't sophisticated enough to really sort out what I was doing or who [...] for or anything like that."[76] Male NCL

73. Jean Middleton, *Convictions: A Woman Political Prisoner Remembers* (Randburg, 1998), pp. 12–29, quotes p. 22. Acker, "Hierarchies", p. 152, notes that claims that women have a sexually unsettling influence in organizations are common.
74. Sylvia Neame to author, 30 September 2020.
75. Stephanie Kemp, *My Life: The Making of an Afrikaner Revolutionary in the South African Liberation Struggle* (Cape Town, 2018), pp. 61–64.
76. Julie Frederikse, interview, Stephanie Kemp, London, 1986, South African History Archive. Available at: http://www.saha.org.za/nonracialism/transcript of interview, stephanie kemp.htm; last accessed 20 April 2019, pp. 6, 10–11; Kemp, *My Life*, pp. 63–64.

activists recount many political discussions, but these did not, evidently, include Kemp.[77]

NLF ACTIVITIES

Unlike those groups, the NLF's division of labour was not gendered, nor were its cells divided by task. Its members formed cells, read, held discussions and lectures, produced articles for *Liberation*, and fundraised. The first two cells were Athlone–Lansdowne and Cape Town central. The Athlone–Lansdowne group met weekly at the Alexander home, with Neville Alexander, Ottilie Abrahams, Solomon, Shipanga, and Kenneth Abrahams, as chair. From February, Shipanga attended sporadically as he was often in Ovamboland preparing for his return as a SWAPO field organizer. September, Dorothy Alexander, and Doris van der Heyden began attending in March, later joined by Leslie van der Heyden, Reginald Francke, and Cyril Jacobs.[78] The group split; Elizabeth van der Heyden led the Athlone cell, and Neville Alexander the Lansdowne group.[79]

Solomon, by then teaching at Walmer Street Primary in Woodstock, formed a Cape Town central cell, which met weekly at his Walmer Estate home. The group initially included Elizabeth van der Heyden and Landers and, briefly, Philip April, as well as Apdusan Lionel Davis, who had completed his Cape Technical College junior certificate and was working as a storeman and clerk. They organized for APDUSA, but received their political education in the NLF, Lionel Davis recalled. Around March–April, Apdusan Yusuf Lucas and high school teacher Achmet Ajam joined the group, which began meeting at Ajam's house in Salt River. Kenneth Abrahams formed small groups in Maitland, led by Daniel Swavel, and in Elsies River, by Giose.[80]

The cells were run in a participatory style, with standardized agendas covering four points – developments in the camp of the oppressed, developments in the camp of the *Herrenvolk* [master race], finances, and general.[81] Each topic was introduced by a different person, broadening speaking opportunities. Women and men led discussions, lectured, or gave short talks – helpful for those with limited public-speaking experience. Neville Alexander lectured on Mao Tse Tung; Ottilie Abrahams kept the group's library and lent September Mao's book to read before the lecture. Ottilie Abrahams lectured

---

77. Baruch Hirson, *Revolutions in my Life* (Johannesburg, 1995), p. 301; Daniels, *There & Back*, p. 105.

78. Neville Alexander, pp. 1706, 1757; September, pp. 1632, 1638; Matsemela, interview, Alexander, p. 64.

79. September, p. 1565; Neville Alexander, p. 1757.

80. BC1538 D5.1.1.13, Lionel Davis, p. 1542, Elizabeth van der Heyden, pp. 1525–1527.

81. The NEUM used the Nazi term *herrenvolk* to describe white South Africans upholding white supremacy.

on South West African politics; Elizabeth van der Heyden on secret communications and on APDUSA; Solomon on the PAC; Landers on partisan warfare; and Doris van der Heyden on the uprising in Paarl, sixty-two kilometres northwest of Cape Town. On 22 November 1962, migrant workers from Mbekweni location had marched on Paarl with axes, pangas, and home-made weapons to attack the police station and free prisoners. Forewarned, the authorities shot at the crowd, killing seven and wounding many others. The government's Snyman Commission issued its interim report in March 1963, and the matter was often in the press.[82]

September, however, minimized her own participation: "I did not know enough about the subject being discussed and I came there to learn". Yet, she spoke clearly and succinctly. Her goal was freedom, she told the court at the NLF trial: "From the state in which we are now, not being able to study the way we want to, the [teaching] profession, to a certain extent, isn't free; to go where we want to without being stopped; freedom from apartheid". Her attitude towards violence was carefully considered: "all methods should be tried first [...] strikes, boycotts, formation of trade unions, demonstrations [...] if we can prove that those methods won't help us in the struggle, then only will we resort to violence, and only then".[83]

The NLF formed a regional committee to coordinate the cells; it held its first meeting in February. Initially, Neville Alexander was to be the NLF's editor and represent the Athlone–Lansdowne group on the regional committee, along with Ottilie Abrahams. But he was drinking heavily and missed meetings. He was suspended, and Ottilie Abrahams became the editor and Athlone–Lansdowne delegate; every member was held accountable for their actions.[84]

The NLF's monthly journal *Liberation* appeared in February, April, and May 1963. The February issue highlighted the January conference recommendations concerning their literature and their paid organizer. The NLF planned to form cells in Wellington, Worcester, Port Elizabeth, Cradock, and South West Africa and, within several months, in the Transkei, Natal, and Johannesburg. Their paid organizer had started building cells in Kimberley and Barkly West, it reported.

The paid organizer Don Davis, born in 1920, served in World War II, studied at the Transvaal Bible Institute and preached interdenominationally in Pentecostal churches. In August 1962, he met Kenneth Abrahams through their mutual friend Giose. His work took him to the rural and semi-rural areas of the north-western Cape and along the west coast. He was a "very unorthodox and eccentric sort of preacher", recounted Neville Alexander,

---

82. September, pp. 1565–1566, 1620–1621; Neville Alexander, pp. 1683, 1709; Doris van der Heyden, p. 1887; Bianca Paigè van Laun, "In the Shadows of the Archive: Investigating the Paarl march of November 22nd 1962" (MA, University of the Western Cape, 2012).
83. September, pp. 1570, 1591, 1596–1597.
84. Neville Alexander, p. 1705; Author interview, Van der Heyden.

and the NLF thought he would be able to identify people amenable to their ideas – figuring out "who was who and what was what in the countryside".[85]

In the meantime, the NLF's propagandizing amongst Apdusans had an impact. In September 1962, Jane Gool complained to Tabata that Alexander and his supporters aimed to "wreck" APDUSA.[86] Late that year, Tabata secretly left the country to seek support from other African countries. The Algerian government promised to help train NEUM soldiers. As a result, in January 1963 – a year after the Abrahams and Alexander suspensions – an extended executive meeting accepted "armed insurrection as the only method of struggle against the Herrenvolk State" and stipulated that APDUSA would organize a people's army. *Liberation* speculated whether the new policy was simply a gesture to prolong the NEUM's life.[87]

Two months later, *Liberation* reported on Transkei politics. Bam had joined the NLF and after his exams spent two months in the Transkei interviewing a range of individuals – civil servants, administrators, journalists, businessmen, protest leaders, and headmen. "I had an hypothesis on what was happening in the Transkei", Bam explained, "and what I was really doing was to test out and confirm some of my own opinions about the Transkei". *Liberation*'s report argued that "because the Transkei is going to be our 'primary field of operation' [...] the work done thus far must be regarded as grossly inadequate". The region would be dependent on urban cells until a wide and effective network could be established, it concluded.[88]

Liberation also carried articles on South West Africa, the NLF's other expected terrain of struggle. "A brief survey of the revolutionary movement in S.W.A" stressed the need for political education over military struggle: "To recruit guerrillas who are still politically raw would be in opposition to our policy of training leaders". Another report the next month referred to an NLF member who had arrived on 28 February and met with SWAPO leaders – presumably Shipanga – and more coming shortly.[89]

As in the YCCC, women and men produced the literature. The articles were typed – Elizabeth van der Heyden recalls a group of them at the Alexander home, she dictating, while Neville Alexander typed – then duplicated through cyclostyling and later a photostat machine. September, the "post office", received and distributed material. The articles were in English; Francke was planning to translate some literature into Afrikaans, which was widely spoken in the western and northern Cape and South West Africa, but this never happened.[90]

---

85. Matsemela, interview, Alexander, pp. 62–63; BC1538 D5.1.1.13, Don Davis, pp. 1499–1500.
86. Rassool, "Individual", pp. 468–469; Levinson, *Five Years*, 149.
87. Kayser and Adhikari, "Land", pp. 324–325; *Liberation*, 1, 1 (February 1963), p. 13.
88. Bam, pp. 1468–1470, 1491–1495, denied writing the report; *Liberation*, 1:2 (April 1963), p. 7.
89. *Liberation*, 1:2 (April 1963), pp. 7–9, and 1, 3 (May 1963), p. 3.
90. Author interview, Van der Heyden; BC1538 D5 1.1 4, Francke, pp. 362–364; BC1538 D5 1.1 11.5, Brian Landers, p. 499; Bam, p. 1411.

Producing and distributing literature required money. To fundraise they sold literature and organized social events, such as concerts, bobops – dances at private homes where one paid to enter – and rummage sales. But their paltry fundraising – 38 Rand on one occasion – was a far cry from that of the SACP, which received US$30,000 from the Soviets in 1960, US$50,000 in 1961, and, as sabotage increased, US$112,445 in 1962.[91] Indeed, the NLF was financially strapped. Its Interim National Executive conceded that their paid organizer had been inadequately trained and they would have to forego his services due to their lack of funds. However, the executive was planning to set up a school for organizers consisting of NLF officials and at least one representative from each cell – how they intended to pay for this was not mentioned.[92]

BUILDING A NETWORK

To expand underground, the NLF needed legal cover organizations. They formed the Rover Soccer and Excelsior Table Tennis Clubs and, drawing on their experience on the CPSU's bursary fund and APDUSA's finance committee, in April 1963, they set up the South African Students Bursary & Loan Fund. Solomon drafted the constitution, which was modified and approved at the first meeting. The fund was established with "a view to raising the low standard of living among the majority of the population", the constitution stated.

> While it shall not be run on a sectional/racial basis it shall [...] assist such students as would not otherwise be able to finance their studies [...] The administrators [...] shall remain loyal to the non-partisan traditions of true educational enlightenment.[93]

Francke was the chair, Landers, the treasurer, and September, the secretary, who circulated funding appeals, organized events, collected monies, paid the expenses, checked the post office box, and signed the paperwork. Alexander was arranging bursaries for South Africans to study at West German universities; the fund was to pay for the students' airfare, as well as subsidize NLF activities.[94]

---

91. September, pp. 1574–1576; Francke, p. 348; Irina Filatova and Apollon Davidson, *The Hidden Thread: Russia and South Africa in the Soviet Era* (Roggebaai [etc.], 2013) p. 341; Magubane *et al.*, "Turn to Armed Struggle", p. 136.
92. *Liberation*, 1:3 (May 1963), p. 13.
93. September, pp. 1577–1579, Dorothy Alexander, p. 1556; Author interview, Marcus Solomon, Kenilworth, Cape Town, 21 June 2018.
94. Author interview, Solomon, 21 June 2018; September, pp. 1580–1581; Neville Alexander, p. 1766, received confirmation from Tübingen for the funding of thirty bursaries at West German universities on 11 July 1963.

By April–May, the NLF had cells in Athlone, Lansdowne, Cape Town, Maitland, Elsies River, and Wellington. It had friendly relations with Cape Town's Fourth Internationalists, namely, Kenneth Jordaan, Enver Marney, and Edmund Troshe, a white European, possibly Dutch, who acted as a courier between Cape Town and Johannesburg socialists.[95] Franz Lee had received a bursary to study at Tübingen and had left for Germany in October 1962. By then, Irmgard Bolle was in the SDS Office for International Affairs with responsibility for Africa. Bolle and Lee set up the NLF's tiny German cell, which sent literature to Cape Town. In mid-May, the Abrahamses left for South West Africa to set up an NLF cell in Rehoboth. Neville Alexander became *Liberation*'s editor.[96]

The state battered its critics. On 2 May 1963, the General Law Amendment Act – the 90-Day Detention Law – came into effect, enabling the police to detain any individual for up to 90 days without a warrant or access to a lawyer. The next month, on 18 June, Bam convened a meeting in Bishop Lavis Township. Bam organized in Langa and Nyanga townships and had formed his own study group with links to the CPSU, Congress Youth League, ANC, and PAC. In keeping with the NLF's united front aspirations, he invited his group to the meeting, which was attended mainly by students and teachers planning to travel during the school break.[97]

It was agreed that people would visit their contacts, assess the local situations, and set up cells where relevant. Elizabeth van der Heyden, the only woman present, was to go to South West Africa; Landers, to Upington; Solomon to George, Cradock and Graaff-Reinet; Alexander to Kimberley and Johannesburg; and Bam to Johannesburg via Natal. They were to explain the NLF's aims and the conduct of its meetings, ensure the supply of and payment for literature and advise their contacts to appoint local people to the bursary fund committee.[98]

A week later, Jordaan drove Alexander, Francke, Van der Heyden, and Solomon to Wellington to supply Adams with literature. Jordaan a teacher at Livingstone, and good friends with Alexander, was admired on the left for his critical Marxist analyses.[99] But he was not an NLF member – he did

95. Matsemela, interview, Alexander, p. 80; Hirson, *Revolutions*, pp. 279, 301; Roseinnes Phahle, "Reminiscences of the Arrest of Fikile Bam & Marcus Solomon in 1963" (August 2019), *South African History Online*. Available at: https://www.sahistory.org.za/archive/reminiscences-arrest-fikile-bam-marcus-solomon-1963-roseinnes-phahle-august-2019; last accessed 8 July 2020.
96. Matsemela, interview, Alexander, p. 77; Francke, p. 379; Doris van der Heyden, p. 1884; Neville Alexander, pp. 1753–1754, 1763; Martin Klimke, *The Other Alliance: Student Protest in West Germany and the United States in the Global Sixties* (Princeton, NJ, 2010), pp. 31, 255, n. 77; Svenja Kunze, Hamburger Institut für Sozialforschung, to author, 3 February 2020.
97. Bam, pp. 1417–1425.
98. Elizabeth van der Heyden, p. 1532; Francke, pp. 365–368.
99. For example, K. A. Jordaan, "The Land Question in South Africa", *Points of View*, 1:1 (October 1959) in Drew, *Radical Tradition*, vol. II, pp. 325–339.

not think guerrilla struggle was relevant to proletarianized and urbanized South Africa, and he and Alexander often argued about this. From Wellington they drove to De Aar. Solomon left for the Midlands, and Van der Heyden, for South West Africa. She had a sister in Swakopmund, where Shipanga resided, and a school friend in Rehoboth, where the Abrahamses lived; Shipanga was travelling, but she met the Abrahamses.

Jordaan, Alexander, and Francke continued via Gong-Gong to Kimberley. The next day Jordaan and Alexander drove to Johannesburg.[100] Alexander and Jordaan stayed with friends in Alexandra Township, and Bam, with family in Soweto. Alexander and Bam "had contacts in Johannesburg", recalled Alexandra resident Roseinnes Phahle. "For the five days they were in Johannesburg, they spent each day and each evening pursuing their contacts and holding meetings with them".[101]

But the NLF's work ended soon after. Don Davis was arrested on 8 July, Neville Alexander on 12 July, and Elizabeth van der Heyden on 18 July. Other arrests followed. In Germany Bolle and Lee set up the Alexander Defence Committee to publicize and raise funds for the trial.[102] The trial of Neville Alexander and ten others began on 4 November 1963; the eleven were found guilty of conspiracy on 14 April 1964. The Cape was supposed to be relatively controllable, Van der Heyden speculated, so perhaps the state was concerned they were starting a new force. "[V]ery slowly in our trial we could see the way things were going. That they were going to hammer us, this group of intellectuals".[103] Indeed, the court concluded: "As intellectuals you seem to have embarked on this course of action with your eyes wide open [...] most of you are teachers [...] you were in a position where you could influence others and persuade them to a course of conduct which you had planned and decided on as the most effective".[104]

A GENDERED SPACE?

This article has considered how gender shaped the political experiences of women YCCC and NLF members. The NLF was predominantly male, recalled Van der Heyden, but "it wasn't a matter of you are in that position because you are a male, you are a woman therefore you must be there [...]

100. Francke, pp. 369–372; Neville Alexander, pp. 1747, 1750.
101. Neville Alexander, pp. 1750–1751; Phahle, "Reminiscences".
102. Archie L. Dick, "Learning from the Alexander Defence Committee Archives", in Aziz Choudry and Salim Vally, eds, *Reflections on Knowledge, Learning and Social Movements: History's Schools* (Abingdon [etc.], 2017), pp. 42–54, 44.
103. Quoted in Scanlon, *Representation*, p. 210; Author interview, Van der Heyden; Don Davis, p. 1513, Elizabeth van der Heyden, p. 1517; Neville Alexander, p. 1767.
104. BC1538 D.5.1.1.17, Verdict, pp. 2026–2027.

we were mostly men, but I think that was because of the mentality of the society at that time – women stayed home".[105]

Several factors explain why the NLF's practice did not follow those social gender norms. First, the organization's relatively flat structure, lack of hierarchy, and small cell size made participation easier for both women and men. While formal education was an advantage in certain types of work, the lack of formal education was not a barrier to reading or speaking. People were encouraged to speak, allowing women to operate equally within the political space. Secondly, all the women had prior experience in student or political bodies. Thirdly, with the exception of September, the women came from homes where they had been encouraged to voice opinions.

However, the visible presence of women in the NLF was a Western Cape phenomenon. While the hierarchical NEUM did not include political space for either discussions of gender or a women's group, a few women intellectuals in Cape Town played public or behind-the-scenes roles, and the few visible black women undoubtedly left an imprint on younger women intellectual-activists.

Although the NLF's idealized notion of revolutionary life was premised on an abstract individual with traits associated with public, vocal male activists, nonetheless women participated as equal abstract individuals. The NLF's stress on intellectual work made it more attractive and accessible to those with university or college education. But political intelligence was not restricted to formal education. Two examples suffice. First, when the police came to September's house before Alexander's arrest, she swiftly hid her documents under her robe and warned him. Secondly, September's comment on the group's security was astute: "All the rules we [the NLF] made, they [the members] ignored every one of them".[106]

From their gendered upbringing and early experiences in hierarchical organizations to their brief experience of equality within the YCCC and NLF, the women were forced into a prison system with an extremely rigid and unequal gender divide. Elizabeth van der Heyden was sentenced to ten years, and Dulcie September, Dorothy Alexander, and Doris van der Heyden to five. While their male comrades were sent to Robben Island, the women were transferred further and further from Cape Town – to prisons that were *"differently awful"*, explains Shanthini Naidoo. They remained at Roeland Street prison for a month before being sent to Worcester prison. Four months later they were moved to Kroonstad for perhaps a year – time got telescoped, in Van der Heyden's perception. They were transferred further to Nylstroom (now Modimolle) prison, where they spent most of the remaining five years. Finally, they were sent further still to Barberton prison, where Van der

---

105. Quoted in Scanlon, *Representation*, p. 208.
106. Author interview, Van der Heyden.

Heyden spent her last five years, her three comrades released after their sentences were completed.[107]

The transfers had profound consequences. First, the distance made it difficult and costly, not just for visits from family, but from lawyers, journalists, and human rights representatives. Marginalized in the public domain, women prisoners became invisible.[108] Secondly, the repeated moves impeded the women's capacity to build political solidarities and friendships across political and sectional divides and thus to organize and manoeuvre against the prison authorities. Subjected to the state's regendering project, the political space available to the NLF's women prisoners shrank far more than it did for their male comrades, whose prison experiences became the measure of anti-apartheid politics.

107. Naidoo, *Women*, p. 194, italics in original; Allison Drew, "Elizabeth van der Heyden", *South African History Online*, 21 June 2020. Available at: https://www.sahistory.org.za/archive/elizabeth-van-der-heyden-allison-drew; last accessed 29 January 2021.
108. Mbatha, "Narratives", p. 93.

IRSH 67 (2022), pp. 209–236 doi:10.1017/S0020859022000037
© The Author(s), 2022. Published by Cambridge University Press on behalf of
Internationaal Instituut voor Sociale Geschiedenis.

Women's Transnational Activism against Portugal's Colonial Wars

Giulia Strippoli ⓘ

*Institute of Contemporary History, NOVA University of Lisbon
Lisbon 1050-99, Portugal*

E-mail: giuliastrippoli@fcsh.unl.pt

Abstract: This article recovers the history of the transnational women's movement
that arose during Portugal's colonial wars (1961–1974). This movement connected
women in Portugal and its colonies and operated independently of the PCP, MPLA,
PAIGC, and FRELIMO. Most research on women's activism in Portugal, Angola,
Guinea-Bissau, Cabo Verde, and Mozambique begins with their relationships to
the male-dominated organizations that operated within national frameworks.
In contrast, by examining the international connections of these women's groups,
this article illuminates their political activities outside national organizations led by
men. It shows that women created transnational solidarity networks struggling against
the Portuguese Estado Novo and the colonial wars and, in doing so, promoted their
own emancipation.

The tenth All-African Women's Conference took place in Dar es Salaam in
1972. Maria Luísa Costa Dias represented the Portuguese Movement of
Democratic Women (Movimento Democrático de Mulheres, MDM), a "unitary, progressive, antifascist movement",[1] which was founded at the end of the
1960s in the context of the mobilization of the unitary movement of democratic opposition, the Commission for Democratic Elections (CDE), against

---

* This work is funded by national funds through the FCT – Fundação para a Ciência e a
Tecnologia, I.P., under the Norma Transitória – DL 57/2016/CP1453/CT0056. I am grateful to:
the researchers of the project "Women's Rights and Global Socialism" for the fruitful debate during our meetings; Allison Drew, Celia Donert, Mallarika Sinha Roy, and Simone Tulumello for
their comments of the draft versions of this article; Andrea Brazzoduro and Immanuel Harisch
for their insights; Regina Marques and Luzia Moniz for our conversations; archivists and archival
employees, and especially Rita Carvalho and Joana Bénard da Costa from AHS; IRSH's editorial
board, production team, and anonymous reviewers; Augusta Conchiglia, Maria do Carmo Piçarra
and José da Costa Ramos for granting me permission to reproduce the images.
1. In these terms, the MDM represented itself. *Pela Paz pela Democracia Mulheres do Mundo
Unidas* (Lisbon, November 1976).

the Estado Novo dictatorship.[2] Costa Dias had a long history of political militancy against Portugal's Estado Novo, a conservative, authoritarian corporatist regime that launched in 1933. Arrested in 1953 and accused of membership of the Portuguese Communist Party (Partido Comunista Português, PCP), Costa Dias spent one year in prison. She was arrested again in 1958; and, after four years and an international campaign, she left Caxias prison in April 1962. She continued to be engaged in political activism from exile in Algeria, where a Patriotic Front of National Liberation (Frente Patriótica de Libertação Nacional, FPLN) had been constituted by various left-wing elements, including PCP members. Costa Dias became an internationally known personality, travelling across Europe, Africa, and Latin America, and denouncing the conditions of Estado Novo's political prisoners. She became the FPLN's delegate abroad and represented the MDM inside the Women's International Democratic Federation (WIDF). Costa Dias's presence at the All-African Women's Conference and the meeting's opening dedication to women struggling – and often fighting – against the Portuguese army in Angola, Guinea-Bissau, and Mozambique exemplify the existence of a larger history of global contacts and encounters among women (Figure 1).

WOMEN'S TRANSNATIONAL NETWORKS: A NEW PERSPECTIVE OF ANALYSIS

This article focuses on the transnational networks of women who were opposed to the Estado Novo dictatorship and to Portugal's colonial wars in Africa (1961–1974). The war began in Angola in February 1961; the second front was opened in Guinea-Bissau in January 1963; and the third in Mozambique in September 1964. On 25 April 1974, the Carnation Revolution ended the Estado Novo and the colonial wars. The dictatorship fell under the coup d'état carried out by the Armed Forces Movement (Movimento das Forças Armadas), composed of officers and soldiers who had fought in the Portuguese Army in the colonial wars in Africa, which was immediately followed by the population's mobilization and mass intervention. Mozambique became independent in June 1975 and Angola in

---

2. The Comissão Democrática Eleitoral (CDE) was formed when the Portuguese elections of 1969 took place, in the context of the first year of government led by Marcelo Caetano, who was prime minister after Salazar's illness. The democratic front was composed of communists, socialists, liberals, and progressive Catholics. Caetano's government and its promises, ambiguities, and failures in terms of modernization and liberalization have been analysed in Fernando Rosas and Pedro Aires Oliveira (eds), *A Transição Falhada, O Marcelismo e o Fim do Estado Novo (1968–1974)* (Lisbon, 2004).

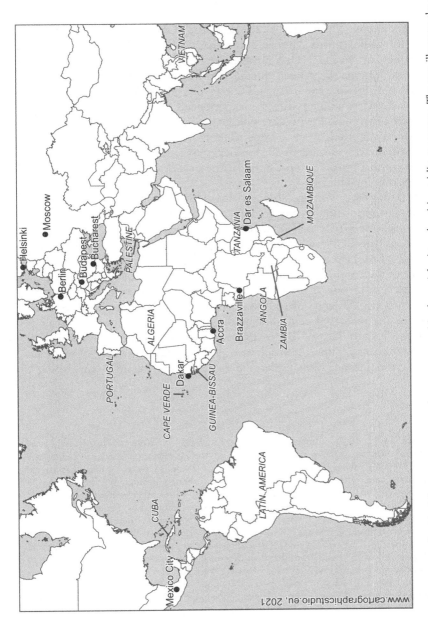

Figure 1. During Portugal's colonial wars women created many opportunities for anti-fascist and anti-imperialist encounters. The map illustrates the places mentioned in the article.

November 1975, while Guinea-Bissau unilaterally declared its independence in September 1973. Against this backdrop, the article discusses the MDM, the Women's Democratic Union of Guinea and Cabo Verde (União Democrática das Mulheres, UDEMU), the Organization of Angolan Women (Organização da Mulher Angolana, OMA), and the Organization of Mozambican Women (Organização da Mulher Moçambicana, OMM). All of these groups were born during the decades of the colonial wars of Portugal – MDM in 1968/1969, UDEMU in 1961; OMA in 1962; OMM in 1973. Activist women directly experienced these wars and engaged themselves against the Portuguese colonialism of Estado Novo and imperialism. Moreover, these four groups shared the socialist inspiration of the WIDF, which was created in November 1945 with four interrelated purposes: to combat fascism; to promote lasting peace; women's rights; and better conditions for children.[3]

By focusing on women, this article offers a wider consideration of anti-colonial opposition to the colonial wars of Portugal, which has previously focused primarily on left-wing groups, students, draft-dodgers, refugees, and on the PCP's winding road to the support of national liberation movements. From the 1920s to the 1950s, the PCP did not support the independence of the colonies: only in October 1957 did the PCP's Fifth Congress declare itself in favour of the complete independence of colonized peoples. The PCP's Sixth Congress of 1965 was a turning point in the party's politics, because of the increased centrality of the colonial question in the struggle against the Estado Novo.[4] By investigating the international relationships between women's groups, the article also aims to indicate the scale of women's resistance and mobilization under the Estado Novo regime,[5] furnishing a

---

3. Francisca de Haan, "Continuing Cold War Paradigms in Western Historiography of Transnational Women's Organisations: The Case of the Women's International Democratic Federation (WIDF)", *Women's History Review*, 19:4 (2010), pp. 547–573. De Haan has offered a critical perspective of the "Cold War paradigm" of Western historiography that has shaped the "not knowing" of left feminist activism, by formulating, among other points, the uncorrected idea that the Federation was oriented by Soviet women and dominated by communist activists.
4. For the ambiguities of the PCP's political line facing the colonies, see Judith Manya, "Le PCP et la question coloniale, 1921–1974" (Ph.D., Université Montesquieu-Bordeaux IV, November 2004); and João Madeira, *História do PCP. Das origens ao 25 de abril (1921–1974)* (Lisbon, 2013). Neves shifted the focus from the identification of anti-colonialism with nationalism to the role of class struggle; see José Neves, *Comunismo e Nacionalismo em Portugal. Política, cultura e história no século XX* (Lisbon, 2008), pp. 166–168. On relationships between the PCP and the liberation movements, see Dalila Cabrita Mateus, *A luta pela independência. A formação das elites fundadoras da FRELIMO, MPLA, PAIGC* (Mem Martins, 1999), pp. 80–84.
5. For a pioneering investigation composed of biographies and testimonies of imprisoned women's resistance to the Estado Novo and prison, see Rose Nery Nobre de Melo, *Mulheres Portuguesas na Resistência* (Lisbon, 1975).

wider perspective than previous studies, which have inscribed their analyses within Portugal's national borders.[6]

The limited literature about Portuguese women and the colonial wars has focused on women who accompanied men to the wars, on those remaining in Portugal while their men were in Africa, or on women such as parachutist nurses who played a role in the wars.[7] African women are strikingly absent in these works: the testimonies of women who accompanied their husbands to the African wars' three fronts reveal their experiences, thoughts, hopes, and fears, but do not refer to African women in Angola, Guinea-Bissau, and Mozambique.[8] Disciplines such as anthropology and ethnology, rather than history, have furnished studies that are focused on women and their struggles in the former Portuguese colonies;[9] but issues such as the scale of women's

6. From the 1980s, several studies have fleshed out the history of different configurations of women's groups. See Vanda Gorjão, *Mulheres em tempos sombrios. Oposição feminina ao Estado Novo* (Lisbon, 2002); Manuela Tavares, *Feminismos. Percursos e desafios (1947–2007)* (Alfragide, 2010); *idem, Movimentos de mulheres em Portugal. Décadas de 70 e 80* (Lisbon, 2000). Other studies have focused on specific aspects of women's opposition, for instance life in the underground. See Ana Barradas, *As clandestinas* (Lisbon, 2004); and Vanessa de Almeida, *Mulheres da clandestinidade* (Lisbon, 2017). Anne Cova focused on the period of the so-called first wave of feminism and the comparison between National Councils of Women in Portugal, Italy, and France, led by upper-middle class women: Anne Cova, "The National Councils of Women in France, Italy and Portugal. Comparisons and Entanglements 1888–1939", in Oliver Janz and Daniel Schönpflug (eds), *Gender History in a Transnational Perspective: Biographies, Networks, Gender Orders* (Oxford and New York, 2014), pp. 46–76. Cova's attention to the comparative approach dates from the beginning of the 2000s, as attested by several publications, in Portuguese and in English. See Anne Cova (ed.), *Comparative Women's History: New Approaches* (Boulder, CO, and New York, 2006). Anne Cova is the Principal Investigator of the project PTDC/HAR–HIS/29376/2017 financed by the FCT, entitled "Women and Associativism in Portugal, 1914–1974", and she coordinates the sub-group Transnational Women's activism in the COST Action CA 18119 Who cares in Europe? programme that is financed by the European Commission. These projects are improving the transnational dimension of studies on women in Portugal and elsewhere.

7. Margarida Calafate Ribeiro and António Sousa Ribeiro (eds), "As mulheres e a guerra colonial", *Revista Crítica de Ciências Sociais*, 68 (2004), Special Issue. See also Sofia Branco, *As mulheres e a guerra colonial. Mães, filhas, mulheres e namoradas. A retaguarda dos homens na frente de batalha* (Lisbon, 2015), which includes individual stories of Portuguese women ("the rear guard of men", according to the subtitle) in a narrative mixing women from the National Feminine Movement (Movimento Nacional Feminino; MNF) – the women's movement that supported the Estado Novo dictatorship – women who accompanied men to Africa, the Red Cross and parachutist nurses, the mothers, daughters, girlfriends left in Portugal, and a few left-wing militants. On the MNF, see also Sílvia Espírito Santo, *"Adeus, até ao teu regresso". O Movimento Nacional Feminino na Guerra Colonial (1961–1974)* (Lisbon, 2003).

8. See the testimonies in Margarida Calafate Ribeiro, *África no feminino. As mulheres portuguesas e a guerra colonial* (Porto, 2007).

9. Stephanie Urdang, *Fighting Two Colonialisms: Women in Guinea Bissau* (New York, 1979); Margarida Paredes, *Combater duas vezes. Mulheres na luta armada em Angola* (Lisbon, 2015); Inês Galvão and Catarina Laranjeiro, "Gender Struggle in Guinea-Bissau: Women's Participation On and Off the Liberation Record", in Nuno Domingos, Miguel Jerónimo, and

activism, the circulation of people and ideas, and the relationships established among women and groups have been largely overlooked.

By focusing on connections among women, this article makes visible the political action of women's groups outside organizations and networks that were dominated by male leaders. Existing scholarship on Portugal's colonial wars has paid little attention to women as political subjects. As the following sections will demonstrate, focusing on women's displacement and connections frees our knowledge about women from the antagonism between male and female subjects or from the opposition between, on the one hand, the doctrines of political parties on women's emancipation and, on the other, women's emancipation in its own right. By demonstrating the existence of the transnational networks through which women shared political objectives, this article seeks to provide new meanings to historiographical categories, such as anti-imperialist opposition to colonial wars, by restoring women as protagonists therein.

This article adds a new dimension to existing scholarship on women's activism from Portugal, Guinea-Bissau and Cabo Verde, Mozambique and Angola, which has insisted on highlighting the implications of the relationships between women's groups and (male-dominated) political parties. Daniela Melo has addressed women's activism in Portugal between the Carnation Revolution and 1977, focusing on the MDM together with two other movements, the Women's Liberation Movement (Movimento de Libertação da Mulher, formed in 1974), and the Antifascist and Revolutionary Women's Group (União de Mulheres Antifascistas e Revolucionárias, formed in 1976). This article focuses on an earlier period than Melo's study, which pays particular attention to the relationships between women's movements and political parties, arguing in the case of the MDM that the connections between it and the PCP have influenced strategies and tactics adopted by the movement.[10] Andreas Stucki has focused on the OMA and the OMM, arguing that the projects of modernization undertaken by the People's Movement for Liberation of Angola (Movimento Popular de Libertação de Angola, MPLA) and the Mozambique Liberation Front (Frente de Libertação de Moçambique; FRELIMO) were only partially consistent with the effective emancipation of women.[11] Despite Stucki's recognition of the international projection of OMA and OMM in Africa and beyond, and of

Ricardo Roque (eds), *Resistance and Colonialism: Insurgent People in World History* (New York, 2019), pp. 85–122.

10. Daniela Melo, "Women's Movements in Portugal and Spain: Democratic Processes and Policy Outcomes", *Journal of Women, Politics & Policy*, 38:3 (2017), pp. 251–275. The same thesis is argued in Daniela Melo, "Women's Mobilisation in the Portuguese Revolution: Context and Framing Strategies", *Social Movement Studies*, 15:4 (2016), pp. 403–416.

11. Andreas Stucki, *Violence and Gender in Africa's Iberian Colonies: Feminizing the Portuguese and Spanish Empire, 1950s–1970s* (New York, 2018).

the occasions that "provided essential platforms for promoting transnational solidarity",[12] the focus remains on the nation-building projects proposed by the MPLA and FRELIMO and on the process through which the two organizations postponed issues of women's emancipation. This article reverts the paradigm: rather than looking at international encounters as occasions for promoting transnational solidarity, it considers such encounters as the multiple signs of the existence of a transnational network of women's movements, whose political life developed autonomously from national projects led by male parties.

In studying Guinea-Bissau and Cabo Verde, Aliou Ly has pointed both to UDEMU's failure and the lack of support from the male leaders of the African Party for the Independence of Guinea and Cabo Verde (Partido Africano para a Independência da Guiné e Cabo Verde; PAIGC) for women's emancipation.[13] Galvão and Laranjeiro used the PAIGC's political documents – especially the speeches and interviews given by Cabral – and women's oral interviews to investigate different perspectives on women's emancipation in the liberation struggle.[14] In emphasizing the harmony and/or distance between existing political parties or organizations and women's activism or emancipation, these works have demonstrated the importance of considering national contexts in which women's groups were born, their ideological background, and how their relationships with previous political organizations could have influenced their histories. However, by emphasizing these connections – the alliances and the oppositions – these studies have circumscribed the political engagement of women mostly to their relations – in accordance or in contrast – with pre-existing political parties. In this sense, the understanding of women's role remained conceptually confined within national boundaries and within the concepts developed by nationalist leaders.

This article adds to these works by shifting the focus from the relationships with the national parties to the relationships between women's groups. PCP, PAIGC, FRELIMO, and MPLA remain in the background compared with women's associations and relationships between women's groups. Even when women's organizations were formed by – or were close to – organizations mainly directed by men, their histories, values, and political heritages should be researched in their own right (Figure 2). Contacts among women's groups in Portugal and in the Portuguese colonies were framed by the socialist

12. *Ibid.*, p. 265.
13. Aliou Ly, "Revisiting the Guinea-Bissau liberation war: PAIGC, UDEMU and the Question of Women's Emancipation, 1963–74", *Portuguese Journal of Social Science*, 14:3 (2015), pp. 365–366. On the same topic of romanticization of gender equality and emancipation of women, to which Ly opposes the PAIGC "masculine ideological narrative", see Aliou Ly, "Promise and Betrayal: Women Fighters and National Liberation in Guinea Bissau", *Feminist Africa*, 20 (2014), pp. 24–42.
14. Galvão and Laranjeiro, "Gender Struggle", pp. 97 and 113.

Figure 2. Women in Angola ensure defence of a village displaced into the bush, 1968.
Archive and copyright: Augusta Conchiglia. Digitization and restoration of negatives: Maria do Carmo Piçarra and José da Costa Ramos.

internationalism promoted by the WIDF and the Pan-African Conference of Women. These relationships were established by various means. Women's groups established contact through letters, telegrams, pamphlets, journal articles, and radio programmes. These materials demonstrate their joint participation in conferences and seminars, the organization of international solidarity campaigns, affiliation to international organizations, and the declarations regarding the need for and procurement of material support. To recreate these networks and connections, and to broaden our historical understanding of opposition to Portugal's colonial wars, this article draws on archival and other sources produced by women's groups themselves and on reports produced by the Estado Novo surveillance and control organizations in Portugal and its colonies.[15]

15. The political police of the Estado Novo regime, called the Polícia Internacional e de Defesa do Estado (PIDE) and, from 1968, the Direção Geral de Segurança (DGS). The PIDE/DGS archive is at the Portuguese National Arquives Torre do Tombo (ANTT). Other sources include the Social History Archives of the Institute of Social Sciences of the University of Lisbon (AHS), the Mário Soares Foundation archive (FMS), the Historical Diplomatic Archive (AHD), the MDM archive, and the United Nations archive.

WOMEN'S ACTIVISM IN PORTUGAL: NATIONAL
PROHIBITION AND INTERNATIONAL PROJECTION

This section discusses the genealogy of the MDM and the international links that Portuguese anti-fascist women established in the context of illegality that was imposed by the Estado Novo dictatorship and the underground travels that ensued. The MDM was founded at the end of the 1960s, despite the Estado Novo ban on the creation of women's associations; this had resulted in the closure of older women's organizations, such as the Portuguese Women's National Council (Conselho Nacional das Mulheres Portuguesas, CNMP), created in 1914 under the umbrella of the International Council of Women and banned since 1947,[16] and the Portuguese Female Association for Peace (Associação Feminina Portuguesa para a Paz, AFPP), created in 1936 and banned since 1952.[17] The internationalism of Portuguese women has a long history, and the underground travels of the delegates demonstrate the network of contacts that women had established with international organizations. When the WIDF was formed in 1945, Maria Lamas represented the CNMP delegation.[18] In 1953 – the CNMP had already dissolved – Lamas was arrested while returning from the World Peace Council in Budapest where she had denounced colonial oppression. As Ana Barradas remarked, "among anti-fascists, few of them would be able to denounce the conditions of women workers, and even fewer, of colonialism".[19]

In 1963, a Portuguese delegation participated in the WIDF's Fifth Congress in Moscow. A year earlier, delegates from Portugal had also been among the 300 representatives of women's organizations from fifty-nine countries who had attended the World Gathering of Women for Disarmament held in

16. Like the other National Councils, the CNMP was a federation of associations of women. Despite its close relationship with Republicans and Freemasons, not all women participating in the CNMP were so aligned. See Cova, "The National Councils of Women", p. 53. The author also underlines the difficulties of associativism in Portugal and the minimal size of the CNMP. Another previous women's organization was the Liga Republicana das Mulheres Portuguesas (1909). The closing of the CNMP by the Civil Governor of Lisbon pushed Maria Lamas to make investigations and to write the book *As Mulheres do Meu País* (Lisbon, 1950).

17. The paradox that permission was given to the AFPP has been noted and analysed, including a reference to the approval of its Statutes that insisted on the enlargement of the organization during the first year of the Spanish Civil War. See Vanda Gorjão, *Mulheres em tempos sombrios. Oposição feminina ao Estado Novo* (Lisbon, 2002), pp. 146–157. The author explains this permission not as a sign of a pluralism tolerated by the regime; rather, the group was tolerated because it was too small to be a threat to the dictatorship.

18. See Regina Marques, *A memória, a obra e o pensamento de Maria Lamas* (Lisbon, 2008), p. 47. For a biography of Maria Lamas see Maria Antónia Fiadeiro, *Maria Lamas. Biografia* (Lisbon, 2003).

19. Ana Barradas, *Dicionário de Mulheres Rebeldes* (Lisbon, 2006), p. 162.

Vienna.[20] By the early 1960s, the WIDF had existed for almost two decades, and over that time different political perspectives had arisen.[21] The Portuguese delegation to the Fifth WIDF Congress consisted of Maria Lamas, Georgette Ferreira, Alice Sena Lopes, Laura Cunha, and Margarida Tengarrinha. They stressed the solidarity of Portuguese women with female fighters from around the world. Tengarrinha emphasized the feelings of the Portuguese women who were there with female fighters from around the world and expressed the delegation's solidarity to "our sisters of liberation movements in Portuguese colonies, in the same fraternal fight against the common enemy".[22]

In April 1965, Free Portugal Radio (Rádio Portugal Livre), the clandestine radio controlled by PCP from Bucharest,[23] mentioned a memorandum that the WIDF had sent to all national organizations of women, inviting them to show their solidarity with Portuguese women and protesting against the Salazar government for its inhumane treatment, including torture, of women in prison. The memorandum mentioned Maria Alda Nogueira,[24] Fernanda Tomas, Serafina Ferreira, Clara Fernandes, Natalia Rodrigues, Olivia Sobral, Albertina Diogo, and Aldina Pato, all of whom had received prison sentences from two to five and a half years.[25] The presence of a Portuguese delegation at these meetings demonstrates that Portuguese women were active internationally before the creation of the MDM in 1969 and the number of groups opposed to the Estado Novo multiplied in the

---

20. AHD, CE39.P3/2034.

21. At the Moscow meeting, the Italian representatives of the Union of Italian women (Unione Donne Italiane, UDI) clashed with the Soviet leaders of the WIDF (mostly members of the Antifascist Committee of Soviet Women) on a topic that had been discussed in previous meetings. From the UDI's perspective, the first objective of the Federation should be the fight for women's rights. For Soviet women, the objective was struggling for peace and against atomic danger, arguing that in the socialist world women had already conquered rights and equality with men. The following year, the UDI abandoned its WIDF membership, but continued to be associated with the Federation. See Maria Michetti, Margherita Repetto, Luciana Viviani *UDI. Laboratorio politico di donne: Idee e materiali per una storia* (Soveria Mannelli, 1999), pp. 317–327.

22. Margarida Tengarrinha, "Maria Lamas, nos Congressos Mundiais de Mulheres", in Regina Marques (ed.), *A memória, a obra e o pensamento de Maria Lamas* (Lisbon, 2008), pp. 81–85.

23. Its programmes were heard and transcribed by political police. Communist leader Aurélio Santos, the radio station's director, later discussed his experience: "Radio Portugal Livre. Uma voz vinda de longe". Available at: http://www.urap.pt/index.php/histria-mainmenu-37/historia/ 50-rdio-portugal-livre-uma-voz-vinda-de-longe; last accessed 12 January 2021.

24. In 1987, Maria Alda Nogueira received the MDM's Distinction for her women's rights activities. Born in 1923 in Alcântara, she and Maria Lamas revitalized the CNMP in 1945. At university, Nogueira joined the PCP, and in 1949 began working for the clandestine edition of the communist journal *Avante!*. Arrested by the PIDE in October 1959, she was released in December 1969 and went into exile. After the Carnation Revolution, she returned to Portugal from Belgium and restarted her activities in the PCP. MDM, *Maria Alda Nogueira. Uma mulher, uma vida, uma história de amor* (Lisbon, November 1987).

25. AHD, UI 7840: Federação Democrática de Mulheres.

late 1960s, when the change of dictator opened new perspectives on ways to defeat the dictatorship.[26]

The MDM was the first women's group in Portugal to be founded as a unitary association of anti-fascist women. However, writing about its own history in the mid-1970s, during the WIDF meeting held in Lisbon in 1976, the organization affirmed that the MDM was "reorganized" in 1969 – suggesting its history preceded its official foundation – in the context of activist democratic opposition in Portugal (the CDE).[27] The MDM referred to the tradition of opposition by previous Portuguese women's organizations: the CNMP; the AFPP; and the female component of the Movement of Democratic Unity, which was formed after the World War II. The self-description affirmed that the organization was made up of "a small group of anti-fascists, democratic with different views, a lot of them with a long past as resistant against the fascist regime".[28] The group later defined itself as a unitary, progressive, anti-fascist movement; in the same year, it joined the WIDF. Then, in 1970, the Federation attributed the Eugénie Cotton[29] honour to the group; and until the Carnation Revolution and the end of Estado Novo, the group continued its activities underground.

In October 1973, still under the Estado Novo, the MDM held its first National Encounter in Cova da Piedade, Almada; 250 women attended the meeting.[30] After the Revolution, in August 1974, the organization declared its support of the WIDF and its commitment to prepare for International Women's Year (Mexico City, 1975) and the World Congress of Women (Berlin, East Germany, 1975).[31] Both the National Encounter of the MDM and this international engagement could count on a past in which Portuguese women had already experienced practices of organization and resistance, and had established relationships of solidarity across Portugal's national borders.

A VANGUARD GROUP AGAINST COLONIALISM: AFRICAN UNITY AND INTERNATIONALISM IN THE WOMEN'S DEMOCRATIC UNION OF GUINEA AND CABO VERDE (UDEMU)

In addressing UDEMU's history, this section underlines how this women's organization enhanced international relationships aimed at African unity

26. Marcelo Caetano replaced António De Oliveira Salazar in September 1968 and opened a short period of reforms in the sense of liberalization, a period dubbed the "Marcelist spring", which was concluded in 1970 with the tightening of repressive measures.

27. The elections of 1969, in the context of the apparent openness and liberalization announced by Marcelo Caetano, were the occasion for political activity and the organization of democratic oppositions.

28. *Pela Paz pela Democracia Mulheres do Mundo Unidas* (Lisbon, November 1976).

29. Founder and first president of the WIDF.

30. Tavares, *Feminismos*, p. 264.

31. *Ibid.*, p. 265.

and affirms that these connections enrich our interpretation of women's political role during the wars.

UDEMU was founded in 1961. Any woman from Guinea-Bissau and Cabo Verde could, from the age of fourteen, participate in the organization, without any distinction based on origin, ethnic group, fortune, social provenance, political opinion, or religious belief. The UDEMU's objective was described as the "complete emancipation of the woman in the 'Portuguese' Guinea and in Cabo Verde islands".[32] The Statutes also affirmed that UDEMU's women were engaged in the struggle for national liberation and complete decolonization, as a first step towards the emancipation of Guinean and Cape Verdean women, and that they recognized the role of the PAIGC as the vanguard in the national liberation struggle.[33]

International connections were integral to UDEMU from its founding; the original statutes refer to its affiliation with the Women's Federation of West Africa and affirmed its right to participate in other international women's organizations. After the 1958 WIDF Congress in Vienna, African delegates decided to create a continent-wide organization. This initiative occurred in the context of the wider movement for pan-African unity, of which the first All-Africa Peoples Conference convened in Accra in December 1958 was a milestone. The creation of this conference was the culmination of previous attempts and meetings and conferences for smaller groups, and from its formation three key phrases marked the official meetings: African women; international solidarity; and peace.[34] In June 1962, a committee of women's organizations from ten countries met in Mali, and the Conference of African Women was launched in Dar es Salaam that July. The Pan-African Women's Organization was formed in 1974 in Dakar, Senegal.[35]

On behalf of UDEMU, Catherine Turpin de Barros took part in the first Conference of African Women, which was held in Dar es Salaam in 1962. Among the manuscripts attributed to Amilcar Cabral is the text of the intervention that was read by de Barros at that conference. Cabral's text stressed that women and men had to be equal in the fight against colonial oppression, and called for the unity of all countries in this struggle:

32. "Estatutos da UDEMU", Fundação Mário Soares/DAC. Documentos Amílcar Cabral. Available at: http://hdl.handle.net/11002/fms_dc_41176; last accessed 2 July 2020. On women from Cabo Verde, see Ângela Sofia Benoliel Coutinho, "Militantes invisíveis. As cabo-verdianas e o movimento independentista (1956–1974)", *Revista Estudos Feministas*, 28:1 (2020), e68316.
33. *Ibid.* To accomplish the objective, the statutes said that a series of works were necessary: the mobilization of women, the defence of their equality with men in the family, support for pregnant women, mothers, and children, the fight for the economic independence of women, and relationships of friendship, solidarity, and fraternal collaboration with similar organizations.
34. See the history of the Conference of African women published by *Awa. La revue de la femme noire*, 1 (1964), pp. 12–13. Available at: www.awamagazine.org; last accessed 29 June 2021.
35. Luzia Moniz, "O Contributo decisivo de Angola para a Organização Pan-Africana de Mulheres", *Jornal de Angola* (2 August 2019).

For women whose country, like ours, is still under colonial domination, the main work is to actively participate in the liberation struggles of their peoples [...] Our fight is just one [fight]; because of that we must unite more firmly day by day, for ideals like liberation, independence, progress, African peoples' happiness.[36]

African unity, to be achieved through mutual understanding, entente, and collaboration among peoples as well as governments, was considered the focus of national liberation. The same document admitted that women were aware that independent Africa had been and would continue for a long time to be almost exclusively governed by men, adding that their aim was not immediate participation in governments. The latter goal, the speech affirmed, would be pursued step by step, at the same pace as their liberation as human beings. By contrast, entente and collaboration among independent African countries towards African unity was urgent. The role of women in national liberation was to be underlined, as was the fact that they were in the vanguard of the struggle, fighting in the PAIGC as militants and as leaders. The need for the unity of African women was part and parcel of the need for African unity: women were not separate from men or from the party, in the same way as colonized countries were not separate from independent ones.

Previous studies have considered this kind of argument as demonstrating the party's ideological shaping of female emancipation: "If for no other reason than for her performance of tasks crucial to family's daily sustenance, the African woman imagined by Cabral on her route to emancipation, should 'take her part in politics'."[37] Here, the declared focus of analysis is women's resistance against male domination. When considered from the opposite perspective, encounters among women provide us with a wider conceptualization of women's history, moving from a depiction of women resisting male domination toward one of women politically organized against imperialism and for decolonization. Taking this perspective, more important than reflecting on Cabral's ideas – whether sincere, rhetorical, realized, or failed – on female emancipation seems to be underlining that Guinean and Cabe Verdean women were active participants in founding events of the history of African women's political organizations. The Statutes of the Conference of African Women, in which Turpin de Barros participated as a delegate – introduced in its preamble issues such as the awareness of African women's responsibilities when facing common problems, the effects of the imperialist system on African women, the strength attributed to solidarity and human values, the opportunity and need of decolonization and the recognition of United Nations resolution on decolonization (December 1960), and the struggle for posterity against

36. I Conferência das Mulheres Africanas, FMS-Documentos Amílcar Cabral. Available at: http://hdl.handle.net/11002/fms_dc_41175; last accessed 2 July 2020.
37. Galvão and Laranjeiro, "Gender Struggle", p. 95.

injustice and ignorance.[38] Moving the focus from PAIGC leaders' ideas about women's role in society to women's participation in the Conference extends the categories of analysis relevant to women who became political delegates in transnational encounters. Conferences and seminars are articulated spaces where women did politics, debated – formally and informally – about women's problems and rights, made efforts to mutually understand each other, established friendships and relationships, and established common political objectives, all the time being aware of common problems and differences.

In 1963, UDEMU accepted the WIDF's invitation to collaborate with the Federation's secretarial office in Berlin; Maria da Luz Andrade was chosen to represent it.[39] According to Stephanie Urdang, the PAIGC ended UDEMU in 1966, after a year of agony. The reasons, according to her research, concerned the allegedly elitist character of the movement. It was based in Conakry, and its members could not leave the city to work in rural areas. Only after independence, in September 1973, did a new group form; this was the Organization of Women.[40] Between 1966 and 1973, therefore, women did not have a specific organization, but rather were integrated into the PAIGC. Guinean women did not engage in combat, but after years of separate revolutionary roles for unarmed women and armed men, women started to receive military training at the Madina Boé camp. However, the war ended shortly after the PAIGC's decision to include women in combat. Urdang also reported that Guinea-Bissau's female leaders referred to Vietnamese and Mozambican guerrilla women as examples of leadership, calling for a change of mentality in Guinea-Bissau. Nonetheless, when the guerrilla militia was transformed into a national army, few women engaged in armed struggles, instead remaining in defence units.[41] Despite this, the revolutionary process for women in Guinea-Bissau ("the revolution within a revolution" and "fighting two colonialisms" were the most popular slogans concerning women) was deep and varied, indicating that women's engagement was not linear and homogeneous. Rather, this process reflected differences between generations, between those who lived in revolutionary zones and those who did not, between Muslim and animist, between mothers and women without children,

---

38. Conferência das Mulheres Africanas (Dar es Salaam, 27 July a 1 August 1962). Estatuto da Conferência das Mulheres Africanas. Associação Tchiweka de Documentação. Available at: https://www.tchiweka.org/documento-textual/0037000001; last accessed 9 September 2021.
39. See the telegram sent from Berlin to Conakry to the WIDF with the name of Maria da Luz Andrade, also known as Lilica Boal, leader of UDEMU and PAIGC: Sem Título, FMS /DAC. Documentos Amílcar Cabral. Available at: http://hdl.handle.net/11002/fms_dc_36699; last accessed 2 July 2020. The Committee of Czechoslovakian women sent the air ticket from Prague to Moscow for the Guinean delegate. See Sem Título, FMS. Documentos Amílcar Cabral. Available at: http://hdl.handle.net/11002/fms_dc_37037; last accessed 2 July 2020.
40. Urdang, *Fighting Two Colonialisms*, p. 268.
41. Stephanie Urdang, *The Revolution within the Revolution* (New York, 1978), p. 16.

between those who considered food preparation as a revolutionary task and those who demanded a different role in the struggle.[42]

Awa. La revue de la femme noire magazine dedicated the cover of its May 1973 issue and a long article inside to women struggling for the liberation of Guinea-Bissau and Cabo Verde.[43] The article suggested that women were engaging against colonial domination in multiple forms and that they could count on international solidarity, including the courses for women that were organized by the WIDF in liberated zones of Guinea-Bissau. The article included a speech given by Ana Maria Cabral about the idea of women's liberation from all forms of oppression, which she considered fundamental for the "true, national and social liberation of the people".[44]

Analysing Guinean women's struggles during the wars and women's role in post-independence, Ly has noted that "women in Guinea-Bissau struggled to find a place for themselves in the war for independence but failed to change male attitudes toward the role of women in peacetime".[45] This kind of analysis has the unquestionable merit of challenging the official narratives that were produced by the movements of national liberation with male leaders. Without questioning these conclusions, this section has tried to demonstrate that the research on women's participation in the colonial wars can go beyond the confrontation between women and male hierarchical attitudes, thus widening our knowledge of women at this time and in this situation, and enlarging our categories of analysis. The links between UDEMU and the WIDF, the participation in pan-African organizations and the presence and speeches of Guinean women at the first international African Arab Women's Seminar, held in Algiers in March 1974,[46] the encounters, in conferences and seminars,[47] with women from the whole world made women's activism visible, and offer us the chance to look at women as political participants in transnational meetings.

---

42. *Idem., Fighting Two Colonialisms*, pp. 119–123. Stephanie Urdang spent two months in Guinea-Bissau in 1974, from mid-April to mid-June (the Portuguese colonial wars ended with the collapse of the Estado Novo on 25 April 1974). She returned for another two and a half months, from June to August 1976, in a totally liberated country. Her work is based on oral interviews and photographs.
43. *Awa* magazine was an independent journal in French, published in Dakar, Senegal, by a network of African women between 1964 and 1973.
44. *Awa. La revue de la femme noire*, 4, New Series (May 1973), p. 4. Available at: www. awamagazine.org; last accessed on 29 June 2021.
45. Ly, "Promise and Betrayal", p. 38.
46. Algiers, 4–6 March 1974. See the numerous newspaper articles dedicated to the event. AHD, UI 7769, I Seminário internacional das mulheres árabes e africanas (recortes jornais).
47. Also consider the presence of Francisca Pereira, UDEMU's leader, at a conference with Angela Davis in 1970, attested by a photograph: "Francisca Pereira durante uma conferência com Angela Davis", FMS/ DAC. Documentos Amílcar Cabral. Available at: http://hdl.handle.net/11002/fms_dc_43603; last accessed 1 September 2021.

BUILDING GLOBAL RELATIONSHIPS: OMA STRUGGLING AGAINST PORTUGUESE COLONIALISM AND FOR EQUALITY

This section focuses on OMA's discourse on gender equality, and on the role of Angolan women in the revolution; it underlines the transnational references and the organization's alliances. OMA was born in 1962 and had its headquarters in Brazzaville, Congo. It was created within the MPLA to mobilize women to fight in the war at different levels, providing political education and combating illiteracy (Figure 3). It was open to all African women born in Angola who were aged fifteen and over. In a document directed "to the Angolan sister", probably written in 1964 because it noted that three years had passed since the start of the colonial war, OMA specifically expressed the value of the presence of women, affirming that Angolan women were more numerous and important than men: they had always done a major part of the work in agricultural and other sectors, often performing extremely difficult tasks. Besides underlining their role in the national economy, the document declared that women had suffered greatly during the war.[48] OMA was a member of the WIDF and of the African Women's Conference, and the organization clearly stated the main reasons that it was part of these international organisms: "to enable us to let the women of the whole world know about the Angolan people's struggle against Portuguese colonialism and, especially, to mobilize feminine public opinion to give us political and material support".[49] Moreover, on more than one occasion, OMA underlined that international solidarity helped the organization, not only in reaching their objectives, but also because of the feelings of closeness that were created among women. After meeting the University Branch of the Union of Women of Tanzania, Umoja wa Wanawake wa Tanzania, OMA's representative was impressed by the large attendance at the meeting, and reported: "such gestures of solidarity not only encourage the Organisation of Angola women to carry on steadfastly until final victory, but they also make us feel close to women in other women's organisations".[50]

In explaining the place of Angolan women in the revolution, OMA made reference to women struggles in other countries, inviting women to focus on the common grounds of their struggle, rather than just expressing a generic "female solidarity": "the fact that we are women does not condition our direct and active participation in the liberation struggle of our country or make it

---

48. See *À Irmã Angolana*, b/d. AHD, UI 7453.
49. "Speech of OMA at the meeting celebrated in Dar es Salaam to commemorate the 2nd. March–ANGOLAN WOMEN'S DAY 1 in 1972", *MPLA News* (1972), PT-AHS-ICS-JL-MNA-61.
50. OMA, *Quarterly Issue*, 1 (1972), ANTT, PIDE/DGS AC SC SR 1446/62 UI 3195.

Figure 3. Luzia (Inga) Inglês, 1968. Between 1999 and 2021, she was secretary-general of the Organization of Angolan Women.
Archive and copyright: Augusta Conchiglia. Digitization and restoration of negatives: Maria do Carmo Piçarra and José da Costa Ramos.

impossible. In Algeria, Cuba or Vietnam women have proved they can do the most difficult works and fight side by side with men".[51]

During the 1970s, the guerrilla activities of Angolan women, including their use of weapons, were proudly proclaimed and became internationally known. In March 1970, for instance, the *Times of Zambia* published an article entitled "Angola's Women Now Start Active Combat", which included a long interview with "Fuxi", OMA's information officer and head of the external propaganda unit. She explained OMA's old and new missions, the latter including the formation of guerrilla units, in which women would complete their emancipation. As with other information about liberation movements, the DGS

---

51. *O papel da mulher da Revolução angolana*, n/d. AHD, UI 7512: Organização da Mulher em Angola.

based in Angola collected this article and sent it to the surveillance headquarters in Lisbon.[52] The stress on women's equality with men, demonstrated by their use of arms, and the reference to other situations around the world where women had fought or were fighting was a recurrent theme in women's organizations. Apart from the valorization of the role of women in society and in guerrilla groups, OMA reflected on different times of women's history to clearly delineate the space and position of Angolan women in the past, present, and future. Criticism of where women had been placed was strong and explicit: "The Angolan woman of today has long since left behind her the tragic and repulsive image of the domestic-woman, the object-woman, the slave-woman. This image remains in history as testimony of the long years of slavery and exploitation."[53]

The turning point was considered to be the revolution, the start of the liberation struggle against colonialism, because with that revolution women became conscious of their role, "overcoming the many complexes inculcated in her for centuries".[54]

The documents produced by OMA tell us that the organization's horizon of reference was large and that it founded its reasons for struggle on more than one issue. In expressing the opportunity of equality between women and men, the reference was not only women's participation in the armed struggle, as their work on a wider canvas was a crucial reason for equality.

WOMEN'S REPRESENTATIONS AGAINST THE WAR: BEING GUERRILLA FIGHTERS AND BEING MOTHERS

The defence of motherhood and its representation have a long history in women's and feminist movements; images concerning motherhood had a large global circulation. This section shows how the issue was expressed in different contexts. On 2 March 1967, five OMA members were captured by the MPLA's adversary, the Angolan People's Union (União das Populações de Angola), while returning from armed action in the interior of the country. In commemoration, 2 March was established as Angolan Women's Day. The five women, Deolinda Rodrigues, Engrácia dos Santos, Irene Cohen, Lucrecia Paim, and Teresa Afonso, were transferred to the Kinkuzu concentration camp and presumed dead (the hypothesis is that they were killed after being tortured in late 1969).[55] They became the women guerrilla heroes

---

52. ANTT, PIDE/DGS SC SR 51/54 Pt 3, Fl. 38.
53. *OMA Quarterly Issue*, 1 (1973). Dar es Salaam, Tanzania, PT-AHS-ICS-JL-MNA-59.
54. *Ibid.*
55. See Departamento de Informação de Propaganda do MPLA, 2 de março. Dia da Mulher de Angola, Lusaka (March 1971), PT_AHS_ICS_AHS_MNA_7.

of the liberation movement and the "mothers of the revolution". This is a fixed point in the discourse and the iconography, in pamphlets, official documents, and journal articles that had national and international circulation.[56] Thus, Angolan women have been both "guerrilla fighters" and "mothers of the revolution", a dual role that is still present in memory and is clearly visible in the monumental statues that represent the "heroines": armed women carrying children.[57] If these definitions of heroism were born from historical episodes in the women's movement, critical analyses of the relationships between gender, nationalism, and liberation struggles have demonstrated how the stereotypes of "mothers of the revolution" and "comrades in arms" were constructed alongside the maintenance of a hierarchical system in which men represented the nation and were seen as superior to women.[58]

In the case of Mozambican women, the representations emphasize the roles of women as guerrilla fighters, in their uniforms; as workers, engaged in everyday occupations and specific tasks; and mothers, or women caring for children. Brochures and pamphlets furnished a series of recurrent images of women's bodies with weapons, with children, and carrying water or other products and materials on their heads.[59] The Portuguese women in the MDM and affiliated to the WIDF also focused on the importance of being mothers; but in their case mothers were not those armed for the revolution, but "mothers and sisters" of soldiers sent to the colonial fronts. The MDM organized one of its first actions against the colonial wars around the image of mothers and sisters of soldiers.[60]

At the 1969 WIDF Congress in Helsinki, MDM was represented by five women, including Sofia Ferreira and Maria Luisa Costa Dias.[61] A brochure produced by the FPLN in Algiers on behalf of MDM was dedicated to the condition and struggles of Portuguese women under the fascist regime.[62] It contains a broad denunciation of women's severe lack of rights: inequality of salaries, working conditions, family roles, and gender discrimination.

56. See for instance the article dedicated to the Angolan women fighters in Zambia: "Angola's Women Now Start Active Combat", *Times of Zambia* (16 March 1970).
57. Monumento às heroínas angolanas, Largo das Heroínas, Luanda, Angola.
58. Paredes, *Combater duas vezes*, pp. 263–291.
59. See for instance the images included in the section concerning the Women's Detachment in the polycopied proceeding *The Mozambican woman in the Revolution*, PT-AHS-ICS-AHS-MNA-58.
60. See the self-portrait made by the MDM on the occasion of the WIDF meeting in Lisbon in 1976 and the brochure *Pela Paz pela Democracia. Mulheres do Mundo Unidas* (Lisbon, November 1976).
61. Sofia Ferreira was a member of the PCP. She was arrested for the first time in 1949 and again ten years later, spending thirteen years in prison. The PIDE accurately reported the Portuguese presence in Finland and then in Berlin at the Peace Congress, and also in 1969. ANTT, Pide/Dgs SC sR 1699/51 NT 2696.
62. *Congrès mondial des femmes. La femme portugaise sous le régime fasciste, Helsinki, 14–17 juin 1969* (Argel, 1969).

According to the new civil code, it was argued, and under the expectations of cohabitation, women were obliged to follow men abroad and to the colonies. Mothers (mostly workers) and children needed elementary rights such as healthcare, housing, and education. MDM clearly affirmed the importance of women in the struggles against the colonial war. It argued that there had been a limited take-up of women's voluntary service in the colonial wars, despite the demagogic propaganda surrounding its introduction; the exception was an extremely limited number of parachutist nurses. MDM provided concrete examples of rebellion, recounting the demonstrations its members had organized on docks where soldiers embarked for the colonies. It also pointed out that women encouraged their children to refuse to be sent to the colonial fronts, as the Portuguese delegates had stated during the WIDF's Helsinki Congress.[63]

This is a focal point for analysing the women's movement's relationship with the PCP. From the beginning of the colonial wars, desertions were a continuous and important phenomenon. Throughout much of the 1960s, the PCP welcomed and approved draft dodgers and deserters. However, in 1967, the Central Committee argued that communist militants should not desert, but rather remain inside the army to engage in anti-fascist propaganda.[64] The MDM's statement in support of desertion at the Helsinki conference did not mean that the MDM was impermeable to communist policy. Indeed, the PCP was the strongest organized force against Estado Novo, and communist women participated in the MDM. Nevertheless, despite the MDM's proximity to the PCP, its position on desertions and refusal of the war was articulated around issues and claims that were born inside women's international organizations rather than in communist parties. Since the WIDF's formation, expressing women's role as mothers was a pivotal issue for women's engagement, and the Federation dedicated particular attention to underlining the connections between the role of mothers, women's engagement in socialist perspectives, friendship among women from all over the world, the rights of children, and the struggle for peace and against imperialism. The international petitions, resolutions, and iconography produced by the women's groups that participated in the WIDF and by the communications organisms of the Federation attest, through texts and images, the strong articulation of these links.[65] At the Helsinki meeting, the MDM referred to women and people in Vietnam, in Palestine, and in Angola, Mozambique, and Guinea-Bissau – the latter

---

63. *Ibid.*, p. 15.
64. "Resolução sobre deserções", *Avante!* (September 1967), p. 4.
65. See the brochure *X° Anniversaire de la Fédération Démocratique des femmes,* and the images on its opening pages, including a reproduction of "The mother", part of the cenotaph dedicated to Soviet Heroes in Berlin, p. 4. See p. 37 for images of women demonstrating in England against the Korean War with the banner "We mothers want our sons at home" and women demonstrating in France against the Vietnam War.

three brought together by their common struggle against Portuguese fascism. The MDM delegates also mentioned women in Greece and Spain, but they expressed special concern for Vietnamese "sisters" because their organization was participating in the WIDF commission of solidarity with women and children in Vietnam.

Portuguese women's international activism focused on Estado Novo practices – mostly regarding political prisons, women's conditions and rights, anti-fascism, anti-imperialism, and struggles against the colonial wars. Being women and the importance accorded to the identity of motherhood were not separable from the fact that they were socialist militants.

MOZAMBICAN WOMEN: AVOIDING SEPARATION FROM MEN AND DENOUNCING TWOFOLD OPPRESSION

This section analyses how the OMM articulated ideas of struggle, oppression, and emancipation, as well as the international circulation of people and ideas beyond Mozambican borders. The first Conference of Mozambican Women did not refer specifically to Portuguese women, but rather to "the fourth front opened in Portugal by the anti-fascist and anti-colonialist patriot".[66] The conference was held between 4 and 6 March 1973, after FRELIMO's Central Committee meeting of December 1972 approved the formation of the OMM. A Women's Detachment (Destacamento Feminino, DF) had existed prior to that.[67] When the DF was born, in 1966 according to FRELIMO's sources, it had precise objectives: the mobilization and organization of the masses; the recruitment of young people of both sexes to be integrated into the armed struggle; the production and transport of materials; and military protection of the civilian population,[68] As Josina Machel, the leader of the DF and a FRELIMO militant,[69] stated: "One of the prime

66. *Cadernos 25 de Junho. Sobre o papel da mulher Moçambicana da Revolução* (polycopied brochure, n.d., personal archive).
67. On DF and its objectives, see the history provided during FRELIMO's Congress, *The Mozambican Woman in the Revolution*.
68. *Ibid.*
69. Josina Abiatar Muthemba Machel was born in 1945 in the province of Inhambane. She participated in the FRELIMO since its foundation. In 1964, during a clandestine mission abroad, she was arrested in Rhodesia with other comrades and imprisoned by PIDE. The group was released the same year. She joined the DF in 1967 and the following year she was delegate of the FRELIMO in the Front's Second Congress. Josina married Samora Machel in 1969, who in 1970 was elected President of the FRELIMO. She carried out many missions in different provinces of Mozambique and abroad. In September 1970, during the Second Conference of the Department of Education and Culture, she denounced the oppressive impact that traditional practices had on women. She also spoke about the emancipation of women in the Second Conference of the Defence Department, held in February 1971. She died in April 1971. For the commemorative brochure made by FRELIMO see: "FRELIMO – 7th April 1972 – 1st Anniversary of the Death of

functions of a women's army is, quite naturally, just like the men's army: participation in combat."[70] The implication was that emancipated women bearing arms shamed men into action. Another women's organization, the Mozambican Women's League (Liga Feminina de Moçambique), held its first Congress in Tanzania in 1966 and joined the DF after the April 1969 decision of FRELIMO's central committee that women were to struggle alongside men, and not only by protecting liberated zones with arms (Figure 4).[71] This was the first and fundamental experience for Mozambican women who were debating and acting on women's issues.[72] Once founded, declared Josina Machel, the OMM was to be integrated into FRELIMO: "the OMM will be an organic part of FRELIMO's structures, where it will be like an arm including all the new sectors of women, whose total and opportune participation was neglected until now".[73] The will of the organization, she added, was to create a centralized and structured movement to channel all potential energies to fight for national liberation: "the new organization will conduct, mobilize, organize and unify women, young and old, married and single, wherever they are, in the villages, in schools, in the FRELIMO's centers abroad".[74]

When Josina Machel died from illness, on 7 April 1971, FRELIMO underlined her role as a militant in the struggle for the liberation of Mozambique, her role as a leader of a women's organization, and her dedication in promoting the role of women against Portuguese colonialism and imperialism. In 1972, the Front established 7 April as the day of Mozambican Women, and the smiling face of Josina Machel in her military uniform became one of the best-known images that achieved international circulation.[75]

The Mozambican sources insist on the avoidance of separation between men and women, focusing on the common struggle against colonialism, racism, imperialism, exploitation, and discrimination, in Western, socialist, and

Comrade Josina Machel, Mozambican Woman Fighter", FMS/Arquivo Mário Pinto de Andrade. Available at: http://hdl.handle.net/11002/fms_dc_84121; last accessed on 30 August 2021.
70. Josina Machel, "The Role of the Women in the Revolution", *Mozambique Revolution*, 41 (1969), apud *The Mozambican Woman in the Revolution*. The same text is published in other brochures and pamphlets; see Women's Section. The Mozambique Liberation Front, PT-AHS-ICS-JL-MNA-54.
71. Machel, "The Role of the Women in the Revolution".
72. Kathleen Sheldon, *Pounders of Grain: A History of Women, Work, and Politics in Mozambique* (Portsmouth, 2002), p. 123. Sheldon also focused on women's role and perceptions of independence and of the construction of socialism in Mozambique. On Mozambican women between April 1974 and June 1975 (the independence of the country), see also the first-person narrative: Michèle Manceaux, *As mulheres de Moçambique* (Vila da Feira, 1976).
73. Machel, "The Role of the Women in the Revolution".
74. *Ibid.*
75. See, for instance, the publication made by the Toronto Committee for the Liberation of Portugal's African Colonies. Available at: http://www.mozambiquehistory.net/people/josina/anniversary_pamphlet.pdf; last accessed 8 December 2021.

Figure 4. Front cover of the brochure *The Mozambican Woman in the Revolution*, edited by the
FRELIMO Women's Detachment, 1969.
Social History Archives of the Institute of Social Sciences, University of Lisbon, reference code
PT-AHS-ICS-CAHS-MNA-058.

colonized countries. Moreover, Mozambican women were aware of the existence of other women's movements around the world. The works of the first
conference of Mozambican Women included a discussion of Western
women's movements, calling the delegates' attention to their problematic
objectives. The examples used were the "much-discussed" (*tão-falados*) movements for the liberation of women in capitalist countries:

> these movements are directing their struggles against the men, accusing them of
> being their oppressors and exploiters. The Conference highlighted the fact that

men who work were also oppressed and exploited like women, and that the system they were acting in inculcated them with reactionary ideas.[76]

However, the insistence on equality with men in the liberation struggle did not mean that Mozambican women did not reflect on their oppression: they explained this, and also how, thanks to the revolutionary process, they had become politically conscious and emancipated. If Angolan women identified colonialism and revolution, or oppression and emancipation, as opposite terms, the Mozambican organization was rather focused on two processes of oppression, colonialism and the traditional system; their combination was the problem. They also saw traditional culture as a source of a psychological inferiority complex that was touching many comrades: this involved initiation rites and also the dowry and polygamy; although different in form depending on the region, these had in common the fact that they inculcated in women the idea of submission to men and a secondary role in society.[77] These issues were circulating in female organizations, and had also become known beyond Africa, as attested by the diversity of sources.[78] Ideas and images were circulated beyond the borders of Mozambique by Mozambican women who represented the OMM in important events. This was the case for the first African Arab Women's Seminar, held in Algiers on March 1974. The OMM was represented by the General Secretary Dominga Vicente, who explained the "multipurpose" role of Mozambican women in the struggle. As Jeanne Martin Cissé, General Secretary of the Conference of African Women, explained, it was the first time that the feminine organizations of Africa, the feminine organizations of Arab countries, and the WIDF had met. In this context, Dominga Vicente underlined how women's groups from dominated countries found inspiring examples in women's groups from African and Arab countries.[79]

This statement by the OMM, and the speech given by OMA representatives in Tanzania, expand the conceptions of women's political activism during the liberation struggles. In concluding an analysis of OMA and OMM, Andreas Stucki states that "African women accepted the assignment, 'a triple burden',

---

76. *Cadernos 25 de Junho.*
77. In the postcolonial context, scholars have underlined the diversity of the society's organization in Mozambique and have criticized the colonial conception of the existence of homogeneous ideas on women. See, for instance, the explanation of a social and institutional role of matriarchy in the north of Mozambique: S. Arnfred, *Conceptions of Gender in Colonial and Postcolonial Discourses: The Case of Mozambique, Gender Activism and Studies in Africa: Codesria Gender Series* (Dakar, 2004), p. 109: "it is pathetic to see how the writers of colonial reports struggle to make the position of women in the matrilinear North fit the pre-conceived image of oppressed subordinated African women in need of liberation".
78. See, for instance, the article, in Spanish, published by the review *Tricontinental*, "Secretariado Executivo da Organização de Solidariedade dos Povos de África, Ásia e América Latina" (6 July 1974). AHD, Folder *Conferência das mulheres moçambicanas*, UI 7770.
79. AHD, Folder *I Seminário Internacional das Mulheres Árabes e Áfricanas*, UI 7769.

as a nationalist leaflet read",[80] thus corroborating the idea that the MPLA and FRELIMO's promises of a new status for women remained only promises, while women firmly stood in their assigned, traditional roles of mothers and educators. The reference to the feeling of being close to other women or to the inspiration coming from other women's groups should widen – if not reverse – these kinds of conceptions. The focus on the multiple traces of women's activism enhances the autonomous channels through which women met transnationally. In this perspective, women's political life can be valued beyond the lens of the traditional role that male parties assigned to them; thus allowing other questions to be raised about further research into the effective impact that encounters beyond borders had on women, as collective groups and as individuals. In turn, this can stimulate other narratives about women during the colonial wars of Portugal, considering them to be the protagonists of a large, internationalist, political network of activists, rather than the contrasting feminine reflection of projects led by the PCP, FRELIMO, MPLA, or PAIGC.

YOUR VICTORY IS OUR VICTORY:
THE STRUGGLE CONTINUES

While celebrating African Women's Day on 31 July 1973 (established by the African Union after the Conference of African Women held in Dar es Salaam in 1962), the MDM declared that the movement was particularly sensitive to issues of concern to African women:

> Among the ranks of African women who are playing such an important role in Africa's struggle for peace, for national freedom and independence, against apartheid and colonialism, for the recovery of their national sovereignty and wealth, for social progress and the strengthening of their achievements, are our sisters of struggle, the women of Angola, Guinea-Bissau, and Mozambique. [...] You can always count on the unfailing presence of Portuguese anti-fascist and anti-colonialist women, firmly in solidarity with your struggle and your activity.[81]

In the previous months of 1973, the WIDF General Secretary Fanny Edelman sent a letter to the Chair of the United Nations Human Rights Commission denouncing Portuguese crimes in Mozambique. The Special Committee of Twenty-Four on Decolonization decided to circulate the communication by Edelman as a petition and to give it the widest possible publicity.[82]

---

80. Stucki, *Violence and Gender*, p. 282.
81. On 30 July 1973, MDM addressed a letter to Mme Madeleine Resha, from the Secretary of Conference of African Women based in Algiers: "To Madame Resha, from the Secretariat de la Conférence des femmes africaines" (Rome, 30 July 1973), Archive MDM.
82. UN Archive. A/AC.109/PET 1249.

Finally legal, the MDM affirmed its aims of creating a national network and promoting international collaboration with "the WIDF, and all women's movements in the world", for unity in struggle, for peace, and for the end of exploitation.[83]

Elisabete Andrade led the delegation of Mozambican women to the WIDF meeting in Warsaw in May 1974, immediately after the Carnation Revolution. In her speech, she addressed Portuguese democratic forces and then Portuguese mothers, to enable them to understand the unfair war against the Mozambican people. She clearly explained the grounds of struggle:

> The enemy of the Mozambican people is not the Portuguese people, itself a victim of fascism, but the Portuguese colonial system. [...] We want to reaffirm, to our sisters in the fight against colonialism, the principle of cooperating fully on the basis of independence, equality, interest, and mutual respect with all the peoples of the world. [...] We wish – once again – to greet the Portuguese women: our victory is your victory, as your victory is our victory.[84]

The WIDF meeting in Warsaw was the first occasion on which MDM was represented after the end of the Estado Novo, with the delegation being led by Maria Luisa Costa Dias, who, interviewed on her arrival in Lisbon, underlined it was the first time the MDM could appear legally and freely after the long years of dictatorship. She also underlined the strong emotions felt at the meeting and the wide welcome at international level that had exceeded her expectations and imagination.[85]

The contacts among women's groups did not end with the conclusion of the colonial wars and of the Estado Novo. In subsequent years, women's groups – and the WIDF – continued their struggles within and beyond national borders, in the context of the democratization of Portugal and the decolonization process in former African colonies.

WOMEN'S ALLIANCES AND SOCIALIST INTERNATIONALISM

The examples in this article show the bases on which women's socialist internationalism in the MDM, UDEMU, OMA, and OMM functioned during the colonial wars, both in practice and in theoretical political terms. Portuguese women and African women from Angola, Guinea-Bissau, and Mozambique met through international organizations, notably the pan-African conferences

83. *O que é o Movimento Democrático de Mulheres* (14 June 1974).

84. Saudação às mulheres portuguesas (May 1974), in MDM, *Solidariedade da mulher portuguesa à mulher moçambicana* (April 1976). Archive MDM.

85. The interview with Maria Luisa Costa Dias on her arrival from Warsaw is part of the RTP archive. The MDM has included part of it in a video dedicated to the WIDF. Available at: https://www.youtube.com/watch?v=1CK7IIilXFk; last accessed 29 June 2021.

and the WIDF. Their exchanges of solidarity and mutual support were possible because of this. These groups seem to have had a lot in common because of their political ideals and the identification of a common political enemy, in the Estado Novo context; but without a previous association that was based on the mutual recognition of a gender identity, this encounter would not have been possible. At the same time, they had more than one commonality because they were anti-fascist and anti-colonialist women. In Portugal, they were against the colonial wars. In Angola, Guinea-Bissau, Cabo Verde, and Mozambique, they fought the colonial wars. In the sources, women refer to other women as "comrades", "friends", "women", and "sisters", concepts that have had and still have a history.[86] Alongside specific references to their diverse contexts, women insisted on the common struggle against fascism and imperialism rather than their common conditions as women. Yet the denunciation of women's oppression was present and strong in all these organizations, for instance in the MDM's pamphlets on women's and children's rights,[87] in the OMM's arguments about the two processes of oppression,[88] and in the OMA's analysis of the equal value of women's work.[89] Reflections on women's conditions and oppression existed and circulated at the international level.

Nevertheless, the closeness among groups was shaped more around socialist issues – struggles for peace, the end of colonialism, imperialism, and fascism – than around the fact of being women. Rights for women and better conditions for children were inscribed within the framework of radical change of society. When women demonstrated that they felt discriminated against or oppressed, they connected this not only with the fact of being women, but also with the fact of being women in a specific context. Taking this perspective, alliances among women were based on political objectives more than on a shared reflection on the meaning of being women. Thus, solidarity among women was more oriented towards a socialist sense then towards a feminine or feminist sisterhood. This does not mean that all these women's groups have always and fully embraced internationalism, but that, in concrete terms, women established left-wing transnational alliances within the frame of socialist internationalism aimed at a radically transformed society. However, this does not

86. See, for instance, the discussion of the concept of global sisterhood proposed by Robin Morgan in C. Mohanty, "Feminist Encounters: Locating the Politics of Experience", in L. Nicholson and S. Seidman (eds), *Social Postmodernism: Beyond Identity Politics*, Cambridge Cultural Social Studies (Cambridge, 1995), pp. 68–86.
87. Even before the MDM's formation, Portuguese women organized and denounced their condition. See, for instance, the pamphlet distributed for the celebration of 8 March 1962, when women from Oporto distributed a text appealing to workers, intellectuals, and housewives, claiming that life for women had become even more difficult. ANTT, PIDE/Dgs SC SR 51/54 Pt 3.
88. Secretariado Executivo da Organização de Solidariedade dos Povos de África, Ásia e América Latina" (6 July 1974). AHD, *Conferência das mulheres moçambicanas*, UI 7770.
89. *À Irmã Angolana*, b/d. AHD, UI 7453.

mean that the fact of being women was irrelevant, because it was precisely this gender identification that allowed the groups' foundation. Since the groups studied here shared a socialist framework with pre-existing, male-dominated political parties, the question arises whether they should be understood as being women's groups with their own – and independent – relationships; or rather, for instance, left-wing groups of women tied to – and hence overly dependent on – pro-Soviet, national political parties, as the literature seems to suggest. Studying the connections of women's groups that were directly involved in the struggles against the Portuguese colonial wars actually makes visible at least four points that are obscured when focusing on the relationship with male-dominated parties. First, women's groups were formed on the basis of both gender and political involvement. Their political life overcame both national borders and their identification with political parties. Second, women created large networks of solidarity under the common impulse of struggling against the Portuguese regime and its colonial wars. Third, when these groups formed, women's emancipation gained a significance that was previously unknown, and this overflowed into the ideological framework of political parties. Women's emancipation became a struggle – a transnational struggle – of women for women's rights. Women struggled as women and as militants. For the first time, in the anti-colonialist struggle against the Estado Novo, the claims for women's emancipation were carried out by women's groups, and these groups established networks of militancy. Fourth, and finally, the significance accorded to emancipation and the networks of solidarity then established constitute a crucial political heritage for the present and future of socialist internationalism.

IRSH 67 (2022), pp. 237–262 doi:10.1017/S0020859021000699
© The Author(s), 2022. Published by Cambridge University Press on behalf of
Internationaal Instituut voor Sociale Geschiedenis

"The Call of the World": Women's Memories of Global Socialist Feminism in India

MALLARIKA SINHA ROY ⓘ

Centre for Women's Studies, School of Social Sciences
Jawaharlal Nehru University
New Delhi 110067, India

E-mail: msroy@jnu.ac.in

ABSTRACT: This article explores the juncture between historical time and space in the
context of socialist feminism, primarily through the memoir of an Indian woman activist who spent four years in East Berlin as the Asian Secretary at the Women's
International Democratic Federation. This primary source material is drawn from a
longer history of Indian leftist women's participation in political mobilizations and
organizational work, the literary tradition of travel writing, found especially in
Bengal, and academic histories of socialist feminism.

THE "CALL" AND THE CALLING

It was such a dilemma! Our everyday life in a little flat, the jasmine sapling in our
balcony, the night-queen bush at the corner of our tiny garden, the chilly plant had
just started blooming, my four-year old Smita's petite hands around my shoulder
and above all my own city, friends, my country. But the call was from dreamland
Europe – the beauty, history, famous museums, architecture of Paris, Rome, snow-
capped Alps and the dark greenery of Black Forest, rippling waves of the
Mediterranean and the modern shining cities of Germany.

And finally, it was a call from the socialist world, a world of which I, and many
like me, have dreamt. It was a call not only to visit, but to live there for a couple of
years – it was, in the truest sense of the term, an invitation to experience the land of
socialist dream. I could see in front of me the legion of socialist women leaders –
Valentina Teseshkova, Dolores Ibaruri, Madam Fucikova, Angela Davis, Vilma
Espin Castro, Bussy Allende, Freda Brown, Madam Nguyen, Isam Abdulhadi –
jewels of socialist women's movement! It was a chance to meet them, to work
with them. How could I refuse it![1]

---

1. Malobika Chattopadhyay, *Biswaloker Ahvane* [hereafter *BA*] (Calcutta, 2011), pp. 13–14. (All
translations are mine unless otherwise indicated.)

Malobika Chattopadhyay experienced these conflicting emotions in 1984, in her hometown of Calcutta, after receiving an invitation to work as the Secretary of the Asian Commission at the headquarters of the Women's International Democratic Federation (WIDF) in East Berlin.[2] Chattopadhyay was a member of Pashchim Banga Mahila Samiti, the provincial wing of the socialist women's organization associated with the National Federation of Indian Women. Her name was put forward by the leadership of her organization for the official position of Asian Secretary in East Berlin. The two quoted paragraphs are excerpted from her travelogue *Biswaloker Ahvane* (hereafter, *BA*),[3] which she compiled as a book from her diaries and scattered memoirs in Bengali literary magazines nearly twenty-five years after her three-year stay in East Germany (1984–1987). Chattopadhyay's book is remarkable for many reasons, and the aim of this article is to explore her text through the nuanced meanings it offers in terms of both the interiority of Indian women socialists and Indian women's participation in international socialist women's organizations. It testifies to the dreams that Indian socialists held concerning European socialism. As a woman, as a socialist, and as an Indian socialist woman, Chattopadhyay explains the subtle ways in which those dreams confronted the realities of living in a European socialist society. She describes in detail the city she inhabited for three years, the countries she visited as part of her job, her colleagues from different corners of the world, and the nature of her work. The book also provides glimpses of her inner world as a traveller in a country that was far from her home, in so many ways. The emotions she struggled with while living on her own for the first time in her life, while in her forties, and the critique she gradually developed of the collective dream she had shared with her comrades at home constitute an inner world of self-realization. By the end of her text, Chattopadhyay hints at the crystallization of a resolution that realities may fail to match the promises of a socialist society, but the dream must carry on. The four sections of this article explore the interwoven details of interiority and public everyday life in her book.

BA has not yet featured prominently in the pantheon of Indian women's writing, perhaps because attention has so far not been paid to the creative and experiential worlds of women who were members of leftist political parties or literary and cultural organizations in India.[4] The first task of this article

2. Malobika Chattopadhyay has been part of the Indian communist movement since her university life as a student in Calcutta in the 1950s. In her book, she mentions her involvement in various student mobilizations. She was active in leftist women's organizations in West Bengal from the 1960s, and even now, an octogenarian who is living on her own after her husband's death, she attends meetings of women's organizations and walks in anti-fascist protest demonstrations.
3. The title of the book can be translated from Bengali as "Call of the World".
4. Bishnupriya Dutt, Urmimala Sarkar Munsi, Lata Singh, and Ania Loomba have recently worked on women's participation in the Indian People's Theatre Association (established in 1943 as an anti-fascist cultural movement). All of them have argued that women's pursuit of creative forms, from theatre to writing, within the Indian socialist movement has remained largely

is to situate this travelogue/memoir in the context of women's involvement in socialist politics in India, especially in Bengal, and explain how Malobika Chattopadhyay emerges as a significant voice in charting the rich but hitherto ignored history of Indian socialist feminists' organizational interaction with WIDF in the context of international socialist feminism.[5] It is equally important to locate this memoir in the cultural history of Bengali women's travel writing. Since the 1870s, this had included a range of experiential narratives, initially travel from the colony to the metropole, and later from postcolonial locations to European metropolitan centres. Definitions of "home" and "abroad" took very different forms when travelling to socialist Europe in the twentieth century, viewed as they were through the lenses of freedom and women's emancipation. Realizations of selfhood through cultural encounters were also deeply political in terms of comparisons and contrasts between expectations and experiences.[6] Exploring the nooks and crannies of one's emotional commitment to social justice, as in Chattopadhyay's text, seems to be how sense was made of the vast gap between "real" and "imagined" socialist Europe.[7]

The simultaneous exteriority of the author's encounters with strangers in an unknown land and the interiority of her emotional responses to those

unaccounted for in both the histories of theatre and performance in India and in the history of the socialist movement. See Bishnupriya Dutt and Urmimala Sarkar Munsi, *Engendering Performance: Indian Women Performers in Search of an Identity* (New Delhi, 2010); Lata Singh, *Raising the Curtain: Recasting Women Performers in India* (Hyderabad, 2017); Ania Loomba, *Revolutionary Desires: Women, Communism, and Feminism in India* (New Delhi, 2019).

5. For contemporary feminist engagements with transnationalism, see Valentine Moghadam, *Globalizing Women: Transnational Feminist Networks* (Baltimore, MD, 2005); Maxine Molyneux, *Women's Movement in International Perspective: Latin America and Beyond* (London, 2003). For the long history of intellectual and political connection between Germany and Indian nationalists since the late nineteenth century, see Kris Manjapra, *Age of Entanglement: German and Indian Intellectuals across Empire* (Cambridge, MA, 2015).

6. Rajkumari Bannerjee's letters from England in 1871, Krishnabhabini Das's *Englande Bongomohila* (A Bengali Woman in England) in 1882, Jagatmohini Chaudhury's *Englande Sat Mas* (Seven Months in England) in 1896, and Hariprabha Takeda's *Bongomohilar Japanyatra* (A Bengali Woman's Travel to Japan) in 1915 are some of the well-known travelogues by Bengali women from the nineteenth and early twentieth centuries. See Simonti Sen, *Travels to Europe: Self and Other in Bengali Travel Narratives, 1870–1910* (Hyderabad, 2005); Inderpal Grewal, *Home and Harem: Nation, Gender, Empire, and the Cultures of Travel* (Durham, NC, 1996).

7. Women's travel writing in postcolonial Bengal earned academic attention and popular appreciation through Nabaneeta Dev Sen, who skilfully deployed the device of self-deprecating humour to critique the marginal positions of the female traveller and the female narrator. See Swaralipi Nandi, "When the Clown Laughs Back: Nabaneeta Dev Sen's Global Travel and the Dynamics of Humour", *Studies in Travel Writing*, 18:3 (2014), pp. 264–278, 270.

encounters compels me to consider *BA* as memoir, travel writing, and an episodic piece of life-writing.[8] In her Introduction, Chattopadhyay writes that
she first travelled to East Berlin with ideological inspiration, hope, and the
dream of seeing and living the socialist society. On her return, she tried to
put her memories into words, and published a few pieces in Bengali literary
journals such as *Desh*, *Eshona*, and *Ekhush Shatak*, but could not complete
a full-length book because of many other involvements.[9] *BA*, as a complete
text, thus becomes significant for its episodic yet autobiographical handling
of a specific set of experiences.

Chattopadhyay writes short, crisp descriptions of life in East Berlin and her
colleagues at WIDF, often interspersing them with snippets of her life in
Calcutta. This intertwining provokes reflections on the history of the women's
movement in India, on the information she gathered from her colleagues about
gender-based discrimination in different parts of the world, and on aspects of
internationalism in socialist women's history. The author's selfhood becomes
enmeshed in these personal experiences as she communicates them to
others, and the fusion between individual and collective memory shapes
Chattopadhyay not only as a narrator of "other" experiences, but also as a
self that is constructed by these experiences. *BA* becomes episodic life-writing
through this interaction, and gains the distinctive characteristics of travel memoir, with the strangeness of the place the author visited and her growing familiarity with it becoming intelligible after a gap of nearly twenty-two years.[10]
The memoir is notable for the details Chattopadhyay provides in terms of
her travels across Europe with her husband when he visits her, as well as her
travels in different countries of Africa, Asia, and Europe as an official delegate
of WIDF during a three-year period; but it also describes East Berlin as it
becomes a home away from home, one that she could compare with everyday
life in Calcutta before and after her time in Europe.

This retrospective quality is what separates *BA* from other memoirs by Bengali
socialist women. Leaders such as Manikuntala Sen, Renu Chakravarty, Kalpana
Joshi, and Kanak Mukherjee remembered their years of participation in the communist movement through autobiographical writings, with the focus often being
on the nature of a collective politics of resistance and sacrifice rather than on individual journeys through political experiences in terms of public and private
lives.[11] In these memoirs, travel features only fleetingly, to indicate the

---

8. See Simon Cooke, "Inner Journeys: Travel Writing as Life Writing", in Carl Thompson (ed.),
Routledge Companion to Travel Writing (London [etc.], 2016), pp. 15–24.
9. *BA*, p. 8.
10. Cooke, "Inner Journeys", p. 18.
11. See Manikuntala Sen, *Sediner Katha* (Calcutta, 1982); Renu Chakravarty, *Communists in
Indian Women's Movement* (New Delhi, 2011); Kalpana Dutt, *Chattagram Astragar
Akramankarider Smritikatha* (Calcutta, 2013); Kanak Mukherjee, *Narimukti Andolan O Amra*
(Calcutta, 1993).

international appeal of socialism and to affirm how activists share ideological bonds across borders. Malobika Chattopadhyay's text allows us, on the one hand, an entry point to the largely forgotten international camaraderie of socialist feminism, where representatives from postcolonial locations found institutional mechanisms that allowed them to interact with each other; on the other hand, it allows us to explore the intertwining of outer and inner journeys of an Indian socialist woman. Simon Cooke has drawn attention to the volatile political aspect of the link between travel writing and self-exploration.[12] Travel as a metaphor for self-exploration can lead to the imposition of an individual's moral landscape on constructing a "strange" foreign land – as in Chinua Achebe's critique of Conrad or V.S. Naipaul's tortuous search for inheritance, which renders India as an "area of darkness".[13] The author's ethical responsibility thus becomes especially important when recovering women's history through the braided characteristics of memory and forgetting.

Women's history does not presume an undifferentiated protagonist who has a neat set of submerged facts and emotions that can be excavated in their entirety. Fragmented documents of memory, history, and imagination are intertwined when reconstituting an individual player, and it is more important to comprehend the fragments than an elusive whole. Memories, when written down, become acts of self-reflection, and taken together these create a chain of representations in which remembering and forgetting become interwoven, as it is impossible to remember every minute detail of one's life, even over a short period of time. The act of representation, as Gayatri Chakravorty Spivak has reminded us, involves two processes – speaking from and speaking for – and the delicate differences between them may be confused unless they are carefully sifted through the ethical responsibilities of representation.[14] In the case of this text and its author, my responsibility concerns both the contexts from which the author drew the aesthetic portrait of her memories of WIDF in East Berlin and a critical review of the context in which the text becomes relevant to women's history. In other words, this article is an effort to understand the ways in which Malobika Chattopadhyay's memories become representative of a particular vision of the world, envisioned from a specific location and bearing the legacy of a social movement that unfolded over a century.

However, it is equally important to outline my motivation for focusing on this text and its author at the outset – as part of the ethical responsibility of representation. Chance encounters or fortuitous events are a not uncommon inspiration for long-term engagement with a specific theme of research, and, in this case, meeting Malobika Chattopadhyay in her capacity as a former

12. Cooke, "Inner Journeys", p. 21.
13. Chinua Achebe, "An Image of Africa: Racism in Conrad's *Heart of Darkness*", *The Massachusetts Review*, 57:1 (2016), pp. 14–27; V.S. Naipaul, *An Area of Darkness* (London, 2010).
14. Gayatri Chakravorty Spivak, "French Feminism in an International Frame", *Yale French Studies*, 62 (1981), pp. 154–184.

Secretary of the Asian Commission in WIDF was one such event. The surprise element of this chance encounter is that Malobika Chattopadhyay was a close friend of my family for over three decades before I knew about her role in WIDF. The access to her text and long conversations with the author consequently did not follow the usual methodology of objective interviews followed by a close reading of the text. Rather, this article draws on personal communication, archival records, reading strategies, and the interrelationship between history and memory.

The first section sets the cultural history of travel and the history of India's connection with WIDF in context. It also develops the specificities of Bengal's cultural connections with Soviet socialism during the Cold War period. The second section describes Chattopadhyay's creation of a home away from home in East Berlin. She remembers her new home, her workplace, her colleagues (many of whom would become friends), her walks in the city, and her conversations with herself as she attempted to understand socialist Europe. These crisp descriptions of people, places, and emotions narrate a complex empathy for socialist ideals and their practices in different geopolitical contexts. The third section focuses on the author's experiences at the Nairobi Women's Forum in 1985, in order to understand the contestations between the socialist and non-socialist world regarding "women's issues", especially the role of international representatives from WIDF. The concluding section focuses on Chattopadhyay's short Epilogue, which situates the book in the post-socialist world of the twenty-first century.

TRAVELLING POLITICS, TRAVELLING WOMEN: FLUID REGIONS OF TRANSNATIONAL SOCIALIST FEMINISM

Women activists in the Indian socialist movement began to travel internationally, develop political associations, and participate in political conferences as early as the 1920s. Ania Loomba has written about Suhasini Chattopadhyay's travels to Europe from the 1920s to the 1940s and Vimla Dang's brief visit to Prague in the 1940s.[15] Indian women also visited Paris in 1946 to participate in the first WIDF Congress.[16] All such journeys indicated participation in a growing transnational socialist feminist organization throughout the Cold War period.[17] Among the 850 delegates present in Paris, there were four from the All India Women's

15. Loomba, *Revolutionary Desires*, pp. 244–245, 252.
16. Yulia Gradskova, "Women's International Democratic Federation, the 'Third World' and the Global Cold War from the late-1950s to the mid-1960s", *Women's History Review*, 29:2 (2020), pp. 270–288, 274–276.
17. Francisca de Haan, "Continuing Cold War Paradigms in Western Historiography of Transnational Women's Organisations: The Case of the Women's International Democratic Federation (WIDF)", *Women's History Review*, 19:4 (2010), pp. 547–573.

Conference who represented different regional and national groups: "Ela Reid came from MARS [Mahila Atma Raksha Samiti, based in Bengal], Jai Kishore Handoo represented the AIWC [All India Women's Conference, led by the Indian National Congress], Roshan Barber joined from the India League's London Office", writes Elisabeth Armstrong, "and Vidya Kanuga (later known as Vidya Munsi) came from the All India Students' Federation".[18] Indian delegates spoke about the specific characteristics of exploitation under colonialism, and argued for the inclusion of anti-imperialist struggles in the fight against fascism. The first WIDF Congress focused on anti-fascist movements, but the voices of Indian delegates made an impact in terms of the broader connections between anti-imperialist and anti-fascist struggles.[19]

WIDF planned to focus on the women of Asia and Africa at its next conference, reflecting a concern for women's conditions in the different contexts of colonialism. A team, consisting of members from Britain, France, the US, and the Soviet Union, visited India, Burma, Singapore, and Malaya in 1948, travelling to Delhi, Bombay, Lucknow, Calcutta, some parts of Assam, as well as a number of Bengali villages. This was part of the preparatory work for the next congress, and it involved meeting the national government of India to get permission to hold it in Calcutta. The Nehru government was at the helm at this time. As Armstrong writes,

> Geographically India lay at the center of a visionary conception of Asia that spanned the pan-Arab nations of Egypt and Lebanon as well as the eastern reaches of China and Indonesia, and in the north, the Asian Soviet republics and Mongolia. Jawaharlal Nehru framed these horizons of Asia in a 1946 radio broadcast.[20]

Calcutta was the selected site for the congress because of its centrality in leading anti-imperialist movements since the nineteenth century as well as its significant role in organizing the Indian socialist movement.[21] Since the seventeenth century, the city had been located on the primary routes of political influence and trade within colonial South East Asia.[22] The long history of the socialist movement in twentieth-century Bengal covers a huge mobile network from Afghanistan to Dutch colonial Batavia.[23]

The meetings between the WIDF team and Indian government officials were not successful, however, and the meetings with the leaders of AIWC

18. Elisabeth Armstrong, "Before Bandung: The Anti-Imperialist Women's Movement in Asia and the Women's International Democratic Federation", *Signs: Journal of Women in Culture and Society*, 41:2 (2016), pp. 305–331, 320.
19. Armstrong, "Before Bandung", pp. 322–323.
20. *Ibid.*, p. 313.
21. For details on the city of Calcutta during the 1940s and 1950s, see Tanika Sarkar and Sekhar Bandyopadhyay (eds), *Calcutta: The Stormy Decades* (Hyderabad, 2015).
22. Sunil Amrith, *Crossing the Bay of Bengal: The Furies of Nature and Fortunes of Migrants* (Cambridge, MA, 2013).
23. Bhupendranath Datta, *Aprakashita Rajnaitik Itihas* (Calcutta, 1953).

did not meet expectations either. In 1948, the Nehru government was explicitly opposed to any communist initiative, and the Communist Party of India (CPI), after a brief period of legitimate existence in the final years of the British Raj because of the support it had offered during World War II, had again been under severe surveillance for organizing militant peasant movements in Bengal. Since the Bengali women leaders of MARS were also involved in these movements, they were expelled from the AIWC; many were in prison when the WIDF team visited. The city of Calcutta was experiencing large protest rallies, led by the communists, and the national government of India was opposed to giving permission for an international socialist feminist conference to be held in the city.[24] The following year, four communist women – Latika, Pratibha, Amiya, and Geeta – succumbed to bullet injuries while leading an anti-government protest rally on the streets of Calcutta.[25]

The WIDF Congress of 1949 was finally co-hosted by the All-China Women's Democratic Federation and MARS in Beijing. The role played by MARS, as a regional organization of India, indicates that transnational socialist feminism was being viewed with a different kind of spatial imagination. In spite of the Indian government's refusal to give permission for the congress and the withdrawal of the AIWC from WIDF, MARS activists found a way to participate and to express solidarity. They also became crucial in articulating the historically informed spatial connections between Bengal, Burma, and Malaya as a regional formation, which could be affiliated with WIDF.[26] Though these regions had recently become territorially defined sovereign nation states when European colonialism formally ended, women were perceiving a regional solidarity that was based on the far longer history of cultural connections. Anti-imperialist solidarity, first raised by Handoo in 1945, was echoed in Beijing when the French delegation presented the Vietnamese delegation with a banner to express their opposition to the ongoing French war in Vietnam, and the Algerian delegation reported how Algerian women as family members of dock workers had stopped French military ships from sailing to Indochina by holding protest marches and pelting the police with stones.[27]

---

24. Sekhar Bandyopadhyay has given a detailed account of the violent peasant movement in Bengal in 1948, which was marked by communal violence and the Partition and continued for the next two years. Pitched battles with the police regularly occurred during the protest processions of Indian communists in Calcutta, in which women volunteers of MARS took part. See for details Sekhar Bandyopadhyay, *Decolonization in South Asia: Meanings of Freedom in Post-Independence West Bengal, 1947–52* (Hyderabad, 2008).
25. On 27 April 1949, police opened fire on a procession at Bowbazar Crossing in Calcutta, killing seven people – among whom were the four communist women.
26. Katherine McGregor, "Opposing Colonialism: The Women's International Democratic Federation and Decolonisation Struggles in Vietnam and Algeria 1945–1965", *Women's History Review*, 25:6 (2016), pp. 925–944, 930.
27. *Ibid.*, pp. 930–931.

It is also important to remember that the working-class women associated with MARS had little concern for territorial nationhood: for them, the struggle against exploitation had only just begun. For them, drawing territorial boundaries for postcolonial nation states meant displacement and escalating vulnerabilities. This sense of solidarity across the social structures of class, caste, region, and religion was at the core of MARS, and it led to the formation of the National Federation of Indian Women (NFIW) in 1954. WIDF's tenth anniversary brochure, published in Berlin in 1956, notes the extensive participation of women from Cameroon, Nigeria, South Africa, and India in the Copenhagen Congress of 1953.[28] This event was therefore crucial in forming NFIW and its continued association with WIDF.[29] The brochure also indicates that India had attained a significant position within WIDF, as Pushpamayee Bose was an elected vice-president.[30]

In 1953, MARS was reconstituted in West Bengal as Pashchim Banga Mahila Samiti (PBMS) (West Bengal Women's Organization) and was affiliated to the CPI. This became necessary owing to the serious losses MARS had suffered when the CPI was banned by the Nehru administration (1948–1952). PBMS also underwent major organizational tension within a decade of its formation because of the Sino-Soviet split in the international forum of communist solidarity. After the Indo-Chinese war in 1962, it became imperative for Indian communists to rethink their affiliation with Soviet Russia. In 1964, a new party – the Communist Party of India (Marxist) (CPI-M) was formed. Members of PBMS did not want to support this as they were involved in issues such as opening girls' schools, children's welfare, mothers' rights, and women's reproductive health rights, along with participating in mass movements.[31] In 1971, however, PBMS split, and the new wing, associated with CPI-M, renamed itself Pashchim Banga Ganatantrik Mahila Samiti (PBGMS) (West Bengal Democratic Women's Organization).

By the end of the 1970s, the Indian women's movement had found its autonomous voice that was able to register protests against violence towards women, and a new feminist scholarship began to emerge with a focus on postcolonial conditions. These efforts were directed towards new tightly knit local organizations with focused agendas that would eventually prepare the ground for a self-consciously feminist critique of the existing leftist political parties.

28. Fédération démocratique internationale des femmes, *10 anniversaire de la Fédération démocratique internationale des femmes* (Berlin, 1956).
29. Declassified government intelligence reports are important sources for tracking the archival sources of this association. Arquivo Histórico Diplomático, Historical Diplomatic Archive, Lisbon, CE39, P3/2034, pp. 16–20 lists Vimla Farooqi as the Indian delegate at the International Women's Assembly for Disarmament, organized by WIDF in Vienna in 1962.
30. 2000/08/27: CIA-RDP78-00915R000600140010-9. Pushpamayee Bose was an active member of the socialist women's movement in India and she became the President of the National Federation of Indian Women in 1954.
31. Kanak Mukherjee, *Narimukti Andolan O Amra* (Calcutta, 1993), pp. 154–178.

The rising challenges in the following decade from majority fundamentalism, limitations of legal reforms and case-based activism exposed "how fragile was the collectivity based on gender politics and how vulnerable it was to challenges of community, class, and caste interests".[32] Amid the beginning of this churning within the women's movement and the challenges from outside, the All-India Democratic Women's Association (AIDWA) was formed in 1981. Elisabeth Armstrong writes that AIDWA shared "deep ties with the Communist Party of India (Marxist)" and remains part of the mass organizations affiliated to the party.[33] However, as one of the largest women's organizations in contemporary India, AIDWA maintains a certain degree of political independence.[34]

The gendered affective political subject, however, survived to a certain extent in the Indian context within the discourses of transnational socialist feminism. An emotional commitment to socialist politics as women, as socialists, and as socialist women has endured in a particular generation. The affiliation with WIDF became a crucial link with international socialist feminism for the next three decades, and Malobika Chattopadhyay notes that before she accepted the position, the leaders of NFIW – Aruna Asaf Ali (Figure 1), Vimla Faruqi, and Bani Dasgupta, who had served at WIDF – informed her about the requirements of the position.[35] Chattopadhyay spoke to these leaders about Indian government policies on women's welfare, on the available data on various aspects of being a woman in India, and on the working of WIDF in Delhi, while her visa and passport were being sanctioned. The opening pages of *BA* are testament to her internal dialogues regarding the seriousness of her responsibilities and her mental preparation for performing the duties that would, for the first time, connect her political ideology and activism with an international institution. Her book, therefore, stands at a crucial historical juncture, between the twilight years of European state socialism, the beginning of a new chapter in South Asian postcolonial feminism, and the initial period of an autonomous women's movement in India.

Chattopadhyay's experiences are also part of the history of the culture of travel, from the perspective of a woman travelling to and from socialist Europe. On her first international journey to Germany, she had a stop at Moscow. She writes:

> Moscow airport is huge, beautiful. It is almost entirely made of glass. But it was silent, lifeless. There were people. Flights were arriving and departing. But

---

32. Samita Sen, "Toward a Feminist Politics? The Indian Women's Movement in Historical Perspective", Policy Research Report on Gender and Development, Working Paper Series No. 9, The World Bank, April 2000, p. 27.
33. Elisabeth Armstrong, *Gender and Neoliberalism: The All-India Democratic Women's Association and Globalization Politics* (New York, 2014), p. 4.
34. *Ibid.*, pp. 2, 4.
35. *BA*, p. 13.

Figure 1. Indian communist leader Aruna Asaf Ali, being felicitated by Freda Brown. Chattopadhyay is on their right along with one colleague.
Photograph from Malobika Chattopadhyay's personal library.

nowhere was a sign of life, of human conversation. Intermittently I could hear noises from the moving footwear of travellers. Police, the officers at immigration, waitresses and airhostesses were cold, nearly rude to everybody. [...] Amidst all my unruly thoughts I could feel an excitement. I am sitting in Moscow, and I shall come to Moscow again in the coming months. Lenin's Moscow, in whose name, we have marched so many times on the streets of Calcutta.[36]

Even though Chattopadhyay admits to herself that she had wasted some money by sending a telegram to the Soviet women's organization to meet her at Moscow, as no one from the organization had come to the airport, her excitement was undeniable. This enthusiasm about an airport transit visit to "Lenin's Moscow" was possible only in the context of the history of the socialist women's movement in India.

Her subsequent visit to Moscow happened in September 1984 as a representative of WIDF at the International Congress of Textile Workers. In her own words:

I was a little anxious about this visit. But anticipation clearly overrode the anxiety. [...] On my way to Berlin, during the stop over at Moscow airport I had my first impressions, but one cannot know or learn about a country from its airport. I set off with a lot of expectations about Lenin's country, Stalin's country and Moscow, the citadel of October Revolution. In the flight I kept on thinking about our days in Calcutta streets, shouting slogans for Soviet socialism. Soviet – the savior of the proletariat, a great friend of India and the third world, the leader of the socialist

36. *Ibid.*, p. 15.

Figure 2. Malobika Chattopadhyay with Uzbek women in Tashkent.
Photograph from Malobika Chattopadhyay's personal library.

bloc! Soviet, where Tolstoy, Dostoyevsky, Gorky, Mayakovski were born – I am going there![37]

Chattopadhyay's sense of disappointment continued, however. Her expectations were not matched in her later visits to Moscow and to Tashkent (Figure 2). The most interesting aspect of her delight during the journey to Moscow in September 1984 is the list of names she mentions – from political personalities to authors, novelists, and poets. While Tolstoy and Dostoyevsky predate Soviet socialism, Gorky and Mayakovski represent different kinds of complexities within the idea of socialist culture in Soviet Russia. The continuous chain of cultural icons that she creates in her imagination is less about Soviet socialist culture inside Russia and more about its reception in India. She had read these authors' works and had known about them ever since her childhood, creating an imaginary world of Russia's socialist society. The affective register of imagining a foreign land, especially an idealized society (idolized to a certain extent), indicates a particular view of colonial modernity in India.

The framework of colonial modernity, utilized by feminist historians of South Asia to explain the effects and impact of the British Empire on women in colonial and postcolonial times, considers the culture and practices

Figure 3 Front cover of the magazine *Women of the Whole World*, the journal of the WIDF. *From Malobika Chattopadhyay's personal library.*

of travel as important axes for the making of the "self" as opposed to the
"other" through constructions of home and the world. "In the European culture of travel", writes Inderpal Grewal, "mobility not only came to signify an
unequal relation between the tourist/traveller and the 'native', but also a notion
of freedom."[38] This idea of freedom was strung in a metonymic chain of meanings alongside "home" and "civilized". "Abroad" referred to despotic rules of
unfreedom suffered by natives, while home was civilized and free. Such spatial
meanings, however, were disrupted when English-educated "natives" used
them during their travels through the imperial centre. The counterflow of
women travellers to England and Europe had produced a distinctive narrative
of freedom in thought and activity, making England/Europe a space where
they could explore their selfhood vis-à-vis gender politics at home and abroad
(Figure 3).[39]

For colonial Bengalis, visits to England and increasingly to Europe were
more about observing the reality of England/Europe as opposed to the hyper-
real image of England/Europe that they had formed through colonial education policy. Their travelogues are interesting because of the preconditioning of
their travel experiences, where the constant comparison between the "real"
and the "image" constituted the narrations of their experiences. A couple of
examples will indicate the process of *"colonization* of experience" (italics in
original).[40] Shibnath Shastri, an eminent social reformer in nineteenth-century
Bengal and a scholar, went to visit Devizes during his travel in England in the
1880s, and when he heard a skylark for the first time in his life he immediately
thought of Shelley.[41] Krishnabhabini Das visited England in 1882, and in her
travelogue she noted unequivocally that she had experienced her greatest freedom during her years there. In a chapter titled "Empress Victoria and her
Household", Das mentions the importance of parliament in imperial governance, citing how the queen was running the entire British Empire with the
help of parliament "with fairness, justice, and discipline".[42] This reference is
suggestive of the "freedom" in "civilized" England, since "parliamentary
rule signified representational politics and the voice of the citizens".[43]
Grewal argues that English women, even without any representation or voting

38. Grewal, *Home and Harem*, p. 136.
39. See for details Michael Fisher, "From India to England and Back: Early Indian Travel
Narratives for Indian Readers", *Huntington Library Quarterly*, 70:1 (2007), pp. 153–172; Kate
Teltscher, "The Shampooing Surgeon and the Persian Prince: Two Indians in Early
Nineteenth-Century Britain", *Interventions: International Journal of Postcolonial Studies*, 2:3
(2011), pp. 409–423.
40. Bhaskar Mukhopadhyay, "Writing Home, Writing Travel: The Poetics and Politics of
Dwelling in Bengali Modernity", *Comparative Studies in Society and History*, 44:2 (2002),
pp. 293–318, 295.
41. *Ibid.*, p. 314.
42. Krishnabhabini Das, *Englande Bongomohila* (Calcutta, [1885] 1996), pp. 58–59.
43. Grewal, *Home and Harem*, p. 136.

rights in the parliamentary system, participated in the discourse of "civilized freedom" when they travelled abroad, precisely because their "home" was defined by those two ideas. However, for "native" women travelling abroad, the ideas of freedom were fraught with competing discourses of progress, tradition, and nationhood. From the 1870s, social reform movements based on the issues of women's emancipation were going through a critical period in British India, as reformers made efforts to forge an agreeable relationship with a gradually emerging nationalism. Krishnabhabini Das's appreciation of imperial good governance and her assurance to her readership that the Empress Victoria did not wish India ill contains an interesting twist in her conceptualization of "home". Das inhabits the intersecting points between home and abroad as she both celebrates and laments the "rulers" of civilized freedom. It seems that the multiple spatial scales of the British Empire of her times constructed her sense of belonging, which contained a yearning for a civilized home that would ensure freedom.

Partha Chatterjee describes such travelogues as "sincere declarations of love by a modern Indian for modern Europe".[44] This "love" is layered more with aspirations towards the object of love than about the surprising elements of experiencing something new. Nearly a century later, Chattopadhyay's travels to socialist Germany, and especially her visits to Soviet Russia, bear a distinctive legacy of the aspirational love for England by the Bengalis. The object of love, however, had been transformed from modern Europe to socialist Europe. While the nineteenth-century modern Bengali's aspirational love for modern Europe was framed by colonialism, the love for socialist Europe was characterized by a sense of solidarity. The affective register had undergone a major shift through a particular kind of familiarity with Russian literature and culture. This shift certainly enjoyed tacit governmental support, which was Soviet aligned in the Cold War period and allowed the flow of Soviet and European socialist literature and cultural ideas and practices.[45]

The translation bureau in Moscow provided excellent books and magazines at affordable prices in various Indian languages such as Bengali, Hindi, and Malayalam. Translators, based in Moscow, often performed the crucial task of introducing socialist aesthetics and culture among publics who were hitherto unaware of them. Here, I would like to refer to Subhomoy Ghosh, who spent six years (1962–1966) as a Bengali translator in Moscow and who wrote short features about his experiences of living in Soviet Russia for

---

44. Partha Chatterjee, "Five Hundred Years of Fear and Love", *Economic and Political Weekly*, 33:22 (1998), pp. 1330–1336, 1334.

45. The CIA document on the Copenhagen Congress in 1960 on "World Assembly of Women to commemorate the fiftieth anniversary of Women's Day" refers to Mrs Rameshwai Nehru of India as a speaker, describing her as "a social worker who is related by marriage to Prime Minister Nehru" along with a leader of NFIW and the President of Indo-Soviet Cultural Secretary. See CIA-RDP78-00915R001200030001-4.

Bengali literary magazines such as *Visva-Bharati Patrika*, *Anandabar Patrika*, and *Desh*. He wrote about Russian ballet, theatre, poetry, music, literature, and architecture alongside politics, and also the reception of Bengali cultural icons such as Rabindranath Tagore and Nandalal Bose in Soviet Russia. Ghosh's short features or "dispatches" were later collected in a book titled *Moskor Chithi* (Letters from Moscow) and explained in accessible Bengali – for example, "Bolshoier Romeo Juliet" (Romeo and Juliet in Bolshoi), "Tolstoy Sadan" (Tolstoy Museums), "Shostakovicer Notun Symphony" (The New Symphony of Shostakovich), and "Leniner Library" (Lenin's Library).[46] The names of literary figures whom Chattopadhyay remembers on her flight to Moscow resonate with the themes of Ghosh's "dispatches". These names and their works became familiar in Indian communist households from the 1950s and 1960s. The affective relations with Russian culture along with socialist politics formed the kernel of emotional political commitment to socialism, where Moscow was not only the name of a modern European city, but also a home from home for Bengali socialists. Chattopadhyay's disappointment with Moscow is thus replete with doubt – whether she had misunderstood the city and its dwellers – and she almost heaves a sigh of relief when East Berlin becomes a second home for her, replacing one dreamland with another.

"ZWEITE HEIMAT": MALOBIKA'S SECOND HOME

On 26 July 1984, Malobika Chattopadhyay arrived at Berlin. Surjit Kaur, who was leaving the position she had come to take, and Gizela, one of the German secretaries at WIDF, received her at the airport. Surjit Kaur's daughter Roli stayed back after her mother left for India, as she was studying in the final year of her undergraduate course in Berlin, and Roli became almost a foster daughter to Chattopadhyay – a relationship that has lasted for three decades. Gizela also became more than a colleague over the months. On Chattopadhyay's first day in Berlin, Gizela and Surjit took her to her accommodation at Albert Hoeschler Strasse, showed her the flat, and taught her how to operate kitchen devices. They had already put some food in the refrigerator for her. The flat was her address for the next three years, and socialist Germany was, in the words of her German colleagues, "Malobika's Zweite Heimat" – second home.[47]

The descriptions of this second home are detailed – the rather large hall with sofa, reading table, television, wardrobe; the bedroom with folded blankets, sheets and pillows; the huge glass front of the hall, covered by a beautiful curtain that reached down to the floor, and the balcony outside the glass front; the

---

46. See Subhomoy Ghosh, *Moskor Chithi* (Calcutta, 1989).
47. *BA*, p. 16.

kitchen with an electric oven; the spacious washroom complete with a bathtub; even the tall mirror on the side of the wardrobe behind the front door of the flat. All are described with crisp precision. Such details serve the purpose of visualizing Chattopadhyay's "home", but they also provide a set of images to envision how she would occupy these spaces for the next three years. References to the flat occur regularly. Her husband visits her in Berlin during the summer and autumn of the next two years; Roli stays with her; Roli and her young friends – mostly Indian students in various universities and technical institutes in East Germany – spend weekends with her. Chattopadhyay gave them the keys when she was at the office, and on her return home she was greeted with tea. During her first Christmas vacation, Roli and her friends came over, cooked for her, took her out for lunch or dinner, or simply for walks, and kept her cheerful as Berlin became covered in thick snow and fog. During the festive seasons, she and her husband accommodated Roli's friends in the tiny space, many of them sleeping on mattresses on the floor; and they played Bengali, Marathi, and Hindi songs on the gramophone, often singing along. With so much detail, the flat becomes a lived space instead of anonymous accommodation in a foreign land.

One of Chattopadhyay's young friends, Radhakrishna Upadhyay, a student of computer science in Ilmanau in southern Germany, once brought his German friend Ube Stoyber to her flat. Ube became close to her, and whenever he came to Berlin with his girlfriend Karin they stayed at her flat. Chattopadhyay's description of this young German man contains a sense of empathy:

Ube Stoyber was an exceptional character. An extremely introvert person and a thorough intellectual. He worked as a male nurse in Ilmanau. But, whatever may be his profession, I have always seen him reading. He would be carrying a volume of Dr. Radhakrishnan's philosophical writings, or a copy of the German translation of Tagore's novel *Home and the World*. He had boundless curiosity and interest about India. When Jyoti [Malobika's husband] came to Berlin he became great friends with Ube. I used to tell Ube that I would send him sponsorship when I return to India, that he should come and stay with us. His rather aloof reply was – such a thing would never happen. They do not have permission to travel outside the socialist bloc.

This introvert, reserved young man had an attraction. Mahesh used to teasingly call him "faqir".[48] He quite liked to be called that. After I came back to India I sent him a letter of invitation. By that time, the Berlin Wall had fallen, there was no "east" and "west" in Germany. When I did not get a reply I asked Mahesh and his friends. Mahesh replied that Ube had passed away. He had a wish to travel outside the socialist bloc and when there was no socialist bloc he had travelled out of this world. We could not bring him to India. Jyoti and I always regretted that.[49]

---

48. A faqir is a deeply spiritual man with few earthly needs.
49. *BA*, pp. 53–54.

The empathy and pathos in this memory of Ube Stoyber is emblematic of Chattopadhyay's compassion for many of her German friends. During a Trade Union Congress on the outskirts of Berlin, she met Ursula Rabe, an English interpreter. They discovered they enjoyed each other's company during breaks from official sessions, and they continued to meet after the Congress. Ursula worked at a bank in quite an important position. She was a little older, but as their friendship developed she became "Ula" to Chattopadhyay. Her office was right opposite the WIDF office in Unter den Linden. They often met at the end of a day's work and had dinner, accompanied by long conversations. Ula's husband had died of cancer and her grown-up sons lived in other cities. Her father had fought in World War II and she hated fascism with a rare passion; but she resented the orthodox restrictive rules of East Germany with an equal passion. She had been to India a couple of times, visiting as an interpreter with German delegations, and wanted to learn more about the country, the culture, the people, and to travel around. Chattopadhyay offered invitation to her on her return to India – "come over when I go back and together we shall go to the Himalayas, the forests, Taj Mahal, Khajuraho, Ajanta [...]" but Ula would always reply with great bitterness that she would never be able to travel outside the socialist bloc.[50] One can hear an echo of Ube Stoyber's reply to her similar offer. The quiet resignation of Stoyber and impassioned bitterness of Ursula Rabe opened Chattopadhyay to the limitations of socialist societies, compelled her to recognize the nature of disaffection from the socialist state among the people of Germany, and to offer, in her individual capacity, solace in friendship.

Glimpses at Chattopadhyay's impressive circle of German friends would remain incomplete without her memories of "Clara and Werner, one was seventy-five, the other was seventy-seven, bound in deep friendship and love with each other. Their story was far more romantic than any Hollywood love story".[51] Chattopadhyay writes the "story" of their lives – young lovers in pre-war Germany who became estranged during the war as Werner had to leave for the Russian front just before their marriage, their decades of loneliness after the war, and their fruitless search for each other, and a chance meeting in Berlin when both were in their sixties – with a rare compassion. It seems that Clara and Werner's love symbolized the national tragedy of war-torn Germany, where the denouement comes after such great sorrow that reunion remains under the shadow of estrangement. Before Chattopadhyay left for India, "they came to my home. A gift of a tea-set and a hand-written card are so precious to me that I have kept them as a reminder of the human capacity to survive the tragedy of war".[52]

---

50. *Ibid.*, p. 42.
51. *Ibid.*, p. 136.
52. *Ibid.*, p. 137.

Chattopadhyay's colleague Hildi Hartings introduced her to Clara and Werner. Hildi, who used to sit in the next room to her office and worked for the Asian Commission, remained a constant presence during the three years of her stay. It was Hildi who took her around the office on her first day, introducing her to other colleagues, and who also took her to shops and markets, helping to make her familiar with the city's roads and transport. Before she became confident enough to go to the office in public transport, Chattopadhyay used to travel there with two of her colleagues – Mita Seperepere from South Africa and Victorin from Congo – in a car organized by the office. Ho An Ga, her Vietnamese colleague, came from a struggling peasant family, while her Mongolian colleague Deze came from a well-off family; both became quite close friends.[53] There are short descriptions of the nature of socialist politics in the countries from which her friends came, with a special emphasis on African countries. There was a special bonding with Mita Seperepere, as they both held Mahatma Gandhi in great respect, and Chattopadhyay's conversations with her colleague are testament to her enduring esteem for anti-Apartheid activists. As she started learning German, mastering everyday conversation after a few months, her closeness to Sabina, Birgitte, Gizela, and Katia – her German colleagues – increased. There are mentions of Rita from Finland, Valeria from Soviet Russia, Therese Noor from Lebanon, and two representatives from Iraq, whose names she does not disclose for reasons of confidentiality and their safety.[54]

Chattopadhyay's work at WIDF is not described in detail in any one place, but rather it is imbricated in everything she saw, did, and felt. She started her work by familiarizing herself with the history of WIDF, pulling out old files from the archives and preparing notes for her future work on connecting the issues of Indian women with WIDF policies. Her first experience of listening to colleagues from different countries through translators was a little intimidating, as she realized that her own interventions and reporting would soon be disseminated in the same manner; that each of her words would be recorded and filed away for future generations of secretaries.[55] Her nervousness, however, soon vanished as she became busy in the office. She started attending emergency meetings when new or complicated issues emerged, participating in discussions and conferences on international contexts of peace and conflict, and attending to special guests.[56] Her time flew by when she had to submit or work collaboratively on a special report. After her trip to Moscow for the International Congress of Textile Workers, Chattopadhyay had to submit a

---

53. *Ibid.*, pp. 21–22.
54. For critical reflections on the relationship between socialist Germany and the Global South through the lens of race, gender and sexuality, see Quinn Slobodian (ed.), *Comrades of Color: East Germany in the Cold War World* (New York [etc.], 2015).
55. *BA*, pp. 23–24.
56. *Ibid.*, p. 36.

report for discussion. When Valeria, the Secretary of International Commission and Soviet Union, praised her report for her ability to connect the ideology of WIDF and the principal themes of the International Decade for Women (1975–1985) with the main issues discussed at the Moscow Congress, she felt the sense of a different kind of achievement.[57] It was her first step towards institutionally engaging with women's global issues – the rest of the world had finally started to take a definite shape.

In the WIDF office on Unter den Linden, events both large and small happened regularly, everything from celebrating a colleague's birthday with flowers and cake, to organizing trips around the city, to visits to museums, opera, or theatre.

Chattopadhyay's visits to the monuments and memorials that dotted the city are informative and lucid, and express part of the cultural life of Berliners. Her rapturous appreciation at watching Brecht's plays at Berliner Ensemble – *The Threepenny Opera* in particular – is followed by her experiences of watching Brecht's translated plays in Calcutta.[58] She does not forget to mention that watching German productions of Brecht's plays inspired her to grasp the genius of Ajitesh Bandyopadhyay, one of the most significant translators and producers of Brecht's plays in Bengali. As she became familiar with the social life of Indians living in Berlin and became acquainted with the Indian ambassador, Chattopadhyay started going to concerts and plays by Indian artists – such as the Calcutta Youth Choir; a play by Utpal Dutt, one of the foremost socialist theatre artists of India; and Indian classical music concerts. Listening to Pete Seeger and Bob Dylan at the Berlin Music Festival takes centre stage in her cultural experiences in Berlin. Such experiences, during which she became a part of the collective social life of her second home, culminate in her participation in various citizens' marches and processions to mark May Day, the anti-Fascism day on 9 September, Martyrs' Day, and Women's Day. Of all these marches, she was most overwhelmed by the one on 13 January to commemorate the martyrdom of Rosa Luxemburg and Karl Liebknecht. Her description conveys the sense of camaraderie that comes through sharing idealism and respecting difference: "In the bitter cold of January, on the snow-covered roads of Berlin thousands of people walked, and I, the only sari-clad figure among them, were a great novelty for the German television."[59] Though her colleagues made fun of her fifteen minutes' fame, she knew that they also appreciated the solidarity of a comrade from a far-flung country.

Participation in such collective cultural experiences, however, was interspersed with solitary walks along Magdalen Strasse to Frankfurter Allee, or

---

57. *Ibid.*, p. 34.
58. See Arundhati Banerjee, "Brecht's Adaptations in Modern Bengali Theatre: A Study in Reception", *Asian Theatre Journal*, 7:1 (1990), pp. 1–28.
59. *BA*, p. 39.

towards Listenberg station, or along Babel Platz. Her trips to West Berlin across the Wall were also experiences of lonely travel, laced with fear and suspicion. She describes the humiliating searches and threatening glances in great detail for her readers at home. Her critical observations about the "Dollar Shops" at the border are significant. For her, they represented the superficiality of capitalist democracy and yet, she admits to her readers, the post-war generation of socialist Germany fell for that enticement as they had, tragically, been dissociated from the history of socialist politics and struggle. Coming from an impoverished Third World country, she could understand the lure of consumerism, but she could not fathom the desperation for consumer goods when basic social justice had already been achieved.

SHOTO POTHE NAIROBITE: A HUNDRED WAYS TO NAIROBI

Before going to the Women's Forum in Nairobi in 1985, Chattopadhyay had earned her stripes as a representative of the Asian Commission of WIDF in various international forums – in Moscow, Athens, and Baghdad.[60] Her observations in each of these conferences contain critical appreciation of the places, people, and issues at stake, but she is astute enough to point at the disconcerting factors without hesitation. In Moscow, she found the conference sessions educational, but the overall social environment stifling. Athens was her introduction to a very different culture, where she found affinities with her home country in loud debates, passionate ideological declarations, and easily formed friendships in conference halls, in collective bus rides from one venue to another, even while travelling through public transport on the city streets. Her Baghdad experiences were an entirely different kettle of fish, to use a colloquial term. The conference took place amid the ongoing war between Iran and Iraq, and she found not only the repeated emphasis on the pride and glory of Iraqi history disturbing, but also the shiny new hotels and sprawling conference venue with an excess of food and beverages perplexing for a country torn by conflict. She marked the exaggerated hospitality of the Iraqi government as a sign of Saddam Hussein's populist politics, rather than his government's adherence towards social justice.

Chattopadhyay also participated in a preparatory conference in Vienna before Nairobi to sharpen the focus of WIDF. A vignette from her experience at this conference introduces the dividing lines between the non-socialist countries and the socialist bloc. This experience is also significant because it almost pre-empts the historic outcome of Nairobi. While participating in the workshop on education, she articulated her thoughts on the development of education in India, and argued that "after two hundred years of British

---

60. *Ibid.*, pp. 31–33, 45–48, 55–66.

colonialism my country is reeling under misery, exploitation, and wretched-ness; what can be the feature of education in my country than disorder and confused policies".[61] After the workshop, Edith Bradshaw, who was part of the delegation from Great Britain, came up to her and said: "Why are you Indians still unable to get out of the colonial hang over? Did India not make any progress during British colonialism? It was the colonial government who made the railways and many other reforms!"[62] Chattopadhyay writes that her response to this was probably a little rude. But she had to tell Bradshaw that the British colonialists crossed oceans and established the empire in India not to introduce reforms. Rather, it was an oppressive regime, killing millions of Indians, which aimed to make as much profit as possible – and it was only for that reason a few hundred kilometres of railways and mechanized ports were constructed. However, the hostility in this exchange of words ended after a prolonged debate in a friendly shaking of hands. The ability to recognize and understand the historical impact of colonialism and imperialism on Third World nations was the key outcome of Nairobi – that political stability and economic policies directed towards social justice were the cornerstones of addressing "women's issues".[63]

The title of the chapter on Nairobi is "Shoto Pothe Nairobite" (A Hundred Ways to Nairobi), underlining the great diversity of the forum. Chattopadhyay writes:

> Groups of women were arriving at the Nairobi airport, were walking on the streets, in the parks, in the markets, in the famous Kenyan safari, in tour buses – women were everywhere. During the ten days of Forum and Conference, the university spaces of Nairobi, every conference venue in the city were filled with women representatives – they argued, debated, gave slogans, sang songs.[64]

This description finds resonance in the way Bina Agarwal remembered Nairobi in 1985 as a celebratory conference, with images "of African women dancing spontaneously on the green spaces between the meeting rooms".[65] Agarwal also confirms that unlike two previous such conferences, in Mexico in 1975 and Copenhagen in 1980, Nairobi celebrated the arrival of "Southern women's movements, including India's", and attracted widely recognized women activists and authors such as Angela Davis, Nawal El

---

61. *Ibid.*, p. 98.
62. *Ibid.*
63. The history of international women's conferences is an interesting site for exploring the tensions and networks of solidarities among delegates from European, North American, and post-colonial countries in Asia, Africa, and Latin America. See Jocelyn Olcott, "Cold War Conflicts and Cheap Cabaret: Sexual Politics at the 1975 United Nations International Women's Year Conference", *Gender and History*, 22:3 (2010), pp. 733–754.
64. *BA*, p. 102.
65. Bina Agarwal, "From Mexico 1975 to Beijing 1995", *Indian Journal of Gender Studies*, 3:1 (1996), pp. 87–92, 87.

Saadawi, and Rigoberta Menchu.[66] That it was a historic occasion was clearly evident. The Nairobi forum became "the site of over 1,000 activities, including panels and workshops; a multitude of cultural events; a film festival; a Tech N' Tools Appropriate Technology Fair; and the Peace Tent an arena of discussions of feminist alternatives for peace".[67] In front of nearly 14,000 representatives from more than 150 countries, it became quite clear in 1986 that it was not possible to have specific "women's issues" with universal applicability, but rather that these issues are interwoven with economic and political contexts, with militarized violence and peace processes, and within the historical trajectories of the participating nation states or non-governmental organizations.[68] Chattopadhyay mentions that in the context of discussions on ecology, the Bhopal gas tragedy, which happened in 1984, was especially condemned, and a resolution was taken to demand compensation from Union Carbide, the owners of the leaking pesticide plant.[69] Women's conditions in conflict-ridden or in post-conflict societies inspired many spontaneous sessions on the impact of civil war in Ethiopia and Afghanistan, the necessity of bilateral talks between Iran and Iraq, between Israel and Palestine, and between India and Sri Lanka, and on the aftermath of imperialist wars in different Asian countries.

In the Nairobi film festival, features on the progress of Cuban women attracted attention; documentaries on women workers in the rubber plantations of Sri Lanka highlighted structural inequalities in the gendered division of labour and the sexual exploitation of African women in the French colonies; and those focusing on the courage of Palestinian women in the resistance movement opened up different historical episodes in women's lives across space and time. Chattopadhyay mentions that the delegates unanimously condemned the Bhopal disaster. She devotes special attention to the Peace Tent and its complexities, indicating the keen political sense that led her to identify important issues that reflected points of confrontation between socialist and non-socialist blocs.[70] WIDF was one of the principal organizers of this

---

66. *Ibid.*, pp. 87, 89.

67. See Nilufar Cagatay, Caren Grown and Aida Santiago, "The Nairobi Women's Conference: Toward a Global Feminism?", *Feminist Studies*, 12:2 (1986), pp. 401–412, 402.

68. The feminist scholarship on the outcome of the Nairobi Forum argues that in the ten years from the first International Women's Forum in Mexico City in 1975 to the Nairobi Forum (with a halfway assessment in 1980 at the Copenhagen Conference), several serious transformations took place in terms of representing "women's issues". See Cagatay *et al.*, "The Nairobi Women's Conference"; Judith P. Zinsser, "From Mexico to Copenhagen to Nairobi: The United Nations Decade for Women, 1975–1985", *Journal of World History*, 13:1 (2002), pp. 139–168.

69. *BA*, p. 104. In December 1984, there was a leak at a pesticide plant owned by Union Carbide in the city of Bhopal in central India, and several thousand people, over generations, were affected by the poisonous gas.

70. *Ibid.*, p. 104.

space. At the front of the huge tent, covered in white and yellow cloth, a plaque read "Nuclear-Armament-Free Zone", while inside cultural events took place to celebrate peace. The fundamental element of all the events at the Peace Tent was opposition to the imperialist-capitalist complex; a view that the ideals of socialism would eventually emerge victorious. Its popularity was not appreciated by the Kenyan government, which made several attempts to close it down, and it remained open only because of women's determined support.

Chattopadhyay also met many of her personal heroines – Vilma Espin Castro (a Cuban revolutionary feminist leader), Valentina Tereshkova (a Soviet woman cosmonaut), and Angela Davis (an American political activist, scholar, and author). Possibly because of her characteristic humility, we are only privy to her endearingly star-struck and overwhelmed expressions when she was invited to sit in the same room as them or share discussion forums, rather than any personal conversations, although the hilarious occasion when she met Angela Davis in the shower is recounted. In her inimitable capacity to traverse the personal and the political with ease and humour, Chattopadhyay narrates her experiences in the common showers at the rest rooms for women delegates:

> It was a long room fixed with a line of showers where women could wash themselves. Women from Asia and Arab countries were trying to bathe under as much cover as they could manage. But the American and European women took showers while animatedly talking to each other completely without clothes. Though many of us, including me, felt quite embarrassed, Angela Davis or Margo Nikitas or Frista from Germany would warmly greet us while bathing![71]

The discourses around women's bodies are hinted at. However, true to the spirit of her travelogue, Chattopadhyay does not intellectualize her experience at the shower. My informed guess is that she avoids stereotyping through this strategy, and this works for the readers too as the humour humanizes icons, with a gentle nudge towards the corporeality of the body and the banality of an everyday ritual.

MEMORIES OF A DREAM? OR, GIFTS OF A LIFETIME

Chattopadhyay added a brief Epilogue to her text, describing her experiences during her journey back to Germany after twenty-two years, in 2009.[72] She felt that very few things had changed spatially in East Berlin other than the removal of the three-storey-high Lenin statue from the centre of the city. Yet, she knew the transformation across the whole country was remarkable. She wanted to understand the changes through her German friends, and she could meet only a few of them. The most poignant meeting was with Hildi

71. *Ibid.*, pp. 105–106.
72. *Ibid.*, pp. 143–150.

Harting, her greatest friend in WIDF. The two women exchanged stories about the changes in their personal lives, but Harting was silent when the unification of Germany came up. Chattopadhyay writes that she could partially understand the reticence of her friend. Harting had never wanted unification at the cost of socialism. The naked aspirations for capitalist opulence among her compatriots and the gradual disintegration of the socialist ethos under the pressure of individualism had turned her bitterness into silence. As her reader, I cannot but juxtapose the resentment of her other friends such as "Ula" Rabe towards the restrictions in socialist Germany with Harting's stern resolve to refrain from discussing unification. Chattopadhyay could not trace Ulrike in 2009. We may wonder whether she was happy in unified Germany, galloping along with the capitalist West.

As she walked down Unter den Linden after two decades, Chattopadhyay remembered her other friends at WIDF, especially Mita Seperepere from South Africa. She had not met Mita in the post-Apartheid era and could only think about Mita's triumphant return to South Africa after long years of exile. She wanted to congratulate her friend for their successful struggle against possibly the most oppressive regime in the twentieth century. It was at least one victory Chattopadhyay could be happy about while sitting on a bench in a park in Berlin. She also remembered Solidad, the young woman from Chile who had fled to Europe after the fall of Salvador Allende and become a Chilean representative at WIDF. Solidad and her husband decided to go back to Chile in 1985 to participate in the Chilean democratic struggle, and told Chattopadhyay before leaving that they must go, knowing fully well the dangers awaiting them, because it was a struggle every Chilean had to fight. "I remembered", writes Chattopadhyay, "that my respect for Solidad increased immensely after listening to her rationale for returning. Solidad, you succeeded in your struggle, finally democracy could again be established in Chile. I hope all of you are well".[73] Faces of her Afghan, Palestinian, Arab colleagues passed in front of her eyes. She wondered "What were they doing in the post-socialist world? Were they continuing with their struggles for an equal and just society? How much are they suffering under the macabre Taliban rule?"[74]

Her heart was heavy, but it was full to the brim, too. When she had started her journey, twenty-two years before, she had been full of doubt; now she was weary with worries about her so many colleagues, nay, friends. These were friendships gifted to her by the camaraderie of international socialist feminism, which in the institutional form of WIDF has vanished from the face of the earth. But the lifelong attachments forged while working in the WIDF office remained. Chattopadhyay was calling out to her far-flung friends, even though

73. *Ibid.*, p. 148.
74. *Ibid.*

they could not hear her. As Rebecca Schneider would say, "the past is a relation" – "the antiphonic back and forth among bodies across different times
and different spaces" dislodges the linear progress of time, and the past reap-
pears at the juncture between present and future.[75] Schneider's reflections
make it possible to situate Chattopadhyay's call to her friends, through the
pages of her travelogue (written in a language that probably none of them
understands), as a gesture that calls the past a relation of friendship, a personal
memory, and a collective with an agenda for women's emancipation. The affinity to feel for the struggles in distant lands and the right to worry about friends
in countries she had not had the chance to visit was the achievement of her
emotional political commitment. In this sense, her gesture of recalling her
friends and her worries about their well-being becomes the gesture through
which the past holds the present, or even the future, accountable. Maybe it
was enough, she thought, "to start to dream anew".[76]

75. Rebecca Schneider, "That the Past May Yet Have Another Future: Gesture in the Times of
Hands Up", *Theatre Journal*, 70:3 (2018), p. 288.
76. *BA*, p. 150.